Three Excavations Along the Thames and its Tributaries, 1994

Neolithic to Saxon Settlement and Burial in the Thames, Colne, and Kennet Valleys

Phil Andrews and Andrew Crockett

Three Excavations Along the Thames and its Tributaries, 1994

Neolithic to Saxon Settlement and Burial in the Thames, Colne, and Kennet Valleys

Phil Andrews and Andrew Crockett

with contributions from
Michael J. Allen, Rowena Gale, Sheila Hamilton-Dyer, P.A. Harding, Pat Hinton, M. Laidlaw, Jacqueline I. McKinley, Lorraine Mepham, R. Montague, Robert G. Scaife, Nicholas A. Wells, and D.F. Williams

Wessex Archaeology Report No. 10
Wessex Archaeology
1996

Published by the Trust for Wessex Archaeology Ltd, Registered Charity No. 287786
Portway House, Old Sarum Park, Salisbury, England, SP4 6EB

British Library Cataloguing in Publication Data
A catalogue for this book is available from the British Library

ISBN 1–874350–18–3
ISSN 0965–5778

Produced by Wessex Archaeology
Printed by Henry Ling (Dorset Press) Ltd

Editor: Melanie Gauden
Series Editor: Julie Gardiner

The publishers wish to acknowledge with gratitude:

- **British Airways**
- **Granada Hospitality Ltd**
- **Wates Built Homes Ltd**

who funded the publication of this volume

Front cover: top, excavation of Romano-British remains at Wickhams Field; left, post-holes belonging to early Saxon hall 721 at Prospect Park; right, Early Bronze Age ring-ditch 23 at Hurst Park

Back cover: Late Neolithic Grooved Ware pottery from Prospect Park (photograph by Elaine Wakefield)

Contents

List of Figures

List of Plates

List of Tables

Acknowledgements

Prospect Park

The archaeological work was commissioned and funded by British Airways, and Wessex Archaeology are grateful to Mr P. Chadwick of Lawson-Price Environmental and Mr C. Bain of MACE for their co-operation and assistance in establishing the project. Thanks are also due to Mr Barwick and Mr Whitehead for allowing access to Fields 13 and 14. Monitoring of the project was undertaken by Mr R. Whytehead, Assistant Archaeological Officer, English Heritage London Region, on behalf of the London Borough of Hillingdon.

The evaluation and excavation were managed by Kit Watson, and the post-excavation by Dave Farwell. Dave Farwell directed excavations in the field, and also prepared the evaluation and assessment reports with the assistance of Kit Watson, Emma Loader, and Jez Fry. Environmental processing was carried out by Jezz Taylor. Site assistance was provided by Steve Campbell-Curtis, Helen Cook, Jez Fry, Kevin Hicks, Emma Loader, Phil McMahon, Madeline Sarley, Maria Schroder, Greig Watson, Joe Whelan, and James Woodhouse. Lorraine Mepham is grateful to Rosamund Cleal for commenting on the Neolithic pottery, and to Lyn Blackmore for discussing the early Saxon pottery in advance of publication of similar assemblages from other sites in west London.

The archive is currently held at the offices of Wessex Archaeology, and will be deposited at the Museum of London in due course (Site Code PPK93).

Hurst Park

The archaeological project was commissioned and funded by Wates Built Homes Ltd of whom John Matthews (Residential Development Manager) is particularly thanked for his assistance in ensuring its successful conclusion. Neil Holbrook (Archaeological Manager, Cotswold Archaeological Trust), acted as archaeological adviser to Wates Built Homes Ltd; his help and advice were greatly appreciated. Monitoring of the project was undertaken by Dinah Saich, Archaeology Officer, on behalf of Surrey County Council.

The excavation and post-excavation work was undertaken by Wessex Archaeology. The project was managed by Jonathan Nowell and directed in the field by Phil Andrews with the assistance of Astrid Hudson. Finds processing was undertaken on site by Steve Tatler, and environmental processing by Sarah Wyles. Phil Andrews would like to thank Darren Saul of John Stacey Plant Hire Ltd for his efficient organisation of the soil stripping and Jonathan Horne for information on the history of the area. Site assistance was provided by Steve Campbell-Curtis, Tim Davis, Bob Davies, Phil Davies, Simon Eddelston, Jane Liddle, Joe McDermott, Jo Pine, Jezz Taylor. Stuart Needham has kindly commented on the polishing stone, and Dinah Saich has provided additional information on the local archaeology. Thanks are also due to Elizabeth Goodman of the Salisbury Conservation Laboratory for conservation of metalwork.

The evaluations were undertaken by the Cotswold Archaeological Trust, directed and reported by Brona Langton. The evaluation geophysical survey was undertaken by Tony Clark and Alastair Bartlett.

The archive, including the finds, has been deposited at Elmbridge Museum, Weybridge (Wessex Archaeology Site Code W7977).

Wickhams Field

Initial archaeological consultations for the development of the motorway service area were carried out by Mobil Oil Company Ltd through their agent David Huskisson Associates. The fieldwork and post-excavation programme were commissioned and financed by Granada Hospitality Ltd through the scheme Project Management team, MACE Ltd.

Wessex Archaeology would like to thank the following for all their assistance and co-operation during the course of the work: Tony Raven, Property Director, Granada Hospitality Ltd; the following members of MACE Ltd: Steve Booth (Project Coordinator); Steve McGuckin (Design Manager); Richard Thorpe; Roger Beswick (Project Manager); David Smith (Assistant Project Manager) and John O'Sullivan (Construction Superintendent). In addition, Wessex Archaeology would like to acknowledge the assistance of Steve Johns (Associate Director, Thorburn Colquhoun Consulting Engineers) and David Huskisson (Director, David Huskisson Associates). Finally, thanks are also due to Peter Fasham, Principal Archaeologist, Babtie Group (as Consultants to Berkshire County Council) for his assistance and advice throughout the project, and to Mr K. McDiarmid of the Englefield Estate.

The project was managed on behalf of Wessex Archaeology by Carrie Hearne. The excavations were directed on site by Andrew Crockett and supervised by Rod Brook and Dave Murdie. Site assistance was provided by Catriona Gibson, Isca Howell, Lucy Howell, Richard May, David Petts, Simon Stevens, and Nick Wells. Robert Scaife would like to thank Alan Clapham and Dr M. Robinson for their comments on the waterlogged seeds report. The radiocarbon determination was provided by the Scottish Universities Research and Reactor Centre (SURRC), East Kilbride. Thanks are also due to Elizabeth Goodman of the Salisbury Conservation Laboratory for conservation of metalwork.

The project archive, including the finds, has been deposited with Newbury Museum (Wessex Archaeology Site Code W668). The artefacts have kindly been donated to the museum by the Englefield Estate.

The authors are particularly grateful to Lorraine Mepham who carried out the finds assessments as well as managing, co-ordinating, and editing the finds reports for all three sites in this volume. The environmental assessments were undertaken by Sarah Wyles and Michael Allen, and the subsequent environmental work managed by Michael Allen. All the figures were prepared by Julian Cross, with the exception of the Neolithic pottery (Figs 22 and 51) which was drawn by Liz James. The plates were prepared by Elaine Wakefield. Melanie Gauden prepared the volume for publication.

The authors would like to record their thanks to Dave Farwell, Carrie Hearne, and Jonathan Nowell for their part in coordinating this volume, and providing assistance and advice at various stages in its production. Finally, Phil Andrews is grateful to Julie Gardiner for commenting on various aspects of this report, particularly the Neolithic sections, and to Jonathan Cotton, Bob Cowie, Mark Birley, and Steven Ford for providing information on a number of sites in west London which are currently under excavation or being prepared for publication.

All levels given in this volume are above Ordance Datum (+m OD), unless otherwise stated.

Abstract

This volume presents the findings from three open area excavations undertaken by Wessex Archaeology during 1994: Prospect Park, near Harmondsworth, London Borough of Hillingdon; Hurst Park, East Molesey, Surrey; and Wickhams Field, near Reading, Berkshire. The sites lay in the Thames, Colne, and Kennet valleys respectively.

At Prospect Park several features containing Neolithic Grooved Ware were encountered. Burial activity in the Middle Bronze Age was indicated by the presence of a ring-ditch and two cremation burials. Part of an extensive, unenclosed Late Bronze Age settlement dated to the 10th–9th centuries BC comprised a number of possible structures, ditches, and pits. A single Romano-British cremation burial was also found. Early Saxon settlement of the 5th or 6th century AD was represented by four sunken-featured buildings, two timber halls, pits, and a well.

At Hurst Park slight evidence for Late Neolithic activity and an Early Bronze Age ring-ditch with associated Collared Urn cremation burials were found on the edge of a former river channel. A single pit of Middle Bronze Age date was encountered. An unenclosed Late Bronze Age settlement of 11th–10th century BC date comprised two areas of distinctive activity apparently associated with huts, and an adjacent field system. Evidence for a probable 1st–2nd century AD Romano-British farmstead included a corndrier and cremation burials. A number of sunken-featured buildings and pits of 6th/7th century date belonged to an Early Saxon settlement.

Slight evidence of Neolithic activity, in the form of a pit and flint artefacts, was also recorded at Wickhams Field where localised colluvial deposits suggested associated woodland clearance. Early Iron Age settlement was indicated by the presence of a trackway, enclosure, and associated pits with a large rectangular pit nearby containing profuse quantities of burnt flint and iron smithing slag. A small, rural, Romano-British farmstead was represented by enclosures, structures, pits, and ditches of 1st–2nd and 3rd–4th century date, the latter phase including a midden. Scattered evidence for a Saxon settlement of 7th–9th century date was revealed by a series of storage pits containing quantities of cereal remains and a pair of timber-lined wells. This settlement may have been associated with the nearby 7th century inhumation cemetery at Field Farm.

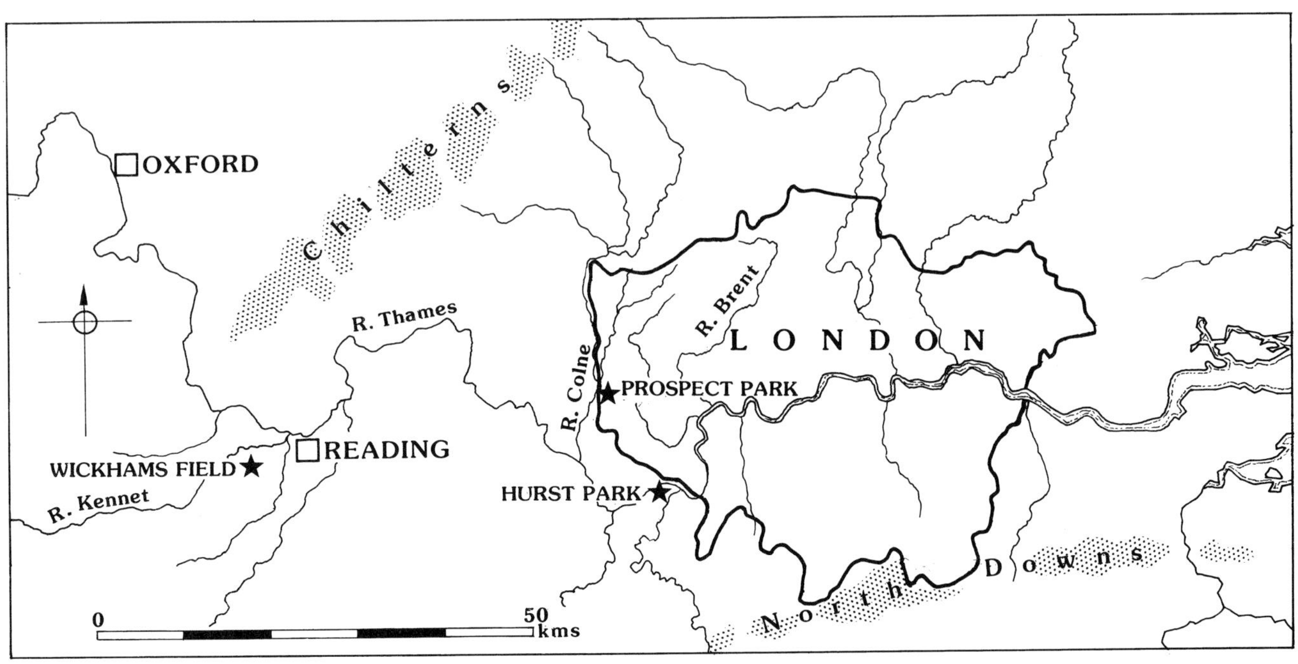

Figure 1 Location of sites discussed in this volume

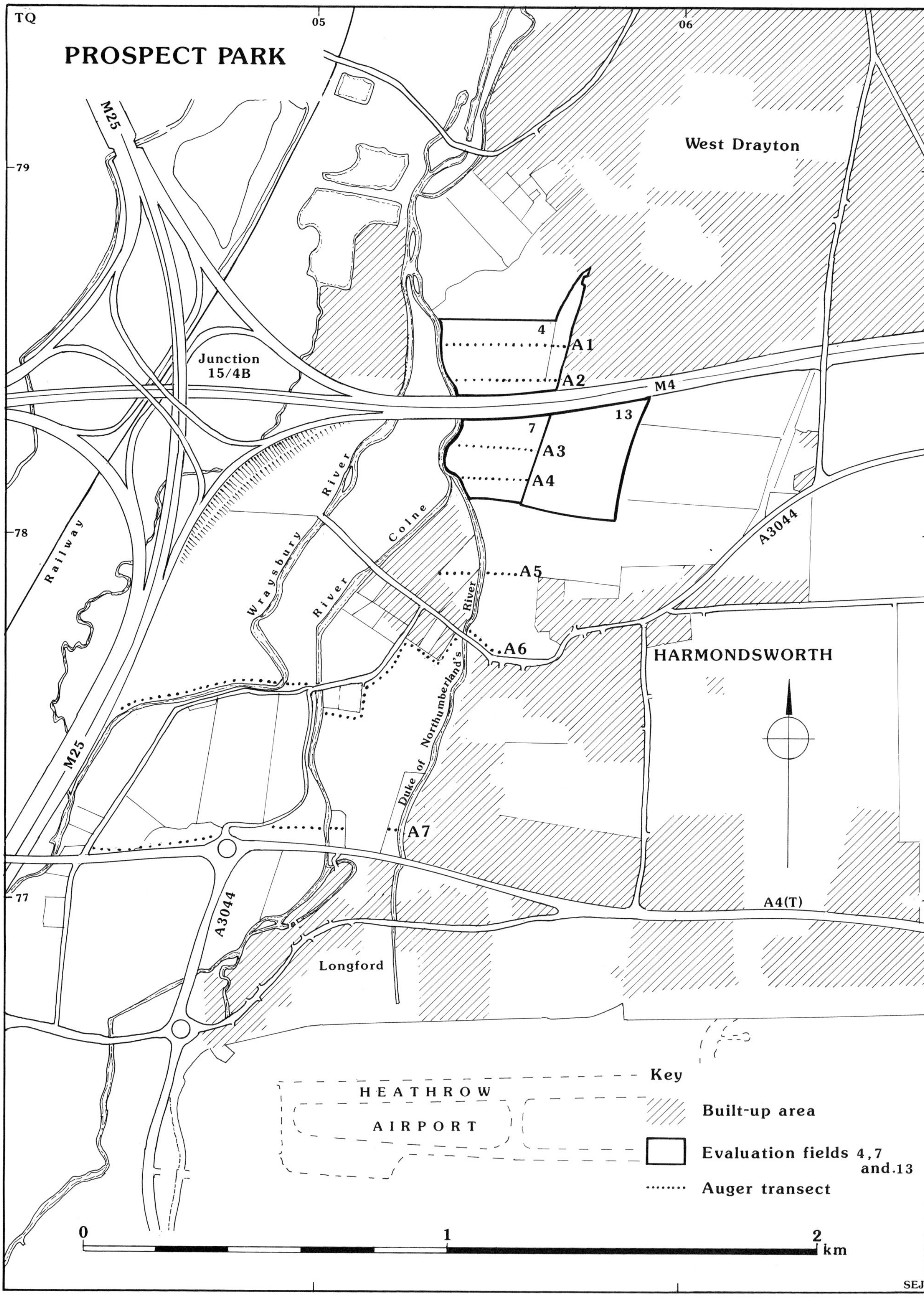

Figure 2 General location plan of Prospect Park, showing evaluation Fields 4, 7, and 13, and auger transects A1–A7

1. Prospect Park, Harmondsworth, London Borough of Hillingdon: Settlement and Burial from the Neolithic to the Early Saxon Periods

by Phil Andrews

with contributions from Sheila Hamilton-Dyer, P.A. Harding, Pat Hinton, M. Laidlaw, Jacqueline I. McKinley, Lorraine Mepham, and D.F. Williams

1. Introduction

In 1993 a desk-based archaeological assessment was undertaken, the results of which suggested that extensive areas of Prospect Park had no archaeological potential having been subject to gravel extraction since 1945 (Chadwick 1993). Elsewhere, although no direct evidence was available, discoveries from the immediate vicinity of Fields 4, 7, and 13, along the northern edge of the land, suggested that these areas had significant archaeological potential. Discoveries included features and finds of Middle Bronze Age, Late Bronze Age, and early to middle Saxon date, as well as evidence for exploitation of the Thames and Colne Valleys from at least *c.* 300,000 BC. Accordingly, British Airways, through Lawson-Price Consultants, commissioned and sponsored the Trust for Wessex Archaeology to carry out a field evaluation programme approved by English Heritage and the London Borough of Hillingdon.

A number of areas containing archaeological features and finds of Neolithic and later prehistoric date were recorded in the evaluation (Wessex Archaeology 1993) and these warranted further investigation. A large-scale excavation was therefore proposed (Chadwick 1994), and this was subsequently carried out by the Trust for Wessex Archaeology between 14th March and 13th May 1994. This focused on Field 13 with a small amount of additional work in Field 7 (Fig. 2). A watching brief, to be reported on separately, was undertaken in 1995 during construction work, and the results from this are also taken account of in the discussion here.

Situation

The majority of the site occupies the floodplain of the River Colne with its associated watercourses (Colne Brook, Wraysbury River, and Duke of Northumberland's River). The floodplain is at *c.* 23 m OD with the land rising, in places in a scarp and elsewhere in a gentle gradient, to a terrace at *c.* 26 m to the north and *c.* 29 m to the east. The site is underlain by sands and gravels which, within the floodplain, are covered by various depths of alluvium (from 0.4 m to in excess of 1.4 m are recorded locally). On the terrace, topsoil rests either directly on gravel in the north or on depths of brickearth in the east. The gravel across much of the site forms part of the Taplow Terrace, with those towards the north-east belonging to the Boyn Hill Terrace.

Land on the gravel terraces has been ploughed since the mid 18th century (Rocque's map 1754) and probably much earlier, which has undoubtedly caused some reduction and damage to the archaeological deposits. The floodplain, however, remained as uncultivated 'moor' and is likely to have been subject to seasonal flooding. Alluvium deposited by various river channels crossing the floodplain may seal archaeological deposits. Land worked for sand and gravel over the past 30 years has been restored variously to lakes or pasture, a process which is continuing and often involves landfilling.

Archaeological Background

The intact floodplain areas of the site are covered with alluvium and their archaeological potential remains largely unknown. Furthermore, the origins of many of the current watercourses are confused, although it is clear that from earliest Postglacial times hunter-gatherers exploited the rich and varied water-side habitats of the lower Colne Valley. A number of Mesolithic and later flint tools have been recovered from the floodplain area as stray finds (Greater London Sites and Monuments Record Number 050426, hereafter SMR No.), and a single flint axe and other lithics were found in the 1980s in Field 7 within the Prospect Park site (SMR No. 050185). During the Neolithic period, areas of the floodplain and adjacent terrace were cleared to enable the construction of major ritual monuments; the Heathrow/Stanwell Cursus once crossed the Prospect Park site (in areas now quarried away) to terminate immediately to the west in an area now under the M25

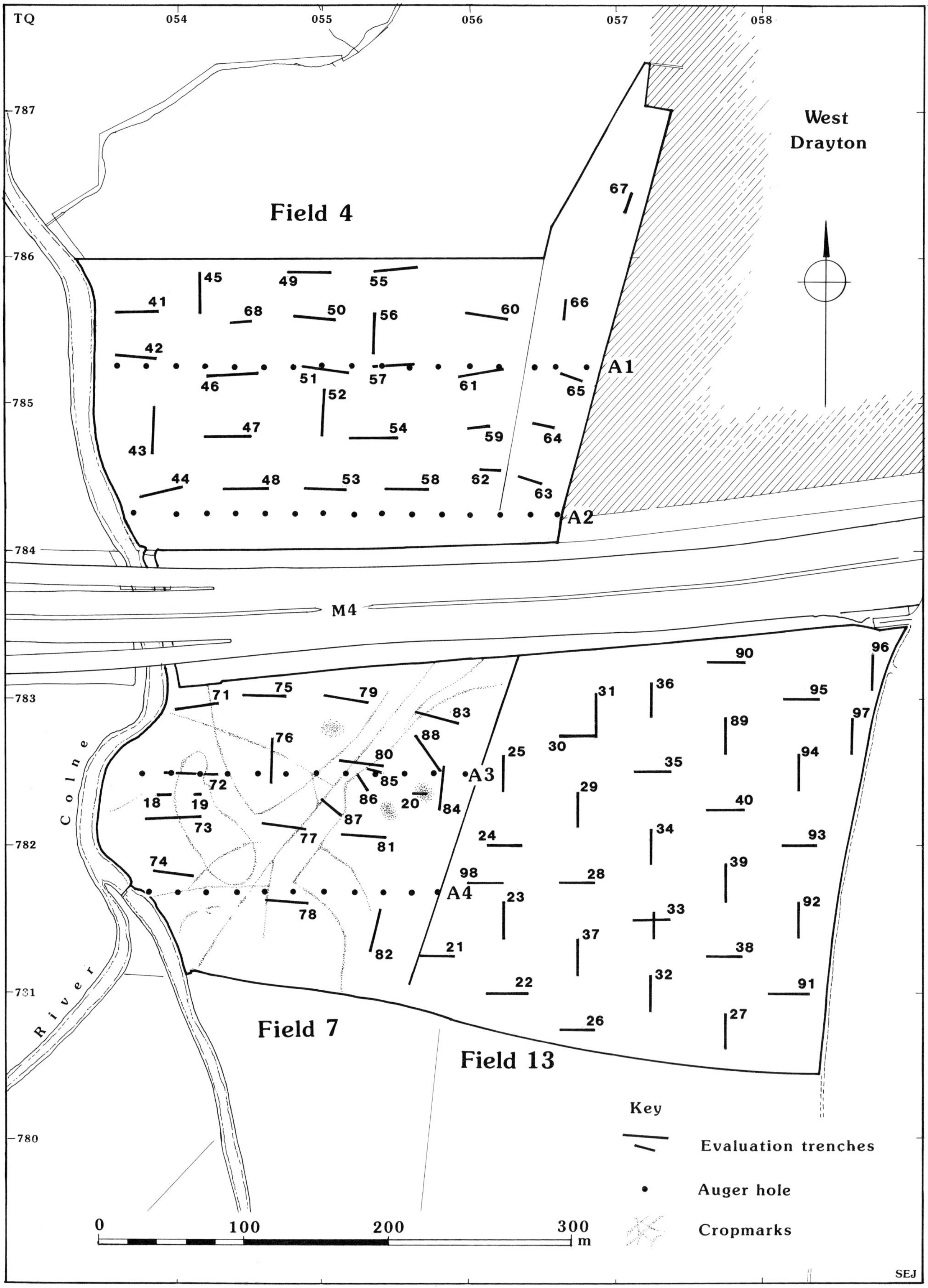

Figure 3 Fields 4, 7, and 13, showing positions of evaluation trenches and auger transects A1–A4

been discovered on the west bank of the Colne Brook between Colnebrook and Horton (Butterworth 1990). No Saxon or medieval finds have come from the floodplain in this area, but as yet unidentified riverside settlements may exist.

The post-medieval development of the floodplain is better understood primarily with information from cartographic sources. Rocque (1754) indicates the area crossed by five channels in the 1750s, of which four fall within the Prospect Park site. The easterly channel, the Duke of Northumberland's River is of uncertain origin; Canham (1978) suggests that this river is an entirely artificial channel built in or about 1543; the Victoria County History (Vol. 2 1911, 310) suggests that it dates to the time of Henry V (1413–1422), and a possibility remains that the river represents a canalised version of an earlier watercourse of natural origin. The possible channels in Field 7 identified on various aerial photographs may be the result of similar drainage and improvement works on the floodplain; equally, a natural origin may be sought.

Evidence for later prehistoric, Roman, and Saxon settlement of the terraces of the Thames and Colne Valleys is more widespread and better understood as a result of a series of watching briefs and excavations (Cotton *et al.* 1986; Cotton 1991; Merriman 1990). At Holloway Lane, Harmondsworth (TQ 079 779), a small Middle Bronze Age pit, an early Saxon sunken-featured building, and a series of 12th–13th century pits and post-holes were found; and Roman *tesserae* were recorded 70 m south-west of Harmondsworth Church (SMR No. 050263). Nearer to Prospect Park, excavations at Manor Farm (TQ 056 778) uncovered several probably prehistoric pits and scoops, part of a possible early Saxon sunken-featured building, and evidence for medieval occupation. At Manor Court (TQ 055 777), Mesolithic and Neolithic features and finds were recorded, along with Romano-British pits and pottery, and Saxon and medieval features. Finally, during the widening of the M4 (TQ 060 783), groundworks revealed a series of Late Bronze Age scoops and a Saxon sunken-featured building.

2. Evaluation

Archaeological evaluation was carried out to establish the date, nature, and extent of the archaeological resource and to assess the nature of the alluvial deposits on the floodplain. The methods employed included auger transects, fieldwalking, test pits, and machine trenching.

Auger Transects Nos A1–A7

The augering was undertaken for two reasons. In Fields 4 and 7 (A1–A4) to define the amount and nature of alluvial deposits and, elsewhere, to confirm or deny the presence of any intact deposits of archaeological potential. Seven auger transects with points at 20 m intervals were carried out using a 40 mm Dutch hand auger. A total of 150 auger points was recorded (Fig. 2). The augering was undertaken for two reasons. In Fields 4 and 7 (A1–A4) the work was to define the amount and nature of the alluvial deposits; elsewhere (within areas known to have been subjected to mineral extraction) to confirm or deny the presence of any intact deposits of archaeological potential at the margins of extracted areas.

Auger Transects A1 and A2

Auger transects A1 and A2 were aligned on the National Grid and ran east–west across the length of Field 4. The transects were 100 m apart. The results showed that gravel deposits were less than 1 m below the present ground surface, with the deepest at 0.95 m; the thickest deposit of alluvium recorded was 0.60 m. Taken overall, these results did not suggest that significant quantities of alluvium existed in Field 4.

Auger Transects A3 and A4

Auger transects A3 and A4 were aligned on the National Grid and ran east–west across the length of Field 7. The transects were 80 m apart. The results showed that gravel deposits were less than one metre below the present ground surface, except at two points. The deepest point was at 1.75 m, with 1.35 m of alluvium, and the other point was at one metre. Taken overall, these results did not suggest that significant quantities of alluvium existed in Field 7 either.

Auger Transect A5

Auger transect A5 was aligned on the National Grid and ran east–west to the west of the Tithe Barn, Harmondsworth. The transect ran across both banks of the Duke of Northumberland's River. The augering encountered disturbed ground and/or gravel deposits very close to the surface. No alluvial deposits were encountered.

Auger Transect A6

Auger transect A6 skirted areas of mineral extraction in the hope of defining untouched deposits of archaeological interest. The augering encountered disturbed ground and/or gravel deposits very close to the surface. Where the transect crossed a 60 m wide neck of land between the Wraysbury River and the River Colne, two auger points encountered more than 0.5 m of overburden. No alluvium was found.

Auger Transect A7

Auger transect A7 ran roughly 500 m to the south of transect A6 and parallel to the A4 trunk road. At the western end of the transect, the points were in undisturbed ground. However, a maximum of only 0.10 m of alluvial material was encountered. The auger points immediately on either side of the River Colne showed undisturbed ground with over half a metre of alluvium

Figure 4 Fields 7 and 13, showing positions of excavated areas and all features

present, with the deepest of the sequence, reaching gravel at 1.8 m. Up to a metre of alluvial clay was found in the area between the River Colne and the Wraysbury River.

Machine Trenching of Field 4

Twenty-eight trenches were excavated in Field 4 (Fig. 3). The general depth of overburden was slight and, on average, gravel was reached at 0.77 m. The average thickness of alluvial deposits was 0.31 m but trenches 45, 49, and 55 were found to contain no alluvium. These trenches ran along the northern edge of the area and served to define the edge of the terrace. The depth of topsoil and alluvium gradually deepened to the south, with localised deeper deposits. Trench 61 was the deepest at 1.5 m and appears to represent a backwater or pond.

Positive evidence for old river channels or other significant deposits was not forthcoming and only a thin, rippled 'skim' of alluvial material along the southern edge of the area was encountered.

Modern and post-medieval debris was noted in the topsoil and localised evidence of agricultural improvement episodes (deep ploughing) were noted in trenches 48, 50, 51, 52, 56, and 58. However, the amount of material and the nature of the disturbances did not suggest that any wholesale levelling and regrading had taken place.

No finds or features of archaeological significance were encountered in any of the trenches. Although limited quantities of brush- and driftwood were recorded and sampled at the base of the deeper alluvial deposits, their environmental potential is low since the levels remain undated and are of generally slight nature. No further work has therefore been carried out on these samples.

Machine Trenching of Field 7

Twenty-one trenches were excavated in Field 7 (Fig. 3). The general depth of overburden was slight, on average gravel was reached at 0.91 m and the average thickness of alluvial deposits was 0.42 m. Trenches 82, 84, and 88 were found to contain no alluvium. These trenches ran along the eastern edge of the area and served to define the edge of the terrace. The depth of soil generally deepened to the west, with localised deeper deposits. Trench 72 had the deepest overburden and gravel was reached at 1.30 m.

There was no positive evidence for old river channels or other significant deposits; only a shallow north–south depression running across the western half of the field was noted. The gravel rose slightly at the western end of the trenches closest to the present river line. It is possible, therefore, that a shallow flood channel ran through at this point but the depth of recorded material was much less than would be expected in an old watercourse.

Modern and post-medieval debris was noted in the topsoil but no evidence of any wholesale levelling or disturbance. Indeed, the waterlogged nature of the western half of the field suggests that agricultural improvement would have been difficult.

Finds or features of archaeological significance were limited to three sherds of Romano-British pottery recovered from the topsoil of trench 77 and two parallel ditches encountered in trenches 80, 85, 86, and 87. The ditches were cut into the underlying gravel and ran roughly from the south-west to the north-east. They were 2 m apart in the north-east and 8 m apart in the south-west. The western ditch was 1.2 m wide and 0.2 m deep, and the eastern ditch 1.5 m wide and 0.6 m deep. Both were filled with grey clay, virtually indistinguishable from the base of the alluvium above them. No finds were recovered from either feature.

Test Pits in Field 13

A pattern of 114 test pits at 25 m intervals was hand dug through the ploughsoil down into the subsoil. They were 0.5 m square and 20% of each was sieved through a 10 mm mesh.

The test pits in the northern half of the field were excavated under optimum weather conditions. By the time the southern half of the field was reached, the weather had deteriorated and the visibility of finds in the wet soil was poor. However, the final distribution of finds suggests that the retrieval of material was not adversely affected. The size of the pits made inspection of the nature of the subsoil and meaningful comparisons across the field difficult. It was noted that the agricultural regime at the time of the survey was ploughing down into the top of the brickearth and/or any surviving prehistoric subsoil.

Considerable quantities of modern and late post-medieval pottery were recovered. The majority of the sherds were small and abraded, suggesting both introduction as part of manuring deposits and intensive agricultural disturbance to at least the top 0.45 m of soil. Quantities of earlier material of archaeological interest were more modest: in total 112 pieces of worked flint, 1993 g of burnt flint, five sherds of Late Bronze Age pottery, two sherds of undiagnostic late prehistoric pottery, and one Romano-British sherd. The pottery showed a localised distribution within a strip 100 m wide along the southern edge of the field but there were no other significant distributions.

Fieldwalking of Field 13

The field had been harrowed but not ploughed. By the time the fieldwalking started, weed growth, added to stubble left lying on the surface, obscured part of the field. However, recent rain had scoured the surface of the soil improving the visibility of artefacts.

In total, 45 pieces of worked flint, 4758 g of burnt flint, and six sherds of pottery were recovered. The latter comprised sherds of Late Bronze Age, Iron Age, probable late prehistoric, Romano-British, and medieval date.

Averages and standard deviations of the amounts of worked and burnt flint were calculated and plotted, but there were no significant distributions. However, the pottery showed a localised distribution along the southern and eastern margins of the field.

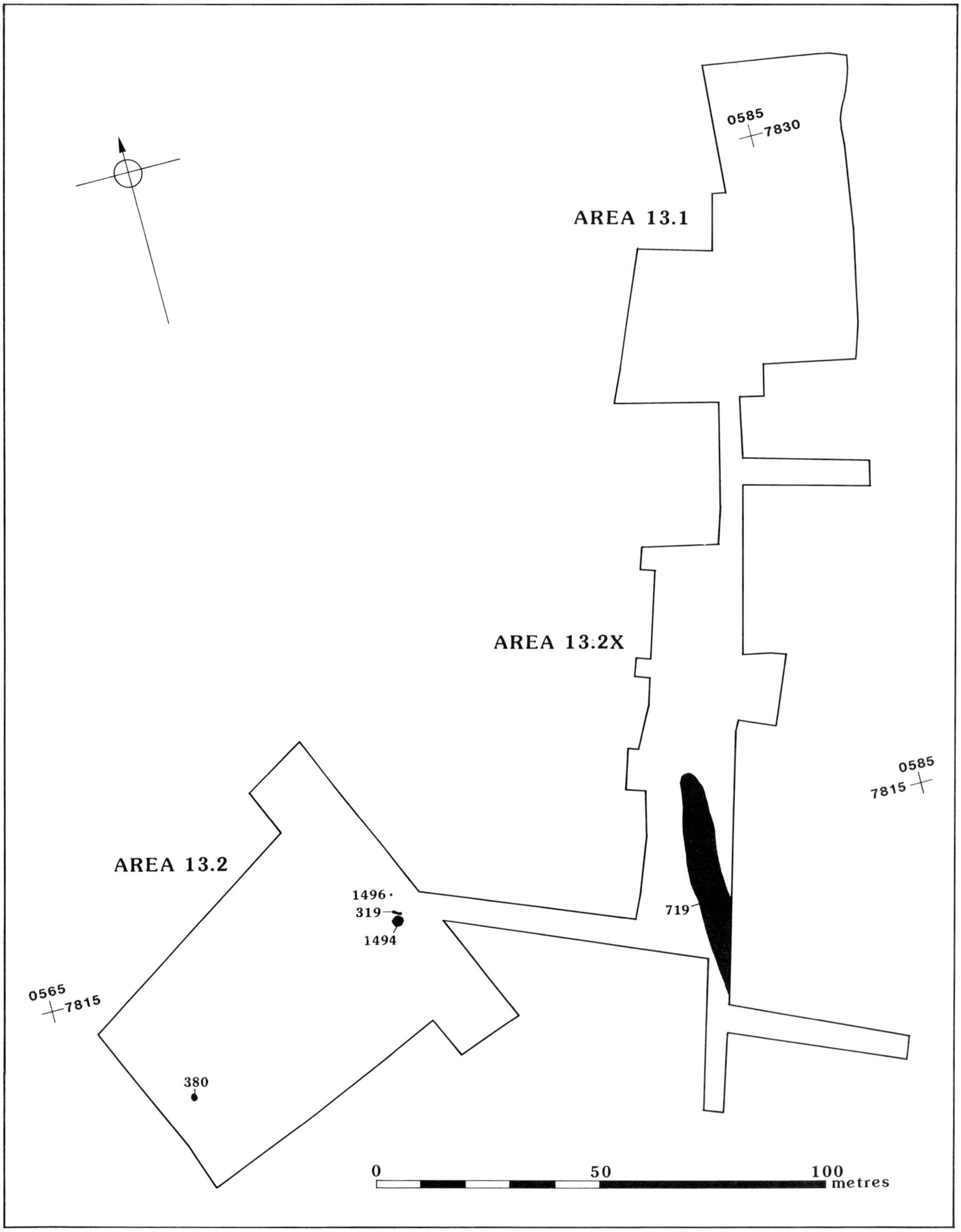

Figure 5 Plan of Late Neolithic features

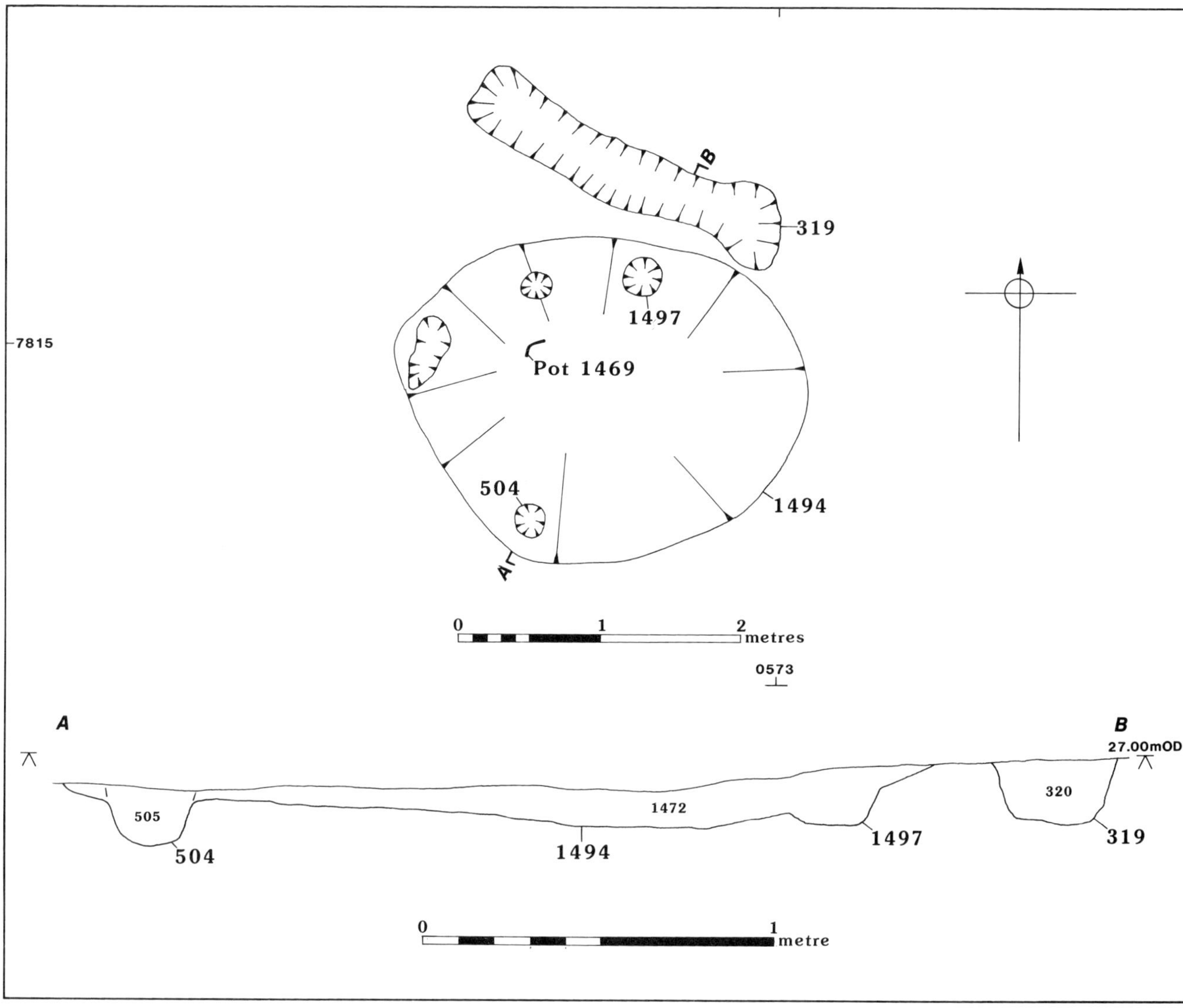

Figure 6 Plan and section of Late Neolithic hollow 1494

Machine Trenching of Field 13

Thirty trenches were excavated in Field 13 (Fig. 3). A regular pattern was adopted in view of the equivocal results of test pitting and fieldwalking.

The first and most obvious piece of information gained from the machine trenches related to the presence of a possible prehistoric agricultural soil. Directly beneath the ploughsoil, and above the natural brickearth, was a fine, generally clean, silty loam which contained a number of abraded sherds of Late Bronze Age date. It can be supposed to be the remnants of a more widespread agricultural surface of that date. This layer was missing over much of the northern and western parts of the site and it is likely that more recent agricultural activity has removed it in the north. To the west, the field drops by about 3 m and it is possible that this layer was confined to the eastern half of the field on the edge of the flatter terrace area.

Six trenches comprising 31, 33, 37, 94, 95, and 96 were found to contain features of archaeological significance.

Late Neolithic and other prehistoric features, including several Late Bronze Age ditches, pits, and post-holes were found in trenches 33, 37, 94, 95, and 96 which fell within the area of the subsequent large-scale excavation; these features are discussed below in the main excavation report. In trench 31 was a shallow slot and depression, but only the former produced finds — two late prehistoric sherds and a flint flake. The generally low level of finds and shallow depth of topsoil in the north-west quadrant of Field 13 suggested that the features in trench 31 should not be taken as indicators of further surviving traces of intensive prehistoric activity in that part of the field.

A series of shallow, linear depressions was encountered in trenches 94, 95, and 96. These ranged from 0.5–3 m in width and were up to 0.15 m deep. These features

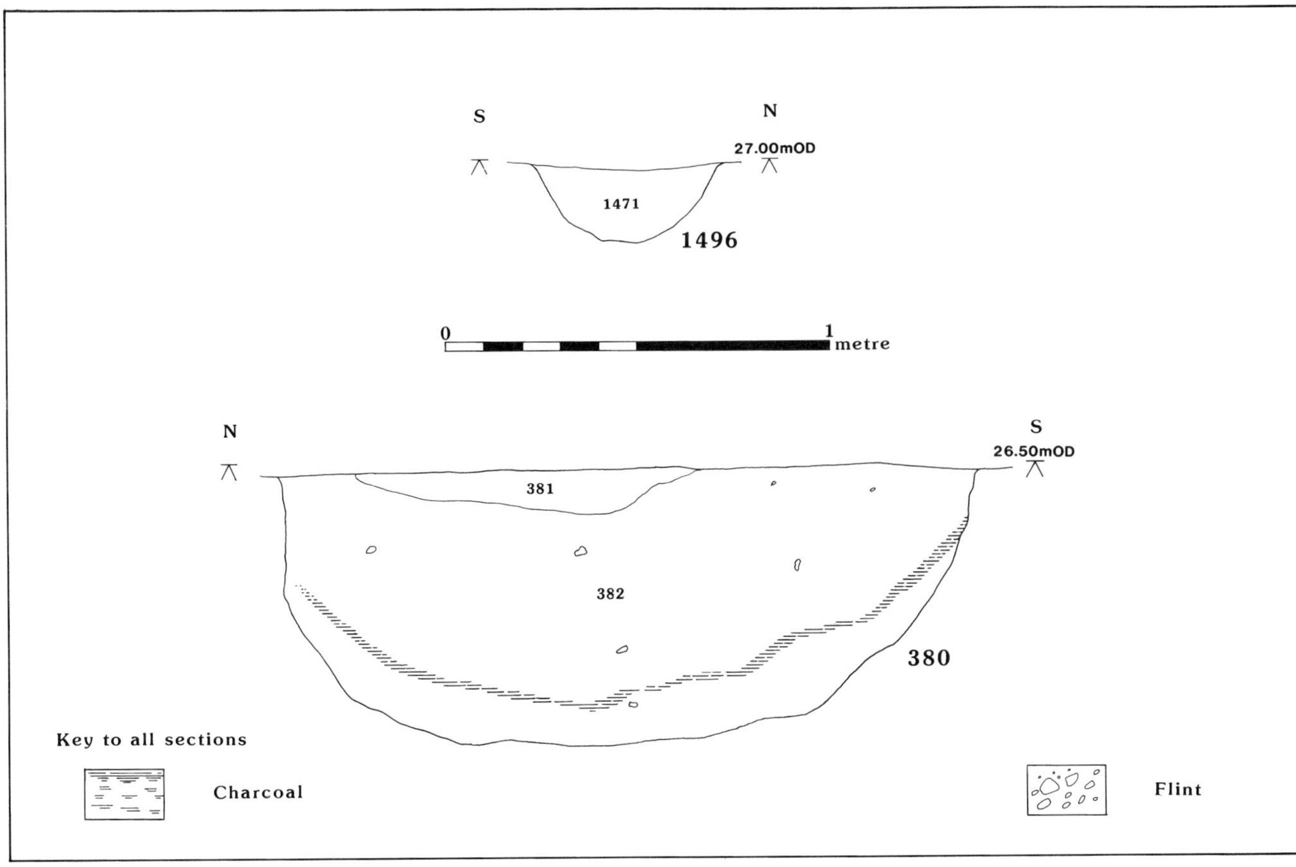

Figure 7 Sections across Late Neolithic pits

were subsequently interpreted as ploughmarks, probably resulting from steam ploughing (*see* below).

3. Excavation

Introduction

On the basis of the results from the evaluations, a large-scale excavation was commissioned by British Airways in Spring 1994 and four themes of investigation were identified. These were:

- 1. To reidentify and attempt to retrieve artefactual material from the two ditches in Field 7.
- 2. To investigate the remains of the prehistoric agricultural system in the north-west corner of Field 13.
- 3. To clarify the extent and character of the Late Neolithic occupation in the southern central area in Field 13.
- 4. To excavate a sample of the brickearth in an attempt to both discover the potential for prehistoric remains within the Pleistocene deposits and to investigate the nature and origins of the brickearth deposit itself. It was anticipated that a buried soil containing Palaeolithic material might survive on the surface of the gravel sealed by the brickearth, and that Mesolithic remains might be present within the brickearth.

Methods

Machine trenching of Field 7

Topsoil was stripped by mechanical excavator down to the level of the gravel in two areas (trenches 7.1 and 7.2, Fig. 4), the archaeological evaluation having established that no archaeological deposits other than negative features survived in this area. Both trenches were positioned in the spaces between evaluation trenches within which ditches had been encountered. The trenches were subsequently enlarged in order to further define the edges of the ditches, and sections were were then dug by hand.

Excavation of Field 13

A tracked excavator using a 1.8 m wide toothless bucket was used to remove the topsoil. Area 13.2 was stripped first to allow a long period of weathering across the surface of the exposed brickearth. Area 13.1 was stripped next, followed by a narrow series of linking trenches between the two areas (Fig. 4). The initial stripping followed the pattern laid down in the brief (Chadwick 1994, fig. 4), with 15 m wide 'arms' in the main areas.

Grids set at 10 m intervals were placed across Areas 13.1 and 13.2 and both areas planned at 1:50. Excavation of features then proceeded. The machine was then used to expand the initial areas where the greatest concentrations of features were encountered. The final stripping operation consisted of a 15 m wide trench which was excavated over the series of linking trenches between Areas 13.1 and 13.2; this area was designated 13.2X.

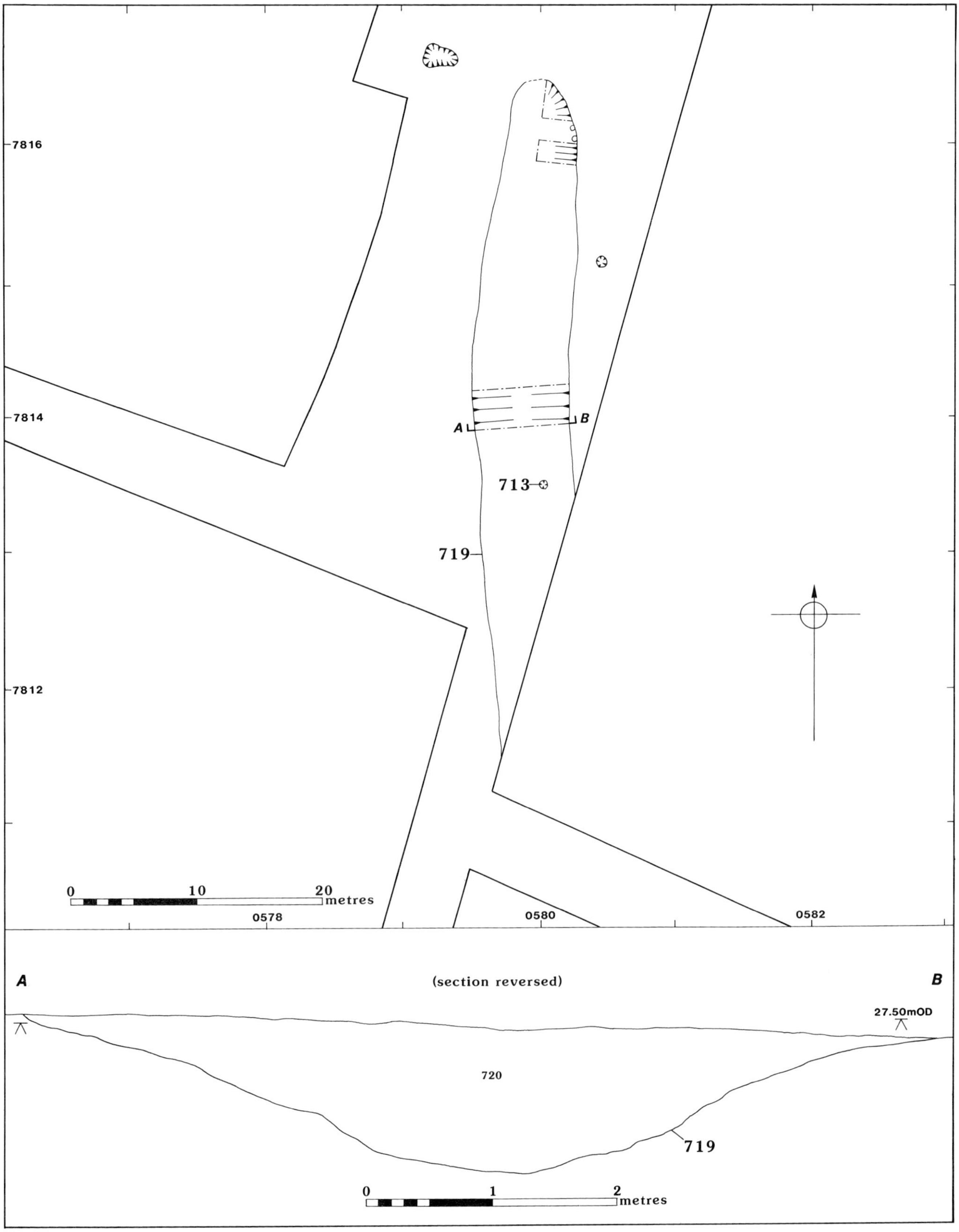

Figure 8 Plan and section of ditch 719

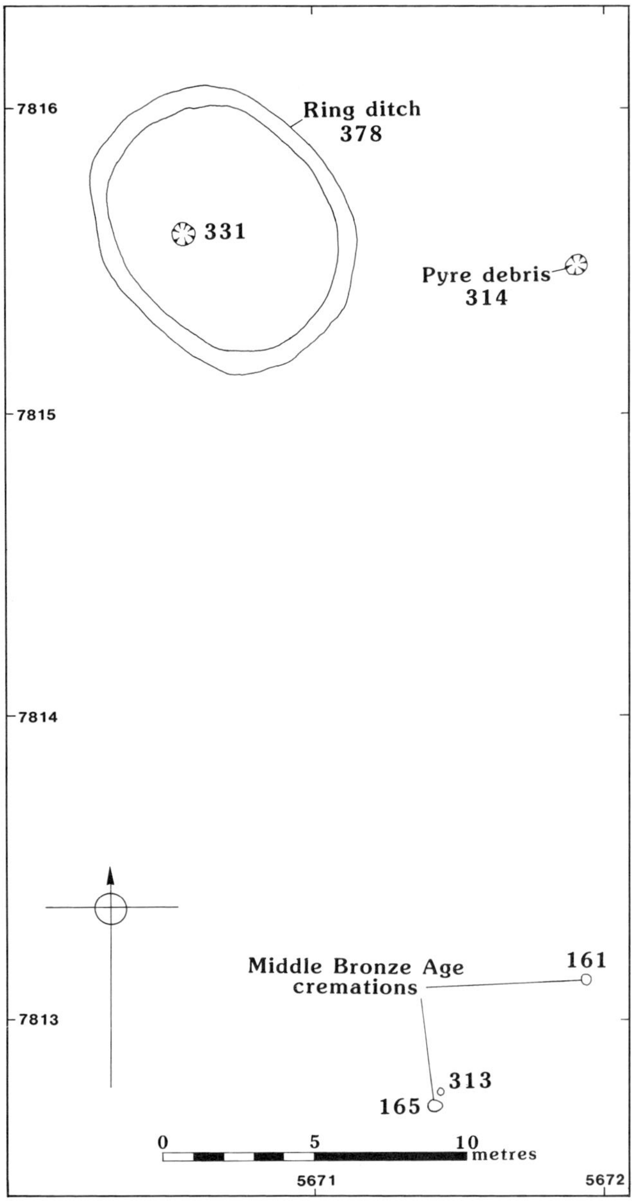

Figure 9 Plan of ring-ditch 378 and Middle Bronze Age cremations 161 and 165

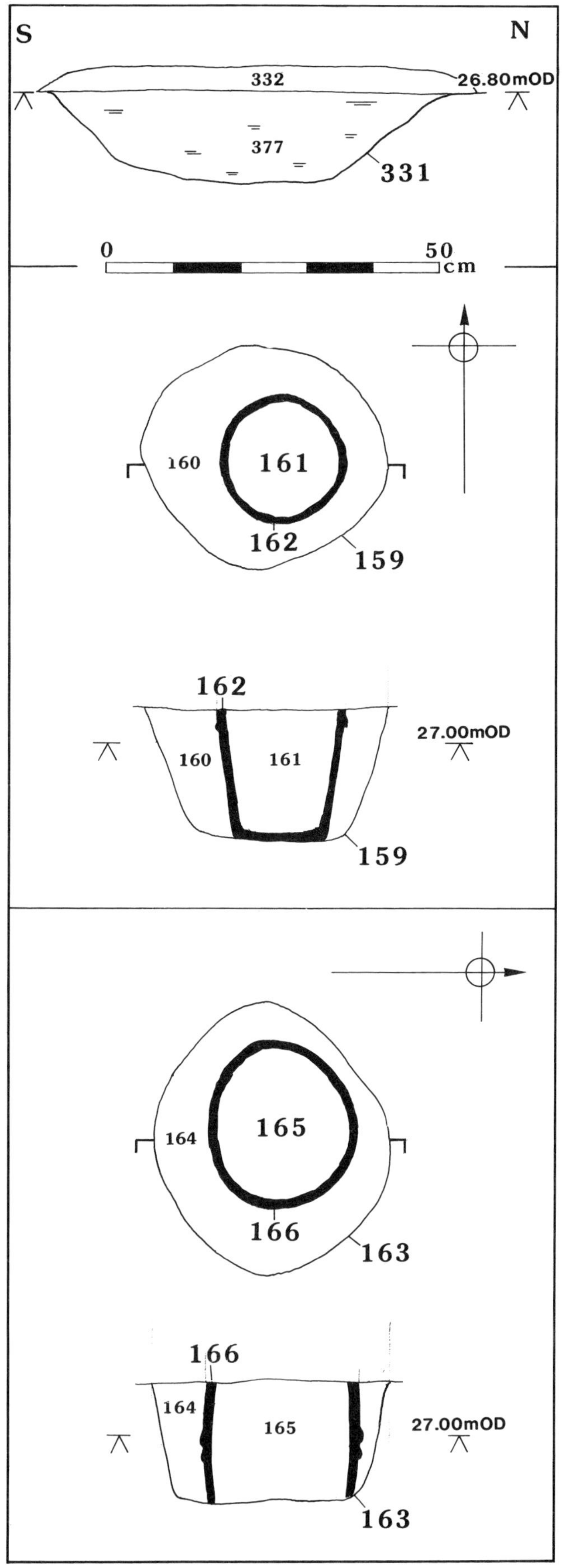

Figure 10 Plans and sections of Middle Bronze Age cremation burials 161 and 165

The remnants of linear disturbances which ran east–west at 7.5 m intervals were recorded across Area 13.1. These were scored through the subsoil into the surface of the brickearth. The scores were 0.05–0.1 m deep and up to 1 m wide. They were similar in section to the form of furrows in a ridge and furrow earthwork. Modern (19th and 20th century) debris was found within these features. A local resident recalled seeing steam ploughing in the field when he was a child and it is likely that the furrows were caused by this activity. If ridge and furrow occurred in the field it would have been obliterated at this time. The disturbed surface was machined down after investigation in order to reveal surviving features beneath. In Area 13.2X the furrows were machined away without record.

Following the excavation of features in Area 13.1, a 4 m deep trench was dug through the brickearth down to the surface of the gravel. This trench, designated 13.3, was oriented east–west, and was 30 m long by 12 m wide

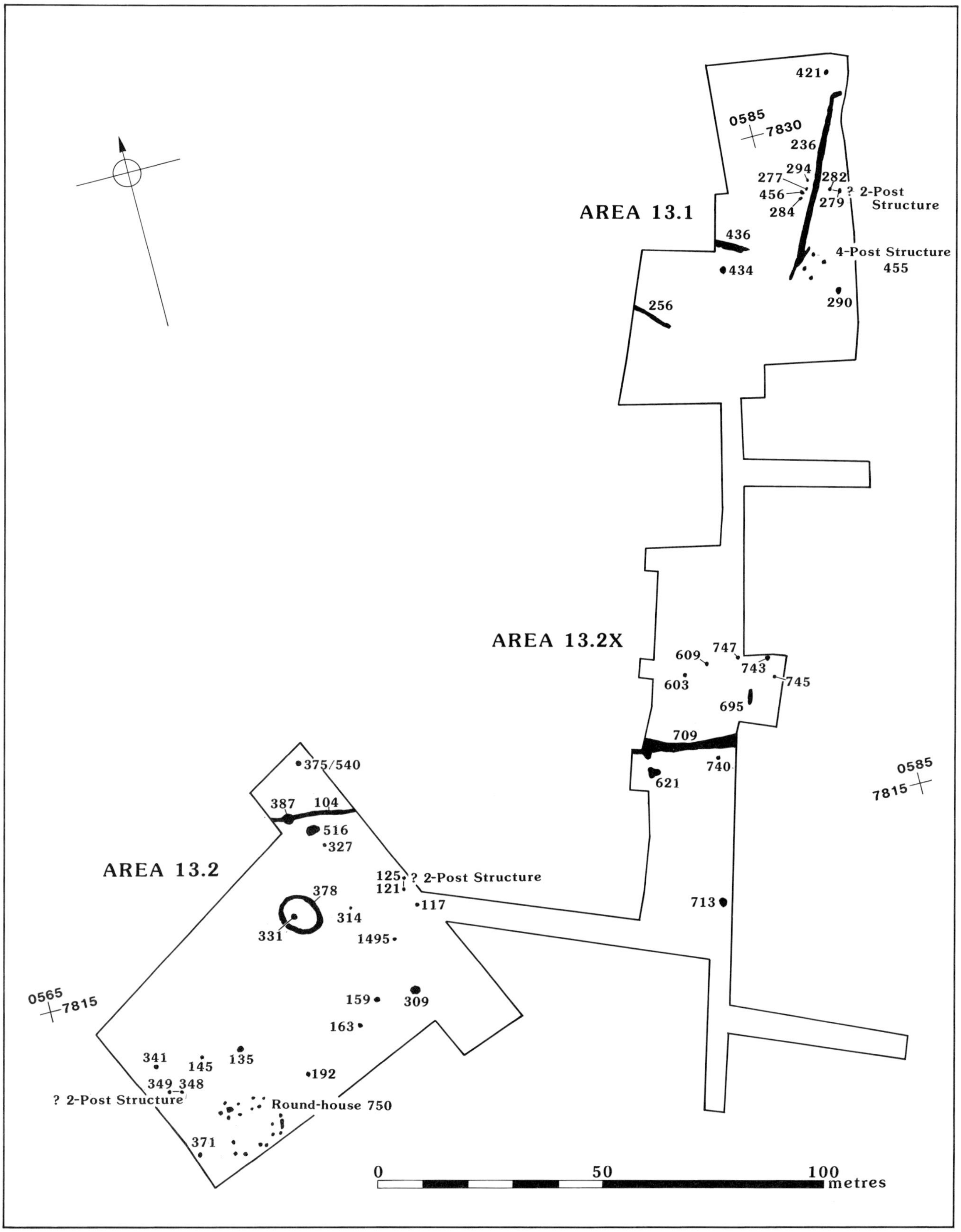

Figure 11 Plan of Middle and Late Bronze Age features

at the top. The northern face was partially battered, the southern was stepped for section recording. A rectangular area of gravel, 28 m long by 2 m wide, was exposed at the base of the trench. The surfaces and sections of the brickearth were photographed and drawn and monolith sampling was undertaken. The brickearth was sampled for the purpose of soil micromorphological analysis. Knowledge of the nature of the material and its deposition process will allow future assessment of the archaeological potential of the medium to be undertaken with greater accuracy.

All discrete features within the stripped areas were half or quarter sectioned, their sections recorded, then completely excavated. Linear features were sectioned at intervals and some were further excavated to maximise the retrieval of artefacts. Some small features, suspected of being of early date, were 100% sampled for the same reason and to gain environmental data.

An appropriate sampling strategy for economic, environmental, and artefactual information was devised during the course of the excavation as the precise archaeological content of the site became clear. High priority was given to the sampling of a selection of well-dated features and features thought to be of early date in order to recover charred plant and cereal remains.

Dating

There was an overall lack of stratified deposits. Not only were there very few physical relationships between features but even substantial features generally lacked internal deposition sequences. The majority of the recorded features were found to be small with single fills and no direct dating evidence.

Most of the features were small and badly eroded. In Areas 13.1 and 13.2X, their average depth was 0.21 m, in Area 13.2 0.17m and, in many cases, it is difficult to interpret their original function (eg whether some represent the bases of small pits or substantial post-holes). Structural associations and the finds recovered from them have allowed some features to be interpreted with a degree of confidence. For the rest, the interpretation relies on a crude index of size and shape: features greater than 0.5 m in diameter have been interpreted as pits, except where an obvious structural interpretation has been apparent (eg post-holes 226, 228, 230, and 275 of structure 455).

Statements of date and function (eg Saxon post-hole) are based on direct evidence in only a limited number of cases. Although almost 38% of the excavated features contained pottery, only 22% contained more than two sherds. Much of the interpretation, therefore, relies on small numbers of badly preserved pottery sherds and/or association with nearby better-dated features. Where features contained reasonable numbers of sherds of pottery, their dates were often mixed as a result of varying degrees of intrusion and residual deposition.

Other than the pottery, only the worked flint among the limited range and quantity of finds recovered assisted in dating the sequence of activity on the site. The period divisions adopted are therefore almost entirely dependent on the pottery. For reasons discussed in the pottery section below, while the prehistoric pottery has been broadly divided into Neolithic (early prehistoric) and Middle and Late Bronze Age (late prehistoric); finer divisions were more difficult to establish, particularly amongst the late prehistoric assemblage. The main periods represented on the site, expressed as broad date ranges are:

- Mesolithic (8500–4000 BC)
- Neolithic (4000–2400 BC)
- Middle Bronze Age (1500–1100 BC)
- Late Bronze Age (1100–700 BC)
- Romano-British (AD 43–410)
- Early Saxon (AD 410–650)

The two ditches encountered in Field 7 during the evaluation were exposed. The northern machined area (7.1) revealed only the terminal of one feature (Fig. 4). In the southern area (7.2) both features were present (Fig. 4). It was apparent that they were not straight or continuous in their courses, but were sinuous in plan and of irregular depth. Both features became ill-defined towards the south-west. They were filled with clean, grey clay. The deeper, western feature had a 0.3 m thick organic-rich fill at its base. The width was 2 m, the overall depth was 0.7 m, and the feature was uncovered over a length of 55 m. The smaller feature was 1 m wide and 0.4 m deep. Both were discontinuous and it is suggested that they were water channels of natural origin. Modern and post-medieval debris was noted in the topsoil but no datable material was found during the excavation of sections through either feature.

The Site

Mesolithic

Five microliths, including two 'rods', indicate some possibly Late Mesolithic activity. All were found towards the southern end of the site but no features were identified.

Neolithic

The earliest datable features on the site were Late Neolithic. Although these were limited in number, the survival of features in the south and west, despite plough damage and the lack of evidence in the north-east where there was a greater depth of subsoil, suggests a concentration of activity in the south (Fig. 5).

Hollow 1494

This was a shallow, sub-circular hollow up to 2.7 m across and 0.15 m deep (Fig. 6). In the bottom, close to the north edge, was a shallow post-hole, 1497, and two insubstantial features which may also have been the remains of post-holes lay to the west of this. Towards the centre was the *in situ* base of a Grooved Ware vessel (1469), the top of which had been removed by ploughing. The fill of the hollow, 1472, was an undifferentiated silty loam very similar to the overlying subsoil. This contained a further 45 sherds of Grooved Ware, probably from two vessels, and a rim of what may be Peterborough Ware.

Plate 1 Prospect Park: section across ditch 719 (2 m scale). Facing south

Two other features may have been part of, or associated with, hollow 1494. Post-hole 504 lay just within the southern edge of the hollow, 2 m from post-hole 1497. It was of similar dimensions to the latter with which it may have formed a pair but contained only a single sherd of late prehistoric pottery. It is possible that post-holes 504 and 1497 were later prehistoric features and unrelated to hollow 1494; a pair of similar but undated post-holes, 399 and 502, lay 3 m to the east and perhaps all may have been contemporaneous.

Immediately to the north of hollow 1494 was slot 319, 1.7 m long, 0.6 m wide, and 0.3 m deep. This contained five sherds of Neolithic pottery.

Other features

Post-hole 1496 lay 4 m to the north of hollow 1494 and was 0.4 m in diameter and 0.2 m deep (Fig. 7). It contained 20 sherds of Grooved Ware from a single vessel, probably burnt after breakage, and perhaps part of one of the vessels found in 1472, the fill of hollow 1494.

Pit 380 lay in the southern corner of the site, some 50 m from hollow 1494. This was oval, measured approximately 1.8 by 1.3 m and was 0.7 m deep. It had two fills, 381 and 382, both of which were dark yellowish–brown clayey silts (Fig. 7). The bottom fill, 382, was slightly more sandy, with a prominent charcoal lens and contained the majority of artefacts. These include five sherds of Neolithic pottery and the largest assemblage of worked flint from any feature on site. This comprises 39 pieces, including five scrapers, a possible triangular arrowhead, and 18 flakes.

Ditch 719

Ditch 719 cannot be ascribed with certainty to the Neolithic period. However, it was cut by a small pit, 713, which contained seven sherds of later prehistoric pottery (Fig. 8; Pl. 1). The full extent of ditch 719 was not determined, but it is estimated to have been approximately 50 m long and up to 7 m wide. It was aligned north–south and was very slightly curvilinear in plan with a rounded terminal at the north end; the assumed southern terminal lay outside the limit of excavation. A cross trench, less than 10 m to the south, showed that it did not continue this far (Fig. 8). When ditch 719 was initially exposed, it was thought possibly to have been a natural feature. However, the profile and clearly defined terminal, rendered this interpretation unlikely. A single section was excavated across the central part of the ditch and two smaller sections at the north end (Fig. 8). These revealed it to survive to a depth of approximately 1 m, with the sides sloping at approximately 20° and a slightly rounded bottom. The fill, 720, was fairly homogeneous and heavily disturbed by root action. It graded imperceptibly from a dark yellowish–brown silty clay loam at the top to a light yellowish–brown sandy clay loam at the bottom. Two soil monoliths were taken from the fill; these showed localised gleying and leaching with no laminations or inwashes of coarser material. The deposits were not heavily weathered, nor was there any evidence of pedogenic features which would indicate geological antiquity. A gradual silting of the ditch is probable but the degree of root disturbance was too great to enable the nature of infilling to be ascertained. The

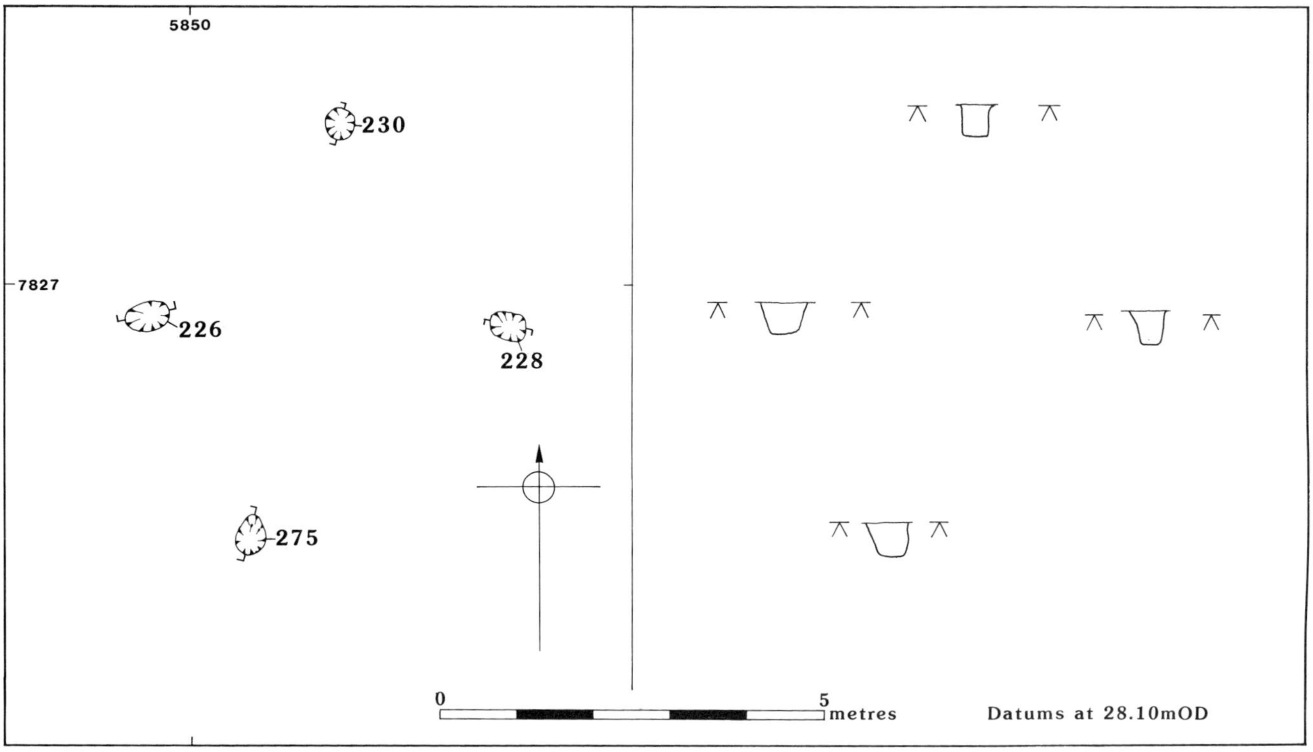

Figure 12 Plan of four-post structure 455

only finds from the ditch were small quantities of burnt and worked flint, the latter including a large, broken, ?unfinished flake tool. Although difficult to date, the worked flint is possibly Late Neolithic.

The concentration of Late Neolithic features in the south and west of the site is further highlighted by the distribution of worked flint and Late Neolithic pottery residual in later features. The quantities of flint are low but tools are well represented and, though difficult to assign chronologically, the principal concentration does coincide with the area of Late Neolithic activity. More than 30 sherds of Late Neolithic pottery have also come from later features in this area, compared with fewer than 10 sherds from the remainder of the site.

Middle Bronze Age

Two cremation burials and a possible ring-ditch have been ascribed to this period, and all of these lay close together in the south-east corner of the site in the same area as the Neolithic features (Figs 9 and 11).

Ring-ditch 378

This lay on a slight knoll which had been reduced by ploughing such that only the deeper features survived over an area approximately 50 m in diameter (Fig. 9; Pl. 2). The ditch was oval in plan and measured approximately 8.4 m by 6.7 m internally, but survived only as a soil stain up to 0.8 m in width. There was no surviving cut in the brickearth and the ditch had evidently been entirely removed by ploughing, leaving only a stain created by darker soil from the ditch filtering down through root holes. Within the ring-ditch, and slightly off-centre to the west, was a small pit, 331 (Fig. 10). This was 0.6 m in diameter and survived to a depth of 0.2 m. The lower fill, 377, was a reddish brown silty clay with some burnt clay and occasional charcoal flecking. Four sherds of late prehistoric pottery were recovered, but no cremated bone and no further evidence was forthcoming from the soil sample taken from this feature. Layer 377 was sealed by a thin spread of redeposited brickearth, 332, which contained occasional patches of reddish brown soil, charcoal flecking, and burnt flint.

Less than 10 m to the east of the ring-ditch lay 314, a shallow feature 0.55 m in diameter and only 0.11 m deep, though it had been heavily truncated. The fill, 315, comprised a mixture of charcoal and burnt human bone fragments with some small pieces of burnt clay. The

Plate 2 Ring-ditch 378, surviving only as a soil stain (1 m and 2 m scales)

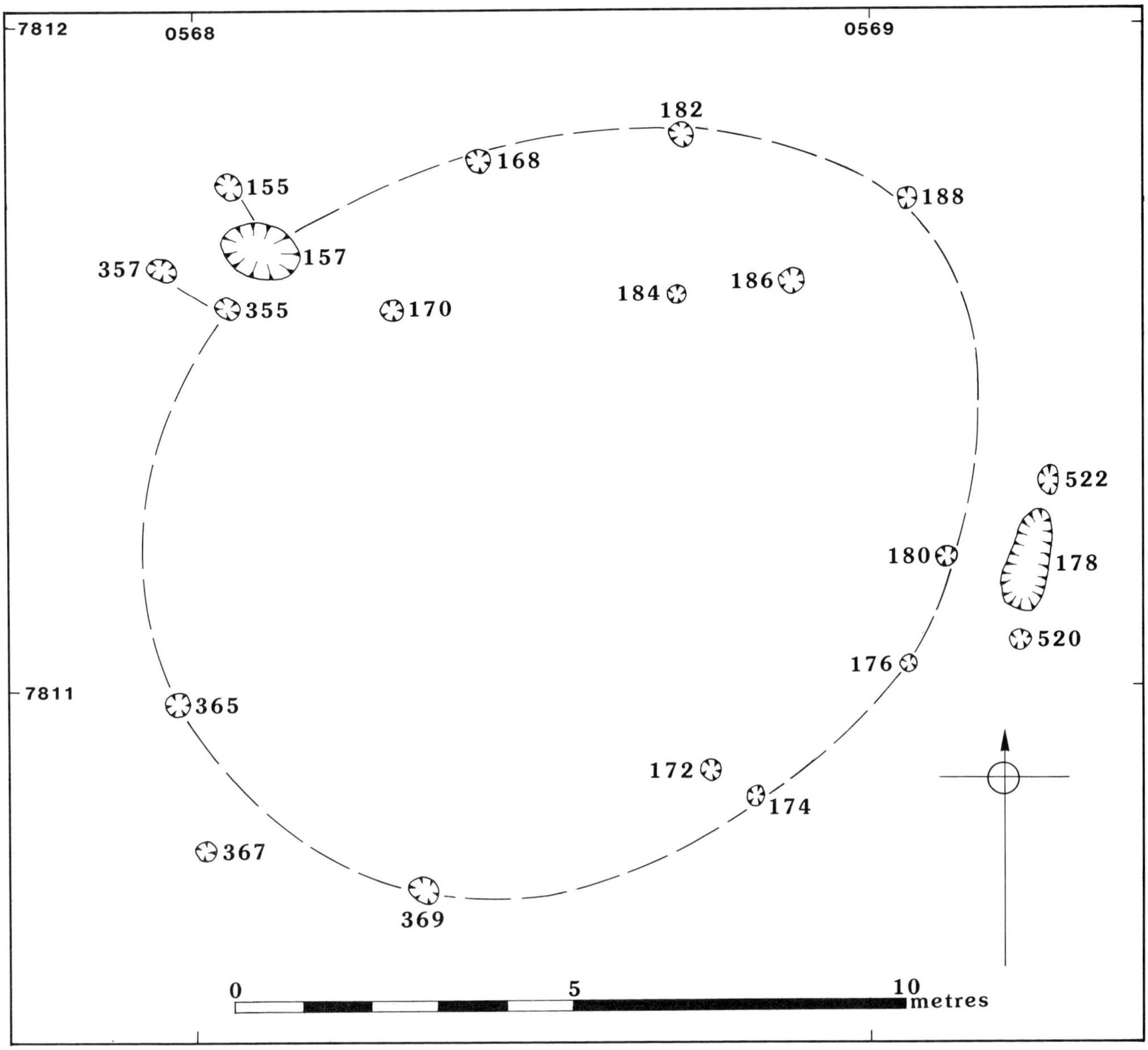

Figure 13 Plan of ?round-house 750

bone, possibly representing two adults, was heavily stained by the charcoal and perhaps was a dump of pyre debris rather than an unurned burial. No dating evidence was recovered from this feature, though its proximity to ring-ditch 378 suggests the possibility that the two were related.

Cremation burials 161 and 165

Two Middle Bronze Age cremation burials, 161 and 165 (Fig. 10) lay approximately 6.5 m apart, and some 25 m south of ring-ditch 378. Both were possibly females, 161 a mature adult and 165 a young adult (*see* below, Human Bone). Both were in urns, one (166) inverted, and placed in shallow pits which had been heavily truncated. The surviving pits were sub-circular, up to 0.4 m in diameter and 0.26 m deep. Although fragmentary, both vessels appear to be of similar bucket-shaped form with a single finger-impressed cordon around the body. Further sherds in similar fabrics which may therefore be of similar date were recovered from ditch 104 and pit 387 to the north and also from pit 713 to the east which cut ditch 719. The pottery in 104 and 387 was certainly residual and probably also in 713; these features are discussed more fully under the Late Bronze Age period below. One further feature, 313, may have been associated with the cremation burials,

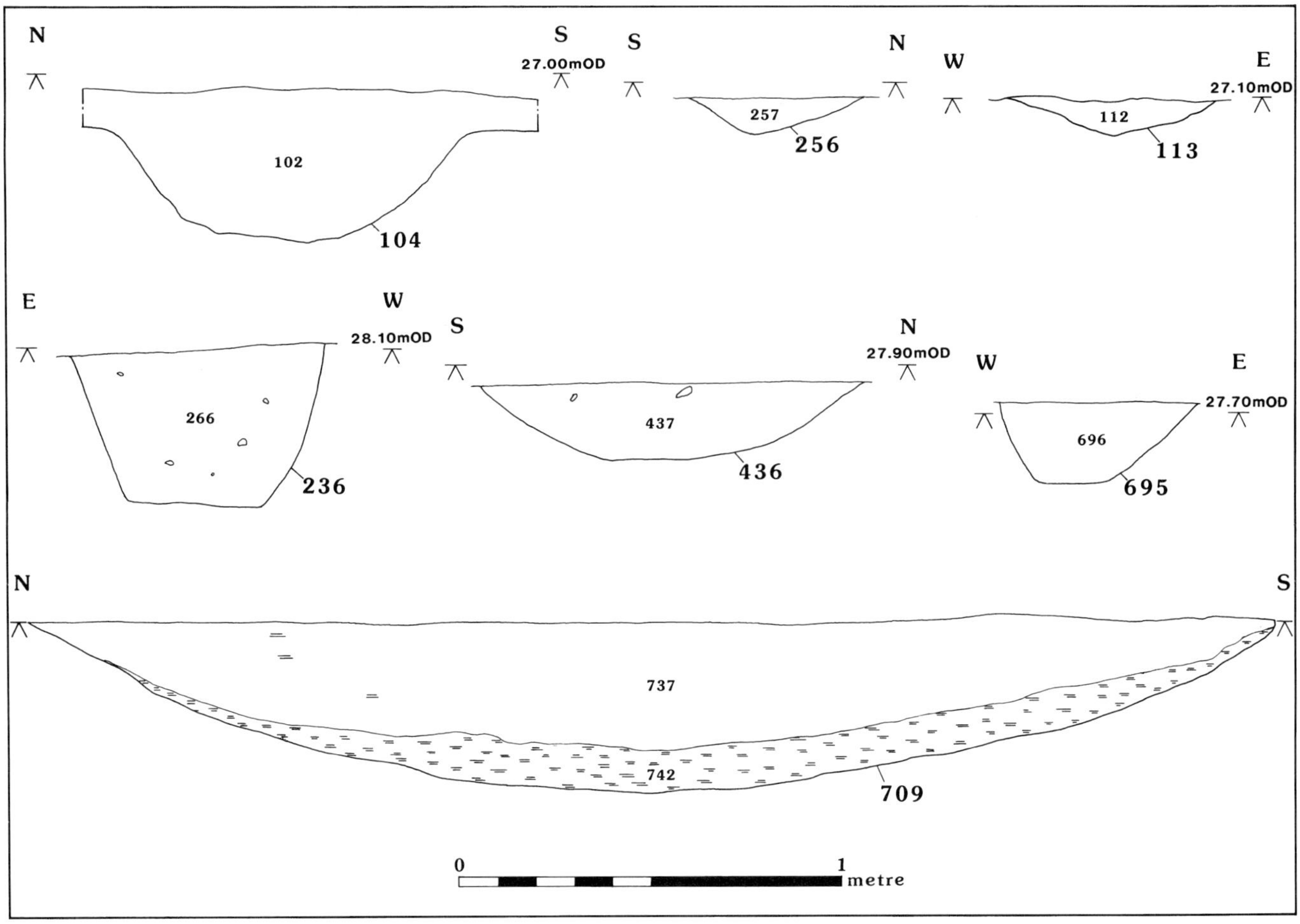

Figure 14 Sections across Late Bronze Age ditches

although it is undated. This was a shallow, sub-circular scoop 0.3 m to the north of cremation burial 165. It was approximately 0.25 m in diameter and 0.07 m deep and filled entirely with charcoal mixed with patches of redeposited brickearth.

Late Bronze Age

In contrast to the restricted distribution of the earlier features, Late Bronze Age features occurred over almost the entire excavated area. Furthermore, these features were clearly associated with occupation (Fig. 11).

Structures

Four-post structure 455, in Area 13.1, is the only structure which can certainly be ascribed to this phase (Fig. 12). The dating of rectangular, post-built structure 721, in Area 13.2X (*see* Fig. 17), is equivocal; although several of the post-holes contained sherds of late prehistoric pottery, the overall plan is considered more likely to represent a Saxon hall and this is discussed more fully below. Various other groups of post-holes have been assigned to the late prehistoric period but it has proved difficult to identify any coherent plans. Several pairs of post-holes may represent two-post structures, and another group could be interpreted as a round-house (structure 750, Area 13.2, Fig. 13).

Structure 455

Structure 455 lay close to the southern end of ditch 236 and comprised four substantial post-holes (226, 228, 230, and 275) up to 4.5 m apart set in a trapezoidal arrangement (Fig. 12). The post-holes were oval in plan, up to 0.6 m across and 0.45 m deep. They contained homogeneous fills, dark yellowish–brown sandy silts with some gravel but no post-pipes were detected. All but post-hole 226, contained sherds of late prehistoric pottery and there seems little doubt that structure 455 was a four-post structure belonging to this period.

Paired post-holes

A considerable number of smaller post-holes were found scattered across the site, many of them undated, but some containing one or more sherds of late prehistoric pottery. The pottery may be residual in some but in others probably not; a single post-hole, 740, to the south of ditch 719 contained 16 sherds. Groups of post-holes containing pottery included 284 and 294, midway along the west side of ditch 236; 603 and 747 to the north of ditch 709; and 145, 341, and 349 in the south-west corner of the site. Some undated post-holes in the vicinity of

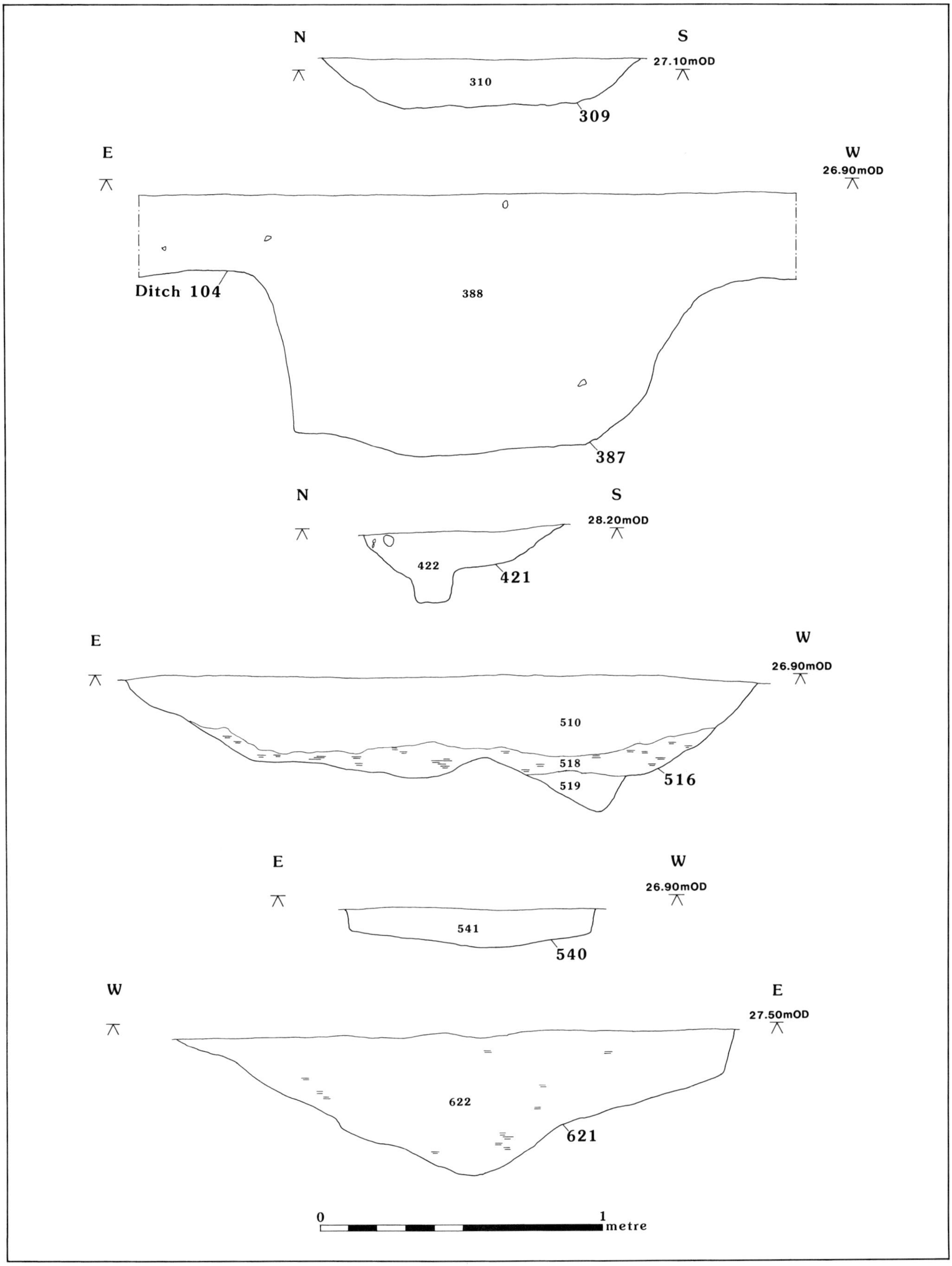

Figure 15 Sections across Late Bronze Age pits

these groups may have been contemporary with them and others are likely to have been completely removed by ploughing. No patterns could be discerned within these groups but several possible pairs of post-holes were noted elsewhere, perhaps representing two-post structures. The paired post-holes were roughly 2 m apart and three examples produced late prehistoric pottery from one of the post-holes: 279 and 282 (in Area 13.1), 121 and 125, and 348 and 349 (both in Area 13.2).

Structure 750

The greatest concentration of undated post-holes lay in the south-west corner of the site, in Area 13.2. Most were less than 0.2 m in diameter and 0.03–0.12 m deep, though there were several deeper examples up to a maximum depth of 0.33 m. Attention is drawn to one group in this area which may represent a circular structure, possibly a round-house or enclosure (structure 750, Fig. 13). No pottery was recovered from any of the post-holes but there were three pits (135, 192, and 371) in the vicinity which contained late prehistoric pottery. The postulated structure 750 was sub-circular, with a diameter of between 11 and 12 m and a possible north-west facing entrance. As many as 11 post-holes may have belonged to this structure, with a further two, 155 and 357, marking an entrance up to 1.5 m wide. The post-holes did not form a continuous circuit, but there is a slight hint of some regularity in their spacing at intervals of about 3 m. These may have marked an inner post-ring, with 155, 357, 367, 520, and 522, along with

Plate 3 Terminal of Late Bronze Age ditch 236 (0.5 and 1 m scales). Facing north-east

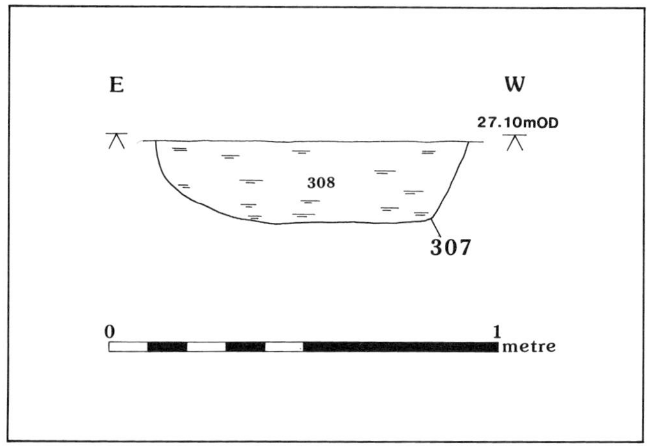

Figure 16 Section across Romano-British pit 307, containing cremated human bone

feature 178, perhaps marking a wall line a metre or so outside the post-ring.

One further possible structural feature was slot 695, which lay within the area covered by structure 721 in Area 13.2X. Unlike the latter, slot 695, which contained 35 sherds of late prehistoric pottery, can certainly be assigned to this period. Slot 695 was aligned north–south, was 3.3 m long, 0.5 m wide, and 0.2 m deep, and was filled with dark yellowish–brown clayey silt. Its function remains uncertain.

Ditches

Five ditches, aligned both across and parallel to the slope, contained late prehistoric pottery. These were 104, 236/254, 256, 436 and 709, with 104 and 709 probably being parts of the same ditch (Fig. 11). Ditch 256 contained a single sherd of pottery and might be a later furrow rather than a ditch (Fig. 14). Four other linear features produced no dating evidence (111, 113, 120 and 250), and only 113 (Fig. 14) might conceivably have been a late prehistoric ditch rather than a feature related to later ridge and furrow agriculture or other recent disturbance.

Ditch 236 with a small spur, 254, towards the southern end produced the greatest quantity of pottery of any of the ditches (Fig. 14, Pl. 3). More than 400 sherds, many of them large and unabraded, came from the entire length of about 40 m which was fully excavated. Ditch 236 was of fairly regular profile, up to 0.8 m across and 0.4 m deep with steeply sloping sides and a fairly flat bottom. It turned sharply to the east at the north end but terminated within 2 m of this corner. The fill throughout was a broadly undifferentiated yellowish–brown silty clay.

Ditches 104 and 709 (Fig. 14) differed considerably in size but may have been part of the same feature running east–west across the centre of the site. If they were part of the same ditch, then it extended for a distance of more than 100 m. Ditch 104 was the smaller, with an average width of 0.9 m and a depth of 0.4 m, whereas ditch 709 was up to 3.2 m wide and 1.1 m deep. The fill was yellowish–brown in colour, ranging from a silty loam in 104 to a silty clay in 709. However, in ditch 709 there was a clear primary fill of dark greyish–brown

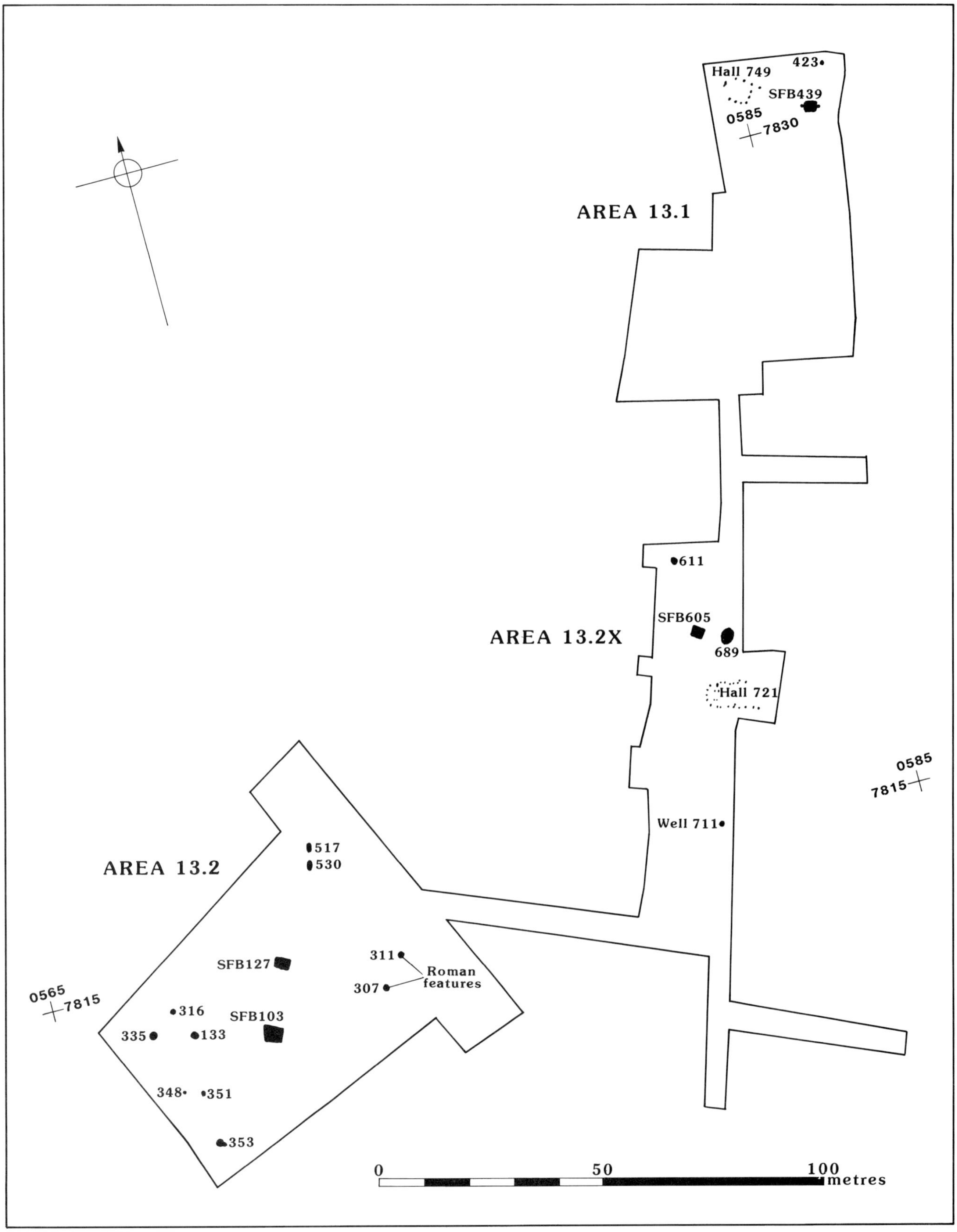

Figure 17 Plan of Saxon features

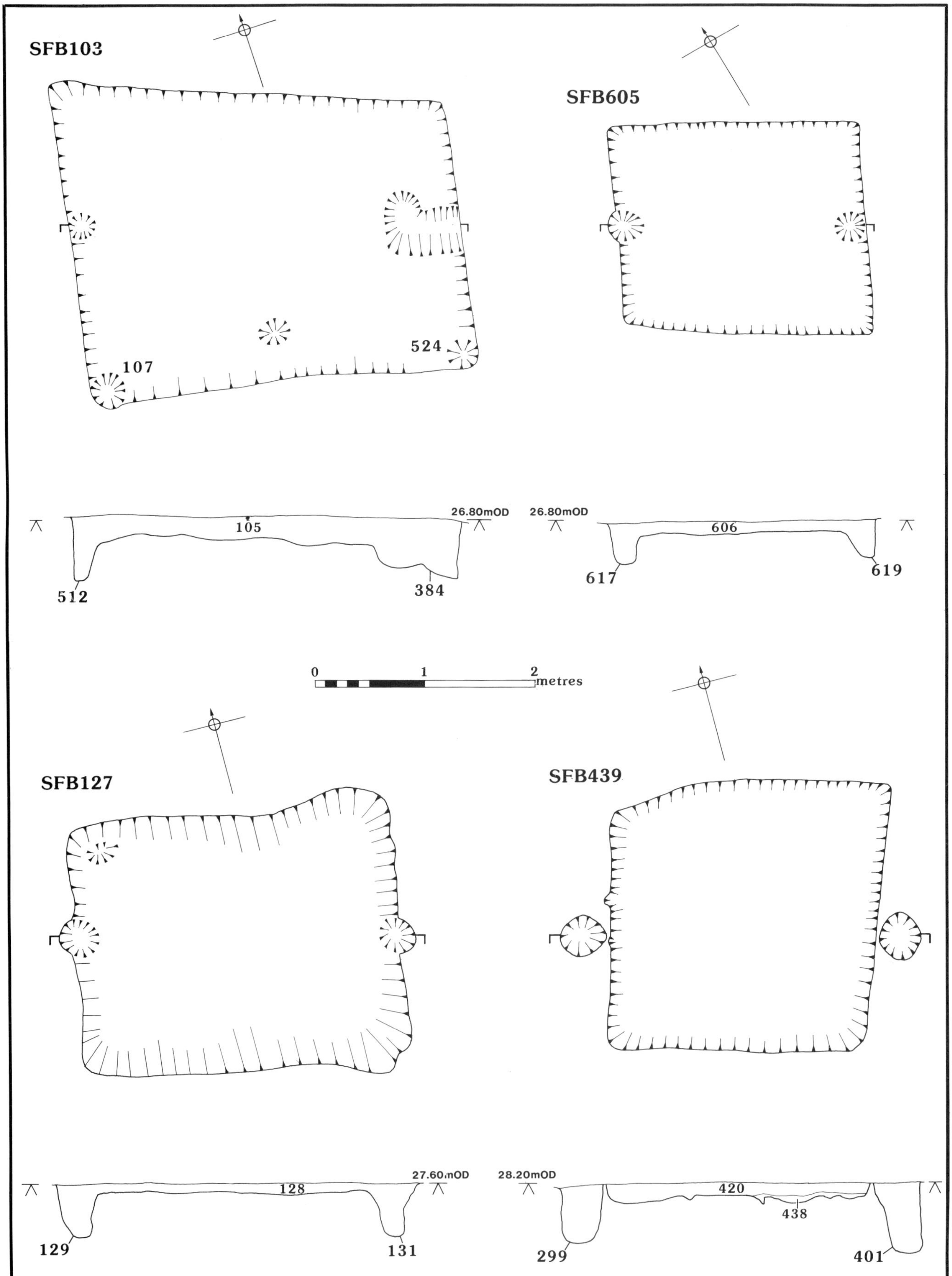

Figure 18 Plans and sections of Saxon sunken-featured buildings

clay containing a considerable quantity of charcoal. Towards the west end of ditch 104 was pit 387 which appeared to cut the ditch, though the fills were virtually indistinguishable. Pit 387, possibly a sump, was oval in plan, measuring 2.35 m by 2 m, and 0.95 m deep. It contained 14 late prehistoric sherds (and seven residual early prehistoric sherds), in addition to the four from ditch 104 and 28 from ditch 709.

A short length of curvilinear ditch, 436, lay towards the north end of the site, 10 m west of ditch 236. This was up to 1.1 m wide and 0.2 m deep and was filled with a brown clayey silt (Fig. 14). This produced three later prehistoric sherds. Ditch 256, by contrast, was smaller, more irregular, and contained only a single sherd of later prehistoric pottery; this feature may have been a remnant of later ridge and furrow.

An undated ditch, 113 (in Area 13.2; not illustrated), which might also have belonged to this period, was aligned north–south and was therefore probably unrelated to the later ridge and furrow. Only a short section of this ditch, which extended for more than 30 m, was excavated. This revealed a shallow feature, 0.4 m wide and only 0.07 m deep filled with dark yellowish–brown silty loam.

Pits

Fifteen features interpreted as pits were scattered across the site. No concentrations were clearly apparent, though there were some marked variations in the quantities of pottery present. Nine of the pits were circular or sub-circular, less than 1 m in diameter and less than 0.3 m deep; it is possible that some of these may have represented post-hole bases, but others (eg 456) contained such large quantities of pottery as to be certain that they were the remnants of pits. Six of the pits were larger, up to 2.5 m across, and included examples that were circular, sub-rectangular, and pear-shaped in plan. These larger pits were generally deeper, up to 0.95 m deep, but one example was only 0.04 m deep. The fills were generally homogeneous brown clayey silts, with only pit 516 containing more than a single fill (Fig. 15). Variable amounts of gravel were present, along with small quantities of burnt flint and charcoal. Fragments of very degraded bone were occasionally noted.

The most prolific pits in terms of pottery were 456 and 621 (Fig. 15), with many of the sherds from these pits being comparatively large and unabraded. Pit 456, which was no more than a shallow scoop, produced 72 sherds; it lay towards the north end of the site, midway along the west side of ditch 236 which produced the largest assemblage of Late Bronze Age pottery from the site. Pit 621 in the centre of the site, south of ditch 709, produced 78 sherds. Of the remainder, only pits 135 (17 sherds) and 387 (14 sherds) produced more than a dozen sherds and both lay towards the south end of the site.

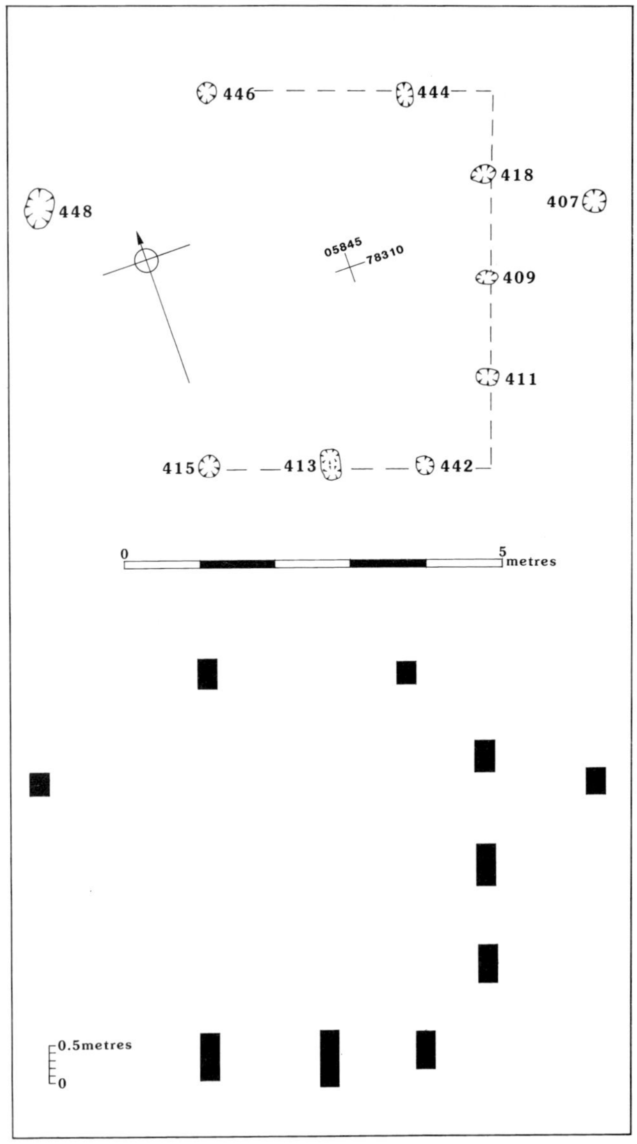

Figure 19 Plan and section of Saxon hall 749

Romano-British

Two small pits, 307 (Fig. 16) and 311, lay close together towards the south end of the site in Area 13.2 (Fig. 17). Pit 311 contained 11 sherds of Roman pottery, all from a single greyware vessel, and a small quantity of cremated bone of an older adult. There seems little doubt that this represents the truncated remains of a Romano-British cremation burial. Pit 307 contained only a single Roman sherd, along with four later prehistoric sherds, and it is possible that the former was intrusive. Pit 311 was no more than a shallow scoop (0.7 by 0.5 m, 0.04 m deep), whereas 307 was somewhat larger at 1.5 m by 0.8 m, and 0.2 m deep. Both pits were filled with yellowish–brown silty loam, and pit 311 also contained a considerable amount of charcoal flecking.

A few residual sherds of Roman pottery were recovered from Saxon features and the subsoil in this area, but little more can be said other than that there is some slight evidence for Roman activity in the area.

Saxon

Four sunken-featured buildings and possibly two post-built halls, all broadly aligned east–west, and a small number of pits and other features, have been assigned to this period. These were dispersed across the entire

Plate 4 Saxon sunken-featured building 103 (2 m scale). Facing south-west

excavated area but there is some evidence of groupings (Fig. 17, Pl. 4).

Sunken-featured buildings (SFBs)

SFB 103
This was the largest example, at 3.4 m by 2.6 m, and surviving to a depth of 0.43 m (Fig. 18). It was sub-rectangular in plan, with gently sloping sides and an uneven bottom. There were two post-holes, 384 and 512, dug centrally at either end against the edge of the pit (Fig. 18). Both post-holes were between 0.5 and 0.6 m deep, with 384 much larger and more irregular in plan. There were two slightly less substantial post- holes, 107 and 524, in the south-west and south-east corners respectively. These were approximately 0.3 m in diameter, similar to post-hole 512, and 0.4 and 0.26 m deep respectively. No post-pipes were apparent, nor any variation between the fills of the post-holes and the pit, all of which contained an undifferentiated dark yellowish–brown clayey silt. This produced 145 sherds of Saxon pottery, along with some residual prehistoric and Romano-British material and was the most prolific SFB on the site.

SFB 127
This lay 15 m to the north of SFB 103 (Fig. 17). It measured 3.2 m by 2.4 m, but was heavily truncated and survived to a depth of only 0.04 m (Fig. 18). It was approximately rectangular, had an irregular bottom, and two post-holes, 129 and 131, centrally placed at either end. Although these post-holes lay partly outside the existing edge of the pit, this is likely to have been an effect of truncation; they would have probably been dug just within the edge. Post-holes 129 and 131 were both approximately 0.3 m in diameter and 0.5 m deep. SFB 127 was filled with layer 128, a homogeneous dark yellowish–brown silty clay. This produced 12 sherds of Saxon pottery, along with seven late prehistoric sherds and one Roman sherd.

SFB 439
This lay at the north end of the site (Fig. 17). It was approximately 2.4 m square, 0.15 m deep, with vertical sides and an irregular bottom (Fig. 18). Post-holes 299 and 401 lay midway along the east and west sides but outside the pit. They were approximately 0.4 m in diameter and between 0.5 and 0.65 m deep. Two fills were distinguishable within the pit. The lower, 438, was a thin spread of dark yellowish–brown silty clay, sealed by 420, a similar but lighter layer; these contained 20 and 42 sherds of Saxon pottery respectively. A single sherd came from each of the post-holes.

SFB 605
This was in the centre of the site in Area 13.2X. It measured 2.4 by 2.1 m and was 0.15 m deep. The sides were near vertical and the bottom flat but uneven. Post-holes 617 and 619, which lay midway along either side, were 0.3 m in diameter and 0.35–0.4 m deep. No post-pipes were apparent and the fill of the post-holes and the pit was a homogeneous dark yellowish–brown clayey silt. This produced 30 sherds of Saxon pottery.

Post-built halls

Hall 749
The plan of this was not entirely clear but it appears that the east end of an east–west aligned post-built structure was revealed in the very north of the excavated area (Figs 17 and 19, Pl. 5). Eight post-holes can be ascribed to this structure, with 444 and 446 marking the north wall; 409, 411, and 418 the east wall; and 413, 415, and 432 the south wall. In addition to these, post-hole 407

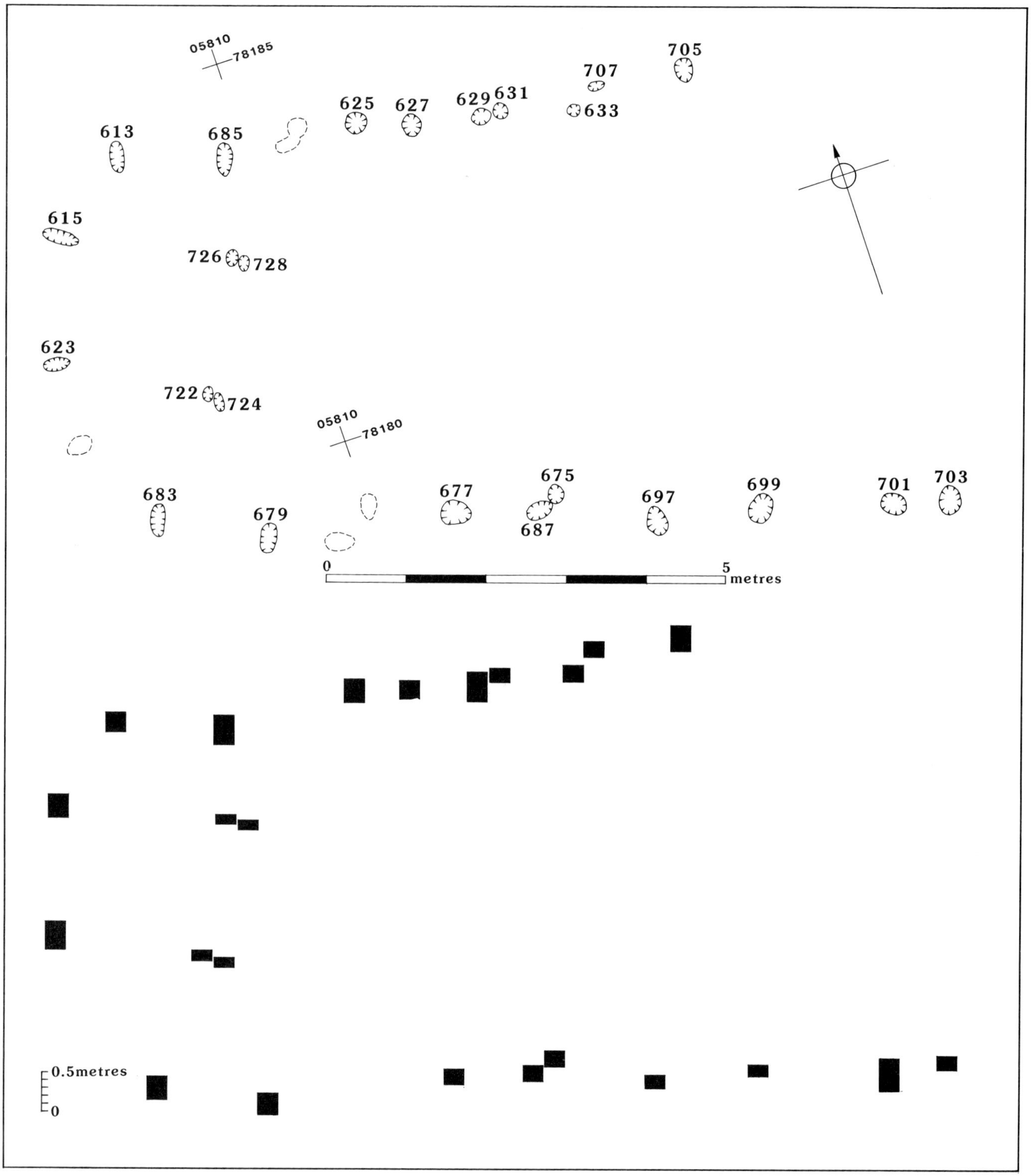

Figure 20 Plan and section of Saxon hall 721

lay immediately to the west, and 448, which may have been an internal post-hole, to the west. The post-holes varied in shape, were between 0.2 and 0.4 m across, and up to 0.3 m deep. If the arrangement of post-holes has been interpreted correctly (shown by a dashed line on Fig. 19), then this represents a structure more than 4 m long and 5 m wide. No post-holes marked the north-east and south-east corners, but there is a hint of regularity in the surviving post-holes which were spaced at intervals of approximately 1.4 m. The fills of most were yellowish–brown silty clay, with no post-pipes apparent. Post-hole 411 contained two sherds, and 446 one sherd of Saxon pottery.

Hall 721

This lay in the centre of the site in Area 13.2X (Fig. 17). It comprised possibly as many as 28 post-holes, though several survived only as shallow depressions. These

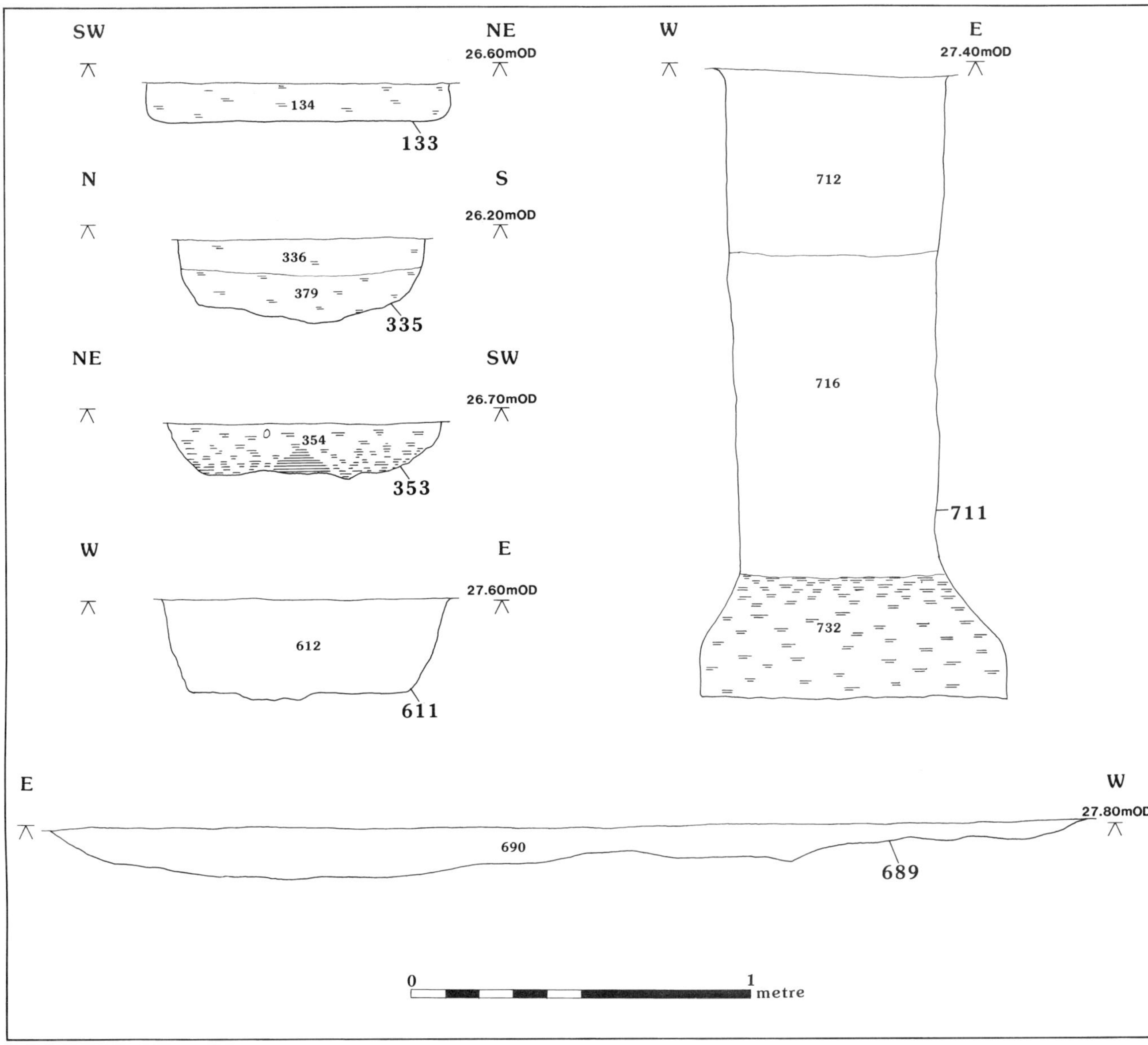

Figure 21 Sections across Saxon pits and possible well

post-holes appeared to mark a rectangular structure perhaps 10 m long and 5 m wide (Fig. 20, Pl. 6). There were no post-holes marking the east end but, at the west end, there was a semi-circular arrangement of post-holes comprising 613, 615, 623, 679, 683, and 685. The post-holes along the north and south sides were irregularly spaced at intervals of between 1 and 2 m but there was some indication of pairings between post-holes in opposing walls. Most of the post-holes were sub-circular or oval in plan, between 0.15 and 0.35 m across, and up to 0.17 m deep. However, the post-holes making up the semi-circular arrangement at the west end were markedly more elongated than the others, with maximum dimensions of between 0.3 and 0.5 m and an average depth of 0.12 m. Post-holes 679 and 685 lay in the south-west and north-west corners respectively of the rectangular part of the structure, with double post-holes 722/724 and 726/728 either marking the west end of this, or more probably an internal division; this group comprised the smallest post-holes assigned to hall 721. The fills of the post-holes were invariably dark yellowish–brown clayey silts with occasional charcoal flecking and there was no evidence of any post-pipes. Three sherds of later prehistoric pottery were recovered from the post-holes but no Saxon material. Slot 695, which lay within the area occupied by hall 721, produced 35 sherds of late prehistoric pottery, and it is suggested that this was an earlier and unrelated feature. This is discussed further below.

Ditches and pits

Linear features 517 and 530 in Area 13.2 may have been the truncated remains of a shallow ditch (Fig. 17). They were aligned virtually north–south, were up to 0.8 m wide and 0.25 m deep but together extended over a distance of only 6 m. Two sherds of Saxon pottery were recovered from these features.

Nine possible pits were excavated: 423 at the north end of Area 13.1; 611, 689, and 711 towards the centre of Area 13.2X; and 133, 316, 335, 351, and 353 in the

Plate 5 Saxon post-built hall 721, with slot 695 in foreground (2 m scale). Facing north-west

west half of Area 13.2 (Fig. 17). Several survived as little more than shallow sub-circular or sub-rectangular scoops, with five less than 1 m in diameter and six less than 0.25 m deep. Virtually all of these smaller pits contained fewer than a dozen sherds of Saxon pottery, along with some residual late prehistoric material. Pit 316 was exceptional in that it was only 0.35 m in diameter and 0.04 m deep, but contained 87 sherds of Saxon pottery. Pit 423 was notable for the large number and range of charred plant remains present.

The pits in Area 13.2X showed the greatest degree of variation in shape and size. Pit 611 measured 1.3 by 0.85 m and was almost 0.7 m deep, but both 689 and 711 were substantially larger (Fig. 21). Feature 689 was a shallow, oval hollow which lay 3 m to the south of SFB

Plate 6 Possible Saxon post-built hall 749

Plate 7 Stepped section through the brickearth down to the underlying gravel

605. It was 3.2 m long, 3 m wide, 0.16 m deep, and filled with a dark yellowish–brown sandy silt containing 12 sherds of Saxon pottery and four residual late prehistoric sherds; it is suggested below that this may have been some form of 'working hollow'. Pit 711, which lay some 40 m to the south of SFB 605, was quite different to any of the others and on balance has been interpreted as a well. This was circular, approximately 0.7 m in diameter at the top, 1.85 m deep, and widening to 0.9 m at the bottom which was flat. The sides above this were near vertical. There were no clear layer boundaries in the fill which graded imperceptibly from a dark yellowish–brown sandy silt (layer 712) at the top, to a slightly lighter clayey silt (716), to a greyish–brown clay (732) at the bottom, the latter likely to have accumulated in standing water. There was a considerable amount of charcoal flecking in the upper part of layer 732 and this layer also showed considerable red staining, probably iron staining. The primary fill, 732, contained five sherds of late prehistoric pottery, but layers 716 and 712 above contained 17 and 11 sherds of Saxon pottery respectively, along with a few late prehistoric sherds.

4. Finds

Worked and Burnt Flint, by P.A. Harding

Introduction

A total of 319 pieces of worked flint was recovered from 57 contexts across the site. Most of the material was found in association with pottery of later prehistoric or Saxon date and may therefore be derived. The largest single group, comprising 39 pieces, including five scrapers, was contained in the primary fill of pit 380 associated with Late Neolithic, Grooved Ware pottery. An additional 12 pieces were found in Late Bronze Age pit 309. No finds were made within or sealed by the brickearth (Plate 7).

Raw material and condition

Flint is readily available in the local gravels and the condition of the surviving cortex suggests that this source was exploited. The flint is of good quality, although nodules are not large. A large, broken, retouched flake from ?Neolithic ditch 719 may have been brought to the site from further afield. Most of the material is in mint condition, although a few pieces show signs of heavy edge damage which is likely to be the result of agriculture. The flint is unpatinated but some pieces are lightly stained.

Technology

Only four cores were found during the excavation. All are undiagnostic flake cores, although one from subsoil context 267 is poorly prepared and has multiple incipient cones of percussion on the striking platform. Cores of this type are often assigned to Late Bronze Age flint technologies.

In the absence of cores, conclusions relating to technology are derived from flakes. A total of 253 flakes and broken flakes was collected from 57 contexts, the largest number being 18 pieces from Late Neolithic pit 380. There is evidence of platform abrasion, faceting, and rejuvenation techniques across the whole site. Hard hammer percussion predominates, although a minority of pieces may have been removed using soft hammers.

Tools

Four microliths, comprising two 'rods', an obliquely blunted point, and a backed bladelet, were found in excavated features.

The most common tool type is the scraper of which 14 were found. Five of these were recovered from the Late Neolithic pit 380. They are mainly end scrapers made on non-cortical, hard hammer struck flakes which were retouched into well made implements. Retouch is direct, continuous, semi-abrupt, and regular/irregular which often extends around to one or both edges. Most of the remaining scrapers are of similar type and may be contemporaneous.

Additional pieces include a fabricator from subsoil context 267, a possible triangular arrowhead from Late Neolithic pit 380, a piercer from Saxon well 711, and two flakes with marginal/microdenticulate edge retouch.

Conclusions

The evaluation established that the earliest activity dated by pottery related to the Late Neolithic; however, a microlith from fieldwalking hinted that Mesolithic occupation may be present. This has been confirmed by the addition of four further microliths. All were found towards the southern end of the site. The inclusion of two rods suggests that this occupation should be placed in the Late Mesolithic. Traces of Mesolithic activity in the Colne valley are known but have previously been restricted to discoveries of tranchet axes (SMR No. 050426 and No. 050185).

Most of the remaining flint is difficult to assign chronologically. The principal activity coincides with the Late Neolithic features and concentration of Grooved Ware pottery towards the southern end of the site. However, the incidence of platform abrasion, faceting, and rejuvenation suggests that there is a residue of the occupation in all areas of the site. The quantities of flint are low but tools are proportionally well represented. Such occurrences are likely to denote domestic activity where tools were used and abandoned in rubbish pits. It is possible that the original tool manufacture took place where the gravels were more readily exposed.

Despite the presence of Late Bronze Age pottery, there is an apparent lack of flintwork which can be assigned to this period. The exception relates to the material recovered from the subsoil in Area 13.1. There is nothing to show why flintwork of this date was better preserved in the subsoil, nor to show why it should be so under-represented elsewhere on the site.

Pottery, by M. Laidlaw and Lorraine Mepham

The pottery assemblage from Prospect Park (excluding a small quantity of medieval, post-medieval, and modern material) consists of 2062 sherds (16,777 g). This assemblage includes pottery of Late Neolithic, Middle Bronze Age, Late Bronze Age, Romano-British, and early Saxon date, and derives from stratified features and contexts excavated during both stages of fieldwork (evaluation and excavation) on the site.

Methods

The assemblage was analysed using the standard Wessex Archaeology pottery recording system (Morris 1992). On the basis of the dominant inclusion type, the assemblage was divided into three broad fabric groups: flint-tempered (Group F), grog-tempered (Group G), and sandy (Group Q). This was carried out with the use of a hand lens (x10 magnification) and a binocular microscope (x20 magnification). Within each of these three groups all sherds were assigned to a fabric type dependent on the frequency and size of inclusions, then counted and weighed by fabric type within each context. Alphanumeric fabric codes have been allocated to each type, which are unique to this site, ie they do not directly correlate to similarly coded fabric types from other sites within this volume. Pottery totals by fabric type and chronological period are listed in Table 1.

Each diagnostic rim sherd was examined and, as far as possible, assigned to vessel form, although a large number of rims have less than 5% of the total diameter surviving. Details of surface treatments, decoration, and manufacture were also recorded. Full records exist in archive.

Terms describing the frequency of the inclusions in the following fabric descriptions are defined as follows: rare (1–3%); sparse (3–10%); moderate (10–20%); common (20–25%); very common (30%); abundant (40–50%). Other percentages throughout are calculated by weight unless otherwise stated. The pottery is discussed by chronological period below.

Late Neolithic

A moderate quantity of sherds (190) has been attributed to the Late Neolithic period, deriving mostly from a group of Grooved Ware vessels in hollow 1494. Four fabric types were identified, one flint-tempered and three grog-tempered:

F1 Moderately fine, slightly micaceous fabric; sparse, poorly-sorted sub-angular flint <5 mm; unoxidised, some oxidisation on surfaces.

G1 Soft, fine, soapy fabric; moderate sub-rounded grog <2 mm; sparse sub-rounded quartz grains <0.25 mm; rare very fine mica; unoxidised with oxidised exterior.

G2 Slightly soapy fabric; moderate, sub-angular grog <2 mm; unoxidised, oxidised interior.

G3 Soft, fine fabric; sparse, sub-rounded grog <2 mm; very rare rounded quartz <1 mm; very rare fine mica; unoxidised.

The majority of the Late Neolithic assemblage comprises sherds in the grog-tempered fabric G1, many of which have impressed and incised decoration characteristic of Grooved Ware ceramics. A minimum of at least four Grooved Ware vessels are represented amongst the assemblage from the evaluation (Fig. 22, 1–9). In nearly every case the decoration comprises bands of parallel grooved lines arranged vertically,

Table 1 Pottery fabric totals

Fabric	*No. sherds*	*Weight (g)*	*% of phase*	*% of total*
Late Neolithic				
F1	8	34	–	
G1	179	926	–	
G2	2	16	–	
G3	1	4	–	
Total	190	980	–	5.9
Middle Bronze Age				
F2	87	3608	–	
F3	3	49	–	
F4	5	50	–	
F11	6	33	–	
Total	101	3740	–	22.6
Late Bronze Age				
C1	1	2	<0.05	
F5	192	1065	14.2	
F6	89	664	8.8	
F7	160	1226	16.3	
F8	77	451	6.0	
F9	502	2599	34.6	
F10	54	334	4.5	
Q1	118	717	9.6	
Q2	73	450	6.0	
Total	1266	7508	–	45.4
Romano-British				
Total	39	291	–	1.8
Early / Middle Saxon				
F400	4	88	2.2	
Q401	3	74	1.8	
Q402	143	1089	27.1	
Q403	56	264	6.6	
Q404	32	519	12.9	
Q405	90	711	18.8	
Q406	4	79	2.0	
Q407	27	321	8.0	
Q408	15	155	3.8	
R400	1	68	1.7	
R401	4	90	2.2	
V400	1	22	0.5	
V401	2	16	0.4	
V402	59	526	13.1	
Total	441	4022	–	24.3
OVERALL TOTAL	2037	16541	–	–

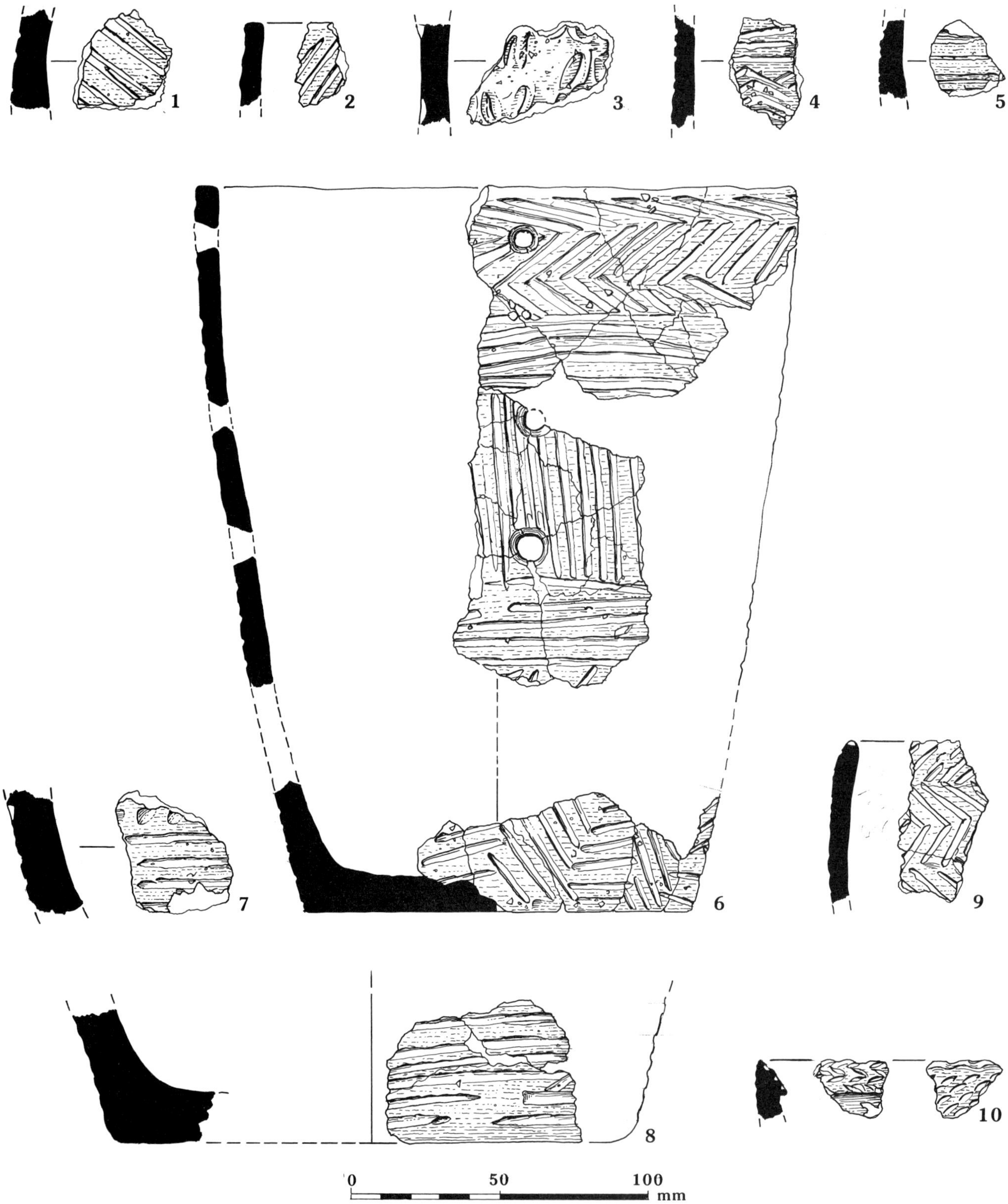

Figure 22 Neolithic pottery — Grooved Ware

horizontally, or diagonally; decoration which is characteristic of the Durrington Walls sub-style (Wainwright and Longworth 1971). One body sherd is decorated with finger-pinching (Fig. 22, 3), and another body sherd combines horizontal grooving with a horizontal row of rounded impressions (Fig. 22, 7). The most complete vessel derives from feature 1496 (Fig. 22, 6), a relatively thin-walled vessel with upright, flattened rim and three post-firing holes drilled through the body wall, probably for binding a break. This vessel had been burnt, probably after breakage. Two other rims are present, one simple rounded form (Fig. 22, 9) and one upright flattened form similar to that already described (Fig. 22, 2).

This small collection of Grooved Ware vessels is significant, particularly so in view of the general paucity of Grooved Ware in the area. The later Neolithic is represented ceramically at Heathrow (Grimes 1960) but largely by Peterborough Ware, which is much more

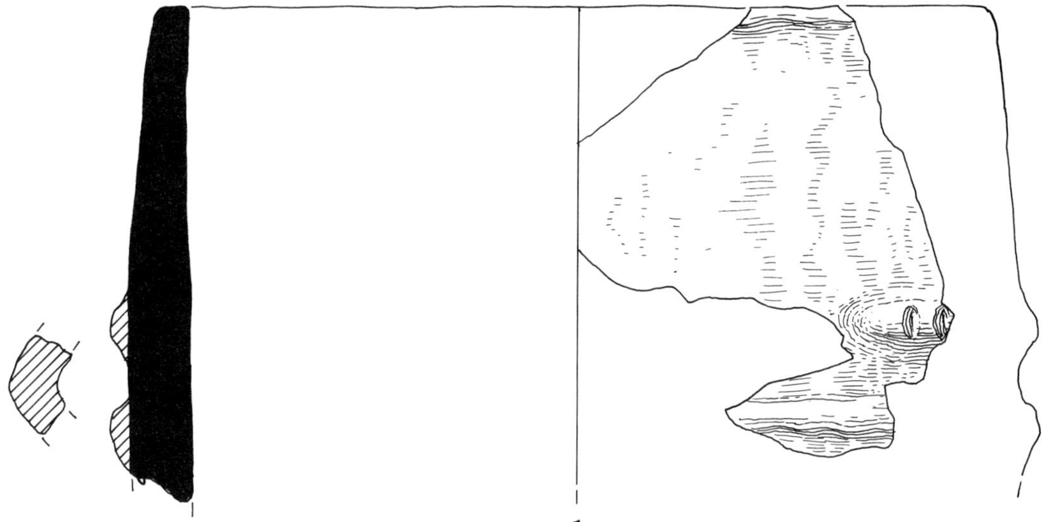

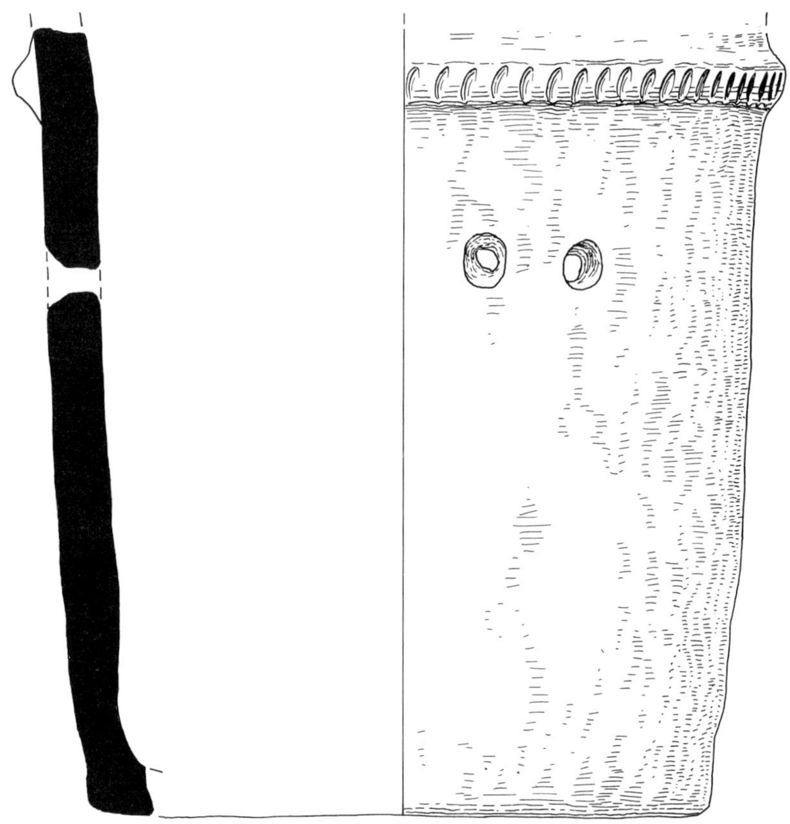

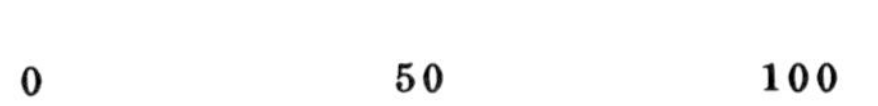

Figure 23 Middle Bronze Age pottery — cremation urns

common generally in the region than is Grooved Ware. Recent excavation in Harmondsworth, however, within 2 km of Prospect Park, has produced a substantial assemblage of over 500 Grooved Ware sherds representing approximately 12 vessels, also in the Durrington Walls sub-style (Field and Cotton 1987).

The four Grooved Ware vessels from the evaluation were found *in situ* within hollow 1494 and the nearby small feature 1496 in Area 13.2 (*see* Fig. 6). A third feature, 319, immediately adjacent and subsequently excavated during the second stage of fieldwork, produced four sherds of Grooved Ware and one possible Late Neolithic plain body sherd (fabric F1), and pit 380, also within Area 13.2, yielded six sherds in fabric F1 and one Late Bronze Age sherd. Other Late Neolithic sherds were recovered in small quantities which were redeposited in later contexts dispersed across the site.

Found in association with the Grooved Ware vessels in hollow 1494 was a single, internally bevelled rim sherd in fabric G3 with impressed twisted cord decoration on the exterior and inside the rim (Fig. 22, 10); this is likely to derive from a Fengate Ware vessel of the Peterborough Ware tradition.

Also assigned to this chronological period were a small number of plain body sherds in the fine, sparsely flint-gritted fabric F1, which have been tentatively dated to the Late Neolithic on the basis of fabric type; the coarse flint inclusions, sparse and very poorly-sorted, in a fine matrix, are often characteristic of Late Neolithic ceramics, particularly Peterborough Ware. Two plain body sherds in the grog-tempered fabric G2 may also be of this period, or could alternatively be of Early Bronze Age date; both were found as redeposited sherds.

Middle Bronze Age

A small quantity of small, plain body sherds (18 sherds) and two partial cremation urns have been attributed to the Middle Bronze Age period. Four fabric types were identified, three coarsely flint-tempered and one noticeably finer flint-tempered. Distinctions between the coarse flint-tempered fabrics F2–F4 and the Late Bronze Age fabrics described in the next section are not always discrete, as several fabrics covered a wide range of variation.

F2 Soft fabric; moderate, well-sorted, sub-angular flint <2 mm; sparse rounded quartz grains <0.25 mm; rare iron oxides <0.5 mm; irregularly fired, generally oxidised surfaces.

F3 Hard fabric; common, poorly-sorted, sub-angular flint <3 mm; sparse rounded quartz grains <0.25 mm; sparse very fine mica; rare iron oxides <0.5 mm; irregularly fired, generally oxidised surfaces.

F4 Hard fabric; common, poorly-sorted sub-angular flint <4 mm; moderate rounded quartz grains—<0.25 mm; sparse very fine mica; irregularly fired, unoxidised core and oxidised surfaces.

F11 Fine, hard fabric; common, well-sorted, sub-angular flint <2 mm; sparse very fine mica; irregularly fired generally unoxidised, some oxidisation on exterior surface.

The bulk of the sherds within this chronological group derive from two cremation vessels. These two vessels, both in fabric F2, are bucket-shaped forms of Deverel-Rimbury type, each with horizontal finger-impressed cordons around the body. The vessel associated with cremation burial 165 survives as the top one-third of a vessel, with a simple rounded rim and a double applied, finger-impressed cordon (Fig. 23, 1). Better preserved is the second vessel (Fig. 23, 2), associated with cremation burial 161, although the upper body above the applied cordon had been removed by post-depositional disturbance. This vessel has two post-firing perforations drilled below the cordon, which are probably repair holes.

Sherds in fabric F11 are noticeably finer, containing well-sorted calcined flint and with smoothed and/or burnished surfaces. Six body sherds from pit 387, all apparently from the same vessel, are well burnished on the interior surface and have shallow multi-directional brushing or wiping on the smoothed exterior surface. Although precise vessel form cannot be determined, the appearance of these sherds suggests that they derive from globular urns of Deverel-Rimbury type.

Comparable Deverel-Rimbury bucket urns have been found at the four Middlesex Bronze Age cremation cemeteries discussed by Barrett (1973); all are flint-tempered, as are the examples from Prospect Park and the decorative elements identified here — finger-impressed cordons and lugs — are found elsewhere. Globular urns, generally found in finer fabrics than the bucket urns, are relatively rare in this region but there are two examples, one each from Yiewsley and Ashford Common (*ibid.*) which, in both cases, are associated with larger quantities of bucket urns. The small collection of two vessels and 18 sherds from Prospect Park may well have originated from a much larger cremation cemetery.

Other plain body sherds in fabrics F2, F3, F4, and F11 were found in very small quantities in ditches 104 and 709, and pit 387. The overall distribution of Middle Bronze Age material is concentrated in Area 13.2X; the only other sherds occur in ditch 709 in Area 13.2X, which appears to be a continuation of ditch 104.

Late Bronze Age

A large quantity of sherds has been attributed to the Late Bronze Age, the majority of which are small, non-diagnostic body sherds. Nine fabrics were identified, comprising five flint-tempered fabrics, one flint-tempered fabric, one shelly and two sandy fabrics. As already noted above, distinguishing between Deverel-Rimbury type fabrics and Late Bronze Age flint-tempered fabrics presented some difficulties.

The terms 'flint-tempered' and 'flint-gritted' are used here to define, respectively, fabrics to which flint has been added deliberately, generally as crushed, calcined fragments, as tempering material; and fabrics in which flint fragments are naturally occurring. Using Barrett's classification (1980), all the flint-tempered fabrics, the shelly fabric C1 and the sandy fabric Q1 may be described as 'coarsewares', while the sandy fabric Q2 could be described as a 'fineware', and the flint-gritted fabric F9 appears to include examples of both 'coarsewares' and 'finewares', although the relative absence of diagnostic vessel forms and surface treatments (*see* below) means that the distinction between 'coarse' and 'fine' cannot easily be sustained here.

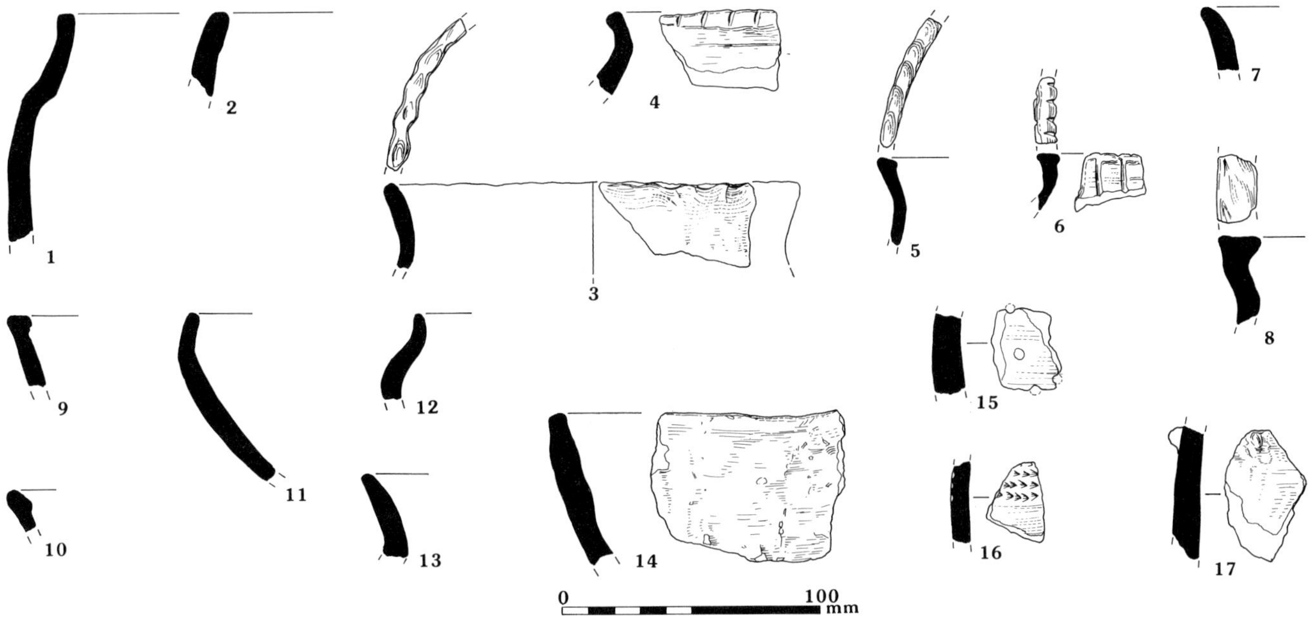

Figure 24 Late Bronze Age pottery

Calcareous fabric

C1 Soft, moderately fine fabric; common, fairly well sorted crushed shell <1 mm; sparse iron <0.5 mm; oxidised, unoxidised core.

Flint-tempered fabrics

F5 Fine, hard fabric; moderate, well-sorted, sub-angular flint <2 mm; moderate rounded quartz grains <0.5 mm; sparse very fine mica; sparse iron ore <0.5 mm; unoxidised, generally with oxidised exterior surface.

F6 Fine, hard fabric; moderate, moderately well-sorted, sub-angular flint <4 mm; moderate rounded quartz grains <0.5 mm; sparse very fine mica; sparse iron ore <1 mm; irregularly fired, generally oxidised.

F7 Fine, hard fabric; common poorly-sorted, sub-angular flint <4 mm; moderate rounded quartz grains <0.25 mm; sparse very fine mica; irregularly fired, unoxidised, some oxidisation on exterior surface.

F8 Fine, hard fabric; sparse, moderately well-sorted, sub-angular flint <3 mm; moderate rounded quartz grains <0.25 mm; sparse iron ore <0.25 mm; sparse very fine mica; unoxidised, oxidised exterior surface.

F10 Fine, hard fabric; abundant well-sorted, rounded quartz grains <0.5 mm; moderate well-sorted flint <2 mm; moderate iron ore <1 mm; unoxidised, oxidised exterior surface.

Flint-gritted fabric

F9 Fine, hard fabric; sparse, well-sorted, sub-angular flint—<2 mm; moderate rounded quartz grains <0.25 mm; sparse very fine mica; sparse iron ore <1 mm; generally unox idised, oxidised exterior surface and outer margin.

Sandy fabrics

Q1 Fine, hard fabric; sparse, well-sorted, sub-angular flint <2 mm; moderate rounded quartz grains <1 mm; sparse very fine mica; sparse iron ore <1 mm; generally unoxidised, oxidised surfaces; some with oxidised outer margin.

Q2 Fine, hard fabric; rare, sub-angular flint <1 mm; moderate rounded quartz grains <0.25 mm; sparse very fine mica; irregularly fired, generally unoxidised.

This rather restricted range of fabrics contains nothing to indicate non-local production and it is likely that most, if not all of the assemblage, results from localised production on or close to the site itself. There is little evidence for the expenditure of any great effort invested in clay preparation, vessel forming, or firing, although the presence of possible 'finewares' does imply some distinction, potentially functional, within the assemblage. All tempering materials would have been relatively easily accessible within the local area; the site is on gravel which forms part of the Taplow Terrace, and which contains abundant flint nodules (Dewey and Bromehead 1915, 72–6), while deposits of London Clay and Bagshot Sands occur within the local area, ie within 10 km of the site. Petrological analysis of Late Bronze Age fabric samples from the nearby site at Heathrow led to a similar conclusion of local production (Williams 1993).

Vessel forms

Diagnostic material is scarce. Only 25 rim sherd fragments were recovered and many of these are too small to attribute to a specific vessel form. A series of nine vessel types has been defined on the basis of the 14 more diagnostic rims. These vessel types have been assigned to Classes I–IV of Barrett's classification (1980, 302–3).

Type 1 Medium-sized, shouldered jar (Class I), upright or slightly everted rim (Fig. 24, 1)

Type 2 Straight-sided or slightly convex jar (Class I), plain rim (Fig. 24, 14)

Type 3 Jar (Class I), unknown form, everted rim, often finger-impressed (Fig. 24, 5–7, 11, 13)

Type 4 Medium-sized jar (Class I), unknown form, internally thickened rim (Fig. 24, 9, 10)
Type 5 Medium-sized jar (Class I/II), unknown form, internally bevelled rim (Fig. 24, 4)
Type 6 Carinated bowl (Class IV), plain inturned rim (Fig. 24, 2)
Type 7 Shouldered bowl (Class IV), everted rim (Fig. 24, 12)
Type 8 Necked bowl (Class IV), everted rim (Fig. 24, 8)
Type 9 Convex bowl (Class IV), plain rim (Fig. 24, 3)

In addition, two small body sherds in fabric F5 from the same context were observed with pre-firing perforations (Fig. 24, 15), possibly deriving from a vessel or vessels with some kind of straining function; these sherds could not be assigned to any particular vessel form.

The correlation of vessel forms to fabric types is given in Table 2. Almost half of the 14 diagnostic rims occur in the flint-gritted fabric F9, and this includes examples of six of the nine forms. Vessels in this fabric tend to be better finished, although roughly tooled burnishing was noted on the single jar of Type 1 in the particularly coarse fabric F7 (Fig. 24, 1).

It is immediately apparent that this small group of identifiable vessel forms is dominated by jar forms (10 examples: Types 1–5), with only four recognisable bowls (Types 6–9). The jars, with the exception of the single rim of Type 5, which is too small to ascertain overall vessel form, are all of Barrett's Class I, ie coarse jars showing limited attempts at surface finishing. The bowls, all in fabric F9, all belong to Class IV. The assemblage is therefore composed of a very limited range of coarseware jars and fineware bowls. This restricted range, however, may be at least partly a reflection of the very small number of diagnostic rim sherds; the Late Bronze Age assemblage from the nearby site at Heathrow, for example, although smaller in size (just over 600 sherds), contained 45 identifiable vessels (Grimes and Close-Brooks 1993, 352–3).

Table 2 Late Bronze Age pottery: vessel form by fabric type (no. of vessels)

	F5	*F6*	*F7*	*F9*	*Q2*	*Total*
Jars						
Type 1	–	–	1	–	–	1
Type 2	–	–	1	–	–	1
Type 3	–	1	1	1	2	5
Type 4	1	–	–	1	–	2
Type 5	1	–	–	–	–	1
Bowls						
Type 6	–	–	–	1	–	1
Type 7	–	–	–	1	–	1
Type 8	–	–	–	1	–	1
Type 9	–	–	–	1	–	1
TOTAL	2	1	3	6	2	14

Decoration and surface treatments

Only a small proportion of the assemblage shows any signs of surface treatments. This consists of burnishing on 31 sherds, mostly in the finer flint-gritted fabric F9, and fairly crude vertical wiping, probably with some sort of vegetable matter, on 29 sherds in the coarser flint-tempered fabrics F5 and F6 (Table 3). Sherds in fabric F9 are generally better finished than the other fabrics; those that are not actually burnished frequently have a surface finish resulting from careful smoothing and the application of a thin slip or slurry to surfaces, which is visible in section.

A small number of base sherds were easily identified because of the high concentration of flint grits occurring on the exterior surface, as identified, for example, at Aldermaston Wharf and Knight's Farm, Berkshire, where it has been suggested that the jars were placed on crushed flint while drying (Bradley *et al.* 1980, 234).

Decoration is likewise scarce. A total of 12 sherds carries some form of decoration, consisting mainly of finger-impressions and slashing or incising on jar rims and finger-impressions on jar shoulders. There are also two sherds in fabric F9, from two separate contexts but probably from the same vessel, with rows of regular triangular impressions (Fig. 24, 16), and one sherd in fabric F7 with a small, applied, pinched boss (Fig. 24, 17).

Chronology and affinities

The assemblage from Prospect Park belongs to the post-Deverel-Rimbury tradition as defined by Barrett (1980), within which it can be seen to fall within the 'plainware' phase in which coarse domestic jars are the most common form represented.

The range of fabrics and vessel forms identified at Prospect Park has its parallels within the slightly smaller assemblage from Heathrow (Grimes and Close-Brooks 1993), although the latter assemblage contained a much higher proportion of fineware burnished bowls (*ibid.*, 352–3 and fig. 36). This may be partly because of the greater number of diagnostic vessel forms at Heathrow mentioned above, and it may be that the vessel type series from Heathrow is more representative. Nevertheless, it may be noted that the Heathrow assemblage produced a similarly restricted range of Class I coarseware jars and Class IV fineware bowls.

Other comparative material comes from sites south of the River Thames in Surrey, particularly Carshalton and Runnymede Bridge (Adkins and Needham 1985; Longley 1980; 1991). Both sites have produced a similar range of large to medium jars and fine burnished bowls, generally undecorated apart from impressed decoration on rims or shoulders. Carshalton in particular has the emphasis on rim decoration as opposed to shoulder decoration which is apparent at Prospect Park. Petters Sports Field also provides good parallels for the range of vessel types observed at Prospect Park, although the emphasis on sandy fabrics at Petters has been taken as an indication of a slightly later date within the post-Deverel-Rimbury phase at a point where the flint-tempered wares had given way to sandy fabrics (O'Connell 1986, 72). The assemblage from Hurst Park, East Molesey, comparable in size to Prospect Park, contains a similar range of coarseware jars but these are

Table 3 Late Bronze Age pottery: decoration and surface treatment by fabric type (no. of sherds)

	F5	*F6*	*F7*	*F9*	*Q2*	*Total*
Surface treatment						
Burnished	–	–	–	26	5	31
Wiped	10	19	–	–	–	29
Decoration						
Applied boss	–	–	1	–	–	1
Incised/slashed rim	–	–	–	2	2	4
Finger-impressed rim	–	1	1	–	1	3
Finger-impressed shoulder	–	–	–	2	–	2
Impressed triangles	–	–	–	2	–	2
TOTAL	10	20	2	32	8	72

accompanied by coarseware bowls, with no identifiable fineware component (Laidlaw, this volume).

Barrett dates 'plainware' post-Deverel-Rimbury ceramics in the middle and lower Thames to the 11th–9th centuries BC (1980, 307), with decorated assemblages becoming more prominent from the 8th century BC. The Carshalton assemblage is dated to the 10th–8th century BC on the basis of ceramic style (Adkins and Needham 1985); Runnymede Bridge has radiocarbon dates of the 9th–8th centuries BC for the Late Bronze Age occupation (Needham 1991, 352–3); while radiocarbon dates from Petters Sports Field place the metalworking phase of that site, contemporary with at least part of the ceramic assemblage, in the 7th or 6th century BC. Within this wide date range, the assemblage from Prospect Park appears to have the closest affinities with the Carshalton assemblage; the Runnymede assemblage contains a higher proportion of decoration. A date range in the 10th–9th centuries BC may therefore be suggested for Prospect Park, contemporary or slightly later than the assemblage from Hurst Park (*see* below, Discussion).

Distribution

Late Bronze Age pottery occurred in small quantities in a number of features across the site. Only two features produced more than 20 sherds: ditch 236 in Area 13.1 and pit 621 in Area 13.2X (Fig. 17). Both features contained a relatively high proportion of the flint-gritted fabric F9, and ditch 236 also contained a noticeably high proportion of sandy wares (65% by weight of the total from the site). No significant patterning can be discerned amongst the small quantities of pottery from other features. Nine of the diagnostic vessel forms identified derive from either ditch 236 (seven examples) or pit 622 (two examples); apart from these two features, there is no obvious clustering of any vessel form, although it may be noted that Class IV bowls are limited to Areas 13.2 and 13.2X, while Class I jars occur also in Area 13.1.

Romano-British

A very small quantity of Romano-British pottery is present (39 sherds), consisting of mainly greywares and smaller quantities of oxidised sandy wares, grogged wares, and two small sherds of south Gaulish samian. With the exception of 10 sherds from pit 311, which is the only feature that can certainly be dated to the Romano-British period, the remaining sherds, all small and abraded, were found redeposited in later contexts.

Early Saxon

The Saxon ceramic assemblage is generally in a relatively good condition, including large unabraded sherds. Fourteen separate fabric types were identified: one flint-tempered, eight sandy (containing either quartz or quartzite), two containing rock fragments, and three organic-tempered.

Flint-tempered fabric

F400 Hard, moderately coarse fabric; moderate, well-sorted, sub-angular flint <1 mm; sparse rounded quartz grains <0.5 mm; sparse iron ore <1 mm; rare fine mica; unoxidised.

Fabrics containing quartz or quartzite as dominant inclusion type

Q401 Hard, fine fabric; common, well-sorted, rounded quartz grains <1 mm; moderate sub-rounded iron ore <1 mm; rare fine mica; rare very coarse organic temper <4 mm; irregularly fired, generally unoxidised core, slightly oxidised surfaces.

Q402 Hard, moderately coarse fabric; moderate, fairly well-sorted, sub-angular quartz /quartzite grains <0.5 mm; sparse fine mica; rare, irregular rock fragments <2 mm; rare sub-angular patinated flint <2 mm; rare organic material <10 mm; unoxidised.

Q403 Hard, moderately coarse fabric; moderate, well-sorted, sub-angular quartz/quartzite grains <0.5 mm; sparse, fine mica; sparse carbonaceous material <3 mm; unoxidised, oxidised margins.

Q404 Hard, moderately coarse fabric; sparse, poorly-sorted, sub-angular quartz/quartzite grains—<1 mm; rare fine mica; rare sub-

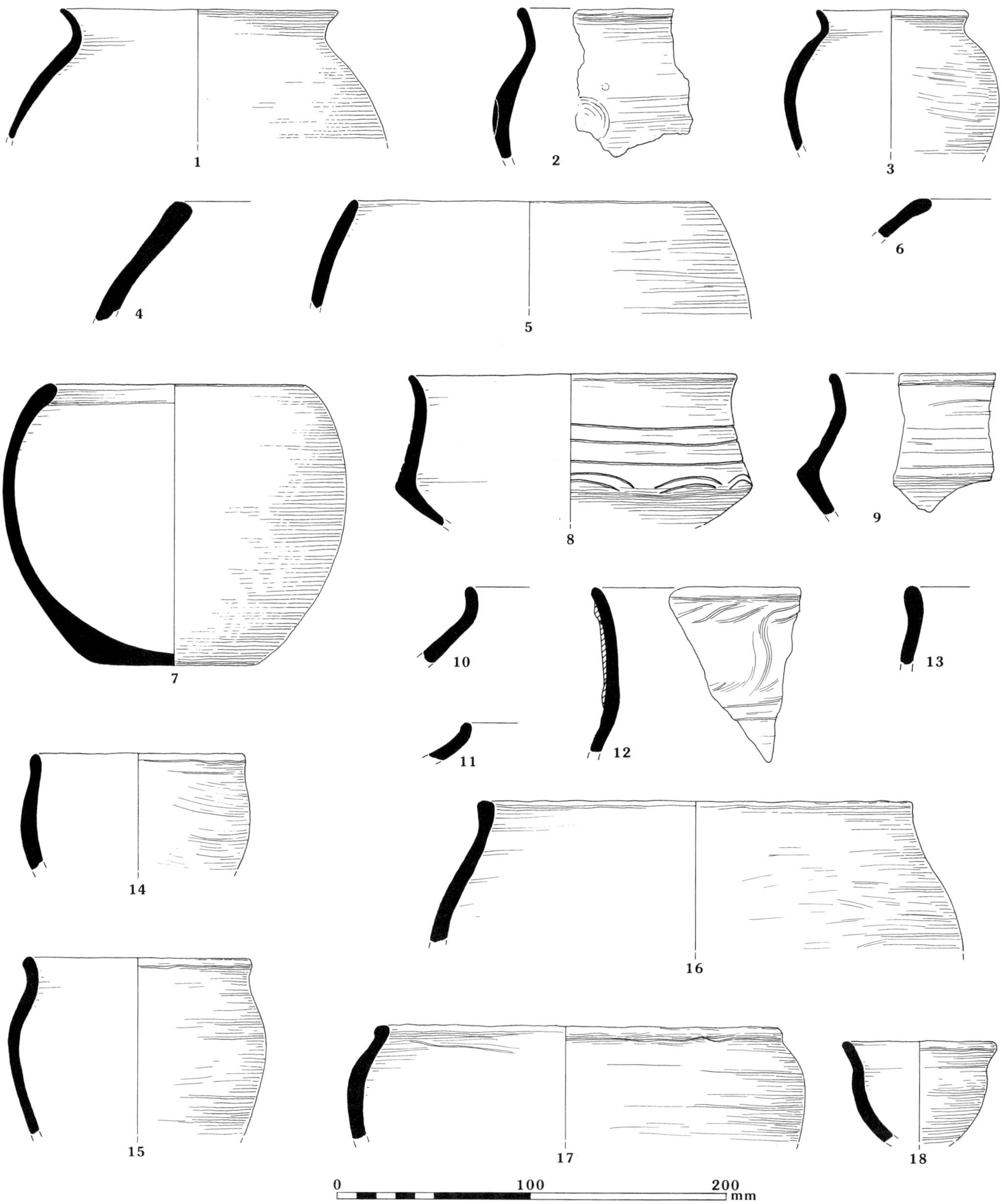

Figure 25 Early Saxon pottery

angular, patinated flint <4 mm; rare, irregular rock fragments <2 mm; sparse very coarse organic temper; rare iron particles <1 mm; unoxidised, generally oxidised exterior surface.

Q405 Hard, moderately coarse fabric; common, well-sorted, rounded/sub-angular quartz /quartzite <0.25 mm; rare fine mica; unoxidised, or oxidised, unoxidised exterior.

Q406 Soft, moderately coarse fabric; moderate, sub-rounded quartz, fairly well-sorted, <0.5 mm; sparse iron particles <1 mm; rare fine mica; oxidised.

Q407 Hard, moderately coarse fabric; moderate, well-sorted, sub-angular quartz/quartzite grains <1 mm; rare iron particles—<1 mm; sparse organic material—<4 mm; rare fine mica; unoxidised, oxidised exterior surface.

Q408 Hard, moderately coarse fabric; moderate, fairly well-sorted, rounded quartz grains <1 mm; rare fine mica; moderate organic temper <10 mm; rare sub-angular/sub-rounded, patinated flint <7 mm; sparse iron particles <2 mm; unoxidised.

Fabrics containing rock fragments as dominant inclusion type

R400 Fine, hard fabric; moderate, well-sorted, rounded quartz grains <1 mm; sparse mica—<2 mm; sparse sub-angular ?felspar—<2 mm; rare organic material <2 mm; unoxidised, oxidised external surface.

R401 Fine, soft fabric; sparse, poorly-sorted, irregular rock fragments <4 mm; rare fine mica; sparse organic temper <5 mm; rare sub-rounded flint pebbles <5 mm; rare iron particles <1 mm; unoxidised, some oxidisation on exterior surface.

Organic-tempered fabrics

V400 Hard, moderately coarse fabric; moderate, poorly-sorted, irregular burnt bone fragments <4 mm; rare sub-rounded quartz <0.5 mm; sparse iron <0.5 mm; rare fine mica; oxidised.

V401 Soft, moderately fine matrix; sparse, poorly-sorted, irregular burnt bone fragments <2 mm; rare rounded quartz <0.5 mm; rare fine mica; unoxidised.

V402 Soft, moderately coarse sandy matrix; moderate strands of organic material (chaff or straw) <5 mm; rare fine mica; unoxidised.

These 14 fabrics represent a markedly diverse range, from the organic-tempered fabric V402, a type considered to be characteristic of the early/mid Saxon period, and a number of sandy fabrics, to more 'exotic' fabrics containing obvious non-local rock fragments (R400, R401, Q402, Q404) and the unusual bone-tempered fabrics V400 and V401. The contrast with the Saxon assemblage from Hurst Park, which includes a range of non-distinctive and almost certainly locally-produced sandy and organic-tempered fabrics (Laidlaw, this volume), is particularly marked.

This range of fabric types is significant, not merely for its reflection of a correspondingly wide range of potential source areas, but also for its chronological and cultural implications. Some fabric types can be identified on the basis of their distinctive rock inclusions as being of definitely non-local and potentially non-British origin. These comprise fabrics R400, R401, Q402, and Q404, which make up half the total Saxon assemblage by weight, a remarkably high proportion.

Fabrics Q402, Q403, Q404, Q405, and Q407 all contain angular fragments of clear, colourless polycrystalline quartz or quartzite, which are quite distinct from the rounded, iron-stained quartz inclusions characteristic of the local Reading Beds. The predominance of these fabrics amongst the sandy wares is interesting, given the rarity of such inclusions in the Late Bronze Age assemblage (*see* above)

Samples of three fabrics (R400, R401, and Q407) were submitted for thin section analysis to D.F. Williams, University of Southampton, and his results are presented below. The results were perhaps unexpected. A non-local origin was confirmed for all of these fabrics, but as an alternative to a non-British origin a potential source in the Charnwood Forest area of Leicestershire has been suggested for fabrics R400 and Q407 and also, possibly, for fabric R401. The implications of these results are discussed further below.

The occurrence of bone as a tempering agent is very unusual but not unique. It is known from a handful of prehistoric vessels of Neolithic and Bronze Age date, from England and Ireland (Smith and Darvill 1990; Cleal in press). In Saxon contexts it has been identified amongst the cremation urns from Spong Hill, Norfolk (Brisbane 1994, group X), although interestingly not from the inhumation or domestic pottery from the same site, nor has any reference to it been found from any other Saxon domestic context.

Other fabrics are considered to be of purely local origin; these include the standard organic-tempered fabric V402, the flint-tempered fabric F400, and the sandy fabrics Q401, Q406, and Q408, which contain rounded, iron-stained quartz grains characteristic of the Reading Beds. These five fabrics together account for less than one-quarter of the total assemblage by weight.

Forms

Diagnostic forms were scarce, with only 18 rims in total recovered from the Saxon assemblage and, because of the lack of complete profiles, it was in some cases difficult to assign rims to particular vessel forms. The rims present have been used to create a type series which is linked as far as possible to vessel forms. Eight rim/vessel forms were thus defined and the correlation of rim form to fabric type is given in Table 4.

The term 'vessel' has been used throughout the descriptions below in preference to 'jar' or 'bowl'. An attempt has been made to group the forms into 'closed' (Types 1–5) and 'open' types (Types 6–8) but it should be made clear that the distinction between the two is not always clear-cut. While 'closed' forms might be taken to correlate to 'jars' and 'open' forms to 'bowls', in an apparently unstandardised assemblage such as this, where there is a wide size range within types and where vessels are likely to have been multi-functional, the definition of such functional terms becomes less meaningful.

'Closed' forms

Type 1: Small to medium rounded vessel, everted rim (Fig. 25, 1–3)
Type 2: Medium to large, rounded vessel, plain, inturned rim (Fig. 25, 4–7)
Type 3: Sharply biconical, necked vessel, slightly everted rim (Fig. 25, 8–9)
Type 4: Medium-sized, globular vessel, upright rim (Fig. 25, 10–11)
Type 5: Necked vessel, possibly biconical as Type 3 (Fig. 25, 12)

'Open' forms

Type 6: Small to medium, slack-shouldered vessel (Fig. 25, 13–15)
Type 7: Small cup with rounded base and everted rim (Fig. 25, 18)
Type 8: Medium-sized, shouldered vessel with beaded rim (Fig. 25, 16–17)

Rim diameters are not available for all vessels but those which are measurable show clearly that there is a wide range of sizes within Types 1 and 6 (external rim diameter range of 75–180 mm and 110–220 mm respectively). The two biconical vessels (Type 3) are of similar size and for other types there is insufficient evidence.

Decoration and surface treatments
A substantial number of the sherds occurring in finer fabrics Q402, Q403, and Q408 are burnished externally and/or internally (*see* Table 5). Decoration is scarce. One of the biconical vessels has parallel horizontal incised lines and arcs above the carination (Fig. 25, 8); the second biconical vessel is corrugated above the carination (Fig. 25, 9). One vessel of Type 1 has a large circular impression on the shoulder (Fig. 25, 2) and the possible biconical vessel of Type 5 is decorated with the unusual technique of applied curvilinear motifs (Fig. 25, 12).

Distribution
A large proportion of the Saxon assemblage (59%) was recovered from the sunken-featured buildings 103, 439, and 605 (126, 59, and 30 sherds respectively). A sizeable group was also recovered from hollow 316 (88 sherds) but this seems to consist of sherds of a single vessel, a rounded vessel in fabric Q402 (Fig. 25, 7). Otherwise sherds occur in small groups in pits and post-holes scattered over the site.

The largest and potentially most interesting group derives from sunken-featured building 103. This group consists largely of sherds in fabrics containing either quartz/quartzite or rock fragments and also includes all three examples of bone-tempered sherds (fabrics V400, V401). Only three sherds in other fabrics are present, all quartz-tempered, probably local wares. There are no organic-tempered sherds of fabric V402. In other words, virtually the entire group is definitely, or potentially, of non-local origin. Vessel forms represented include Types 2, 3, 6, and 8 (Fig. 25, 4, 5, 8, 15–17).

Sunken-featured building 127 produced a similar range of fabric types but the quantities are much smaller (12 sherds). Sunken-featured buildings 439 and 605, on the other hand, show some significant differences. Both produced fabrics containing either quartz/quartzite or rock fragments but the proportion of these wares is less than for SFB 103 (59% and 69% respectively). Local quartz-tempered fabrics are still rare but both features contained sherds of the organic-tempered fabric V402. The range of vessel forms is correspondingly wider and includes examples of Types 1, 2, 4, 6, and 7 (Fig. 25: 3, 6, 10, 14, 18).

Discussion of the early Saxon pottery
This small but significant group of pottery can be added to a growing body of evidence for early Saxon ceramics in London and the surrounding area. Several sites producing pottery from the period of the 5th to mid-7th century AD have now been excavated (Blackmore 1993, fig. 1) with a distribution extending from central London westwards along the Thames and down its tributaries into Surrey and Middlesex. Prospect Park falls at the western limit of this distribution. Detailed analysis and

Table 4 Early Saxon pottery: vessel form by fabric type (no. of vessels)

Vessel form	*F400*	*Q402*	*Q403*	*Q404*	*Q407*	*Q408*	*Total*
'Closed' forms							
Type 1	–	–	2	–	–	1	3
Type 2	–	1	1	1	–	1	4
Type 3	–	1	–		1	–	2
Type 4	–	–	2	–	–	–	2
Type 5	1	–	–	–	–	–	1
'Open' forms							
Type 6	–	–	2	–	–	1	3
Type 7	–	–	1	–	–	–	1
Type 8	–	1	–	–	–	–	1
Total	1	3	8	1	1	3	17

Table 5 Early Saxon pottery: decoration and surface treatment by fabric type (no. of sherds)

	F400	*Q402*	*Q403*	*Q404*	*Q405*	*Q407*	*V402*	*Total*
Surface treatment								
Burnished	–	10	10	1	6	6	7	40
Decoration								
Incised	–	1	2	–	1	–	–	4
Impressed	–	–	1	–	–	–	–	2
Furrowed shoulder	–	–	–	–	–	1	–	1
Applied	1	–	–	–	–	–	–	1
Total	1	11	13	1	7	7	8	48

publication of these early sites is still pending and the current state of knowledge does not allow a comprehensive overview of the ceramic developments of the period. Any discussion of the pottery from Prospect Park, therefore, must necessarily be provisional and will doubtless need revision in the light of future work, but it is hoped that this report will highlight some of the trends in ceramic production and distribution in operation and provide useful comparative data for future analyses.

Comparable examples for the range of fabrics and forms identified at Prospect Park were sought amongst the, as yet, unpublished material from some of the early Saxon sites already identified, in particular the nearby site at Harmondsworth (Museum of London Accession No. MFH88), and from Hammersmith (HAM90), and Twickenham (UTH94). It was observed that while there is some overlap with fabric types from Harmondsworth and Twickenham, mainly in the range of fabrics containing either polycrystalline quartz/quartzite or the rounded, iron-stained quartz characteristic of the Surrey sands, the best parallels are with the assemblage from Hammersmith. At the latter site fabric types were noted containing polycrystalline quartz/quartzite and also rock fragments similar to those identified in fabric R400. Decoration amongst the Hammersmith assemblage, however, is more frequent than at Prospect Park, including vertical combing, rustication and grooving, and the coarse-slipped surface treatment of Germanic *Schlickung* type, which was not observed at Prospect Park. Vessel forms were also similarly represented, although the rounded, closed vessels with inturned rims (Type 2) at present appear to be unique in the London area to Prospect Park.

The occurrence of a significant proportion of non-local fabric types appears to be a consistent trend amongst several of these early sites and the petrological analysis of the sherds from Prospect Park goes some way towards an attribution of these fabrics to source areas, although this analysis has in some ways raised more questions than it has answered. A reasonable supposition to explain the presence of such a high proportion of non-local fabric types amongst early Saxon assemblages within the London area could be that the earliest Saxon settlers in the area would have brought with them pottery from their native country, later to be replaced by pottery made locally but still at this point heavily influenced by the native (ie non-British) ceramic traditions. Continental parallels for vessel forms and decorative techniques found on the early Saxon sites in the London area are wide-ranging across the Germanic areas of northern Germany, the Low Countries, and Denmark. This supposition, however, is not entirely supported by the results of the petrological analysis carried out for Prospect Park; the evidence is as yet ambiguous. No alternative models are presented here; there is a need for a far more wide-ranging programme of petrological analysis on early Saxon ceramics from the London area and elsewherebefore any such models may be advanced.

Dating for other early Saxon sites in London is by no means certain as yet but Harmondsworth and Hammersmith are tentatively dated on ceramic grounds to within a range of 5th to mid 6th century (Blackmore 1993, 131) and it seems likely that Prospect Park falls within the same date range. The high proportion of non-local fabric types at Prospect Park could be taken as an indication of an early date within this range, perhaps within the 5th century, but other evidence is conflicting. Few of the vessel forms are closely datable but types which are defined by Myres as amongst the earliest in the sequence include the sharply biconical forms (1977, 2–3). On the other hand, the rounded, inturned forms (Type 2) are not regarded as characteristic of early groups and Myres dates these generally to the 6th century (*ibid.*, 7–8). Both types occur in 'non-local' fabric types at Prospect Park. The absence of coarse-slipped *Schlickung* type pottery could also be chronologically significant. On the continent it seems to occur in 5th-century contexts (eg van Es 1967) and has been found on sites in London and elsewhere, for example Mucking, Essex, in 5th- to early 6th century contexts; it is suggested that this tradition can be taken as a type-fossil for the 5th century (Hamerow 1993; Blackmore forthcoming). Given the rather contradictory nature of the dating evidence available for Prospect Park, therefore, the general date range of 5th to mid 6th century is proposed with no attempt at refinement.

The proposed model for ceramic production and distribution in the early Saxon period of non-local ceramics, gradually replaced by local wares, raises some interesting questions regarding the internal chronological sequence at Prospect Park. The varying proportions of non-local fabrics in the four sunken-featured buildings is discussed above. If these fabrics represent the earliest ceramics on the site, a tentative sequence could be proposed in which sunken-featured buildings 103 and 127 are the earliest structures on the site, augmented at a slightly later date by sunken-featured buildings 439 and 605, which both contained a significantly higher proportion of local wares. On the other hand, such variations might have some functional significance.

List of illustrated pottery

Fig. 22: Late Neolithic

1. Grooved Ware decorated body sherd. Fabric G1. Context 310, pit 309.
2. Grooved Ware decorated rim sherds. Fabric G1. Context 310, pit 309.
3. Grooved Ware decorated body sherd; pinched finger impressions. Fabric G1. Context 310, pit 309.
4. Grooved Ware decorated body sherd. Context 382, pit 380.
5. Grooved Ware decorated body sherd. Fabric G1. Context 102, ditch 104.
6. Rim, body and base sherds of decorated Grooved Ware vessel; post-firing drilled holes through body wall. Fabric G1. Context 1469/1471, hollow 1494/post-hole 1496.
7. Grooved Ware decorated body sherd. Fabric G1. Context 1472, hollow 1494.
8. Grooved Ware decorated base angle sherds. Fabric G1. Context 1472, hollow 1494.
9. Grooved Ware decorated rim sherds. Fabric G1. Context 1472, hollow 1494.
10. Fengate Ware rim sherd; impressed decoration on exterior and inside rim. Fabric G3. Context 1469, hollow 1494.

Fig. 23: Middle Bronze Age Urns

1. Bucket urn, body sherds, lug and rounded simple rim fragment. Fabric F2. Urn 166, cremation 165.
2. Bucket urn, upper body rim missing, two perforations below finger impressed cordon drilled after firing. Fabric F4. Urn 162, cremation 161.

Fig. 24: Late Bronze Age

1. Shouldered jar (Type 1). Fabric F7. Context 622, pit 621.
2. Convex jar (Type 2), plain rim. Fabric F9. Context 237/417, ditch 236.
3. Everted rim, jar of unknown form (Type 3); incised on outer edge of rim. Fabric Q2. Context 267, layer.
4. Everted rim, jar of unknown form (Type 3); pinched along rim. Fabric Q2. Context 450, ditch 236.
5. Everted rim, jar of unknown form (Type 3); finger impressed on top of rim. Fabric F6. Context 296, layer.
6. Everted rim, thickened and flattened, jar of unknown form (Type 3); incised on external surface and internal surface of rim. Fabric F9. Context 417, ditch 236.
7. Everted rim, jar of unknown form (Type 3), finger impressed lightly on exterior of rim. Fabric F7. Context 310, pit 309.
8. Upright, internally expanded rim, jar of unknown form (Type 4); impressed decoration on top of rim. Fabric F9. Context 417, ditch 236.
9. Upright rim, internally expanded, jar of unknown form (Type 4). Fabric F9. Context 417, ditch 236.
10. Jar rim, unknown form, internally bevelled (Type 5). Fabric F5. Context 257, cut 256.
11. Biconical bowl (Type 6), inturned plain rim; burnished externally. Fabric F9. Context 622, pit 621.
12. Small shouldered bowl, upright rim (Type 7). Fabric F9. Context 231, four-post structure 455.
13. Everted rim, necked bowl (Type 8). Fabric F9. Context 417, ditch 236.
14. Convex bowl (Type 9), upright plain rim. Fabric F7. Context 746, pit 745.
15. Perforated body sherd. Fabric F5. Context 450, ditch 236.
16. Decorated body sherd; impressed decoration. Fabric F9. Context 417, ditch 236.
17. Decorated body sherd; applied, pinched boss. Fabric F7. Context 417, ditch 236.

Fig. 25: Early Saxon

1. Rounded jar (Type 1), everted rim. Fabric Q406. Context 612, pit 611.
2. Rounded jar (Type 1), everted rim; circular impression on shoulder. Burnished external surface. Fabric Q408. Context 354, pit 353.
3. Small, rounded vessel (Type 1), everted rim. Fabric Q403. Context 420, SFB 439.
4. Large rounded vessel, inturned plain rim (Type 2); external surface burnished. Fabric Q408. Context 105, SFB 103.
5. Medium, convex vessel, plain inturned rim (Type 2). Fabric Q404. Context 105, SFB 103.
6. Rounded vessel (Type 2), thickened, inturned rim; possible finger impression on external surface. Fabric Q402. Context 420, SFB 439.
7. Rounded vessel (Type 2), inturned rim; burnished internally. Fabric Q403. Context 317, Cut 316.
8. Sharply biconical vessel (Type 3); external surface burnished and decorated with incised parallel bands. Internal surface burnished on upper body and rim. Fabric Q402. Context 105, SFB 103.
9. Sharply biconical vessel (Type 3); burnished externally. Fabric Q407. Context 105, SFB 103.
10. Rounded vessel, upright rim (Type 4); external surface burnished. Fabric Q403. Context 420, SFB 439.
11. Rounded vessel (Type 4), upright rim. Fabric Q403. Context 417, ditch 236 (intrusive).
12. Necked vessel (Type 5), possibly biconical; applied decoration. Fabric F400. Context 424, post-hole 425.
13. Slack-shouldered vessel (Type 6), thickened rim. Fabric Q403. Context 128, SFB 127.
14. Small, slack-shouldered vessel (Type 6); external surface burnished. Fabric Q403. Context 268, Pit 273.
15. Slack-shouldered vessel (Type 6); Fabric Q403. Context 420, SFB 439.
16. Slack-shouldered vessel (Type 6); Fabric Q408. Context 105, SFB 103.
17. Wide-mouthed, shouldered vessel (Type 7), beaded rim. External surface burnished on shoulder. Fabric Q402. Context 105, SFB 103.
18. Small cup (Type 8), rounded base and everted rim; external surface burnished. Fabric Q403. Context 420, SFB 439.

A Note on the Petrology of Three Sherds of Early Saxon Pottery, by D.F. Williams

Petrology and fabric

Three sherds of early Saxon pottery, which all appear to have unusual fabrics for the area, were thin sectioned and studied under the petrological microscope. Initially, all three sherds were examined under a binocular microscope (x20). Munsell colour charts are referred to together with free descriptive terms.

[1] Fabric R400
Fairly thin-walled, reasonably hard, roughish sandy fabric containing distinctive large plates of golden, or sometimes silver, mica and small fragments of granite. Very dark grey (5YR 3/1) outer surface and core, reddish–brown (between 5YR 6/4 and 5/4) inner surface. Thin sectioning shows that scattered throughout the clay matrix are large, discrete grains of potash and plagioclase feldspar, grains of quartz, some of them polycrystalline, and small fragments of a granite, or perhaps a grano-diorite rock.

This sherd is obviously not a local product. Similar granitic-tempered pottery has previously been noted by the writer from a number of early–middle Saxon sites situated mainly in the Midlands and eastern part of the country (*see*, for example, Williams 1993a; 1994). The actual source for this distinctively-tempered pottery has yet to be conclusively tied down, but an origin is very probably to be found near the acid-intermediate igneous intrusions of the Charnwood Forest area to the south-west of Leicester (including the Mount Sorrel grano-diorite). A similar source may be possible for the Prospect Park sherd but, given its early date, a continental origin (ie North Germany) should not be ruled out at this stage.

[2] Fabric Q407
Medium thick, hard, rough, very sandy fabric, light brownish–grey (2.5YR 6/2) outer surface, dark grey inner surface and core. Thin sectioning shows a fairly fine textured clay matrix containing moderately sparse, silt-sized quartz grains and shreds of mica. Scattered throughout the fabric are ill-sorted sub-angular quartz grains ranging in size from about 0.20–1 mm across. Also present are a few pieces of sandstone, quartzite, a number of discrete grains of feldspar, and what appear to be weathered fragments of ?igneous rock.

The presence of discrete feldspar grains and the possible identification of weathered igneous material raises the possibility that this sherd may also come from the general region of no. 1 above, although not necessarily from the same source.

[3] Fabric R401
Thick, fairly hard, rough, sandy fabric with a few large scattered inclusions of quartzite and flint, darkish grey (between 10YR 5/1 and 4/1) outer surface, darker grey inner surface and core. Thin sectioning shows frequent sub-angular quartz grains ranging up to 0.50 mm across but mostly well below this in size, together with pieces of quartzite, a little flint, fine-grained sandstone, flecks of mica, some elongated voids, indicating organic material was present at some stage, and iron oxides.

This sherd is unlike the local prehistoric range of fabrics from the nearby site of Caesar's Camp at Heathrow (Williams 1993b) and so it is possible that once again it may be an import to the site. Quartzite, for example, is present in the Charnwood Forest area, and occurs as pebbles in the surrounding Triassic formations and Boulder Clays (Worssam and Old 1988). However, the range of inclusions present in this sherd are not especially uncommon and, at this stage, other more local sources cannot as yet be ruled out.

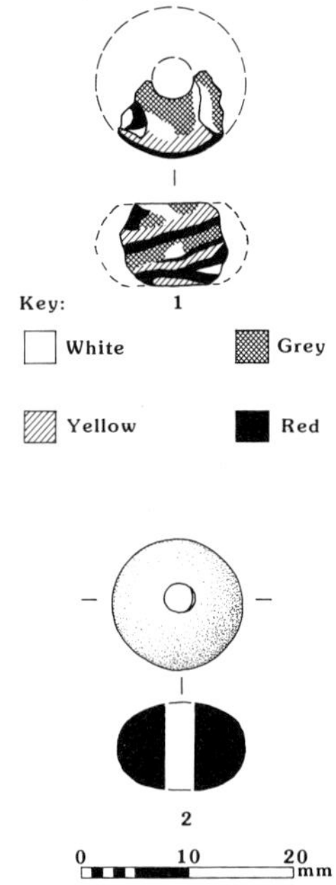

Figure 26 Glass and ceramic beads

Glass and Ceramic Beads, by M. Laidlaw

Three beads were found, comprising one fragment from a polychrome glass bead, one miniature monochrome glass bead, and one fired clay bead. All were recovered from Saxon sunken-featured building 103.

The polychrome glass bead (Fig. 26, 1) is a flattened spherical form of which approximately 25% survives. The fragment is too small to discern the full decorative motifs but wavy lines of red, yellow, and white can be seen on an opaque background. Comparable glass beads are generally dated to the end of the 6th or the 7th century AD (eg Cook and Dacre 1985, 82–3).

The miniature monochrome glass bead, recovered from a bulk soil sample, is also flattened spherical in form, 2 mm in diameter and with a central perforation. Tiny beads such as this are not common on Saxon sites but their rarity may in part be the result of recovery techniques employed during excavation. Dickinson has concluded that miniature beads were used throughout the early Anglo-Saxon period (1973, 253).

The flattened spherical fired clay bead (Fig. 26, 2) is 11–12 mm in diameter with a central perforation 3 mm in diameter. The bead is well-made and very hard-fired. While this object does not readily find parallels on other Saxon sites, its provenance and association with the two glass beads suggests a similar date. However, it may have been a residual Bronze Age find.

Illustrated Beads (Fig. 26)

1. Glass bead fragment; polychrome, interlacing wavy lines of red, yellow, and white on opaque background, diameter of perforation 4 mm, estimated original diameter of bead 10 mm. Obj. No. 6016; context 383; post-hole 384; SFB 103.
2. Ceramic bead; flattened spherical, diameter of bead 11–12 mm, diameter of perforation 3 mm. Context 105; SFB 103.

Ceramic Building Material, by M. Laidlaw

Seven pieces of ceramic building material were recovered from Saxon contexts. These include three tile and brick fragments from the sunken-featured building 103 and one fragment of roofing tile from well 711, all tentatively identified as Romano-British, although no clearly diagnostic material is present. In both cases, Romano-British pottery came from the same contexts as the ceramic building material. The remaining two brick fragments and one small tile fragment, all from well 711, are post-medieval.

Fired Clay, by M. Laidlaw

Small, non-diagnostic fragments of fired clay were recovered from excavation Areas 13.1, 13.2, and 13.2X (a total of 311, 1407 g). Most fragments are oxidised in a fine to coarse quartz fabric with occasional flint inclusions. A small number of surfaces were visible, suggesting the fragments were probably structural in origin from either wattle and daub structures or hearth linings. Wattle impressions, however, were only visible on a very small number of pieces.

On the basis of associated pottery, 90 fragments of fired clay have been attributed to the late prehistoric period, the largest concentration of which was found in ditch 236. The remaining fragments were dispersed in small quantities within various pits and post-holes across the site.

A large quantity of fired clay fragments (201) was retrieved from features attributed to the early Saxon period. One third of the total fired clay assemblage came from sunken-featured building 103, 24 fragments from well 711, and smaller quantities found in sunken-featured buildings 127, 316, and 605, and various pits dispersed over the site. Twenty fragments were from features which could not be positively dated.

5. Environmental Evidence

Cremated Human Bone, by Jacqueline I. McKinley.

Introduction

Cremated human bone from six contexts was received for examination, comprising two Middle Bronze Age urned burials and their respective pit backfills, one Romano-British and one undated context. One of the urned burials (161) was emptied in spits by the writer.

Methods

All possible cremation-related features were subject to total recovery in excavation. The 'samples' were wet-sieved to 1 mm fraction-size. All bone was extracted from the >5 mm fraction, the <5 mm fraction being retained for scanning.

Osteological procedure

Analysis followed the writer's standard procedure for the examination of cremated bone (McKinley 1989, 1994a).

The bone extracted from each context was passed through a sieve stack of 10, 5, and 2 mm mesh size. The relative weights of bone from each sieve and the maximum skull and long bone fragments, illustrates the degree of bone fragmentation in each context (table in archive). Identifiable bone was separated for further examination being divided into skull, axial skeleton, upper, and lower limb categories. This may demonstrate any deliberate bias in the skeletal elements collected for burial. 'Identifiable' bone is defined as fragments which may be identified to a particular bone or group, eg femur, proximal finger phalanx, thoracic vertebra.

Animal bone fragments (mostly cremated) were extracted and forwarded to the archaeozoologist.

Some of the 2 mm fraction residues contained quantities of pea-grits etc. Consequently, the 2 mm fraction weights presented in archive tables and the total weights of bone in Table 6, include, in some instances, the weight of this extraneous material and are not representative of the bone weight alone.

Full details of all identified bone are presented in the archive including:

- The number of identified bone fragments with descriptions of morphology and pathological lesions.
- Bone measurements taken in addition to those presented in the archive table.
- Variations in the colour of individual bone fragments from the buff/white of full oxidation.
- Any coloured staining to bone fragments or adhering substances. A brief note on animal bone fragments recovered and pyre/grave goods removed during the osteological examination.

Number of individuals

The number of individuals represented in a context was ascertained either from obvious age-related differences in size and development of the bone as between immature and adult individuals, or by duplication of identifiable bone fragments (McKinley 1989, 1994a for further discussion).

Age

Age assessed from the stage of tooth development (van Beek 1983), ossification/epiphyseal bone fusion (Gray 1977; McMinn and Hutchings 1985; Webb and Suchey 1985), cranial suture fusion, and other age-related degenerative changes to the bone (Bass 1987). The age categories used are as follows:

- subadult 13–18 years
- young adult 19–25 years
- mature adult 26–45 years
- older adult 45 years +

Table 6 Cremated bone: summary results

Context	*Period*	*Dist.*	*Type*	*Total wt. (g)*	*No. Ind.*	*Age*	*Sex*	*Pathology / morphological variation*	*Animal*
160 (165)	MBA	*	pd	127.5+	–	adult	?	–	present
161	MBA	*	u	660.8+	1	older mature adult	??female	new bone: r. malar	?imm.
164 (161)	MBA	*	pd	114.1+	–	mature adult	?	–	–
165	MBA	*	u	841..2	1	young adult	?female	o.p.– auricular surface; m.v.– ?retention deciduous molar	–
312	RB		cb/?pd	51.8+	1?	older mature/older adult	?	exo – femur shaft	–
315	?		?pd	135..5	–	1) adult ?2) adult			u/b

Key:

Period
MBA Middle Bronze Age
RB Romano-British

Dist
* undisturbed

Total wt
+ 2 mm fraction includes extraneous material

Pathology / morphological variation
exo exostoses
o.p. osteophytes
m.v. morphological variation
r. right

Animal
u/b unburnt
imm. immature

Type
u urned cremation burial
cb cremation burial mode of deposition unknown
pd pyre debris

Where insufficient evidence was present to aid age assessment there may be overlaps between categories.

Sex
Sex was ascertained from the sexually dimorphic traits of the skeleton (Bass 1987), including the maximum cranial vault thicknesses '1a' and '1b' according to Gejvall (1981). As with age assessment, a combination and scoring of traits was used in order to overcome any methodological bias or variations in sexual dimorphology within the group. Levels of reliability reflect the quantity and quality of available traits on which to base the assessment; '??' denotes possible, '?' denotes probable.

Vessel emptied in spits
Annotated plan and section drawings were made during excavation of the fill of the vessel 162 (context 161) at 20 mm intervals. The bone from each context was examined by half section/spit to ascertain any deliberate order of deposition within the urn.

Results
A summary of the results is presented in Table 6. Contexts comprising only a few grams of scattered/redeposited bone or no 'identifiable' bone fragments have not been included in these tables. Weights of bone from all contexts containing bone are presented in archive. All weights are given in grams (g) to one decimal place. All measurements are given in millimetres (mm). Unless stated otherwise, all bone, human and animal, is cremated/burnt.

Disturbance and condition of bone
The Middle Bronze Age burials were slightly disturbed, the uppermost portions of the urns having been slightly clipped by ploughing. The Romano-British burial was severely truncated (depth of feature 0.04 m), and the undated context also appeared to have been truncated (0.11 m deep).

After sieving, the bone appeared in good condition. However, it was noted during excavation of context 161, that the soil matrix was very hard and that the bone was in poor condition, suffering considerable fragmentation during excavation. It may be significant to note the relative absence of spongy bone identified from this burial.

Demography
A minimum of three individuals was identified, two from the Bronze Age contexts, both adult females, and one from the Romano-British ?burial. The remains of two individuals were present in the undated context,

there being duplication of the right petrous temporal. The nature of this undated context, a homogeneous mix of cremated bone and charcoal with no other inclusions, suggests it does not represent a burial but is probably pyre debris, either deliberately dumped in the feature or redeposited. The bone may, therefore, relate to the same cremation(s) episode represented by one or more of the burials, excluding 161 where the identified fragments were duplicated. Alternatively, the debris may be related to a cremation or cremations from which the burials were not recovered in excavation.

The small size of the group precludes further demographic comment. It is probable that further burials were originally present and have either been completely truncated or were outside the limits of excavation.

Pyre technology and ritual

Efficiency of cremation
The efficiency of cremation was good, the vast majority of bone being the buff–white resulting from full oxidation (Shipman *et al.* 1984). A few fragments of bone from the Middle Bronze Age burials showed some variation in colour, being slightly blue–grey, but the variations were very minor and of no significance.

Collection
In both Bronze Age burials 13–15% of the total bone weight was recovered from pyre debris incorporated in the backfills of the graves. The total weight of bone from each burial represents a maximum of 77% (161) and 96% (165) of the total weight of bone expected from an adult cremation (McKinley 1993a), probably nearer to 48% and 60% respectively. Incomplete recovery of bone for burial is a normal feature of the cremation rite.

The majority of the bone in the Bronze Age burials was recovered from the 10 mm fraction, *c.* 40%. The maximum fragment size recorded in analysis was 52 mm (burial context 165). However, it was evident that substantial fragmentation of the bone had occurred during removal from the burial medium. During excavation by the writer of the vessel fills 161 and 165, the maximum fragment sizes recorded were 70 mm from the former (reduced to 41 mm by time of analysis) and 100 mm from the latter. These observations demonstrate that cremated bone, brittle by nature and dried-out by the soil, may be reduced by up to half its length in excavation, despite great care taken in removal. There was no evidence to suggest any deliberate fragmentation of bone prior to burial (McKinley 1994b).

Bone from the Romano-British and undated contexts showed a lower percentage of bone in the 10 mm fraction, 20% and 30% respectively, and smaller maximum fragment sizes, 22 mm and 34 mm, than the Bronze Age burials. It has been demonstrated elsewhere (McKinley 1994b) that the form of deposition and level of disturbance have an effect on the size of bone fragments. The condition of the bone in 312 is probably a consequence of the severe truncation of the feature.

It is normal to observe a (apparently random) selection of bone from each skeletal area within a burial, irrespective (other than in extreme circumstances) of the overall quantity of bone included. The percentages of identified bone in each area is rarely exactly equal for a variety of reasons including disturbance, ease of identifying different skeletal areas and bone survival (McKinley 1994a). The percentage of axial bone in each context was small, 3–4% of the identified bone weight. It was also noted in general that few fragments of spongy bone tended to be present. In view of the observation made by the writer during excavation of the urn fill 161, it is felt this absence is probably due to poor survival of spongy bone rather than deliberate selection.

Excavation of fill 161 in vessel 162 showed a mixture of skeletal elements throughout the burial. There is no evidence to suggest that collection of the remains commenced at one end of the pyre and progressed to the other, although the presence of both petrous temporals in one small area of the vessel may indicate they were picked up together. It cannot automatically be assumed, however, that the burial urn also formed the receptacle for collection of bone from the pyre; the bone may only have been transferred to the urn for burial.

Cremated animal bone
A small quantity of cremated animal bone was recovered from the backfill (160) of burial context 165 and a fragment of unidentified animal bone was also present in burial context 161. The inclusion of cremated animal bone in Bronze Age burials is not unusual (McKinley 1993b).

Pyre debris
Although no evidence of pyre sites was recovered, the presence of pyre debris in the backfills of the Bronze Age and Romano-British burials, and the pyre debris 315, would suggest that the cremations were conducted in the general vicinity of the burials. Evidence for such proximity of the pyre site to place of burial has been recorded at other sites both of the Bronze Age (eg Grinsell 1941; Christie 1967; Barnett 1994) and Romano-British periods (eg East London Cemeteries (McKinley 1995a) and Baldock 15 (G. Burleigh pers. comm.).

Pathology

A summary of the pathological lesions and morphological variation observed is given in Table 6.

In burial 161, a fragment of right malar showed a small area of fine surface new bone on the posterior side of the inferior lateral border. The inferior portion of the temporo-malar canal was exposed (damaged) and had a lining of the same fine new bone. The lesion suggests some form of infection. Formation of slight osteophytes and exostoses noted in 165 and 312 are most probably the result of age-related wear-and-tear.

Animal Bones, by Sheila Hamilton-Dyer

A total of 93 bone fragments was recovered from 27 contexts. These comprise 63 individual bones and teeth of which 34 were identified to species (horse, cattle, sheep/goat, pig, and dog), 11 could be identified only as sheep/pig and cattle/horse sized fragments and, a further 18 could not be identified further than mammalian (Table 7). The preservation is generally poor, in

Table 7 Animal bone, species distribution

Period	*Horse*	*Cattle*	*Sheep/Goat*	*Pig*	*Dog*	*LAR*	*SAR*	*Mammal*	*Total*
Neolithic	–	1	–	–	–	–	–	–	1
Late BA	10	5	–	–	–	–	–	–	15
Saxon	1	11	2	1	1	7	2	17	42
Undated	1	1	–	–	–	1	1	1	5
Total	12	18	2	1	1	8	3	18	63
%	19	28.6	3.2	1.6	1.6	12.7	4.8	28.6	

some cases the surface had been intact but even minimal handling has resulted in significant damage. The high percentage of loose teeth underlines the poor bone survival, with 23 loose teeth forming 36% of the total bones and 68% of the remains identified to species, just 11 non-tooth fragments were identified. Eight fragments had been charred, this also appears to help in preservation of bone.

Neolithic

The single, fragmented bone from this phase is a cattle pelvis from pit 380.

Middle/Late Bronze Age

All of the horse remains from this site are teeth, and ten of the 12 come from this phase. Close examination indicates that nine of the teeth, all from ditch 236, are likely to have come from one individual maxilla of an adult but not aged animal. The cattle remains were also teeth.

A few very small fragments of mammalian bone were recovered from cremation burial 161, but these could not be positively identified to species. A deciduous upper canine of a piglet came from the possible pyre debris 315. Resorption of part of the root indicates that this was naturally shed rather than coming from a dead piglet. The tooth is not calcined or charred black but is of a golden–brown colour and may be heat affected or soil stained.

Saxon

The bulk of the remains come from contexts in this phase. Five species are represented with the majority of identified fragments being of cattle. Fragments of a cattle humerus, metatarsus, astragalus, and jaw are present, as well as seven loose teeth. The single horse fragment and the two sheep/goat fragments are of loose teeth. Pig is represented by the fragmented maxilla of an immature animal. A small fragment of limb bone shaft from context 128 is believed to be part of a dog radius. The remaining 26 fragments have not been identified to species. The composition of this small group is typical of Saxon assemblages with cattle dominant, sheep and pig of secondary importance, and occasional remains of horse and dog. Undated material is composed of a horse and a cattle tooth and three unidentified fragments.

Charred Plant Remains, by Pat Hinton

Method

Samples were processed by Wessex Archaeology following standard flotation methods with the flots retained on a 0.5 mm mesh and the residues on a 1 mm mesh. All the residues were fractionated and sorted for carbonised plant remains (by S.F. Wyles), and then both the unsorted flots and material extracted from the residues were sorted by the writer with a stereo-microscope at 7–40x magnification.

Results

All samples included at least a few modern seeds and root fragments and the majority contained only small amounts of charred plant remains, often in poor condition. Only one sample, from a Saxon feature, included a wider range of cereals, chaff, and weeds (Table 8b).

Late Neolithic

The one sample from this phase, from pit 380, contained very few seeds but there were several very small, shiny, vacuolated fragments. They are listed as cereal grain fragments because in other samples they sometimes include shapes indicative of distorted cereal grains, such as a trace of a ventral furrow.

Apart from a single grass seed, the only contents are fruit stones of *Crataegus monogyna* (hawthorn) and fragments of *Corylus avellana* (hazel) nut shells. These suggest a characteristic Neolithic picture of wild plant food gathering and denote the establishment of scrub vegetation.

Late prehistoric

The material from the pyre debris in pit 314 shows a similar pattern to the Late Neolithic assemblage. As before, there is very little evidence of agriculture and grass and woodland plants are again represented.

However, the samples from pit 331, within the possible Middle Bronze Age ring-ditch 378, show an increase in cereals, notably probable *Hordeum vulgare* (hulled barley), *Triticum* (wheat) species, and *Avena* sp. (oats) (Table 8a). The better preserved wheat grains are identified by their short plump forms and more steeply inclined radicle depressions as *Triticum* cf. *aestivum* s.l., a free-threshing bread wheat and the almost square

Table 8a Charred plant remains (Late Neolithic to Romano-British)

		Late Neolithic	*Middle–Late Bronze Age*			*Late Bronze Age*				*Romano-British*
	Feature	Pit 380	Pit 414	Pit 331		Post-holes 277	230	275	Slot 695	Pit 423
	Context no.	382	315	332	377	278	231	276	696	312
	Sample no.	5022	5007	5014	5017	5020	5011	5012	5037	5006
	Sample volume (litres)	10	10	5	10	10	10	10	8	5
CULTIVATED										
Hordeum vulgare L.– grains	hulled barley	–	–	(1)	–	(1)	–	–	–	–
Triticum cf *spelta* – grains	spelt	–	–	–	–	–	1	–	–	3
Triticum cf dicoccum/*spelta* – glume base	emmer/spelt	–	–	–	–	–	–	1	–	–
Triticum dicoccum / spelta – rachis internode		–	–	–	–	–	–	1	–	–
Triticum cf *aestivum* sl – grains	bread wheat	–	–	12	14	–	–	1	–	–
Triticum sp	indeterminate wheat	–	–	5	7	–	2	3	–	–
Avena sp – grains	oats	–	–	>4	1	–	–	–	–	–
Avena sp – awn fragments	indeterminate cereals	–	–	2	–	–	–	–	–	–
Cerealia – grain fragments		<0.25ml	<0.5ml	<0.5ml	<0.5ml	<0.5ml	<0.5ml	<0.5ml	<0.5ml	<0.5ml
ARABLE, WASTE & GRASSLAND										
Chenopodium cf *polyspermum*	many-seeded goosefoot	–	–	–	–	–	–	1	–	–
Rumex cf *crispus*	curled dock	–	–	1	–	–	–	–	–	–
Vicia / Lathyrus sp	tare/vetchling	–	–	–	–	–	–	–	1	1
Bromus cf *secalinus*	rye brome	–	–	–	–	–	–	2	–	–
Poaceae – *Phleum* type	timothy grass	1	–	–	–	–	–	–	–	–
Poaceae – indet.	small-seeded grass	–	–	–	–	–	–	–	(1)	1
WOOD MARGINS/SCRUB										
Corylus avellana L. – nut shell frags	hazel	10	1	–	–	–	–	1	–	–
Crataegus monogyna L. – fruit stone	hawthorn	≥4	>6	–	–	–	–	–	–	–
cf bud		–	1	–	–	–	–	–	–	–
Unidentified		–	1	–	–	–	–	–	–	–

Table 8b Charred plant remains (Saxon)

		Well 711		*Pit 423*	*Pit 316*	*Sunken-featured buildings*			
						439	605	103	605
	Context no.	712	716	424	318	400	620	105	606
	Sample no.	5038	5042	5018	5009	5015	5030	5019	5029
	Sample volume (litres)	10	10	10	1	8	5	10	10
CULTIVATED									
Hordeum vulgare L. – grains	hulled barley	–	2(1)	3	1(2)	2(3)	2	1(2)	1(1)
Hordeum vulgare – rachis frags		–	–	2	–	–	–	–	–
Triticum cf *dicoccum* – glume bases	emmer	–	–	27	–	–	–	–	–
Triticum cf *spelta* – grains	spelt	–	–	1(4)	–	–	–	–	–
Triticum cf *spelta – glume bases*		–	–	89	–	–	–	–	–
Triticum dicoccum / spelta – grains	emmer/spelt	–	–	8	–	–	–	–	–
Triticum dicoccum / spelta – glume bases		–	–	87	–	–	–	–	–
Triticum dicoccum / spelta – rachis internodes		–	–	>25	–	–	–	–	–
Triticum cf aestivum sl – *grains*	bread wheat	1	–	5(1)	1(2)	1(2)	1	1(1)	(1)
Triticum sp	indeterminate wheats	1	–	>7	–	–	–	1	(1)
Avena sp – grains	oats	–	–	–	1	1	–	(1)	–
Avena – awn fragments		–	–	5	–	–	–	2	–
Cerealia indet. – grain frags	indeterminate cereals	<0.5ml	<0.25ml	<0.5ml	<0.5ml	<0.5ml	<0.5ml	<0.5ml	<0.5ml
ARABLE, WASTE & GRASSLAND									
Chenopodium cf *polyspermum*	many-seeded goosefoot	–	–	1	–	2	–	–	–
Chenopodium album L.	fat hen	–	–	(2)	–	4	–	–	–
Stellaria media / neglecta	chickweed	–	–	2	–	–	–	–	–
Persicaria lapathifolia (L.) Gray	pale persicaria	–	–	–	–	–	–	6	–
Fallopia convolvulus (L.) A. Love	black bindweed	–	1	–	–	–	–	–	–
Rumex cf *crispus*	curled dock	1	–	–	–	–	–	–	–
Capsella bursa-pastoris (L.) Medikus	shepherd's purse	–	1	–	–	1	–	–	–
Vicia cf *tetrasperma*	smooth tare	–	–	3	–	1	–	–	–
Vicia hirsuta (L.) Gray	hairy tare	–	1	1	–	–	–	–	–

Table 8b continued

		Well 711		Pit 423	Pit 316	Sunken-featured buildings			
						439	605	103	605
	Context no.	712	716	424	318	400	620	105	606
	Sample no.	5038	5042	5018	5009	5015	5030	5019	5029
	Sample volume (litres)	10	10	10	1	8	5	10	10
ARABLE, WASTE & GRASSLAND contd.									
Trifolium cf *repens*	white clover	1	–	1	–	–	–	–	–
Vicia / Lathyrus sp	tare/vetchling	1	–	–	–	–	–	1	–
Odontites vernus (Bellardi) Dumort	red bartsia	–	–	3	–	–	–	–	–
Galium aparine L.	cleavers	–	–	2	–	–	–	–	–
Bromus cf *secalinus*	rye brome	–	–	≥4	–	–	–	–	–
Poaceae indet.	small-seeded grasses	–	–	(1)	–	–	–	–	–
WOOD MARGINS/SCRUB									
cf *Quercus* sp – bud fragment	oak	–	–	–	–	–	–	1	–
Corylus avellana L. – nut shell frags	hazel	1	–	3	–	–	–	–	(1)
Prunus spinosa L. – fruit stone	sloe	–	1	–	–	–	–	–	–

Key to Tables 8a and 8b: ( ) = identification uncertain

outlines of some are characteristic of *Triticum compactum* type (club wheat).The few oat grains and awn fragments are insufficient in themselves to indicate a cultivated or wild species. It is likely they occurred as a weed of the other cereal crops.

Bread wheat is again present in the Late Bronze Age post-holes associated with the possible four-post structure and there is also slender evidence, in the form of chaff fragments, for the glumed wheats *Triticum dicoccum* or *T. spelta* (emmer or spelt), the only traces of these in the prehistoric phases at Prospect Park.

Other seeds from the late prehistoric samples are so few, that any attempt to interpret the agricultural and environmental background of this period from them is almost impossible. *Rumex* and *Chenopodium* spp. (docks and goosefoots) are ruderals of usually nutrient-rich disturbed ground or may occur as field weeds. *Bromus* cf. *secalinus* (probable rye brome) is a frequent weed of late prehistoric and Roman crops and is very often associated with spelt. Adjacent woodland or scrub is attested by hazel.

Romano-British

The only sample from this phase, a possible cremation context, produced very few cereals, of which the only identifiable grains were most probably spelt. Two other seeds, of a grass and *Vicia/Lathyrus* (tare/vetchling) species add little information.

Saxon

As in the earlier periods, plant remains are sparse and often fragmentary. In the samples from well 711, hollow 316, and the sunken-featured buildings, hulled barley, bread wheat, and oats are the only identified cereals, although there were a few indeterminate wheats. All samples had very small amounts of the small tarry fragments, similar to those described above, of which most are very likely to be severely burned cereal remains.

The wild plants have no particularly characteristic habitat preferences other than crop fields or other open grassy or disturbed places. Adjacent woodland in this phase is indicated by a fruit stone of *Prunus spinosa* (sloe) and a small fragment of probable hazel nut shell. A fragment of a bud resembles *Quercus* sp. (oak) in the arrangement of the bud scales.

Pit 423 yielded greater numbers and a wider range of cereal species, although most are represented by few grains and larger proportions of chaff. Apart from one spelt and some of the bread wheat grains, which are within a normal size range, all the cereals are undersized and some are malformed. These are probably 'tail grain' or the small and very light items which are removed, with the smaller seeds, by the winnowing and sieving of harvested cereals. Weeds too are present in slightly larger numbers in this sample and the whole assemblage appears to have originated in discarded crop processing refuse.

Information from the non-cultivated plants, which are either field weeds or plants of grassy or disturbed places, is again limited. Hazel, which occurs so commonly in archaeological deposits, once again may represent either gathered food or chance inclusion, but also signifies the proximity of light woodland or scrub.

The composition of the assemblage from pit 423, with the presence of probable emmer in addition to spelt and bread wheat, might suggest that it derived from an earlier period (eg later prehistoric). The sample, however, appears to derive from a single source (discarded crop processing waste) and all three cereal species are also present, though in different proportions, in the early Saxon phase at Hurst Park (this volume).

Discussion

Comparing the cereal remains from all periods at Prospect Park with those from Hurst Park (below) reveals a major difference in the absence of free-threshing bread wheat at the latter site until the Roman and Saxon phases and its earlier appearance at Prospect Park in the Late Bronze Age. A second difference is that *Secale cereale* (rye) was identified, as a minor element, in the Saxon phase at Hurst Park but was not found at Prospect Park.

Another comparable site in this region is Runnymede, where the Late Bronze Age cereals (Greig 1991a) are similar in their lack of bread wheat to those from Hurst Park. Rye was identified at Runnymede and at Hurst Park but not before Saxon times at the latter. Hulled barley and oats were present at all three sites. Runnymede and Hurst Park were both situated close to the river and the light sandy gravels would have been appropriate for barley, oats, and rye, and probably for emmer and spelt, but less suitable for bread wheats which thrive on medium to heavy loamy soils, perhaps available at Prospect Park. This suggestion is further borne out by the similar assemblage of cereal remains from early Saxon features at Holloway Lane, a short distance to the east of Prospect Park. There, bread or club wheat, and a glume wheat, probably spelt, were also present in the small and poorly preserved assemblage. Barley and oats were recorded but rye was absent, and the weed seeds and chaff have been interpreted as waste from cleaning of the grain prior to use rather than crop processing waste (Rackham 1994, 126–7).

6. Discussion

The section cut through the brickearth in Area 13.3 (Pl. 7) revealed an interesting sequence of periglacial features which will be reported on in detail elsewhere. However, no Palaeolithic remains or buried land surface were revealed at the interface of the brickearth and underlying gravels, and no stratified deposits were observed within the brickearth itself.

Five microliths, including two rods, indicate a (?late) Mesolithic presence in the area and represent the earliest datable finds from the site.

Neolithic

There is clearly evidence for Late Neolithic activity on the site but the nature of this remains somewhat enigmatic. A circular hollow, 1494, and the various surrounding features may represent a structure, and the minimum number of four Grooved Ware vessels depicts an important group, particularly in view of the relative paucity of other Late Neolithic fabric types from the site. Most of the assemblage came from hollow 1494 but it is not possible to be certain about what form any postulated structure took. Slot 319 and various post-holes, possibly including 504 and 1497, with 1496 to the north, may have been part of a single structure. All these features lay within 8 m of each other and others may have been completely destroyed. However, no reconstruction can be attempted based on this slender evidence. Post-hole 1496 is particularly interesting because of the number of Grooved Ware sherds in the fill, possibly from one of the vessels in hollow 1494. Large sherds of Grooved Ware have been found in the tops of post-holes for timber settings inside henge monuments where they had probably been placed around the posts; a similar explanation for the sherds in post-hole 1496 is possible. However in the absence of any other artefact belonging to the so-called Grooved Ware package, there is no particular reason to suggest a ritual theme for the feature found here.

The function of pit 380, which was relatively large, is not known; it need not have been contemporary with the other Late Neolithic features and could have served a domestic purpose. The proportionally high representation of tools in the flint assemblage supports this suggestion. The apparent absence of features in the area between hollow 1494 and pit 380 could have been the result of the slightly higher ground there having been reduced by ploughing, thereby removing any shallow features.

Finally, the significance of ditch 719 must be considered. No certain dating evidence came from the small volume excavated but it must have been late prehistoric or earlier for it was cut by a small pit containing Late Bronze Age pottery, after it had become completely infilled. The ditch, although not deep, was of substantial width and a natural origin is considered unlikely. One possibility is that it was the side-ditch on the west side of a ploughed out earthen long barrow. The profile of ditch 719 was not as steeply sloping and flat-bottomed as might be expected for a side-ditch to a long barrow but the nature of the natural brickearth and its greater susceptibility to weathering and erosion compared with chalk, for example, may be a factor to be taken into account. Similarly, the nature of the brickearth might, coupled with biological action, result in the homogeneous soil profile observed in section with no clearly defined primary fill apparent.

Ditch 719 was subject to further investigation during the watching brief. A probable terminus to the south was identified in the previously unexcavated area, though the difference between the natural and the ditch fill was very indistinct. Limited further excavation produced only a few small pieces of burnt flint. The nature of this feature, its fill, the general paucity of finds, and the absence of a corresponding ditch to the east means that the argument for the existence of such a monument remains unproven.

Middle Bronze Age

The interpretation and dating of feature 378 as a ring-ditch representing a prehistoric barrow is not unequivocal but is considered most probable. A diameter of less than 10 m would make it rather small but, considering its size and shape, it is more likely to have been prehistoric than Saxon; the latter might be expected to be smaller and more regular. A date to anywhere between the Late Neolithic and Late Bronze Age can be suggested, though it has been broadly assigned to the later prehistoric (?Middle Bronze Age) period. No dating evidence came from the ditch which had been entirely truncated and survived only as a soil stain. Pit 331 which may have been associated, perhaps the central burial pit, contained four sherds of late prehistoric pottery. It is possible that this was a later pit which coincidentally had been dug within the area enclosed by the ring-ditch, and survived later ploughing, but on balance this is considered less likely. The small amount of burnt clay recovered from pit 331 could have been derived from a variety of sources, including the base of a cremation pyre, although no cremated bone was found. However, feature 314 to the east of the ring-ditch has been interpreted as a dump of pyre debris and may have been contemporaneous and associated with the ring-ditch. The two urned cremation burials could have been survivors of a once greater number grouped around the putative barrow, and subsequently removed by truncation. A possible parallel for ring-ditch 378 is that excavated at Fenning's Wharf, near London Bridge, in 1984 (Cotton 1991, 154); a central pit contained later Bronze Age finds, and cremated bone was recovered from the ring-ditch.

Late Bronze Age

There is evidence for Late Bronze Age activity across the entire site and it is clear that only a limited area of the complex has been excavated. The settlement appears to have been open and occupation dispersed. The overall extent remains unknown, except to the west where the evaluation trenches have demonstrated a fall-off in features on the slope down to the floodplain of the River Colne. In various places, most notably in Area 13.2, some shallow features will not have survived plough damage.

The ceramic evidence suggests a sequence of activity spanning the 10th–9th centuries BC but it has not proved possible to phase this more closely from either the stratigraphy (there were virtually no intercutting features) or the pottery.

Evidence of several boundaries marked by ditches broadly aligned east–west and north–south was found. It is likely that these marked large plots or fields along the edge of the river terrace, each probably covering several thousand square metres, but no complete examples were revealed within the excavated area. Pit 387 towards the west end of ditch 104 may have been a sump or well; it could have acted as a receptacle into which water drained, thereby providing a source for human or animal consumption. Similar features interpreted as sumps have been found on recent excavations to the east at Cranford Lane (Mark Birley, pers. comm.).

Numerous post-holes were recorded across the site but most were undated and only one structure has been identified with certainty. Four-post structure 455 may have been a granary; this is the most common interpretation of such structures, although they could have been used for other purposes, such as storing hay. There were also possibly as many as six two-post structures; these are generally interpreted as racks. One possible circular structure, perhaps a round-house, has been remarked upon, lying in the south-west corner of the excavated area but there is no dating evidence and any interpretation must remain conjectural. The postulated structure would have been large, but diameters of up to 13 m are suggested for some of the Late Bronze Age circular buildings at Reading Business Park (Moore and Jennings 1992, 14). The apparent lack of round-houses within the excavated area is considered likely to represent a real absence; two probable Saxon post-built rectangular halls have been identified and there seems no reason why any round-houses should not have been recognised, even allowing for a certain degree of truncation. If so, then it would seem that many of the pits were dug in areas away from the houses.

The number of pits was not large and the majority were relatively insubstantial features containing only small quantities of finds. None appeared to have been dug for storage, but their function, with the possible exception of 'sump' 387, remains unknown.

The main focus of what is likely to have been a Late Bronze Age farming settlement probably lay beyond the north-east limit of the excavation. It was in this area that the four-post structure lay and where the greatest quantities of pottery were recovered, much of it as large and relatively unabraded sherds, particularly in ditch 236.

The results of the subsequent watching brief confirmed these conclusions. This revealed a shallow Late Bronze Age ditch lying approximately along the 26 m contour, on the edge of the slope down to the River Colne. The ditch marked a boundary to the settlement on the west side, and there was at least one probable entrance which could have provided access for grazing animals to the floodplain below. A second four-post structure lay immediately to the east of this ditch. Elsewhere, only a few generally shallow ditches were recorded, and a small quantity of finds recovered.

Romano-British

The only indication of Romano-British activity on the site was a single cremation burial and a very thin scatter of pottery. This may have been an isolated burial, or a survivor of a once larger number which had been entirely destroyed by ploughing. However, the watching brief revealed a group of one certain and a further four possible Roman cremation burials to the south-west of the excavated example. Further west again, on the slope down to the River Colne, were two inhumation burials which may also have been Romano-British; they were aligned north–south and one grave contained coffin nails. No evidence of Romano-British settlement has been found in the immediate vicinity but features and finds have been recorded at Manor Court, Harmondsworth, some 400 m to the south, and it is possible that the burials at Prospect Park were associated with a settlement there.

Early Saxon

Saxon settlement of the site is clearly attested and, as in the later prehistoric period, this extended across the entire excavated area within Field 13 along the edge of the river terrace. It is unclear whether all the structures were contemporaneous, whether one replaced another, or whether the settlement shifted over time. There were no intercutting features and,though there is a hint that SFBs 103 and 127 may have been earlier than SFBs 439 and 605, the pottery, cannot be dated closely enough to be of help in this respect.

Two groups of sunken-featured buildings, 439 and 605, and 103 and 127, lay approximately 100 m apart and all were broadly aligned east–west. SFBs 127, 439, and 605 were of the two-post type, with 439 differing slightly to the others in this group in having the post-holes just outside the pit. The post-holes in SFBs 127 and 439 were 2.9 m apart (centre to centre) but in 605 were only 2.1 m apart. SFB 103 was larger than the others, with the central post-holes 3.3 m apart and additional post-holes in two of the corners, though these were less substantial than the central pair. The absence of post-holes in the other two corners makes it unlikely that this SFB was of the six-post type, though it did differ from the others in size, shape, and superficial structural arrangements.

No floor surfaces were apparent within the truncated SFBs, which may originally have been 0.5 m or more deep and it is not certain whether they had revetted sides and raised floors as has been suggested for some examples elsewhere, as at West Stow, Suffolk (West 1985, 116–121). However, the finds from them are likely to represent later rubbish deposition in abandoned and perhaps dismantled structures.

SFB 439 may have been associated with hall 749 which lay less than 15 m to the east, and SFB 605 with hall 721 10 m to the south. Both putative halls were of post-hole construction, 5 m wide and perhaps twice as long. The semi-circular arrangement of post-holes at the west end of hall 721 remains somewhat puzzling but their size and layout suggest that they may have held angled posts forming a semi-circular arrangement that formed an integral part of the original structure, rather than some form of lean-to or later addition. No parallels are known for this structure, although square end annexes were to become characteristic of large 7th-century timber halls (Blair 1994, 20). Any internal features such as hearths and floor surfaces are likely to have been completely truncated. These halls, like the SFBs, were aligned approximately east–west.

Hall 749 seems certainly to have been Saxon but the dating of hall 721 remains equivocal. It has been assigned to the Saxon period for two reasons. First, because of its plan, which does not closely resemble any later prehistoric post-built rectangular structures (eg Lofts Farm, Essex; Brown 1988) and is more easily compared with Saxon halls elsewhere (eg West 1985, fig. 10, hall 2), as well as hall 749 here. The second reason for assigning this feature a Saxon date is its close proximity to SFB 605 and pit 689, with which it may have formed a group. The principal arguments against a Saxon attribution for hall 721 are its relationship to slot 695 and the associated dating evidence. Slot 695, assigned a late prehistoric date, appears in plan to have been part of hall 721, perhaps a partition, though the juxtaposition of features may be purely coincidental and the slot would represent a different form of construction technique. The ceramic evidence alone suggests that hall 721 was a late prehistoric structure, but the three sherds recovered from its post-holes could have been residual, for slot 695 and several of the surrounding features (eg ditch 709 and pit 621) contained notable quantities of late prehistoric pottery. Perhaps the absence of Saxon pottery should not be surprising, given its paucity in hall 749 post-holes, but it cannot be stated with certainty whether hall 721 was a late prehistoric or Saxon structure.

No post-built halls were recognised in the vicinity of SFBs 103 and 127. However, heavy truncation around SFB 127 and to the north of SFB 103 is likely to have completely removed any post-holes, and some of the undated post-holes to the south may have belonged to an unrecognised, associated structure.

If the SFBs were generally associated with post-built halls on the site, then the latter may have provided the principal living accommodation, with the SFBs being used as workshops or for storage. However, finds such as loomweights, for example, were found in only one of the SFBs (excavated during the watching brief).

The watching brief revealed a further seven SFBs, but no additional halls or other features were recognised. One group of three SFBs lay close to the north edge of the site approximately 100 m to the west of SFB 439, and a further group of three some 50 m to the south of these. All were of the two-post type, aligned east–west, and generally similar to the examples excavated earlier. There were some minor variations in their shapes and sizes, and one was substantially larger with a depth of approximately 0.5 m. Apart from pottery and animal bone, the finds include a small number of loomweights and spindle-whorls, a lead spearhead, and a small amount of possible smithing slag.

With the possible exceptions of linear features 517 and 530, there was no evidence for any boundaries delineated by ditches. However, such boundaries seem only to appear in early Saxon settlements of the late 6th and 7th century, and not before (West 1985, 151) and this might provide a further indication, along with the pottery, of an early (5th–6th century) date for the Saxon settlement at Prospect Park.

Pits were generally shallow and lay within 25 m or so of the structures, with perhaps two or more pits to each SFB. Most, whatever their original purpose, were ultimately used for rubbish disposal. This rubbish is likely to have included quantities of food waste but, because of the acidic soil conditions, only very small quantities of fragmentary animal bone has survived. With two exceptions, 689 and 711, there is no evidence of any of the pits having been dug for a specialised function. Hollow 689, perhaps associated with SFB 605 and hall 721, may have been a 'working hollow', but if so, for what reason is unknown. Pit 483 was the only one which contained well-preserved environmental remains, in this case providing some evidence for crop processing. Pit 711 was almost certainly a well; its depth, profile, and lower fill in particular would suggest this. The slight belling-out at the bottom appears to have been deliberate, rather than a result of collapse, though no trace of what is likely to have been a wattle lining survived; a pit such as this dug in brickearth would not have remained open long unless it was lined with wattle or timber to prevent collapse. The primary fill of grey clay is likely to have accumulated in standing water, a suggestion supported by the concentration of charcoal flecking in the upper part of this fill, which perhaps had floated to the surface. Only a few residual sherds of late prehistoric pottery came from the primary fill, with all of the Saxon pottery coming from higher up in the shaft and probably representing rubbish deposition after the well had fallen into disuse. The height of the top of the primary fill suggests that the water table at this time lay between 1.5 and 2 m of the surface, at a height of around 29.6 m OD.

Excluding the few finds made during the watching brief (see above), no metalwork was recovered from any of the Saxon features, which is somewhat surprising, and the only finds besides the pottery were three beads, all from SFB 103. The ceramic assemblage, however, is noteworthy for it contained sherds from several non-local vessels (based on petrological analysis), which may be as early as 5th century. One possible source in the Midlands area has been suggested but, given the early dating proposed, a continental (ie North German) origin cannot be ruled out. This would provide further support for an early date for the settlement, but the implications of its presence here remain to be explored (*see* above, Pottery).

2. Hurst Park, East Molesey, Surrey: Riverside Settlement and Burial from the Neolithic to the Early Saxon Periods,

by Phil Andrews

With contributions from Michael J. Allen, Rowena Gale, M. Laidlaw, Jacqueline I. McKinley, and R. Montague

1. Introduction

In 1991 Wates Built Homes Limited received planning consent from Elmbridge Borough Council to build homes and landscape a large part (approximately 9 hectares) of the site of the former racecourse at Hurst Park, East Molesey, Surrey. The site, centred at TQ 1450 6890, located to the north of East Molesey on the south bank of the River Thames, some 150 m south of the present course of the river (Fig. 27), lies approximately 1 km upstream from Hampton Court Palace. Prospect Park lies approximately 12 km to the north-west.

Planning consent was conditional on the site being 'inspected and records made of any archaeological features before they are damaged by construction works'. No archaeological works had previously been undertaken on the site, nor any finds of archaeological interest recorded. However, the Sites and Monuments Record lists a number of chance finds in the area dating from the Neolithic and Bronze Age periods, mainly found on adjacent eyots in the River Thames. Furthermore, any previously undeveloped area of gravel terrace bordering the Thames can be regarded as of potential archaeological importance and, on this basis, a programme of

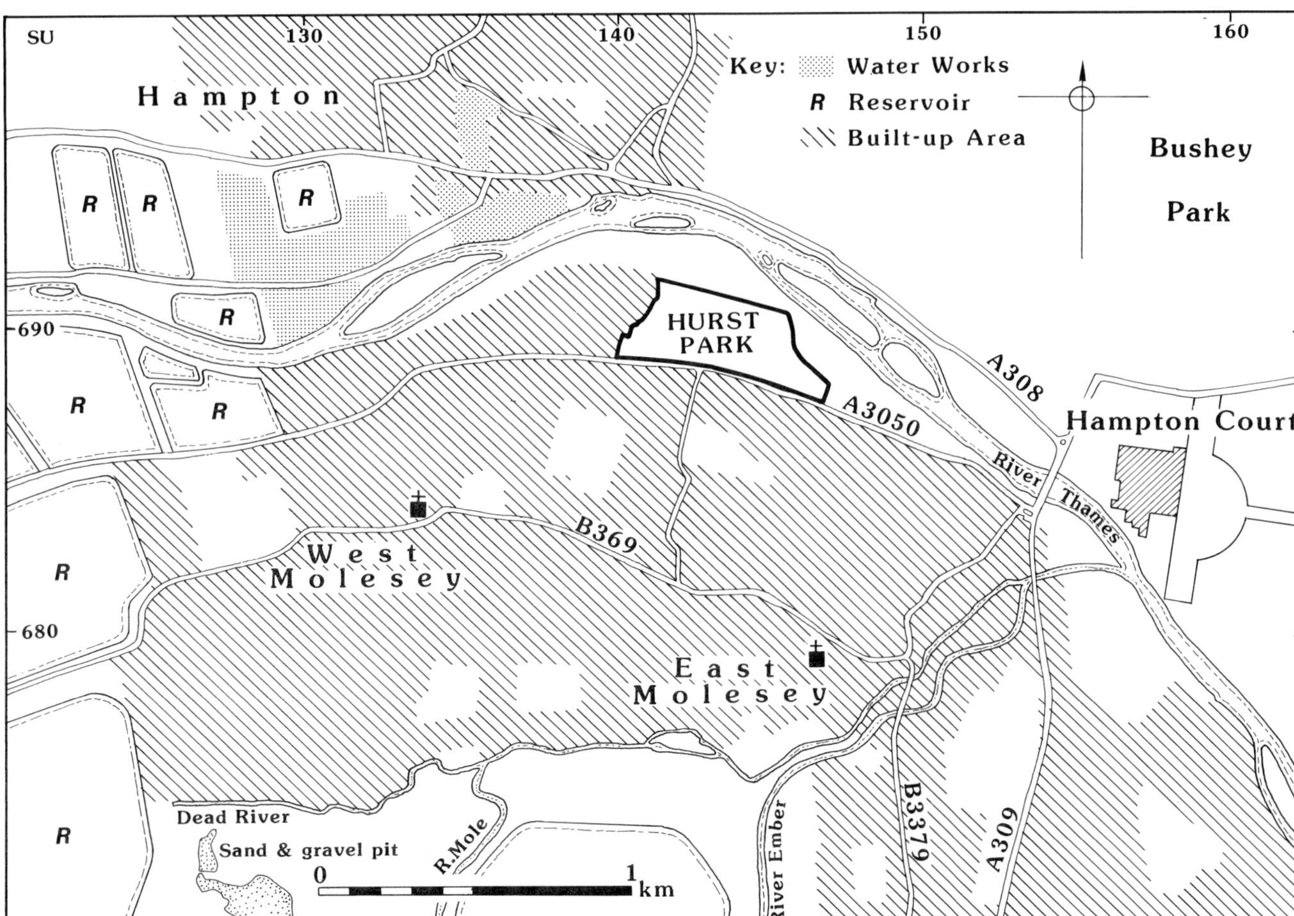

Figure 27 Hurst Park, general location plan

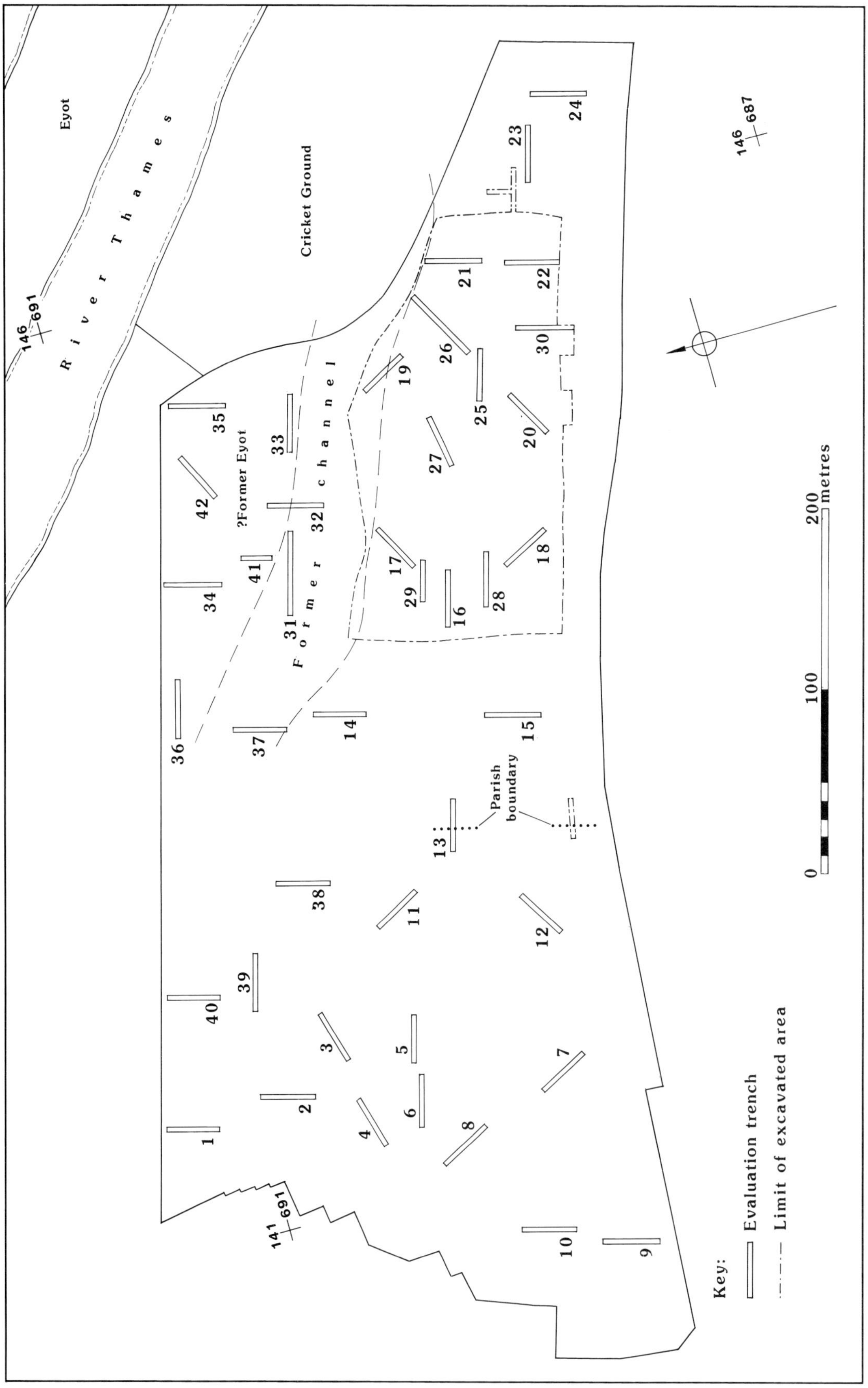

Figure 28 Site plan showing positions of evaluation trenches and excavated areas

Figure 29 Plan showing all excavated features

archaeological evaluation was commissioned to assess the potential of the site.

The main phase of evaluation work, carried out by the Cotswold Archaeological Trust, took place in April–May 1994 following a geophysical survey undertaken by A.J. Clark in April 1994. A second, more limited phase of evaluation work was carried out at the end of May 1994, also by the Cotswold Archaeological Trust. The evaluation work revealed archaeological features and finds of Mesolithic, Neolithic, and Bronze Age date, with an apparent concentration of activity at the east end of the site.

Following the evaluation it was decided that preservation *in situ* of the archaeological deposits within the area to be landscaped, which included all but the very western end of the site, would not be appropriate, since none were deemed to be of national importance. Consequently, a large scale excavation was proposed, focused on the eastern end of the site. Accordingly, Wates Built Homes Limited commissioned the Trust for Wessex Archaeology to implement a programme of work approved by Surrey County Council Archaeology Section. This was carried out between July 12th and August 26th 1994. The main area of investigation was at the east end of the site, with a limited amount of trenching towards the centre. Following completion of the excavation, a watching brief was maintained over the remainder of the area during earthmoving operations in September 1994.

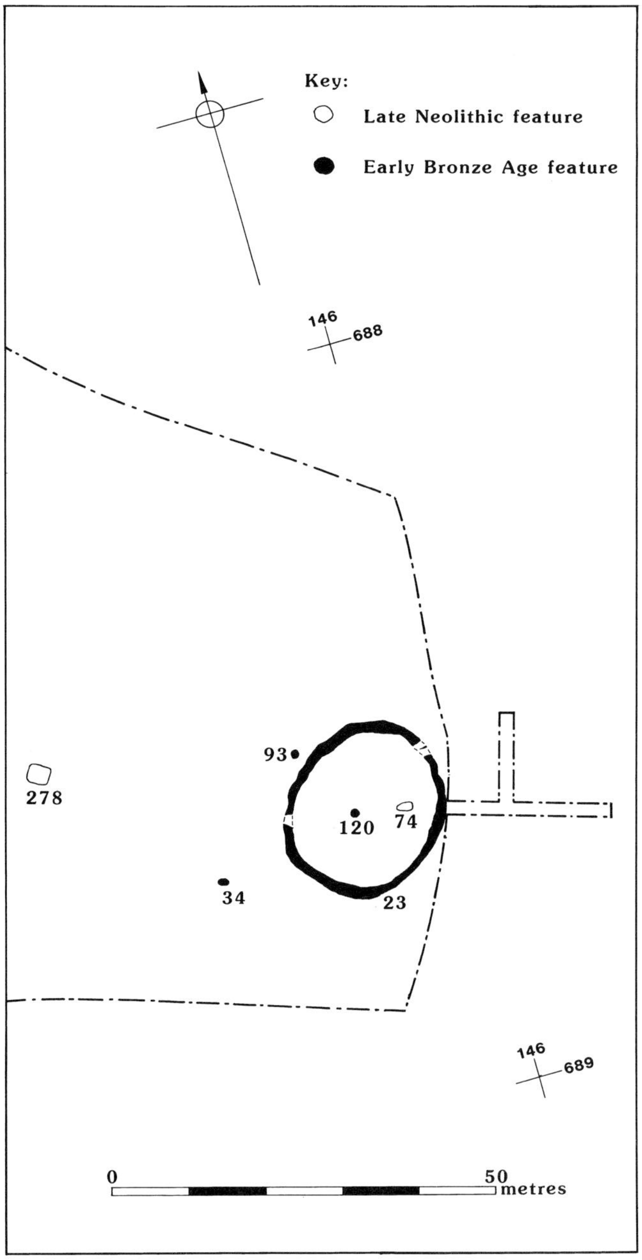

Figure 30 Plan of Late Neolithic and Early Bronze Age features

Situation

The site occupies part of the floodplain terrace of the River Thames between two of its tributaries, the River Mole, less than 0.75 km to the east, and the River Wey, approximately 7 km to the west. The ground is relatively flat, at a height of approximately 8 m OD, with only a slight (<2°) fall northwards towards the River Thames. The highest ground, at 8.80 m OD, lies towards the south-east corner of the site, sloping down to 6.90 m OD to the north and 7.80 m OD to the west. The water table was recorded at a height of 6.40 m OD in May 1994.

The superficial geology of the area comprises river gravels, probably of Devensian date; an upper, dark yellowish–brown fine gravel, *c.* 0.2 m thick, overlies a lower, strong brown gravel at least 0.7 m thick, both in a sandy matrix. In places, a yellowish–brown coarse, fluvial sand deposit, at least 0.5 m thick, lay beneath the upper gravel, and at the extreme east end of the site was exposed at the surface. Across the northern part of the site the upper gravel was sealed by an alluvial deposit comprising a homogeneous light olive–brown silty clay with occasional sand inclusions and some evidence of gleying. The observed deposit was up to 1 m thick, and filled a natural channel that ran east–west and was approximately 50 m wide (Fig. 28). In the north-east corner of the site the surface of the gravels rose and the silty clay deposit petered out, possibly defining the south edge of a former eyot. When the channel became infilled by natural silting is unknown as the channel deposits were devoid of archaeological material. However, the channel deposits did in part seal the fill of a Late Bronze Age ditch and were themselves cut by at least one post-medieval ditch. No organic material was encountered within the alluvial deposits and, therefore, the recovery of environmental data was low.

The course of the channel remains uncertain but it is conceivable that it was the southernmost of a series of braided channels or watercourses through which the Thames formerly flowed, perhaps periodically during times of flood. Alternatively, it may have been an area of lower, marshy ground which occasionally flooded. Today, there are some marshy, reed covered patches in the area formerly occupied by the channel but the area is now drained by ditches and the threat of flooding has been removed as a result of the Thames flood alleviation programme. Water levels are now controlled by a series of sluices and barriers and the Thames is no longer tidal up to this point.

The site became popular in the 18th century for various sporting pursuits, culminating in 1890 with the establishment of a horse racing track — Hurst Park racecourse. This closed in 1961 and the land was sold for redevelopment in 1962. Some houses were built soon after at the extreme west end of the site but the majority of the area was left open. Extensive removal of turf and topsoil is reported to have taken place, which would explain the apparent lack of topsoil observed, and the site subsequently became covered with rough grass and scrub.

Archaeological Background

No archaeological work had previously taken place on the site or in the immediate vicinity, though chance finds of Neolithic and Bronze Age date are recorded from the area in the Sites and Monuments Record. Particularly noteworthy is the concentration of Neolithic axes from the River Thames in the Kingston area. Twenty-five polished and fine-flaked flint axes plus seven stone axes (including Grouped axes from Cornwall and Langdale) had been recorded from the river between Kingston and Hampton by 1978 (Adkins and Jackson 1978; see also Field and Cotton 1987, fig. 4.7).

Despite the absence of any certain evidence for early settlement at or around Hurst Park, the site was considered to be of high archaeological potential because of its riverside location between the confluences of the Rivers Mole and Wey with the Thames. Archaeological work in Kingston-upon-Thames less than 3 km to the east has revealed considerable evidence for settlement at various times from the Neolithic through to the medieval and post-medieval periods, and an important Bronze Age site lies close by at Kingston Hill. Less than 6 km upstream to the west of Hurst Park are the Anglo-Saxon cemeteries at Shepperton, and further west again the major Neolithic and Late Bronze Age riverside settlements at Runnymede Bridge. These and other sites are discussed more fully in Chapter 9, but serve to illustrate the rich archaeological potential of the area.

Prior to excavation, the only known feature of historical interest at Hurst Park was the parish boundary between East and West Moulsey (now Molesey) which is shown crossing the area on a map of 1781 (SRO 81/3/1/B27/WS). This map shows land to the east of the boundary under cultivation, and to the west as uncultivated scrub.

2. Evaluation

An archaeological evaluation was carried out to establish the date, nature, and extent of any archaeological

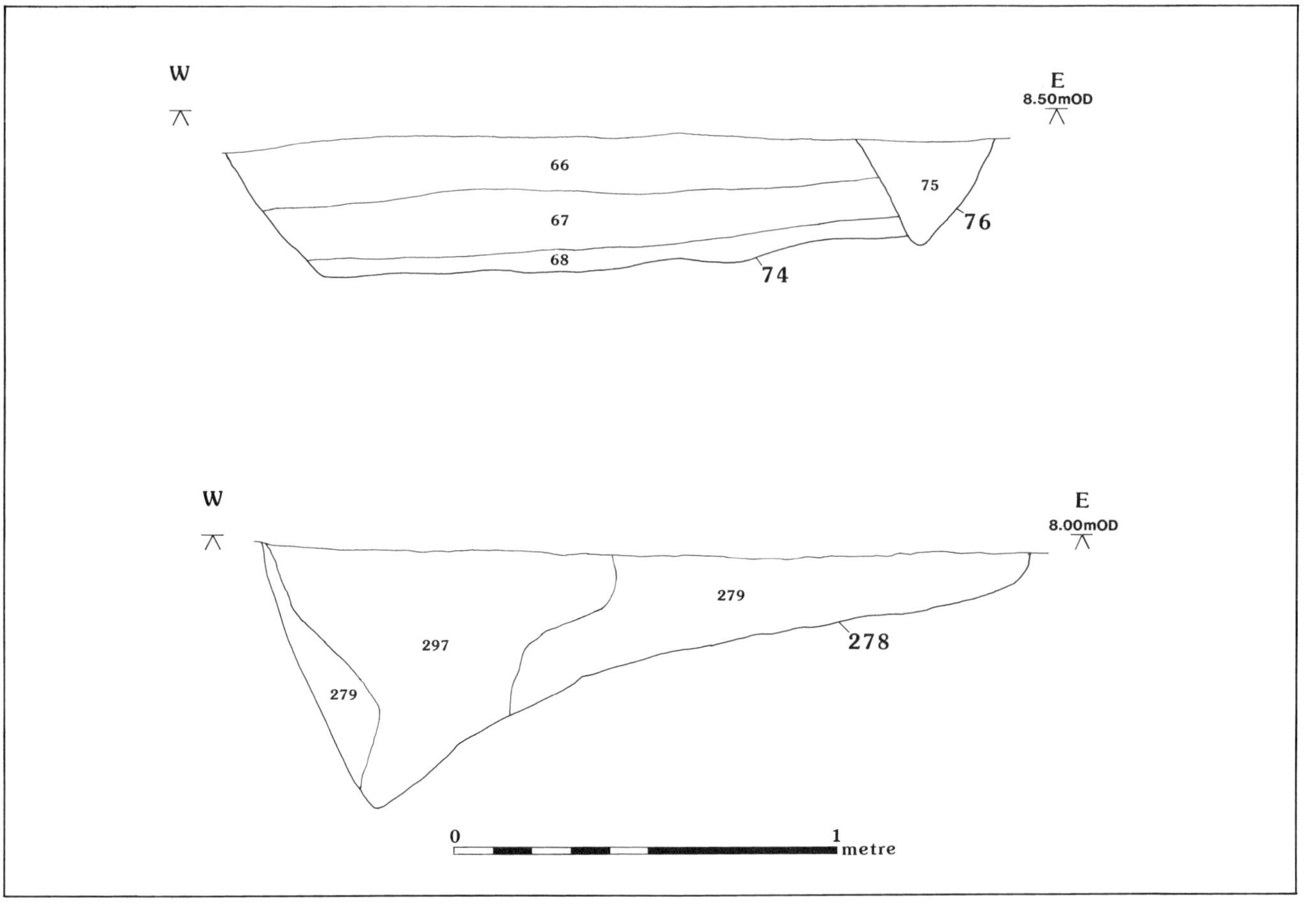

Figure 31 Sections across Late Neolithic pits

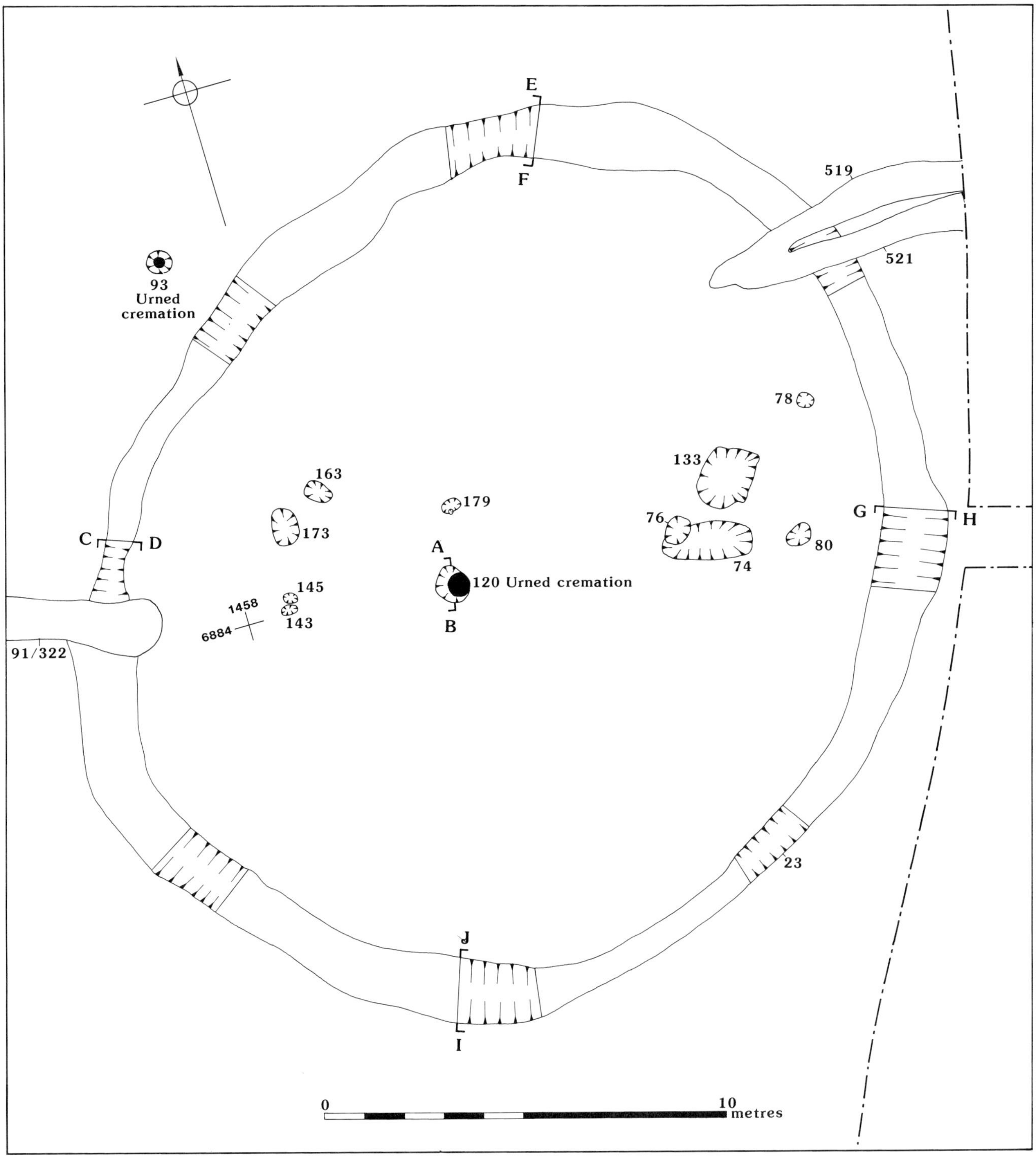

Figure 32 Plan of Early Bronze Age ring-ditch 23

activity on the site. The methods employed included geophysical survey and machine trenching (Fig. 28).

Geophysical Survey

A geophysical survey was undertaken by A.J. Clark in April 1994. The work involved initial magnetic susceptibility measurements on samples taken from the topsoil over an area of approximately 13 hectares. The samples were taken at 20 m intervals using a coring auger. Magnetic enhancement of soil particles may occur when they are subject to heat, perhaps as a result of human activity, most commonly hearths or fires, and this can therefore provide an indication of settlement on a site in the absence of other evidence. On the basis of the results from this survey, a small group of samples was selected for detailed analysis and an area of 7200

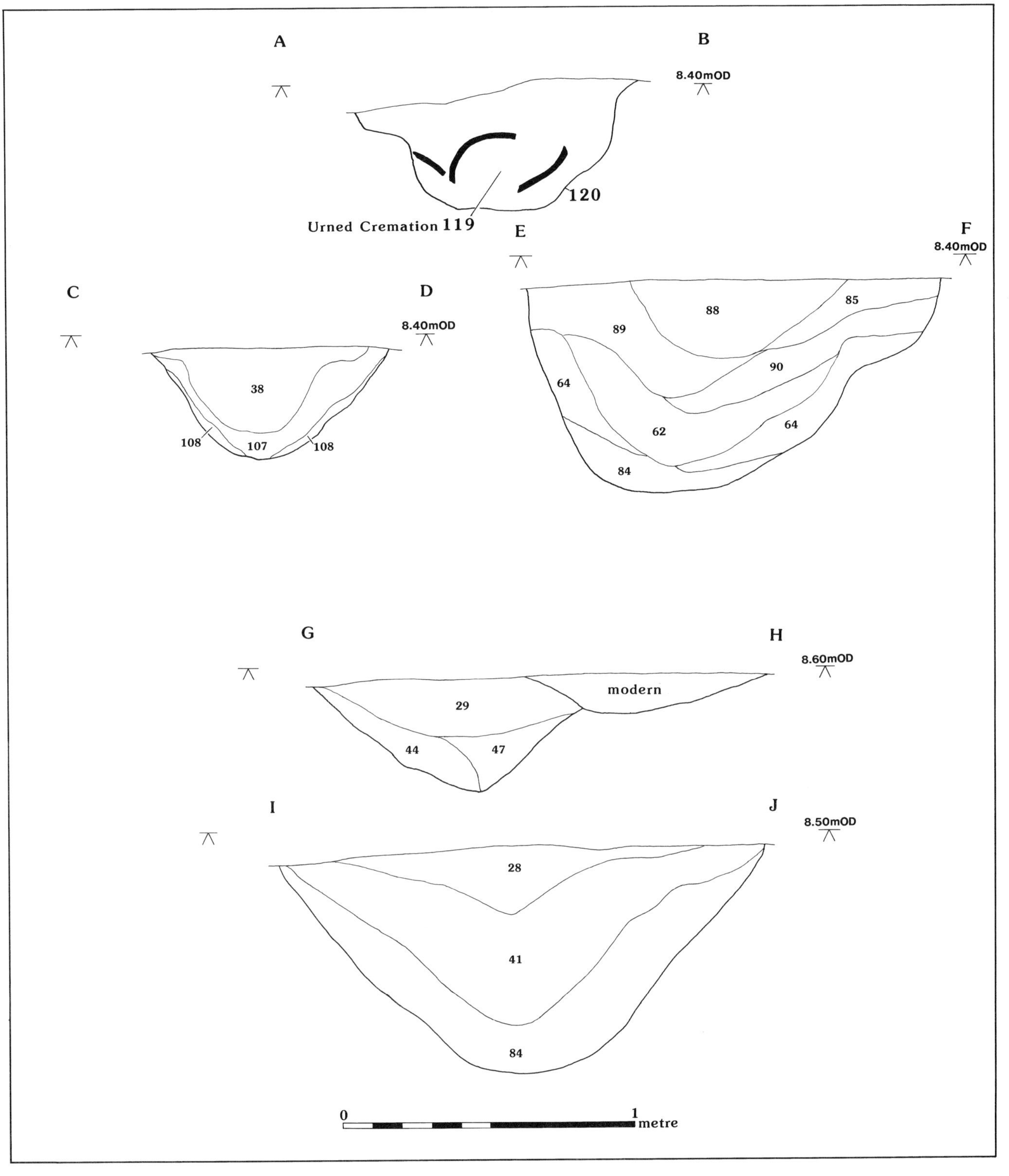

Figure 33 Sections across Early Bronze Age ring-ditch 23

m^2 for intensive magnetometer survey. The results of these surveys are summarised here and a full report is contained within the archive.

An area in the south-east part of the site showed magnetic susceptibility enhancement considered to result from human occupation or activity, probably of an earlier date than the racecourse. A band of low susceptibility values running east–west towards the northern limit of the site coincided with low ground, some of which was marshy. Testing with an auger showed dark silty soil down to a depth of *c.* 0.75 m, overlying gravel, and this broadly coincided with the course of a former river channel.

A marked change in susceptibility between Trenches 12 and 15 was probably associated with the parish boundary. The existence of fields (shown on the 1781 map) on the East Molesey side probably contributed to the spread of the magnetically enhanced soil up to this boundary and it was considered likely that this magnetic enhancement occurred before the fields were established, rather than as a result of intensive activity associated with the fields themselves. The excavation subsequently demonstrated a close correlation between the extent of this magnetic enhancement and the distribution of archaeological features.

The magnetometer survey, using a fluxgate gradiometer, was heavily affected by interference, and did not produce any clear evidence of archaeological features. The interference was subsequently shown to have been caused by pipes associated with the racecourse and the lack of evidence for archaeological features was a result of their shallow depth and gravelly fills similar to the natural.

Machine Trenching

Following the geophysical survey, two sets of machine trenches were excavated in April–May and May–June 1994 respectively (Fig. 28). The first set (T1–30) comprised 25 trenches, each 30 m long and 1.8 m wide, which were distributed across the entire site with the intention of sampling the whole area. A further five trenches were positioned to enhance the understanding of the data uncovered by the geophysical survey and the archaeological features in the trenches.

As a result of the archaeological discoveries made in the first set of trenches, Wates Built Homes Ltd began exploring design changes that would have left the main focus of archaeological activity at the east end of the site undisturbed. This would have involved lowering the ground surface north of the area already evaluated. A further set of 12 machine trenches (T31–42), 30 m long and 1.6 m wide were therefore cut across this northern area. Ten trenches were positioned on plan prior to fieldwork commencing and a further two trenches were added to enhance the understanding of the archaeological data revealed. Together, the two sets of trenches covered a total area of 2196 m^2 representing approximately 2.5% of the entire site.

The results are only summarised here as much of the data has been incorporated in the main excavation report below. The existence of an east–west channel, identified during the evaluation, is discussed above.

The evaluation produced a small assemblage of struck flint, mainly from the eastern half of the site. A few pieces were recovered from features; however the subsequent excavation suggests that virtually all of this material was probably residual within later deposits. Apart from a single Late Mesolithic tool, the rest of the assemblage was assigned a broad, possibly Late Neolithic, date and thought to be indicative of settlement activity rather than tool production. This is in contrast to the material from the main excavation which suggested the reverse.

Four trenches (T21, 25, 26, and 30) contained features which were tentatively dated to the Late Bronze Age and all of these trenches lay within the area of the subsequent excavation (Fig. 28). The features comprising pits, post-holes, and at least one ditch, suggested

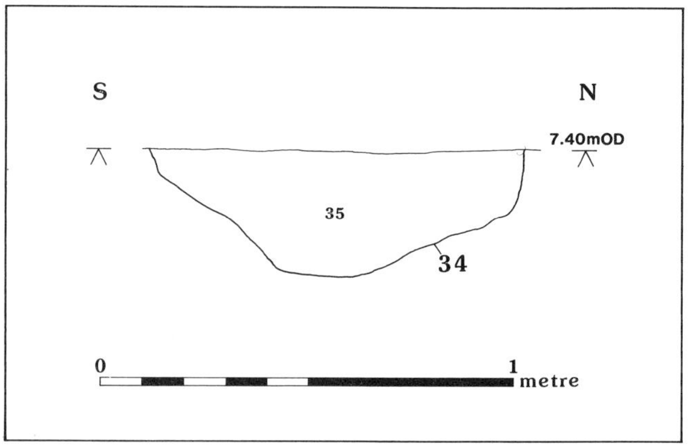

Figure 34 Section across Early Bronze Age pit 34

the presence of a settlement, perhaps a farmstead within an enclosure, towards the south-east corner of the site.

Virtually all of the features away from the south-east corner of the site were undated; those which did contain dating evidence were either late post-medieval or modern. The undated features comprised a scatter of post-holes, shallow pits and scoops, and ditches, the latter perhaps field ditches. No patterns of features could be discerned within the relatively small areas exposed, but it is considered, following the results of the excavation and watching brief, that the majority of these features were likely to have been of comparatively recent date, many probably associated with the racecourse. One possible exception was an east–west aligned ditch in Trench 35. This was a quite substantial feature, measuring approximately 2 m across and 0.76 m deep, including a 0.3 m deep slot running centrally along the bottom. It contained two Neolithic flint tools, but caution should be exercised in interpreting this as a Neolithic ditch; a similar ditch, which also produced some worked flint, was shown to be a post-medieval/early modern feature when further investigated during the main excavation.

3. Excavation

On the basis of the results of the evaluation, which indicated possible Late Neolithic as well as Late Bronze Age settlement in the south-eastern part of the site, a larger, open area excavation was proposed in order to record and better understand the nature of this activity.

Methods

An area of approximately 2.8 hectares was stripped under archaeological supervision using two 360° excavators with toothless buckets (Figs 28 and 29). A site grid at 10 m intervals was then established and features cutting the exposed sands and gravels planned at a scale of 1:50. Selected areas were hand cleaned before detailed investigation of specific features or groups of features. Discrete features (eg pits and post-holes) were half-sectioned and linear features (eg ditches) sampled in at least two places (representing *c.* 2% of their exposed

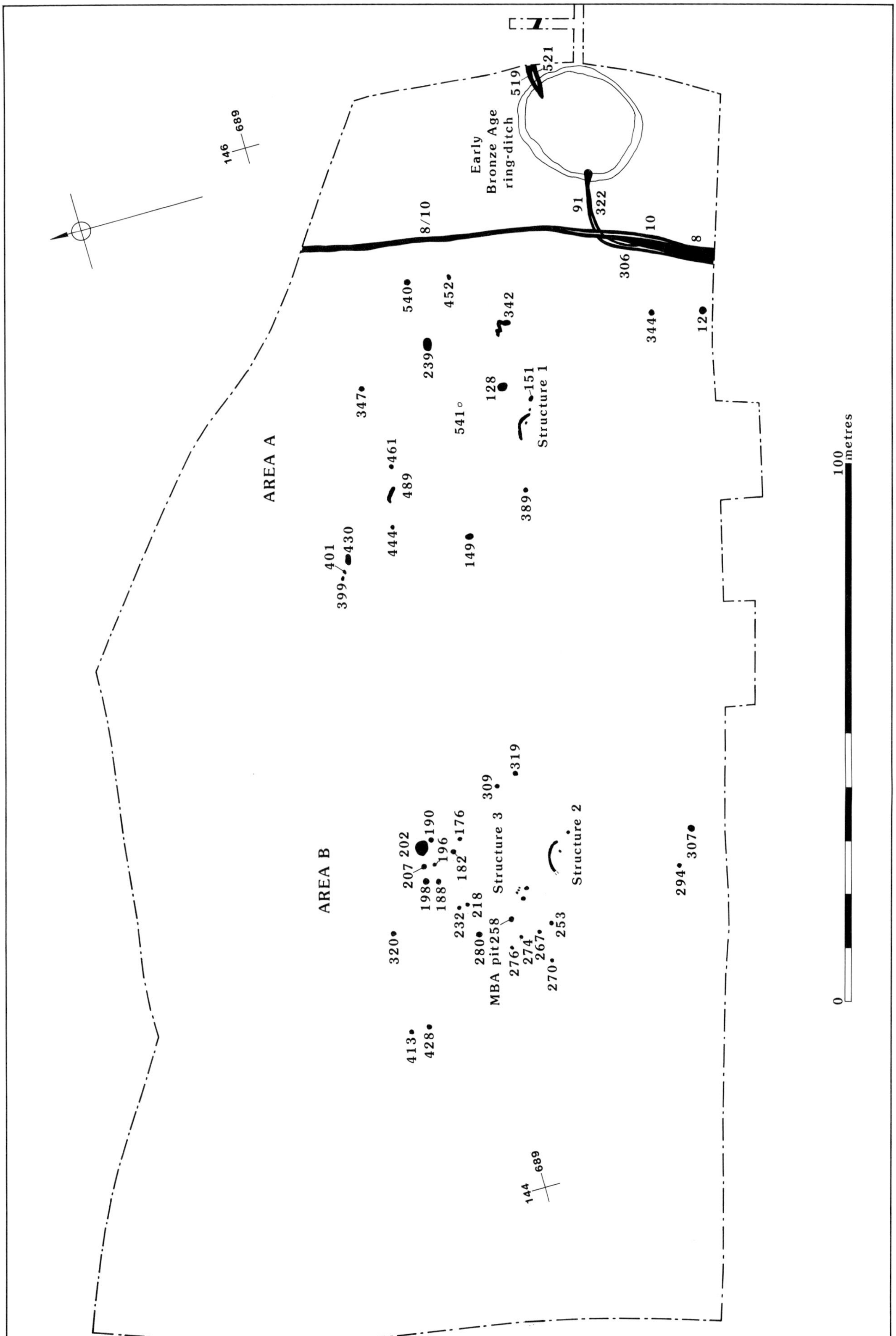

Figure 35 Plan of Late Bronze Age features

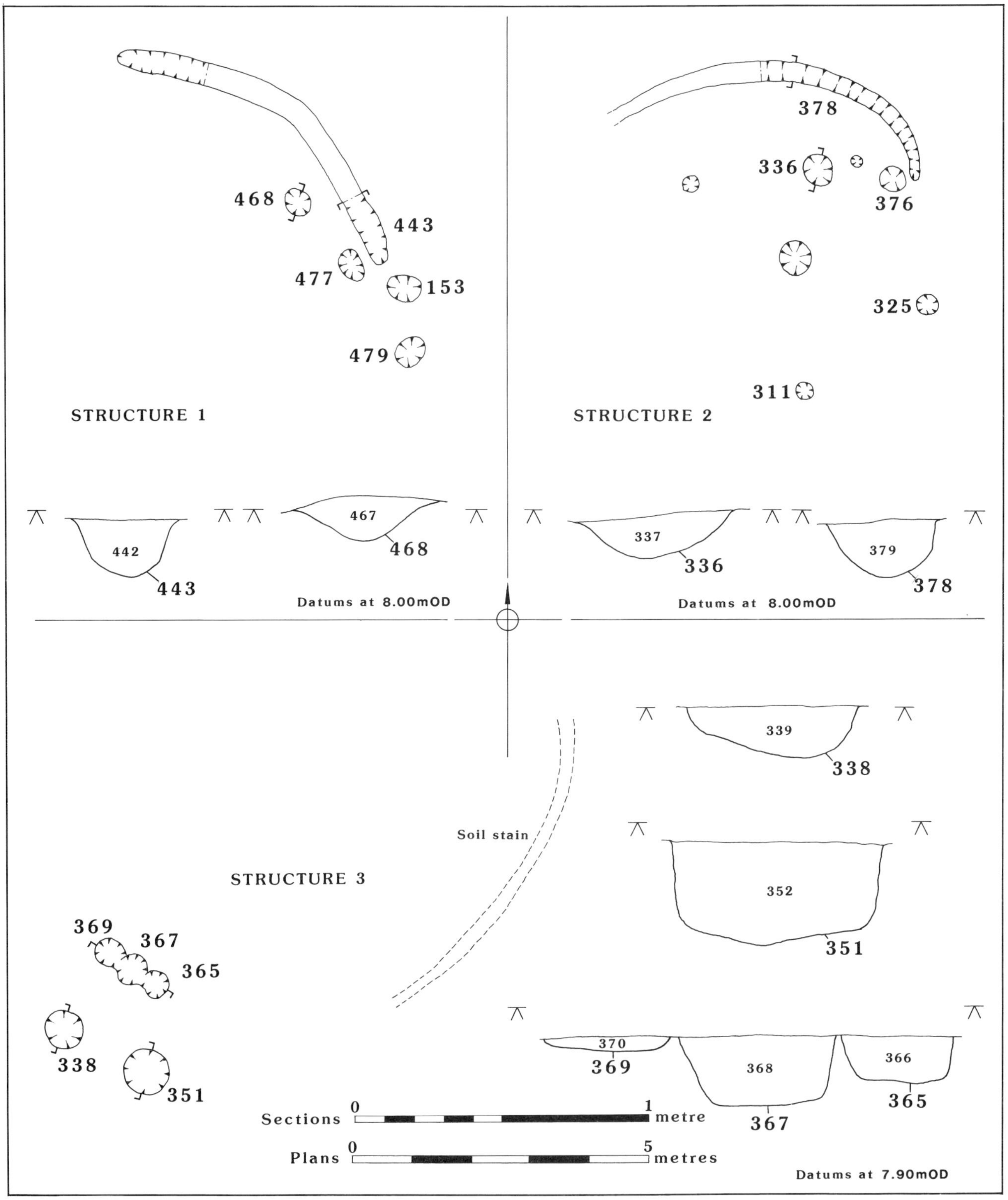

Figure 36 Plans and sections of Late Bronze Age structures 1–3

length) in order to determine their character, form, stratigraphic sequence, and to recover datable artefacts. Certain features such as burials, or features which yielded sealed assemblages which could be related to the structural sequence (eg sunken-featured buildings), were fully excavated. Bulk samples of up to 30 litres were collected from a range of features of various periods for environmental and artefactual evidence. No water-logged deposits were encountered.

Following completion of the main phase of excavation, a limited amount of additional machine trenching was carried out to answer specific questions. At the east end of the site a T-shaped arrangement of trenches was dug in order to determine whether any further ring-ditches lay in this area. Beyond the west end of the site a single trench was excavated to ascertain whether there was evidence for a fence or ditch having defined the parish boundary between East and West Molesey.

A watching brief was carried out in September 1994 when the area to the west of the excavated site was stripped of topsoil and subsoil. No further deposits of archaeological interest were seen and the few features present appeared to be of comparatively recent date (19th–20th century).

Dating

There was an overall lack of stratified deposits, with very few physical relationships; even the more substantial features lacked internal deposition sequences. Many of the features were small and it was clear that a considerable degree of truncation had occurred, particularly towards the central–southern part of the site. This may have resulted from ploughing, probably at various times from the late Saxon period onwards, and also during the laying out of the racecourse in the 19th century. The shallow depth of some of the surviving features (particularly the Romano-British cremations) suggests that as much as 0.4 m or so of the top of the gravel may have been removed from what originally was a slightly raised area of gravel terrace on the edge of the floodplain.

Many of the smaller features were difficult to interpret and it is unclear whether some were large postholes or the bases of small pits. In some cases, the interpretation and dating has relied on their association with nearby, better-dated features. However, structural associations and finds have allowed most of the larger features and some of the smaller features to be dated and interpreted with a reasonable degree of confidence. Approximately 33% of the excavated features contained pottery, and of these, 23% contained more than two sherds. There were varying degrees of intrusiveness and residuality, particularly in some of the features containing larger quantities of pottery, but this has caused relatively little difficulty in dating contexts.

Other than pottery, there was relatively little amongst the limited range and quantity of flint, metalwork and other finds which assisted in dating the sequence of activity on the site. The phasing adopted below is, therefore, almost entirely dependent on the dating provided by the pottery.

- Mesolithic (8500–4000 BC)
- Late Neolithic (3000–2400 BC)
- Early Bronze Age (2400–1500 BC)
- Middle Bronze Age (1500–1100 BC)
- Late Bronze Age (1100–700 BC)
- (Early) Romano-British (AD 43–150)
- Early Saxon (410–650)
- Post-medieval/early modern (1500–)

The Site

Mesolithic

The Late Mesolithic period is represented by a single geometric microlith found redeposited in a later context (from evaluation Trench 20, within the area of the subsequent excavation).

Late Neolithic

Two features have been assigned with some certainty to this period on the basis that they contained very small quantities of Late Neolithic pottery and no material of a later date. Both lay towards the east end of the site (Fig. 30).

Pit 278 was a sub-rectangular feature, measuring 3.7 m by 2.6 m, with an average depth of approximately 0.4 m (Figs 30 and 31). It had steep sides, a very irregular bottom, and was filled with yellowish–brown sandy loam. A small assemblage of seven pottery sherds was recovered, including six sherds of Peterborough Ware.

Feature 74, within the area subsequently enclosed by a Bronze Age ring-ditch, contained three sherds of Grooved Ware (Figs 30 and 31). This was a shallow, oval scoop, 2 m long and 1 m wide, filled with gravelly sand. It had the appearance of a tree throw hole but its interpretation remains uncertain.

Approximately 20 irregularly-shaped features, up to 2 m in diameter and 1 m deep, were concentrated towards the north-west corner of the site, adjacent to the channel. A few lay further away, including one which had been cut by Saxon sunken-featured building SFB 186. All were filled with a slightly 'dirty' sandy gravel and none of the three excavated examples produced any finds. It is suggested that these were tree- holes, possibly representing Late Neolithic or Early Bronze Age vegetation clearance.

No other Neolithic features were identified but three sherds of coarse, flint-tempered pottery, which are possibly Late Neolithic, were found in feature 490, a Late Bronze Age gully which also lay towards the east end of the site.

A small quantity of flint was recovered, mainly from the central and eastern parts of the site. This generally mixed assemblage includes a few tools but is difficult to date. However, there is a small early prehistoric component, and some Neolithic worked flint came from a ditch in Trench 35 in the north-east corner of the site which was excavated during the evaluation. No pottery was found, and it is possible that this ditch was a later feature and the flint redeposited. The presence of this flint might indicate activity on what has been interpreted as a former eyot between a series of river channels (Fig. 28), immediately to the north of a possible settlement on the edge of the floodplain, though the two need not have been contemporaneous.

Early Bronze Age

Ring-ditch 23

A sub-circular ditch, 23, was revealed at the extreme east end of the site, and it immediately became clear that this was a ring-ditch representing the remains of a bell barrow (Figs 30 and 32; Pl. 8). It lay at a height of approximately 8 m OD and straddled a change in the natural geology from sandy gravel on the west side to sand on the east. The surface of the sand and gravel is likely to have been removed by subsequent activity in this area and no mound material nor any buried soil survived. The dry conditions at the time of excavation made the detection of any small internal features

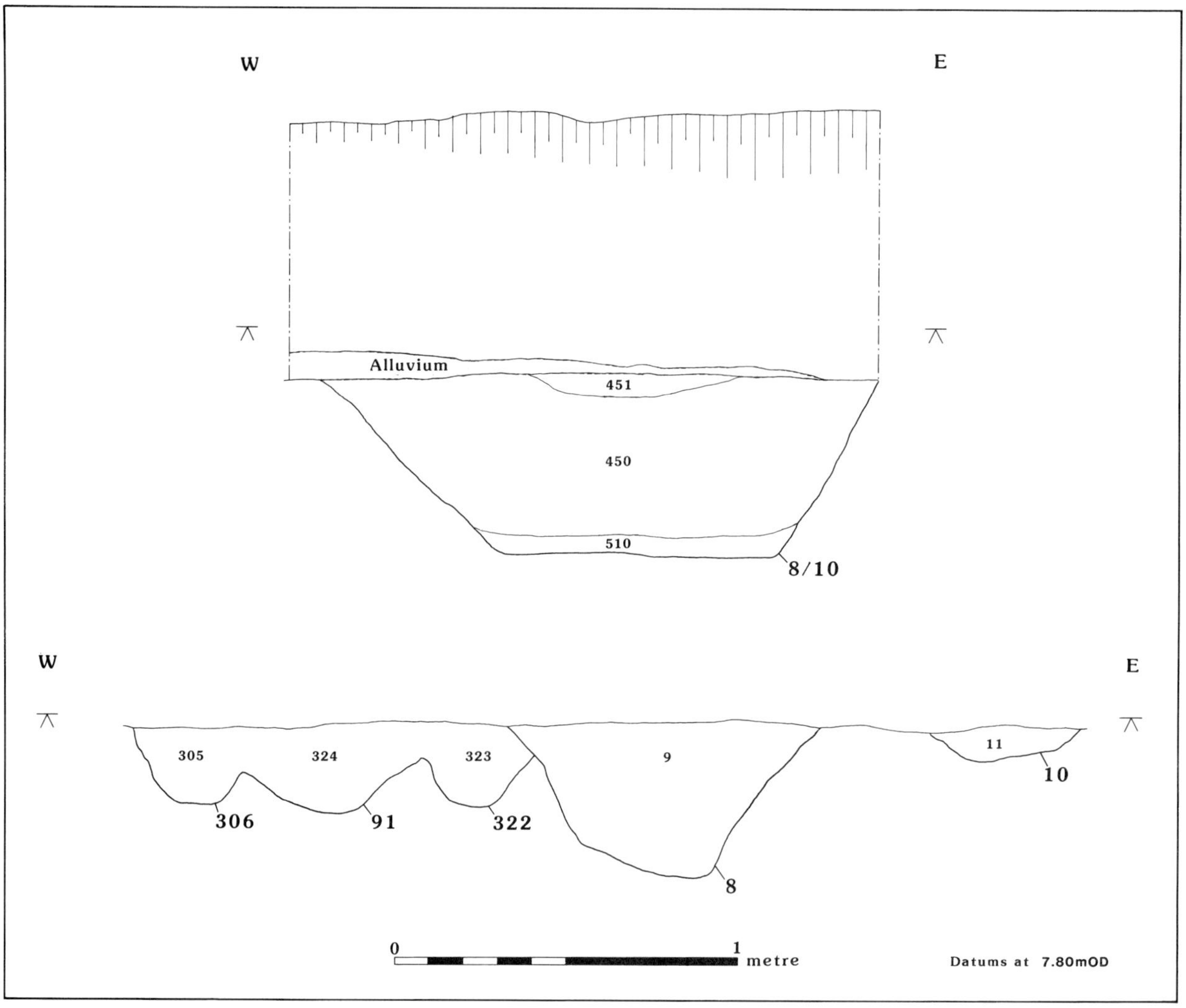

Figure 37 Sections across Late Bronze Age ditches

cutting the sand extremely difficult and it is possible that any stake-holes in this area went unrecorded.

The ditch was slightly ovoid in plan with a maximum internal diameter of *c.* 21 m and a minimum of *c.* 18 m (Fig. 32). It was sectioned in eight, approximately equi-

Plate 8 Ring-ditch 23, defining an Early Bronze Age bell barrow; Late Bronze Age ditches 8/10 beyond (2 m scale). Facing west

distantly placed cuttings, each 2 m long, representing 25% of the total circumference of the ditch. The ditch varied considerably in width, from 0.8–1.6 m, with the narrowest sections in the west and south-east. The latter may reflect a greater degree of truncation of the sandy natural in that area but this explanation is less likely in the more gravelly natural on the west side. Differential weathering seems also not to have been a factor in determining the profile, as the ditch would have been weathered and eroded more where it cut through the natural sand. The depth of the ditch, which had a rounded bottom, also varied, from *c.* 0.4–0.8 m, with the sides sloping at 45° or more. The primary fill comprised sand which, in most of the eastern half of the ditch, was virtually indistinguishable from the natural, suggesting rapid initial infilling. The layers above this were also sands, generally darker in colour and containing variable amounts of gravel. There was slight evidence in the north and east sections through the ditch fills that more erosion had taken place on the inner than outer face of the ditch. However, some of this material may have derived from the central mound or bank. In some areas, most notably to the north, a series of slightly darker

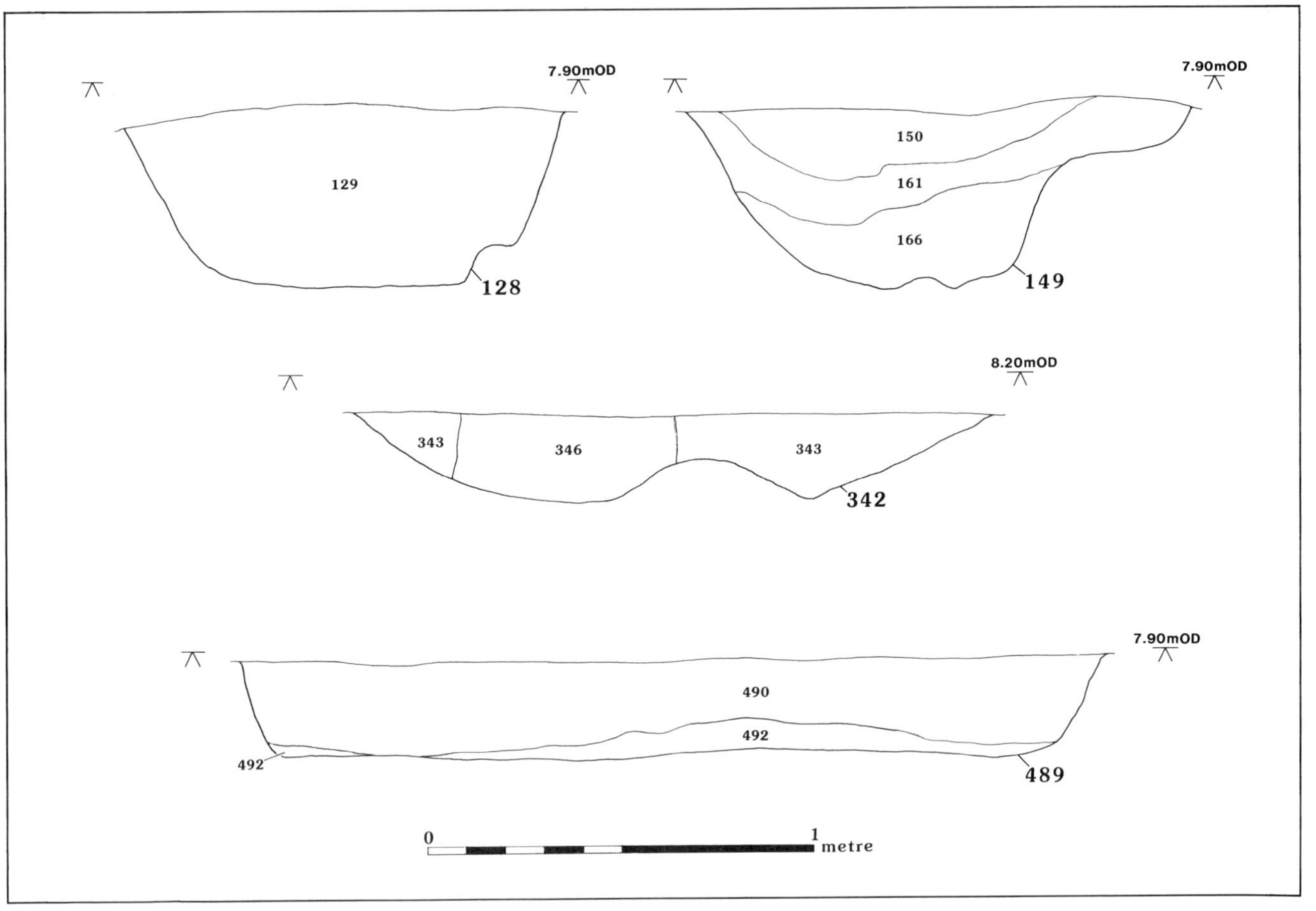

Figure 38 Sections across Late Bronze Age pits and slot 489 in Area A

layers and lenses was recorded, probably representing periods of slower infilling.

Few finds were recovered from any of the excavated ditch sections. A single sherd of Early Bronze Age pottery came from the upper fill on the west side and two Late Bronze Age sherds from the top of the upper fill on the east side. Three flint cores, one from the bottom fill and one flake were also recovered from the ditch sections on the east side.

The ring-ditch was cut on its east and west sides by two ditches, 519/521 and 91/322 respectively, comprising part of a Late Bronze Age field system. These later ditches terminated some 2 m inside the ring-ditch, suggesting that it may have defined a bell barrow, the later ditches crossing the silted-up ring-ditch, a berm up to 2 m wide, and terminating against a still upstanding low bank which was incorporated into the later field system (Fig. 32).

Central burial 120

Slightly south-west of the centre of the ring-ditch was a small sub-circular pit, 120, filled with a comparatively compact dark brown soil mixed with some gravel (Figs 32 and 33; Pl. 9). The pit was just under 1 m in diameter and 0.5 m deep, with irregular, stepped sides and a flat bottom. Placed in this pit was an inverted, Secondary Series Collared Urn (Longworth 1984, 35) which has been attributed to Burgess's 'Late' style. The urn was complete but it was in a very fragmentary condition. The

Plate 9 Central cremation burial 120, showing inverted Collared Urn crushed in situ (0.2 m and 0.5 m scales). Facing east

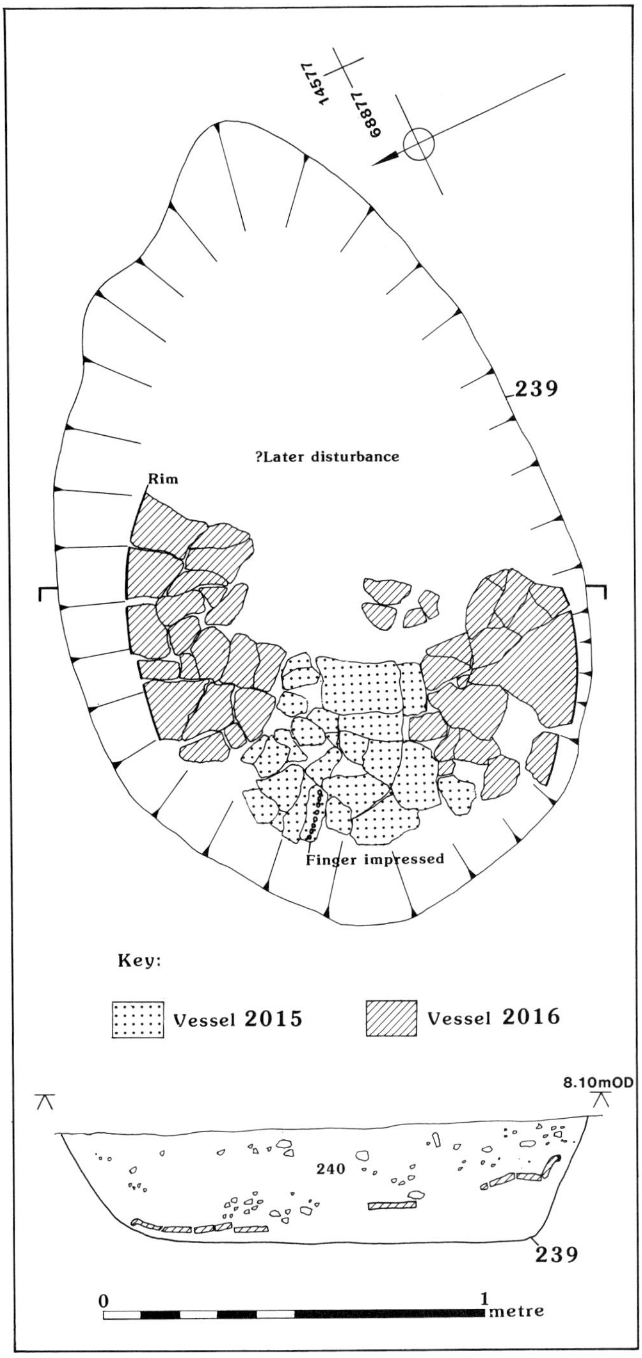

Figure 39 Late Bronze Age pit 239

fragmentation may possibly have occurred as a result of it having lain directly underneath the racecourse and been subject to heavy, repeated vibration. The cremated human skeletal remains from the Collared Urn comprise two adults (an older mature adult female and an adult ?male), accompanied by three seg mented, faience beads.

Satellite burial 93

This lay less than 2 m to the north-west of ring-ditch 23, in an area of sandy natural (Fig. 32). It had been heavily truncated and the soil conditions were so dry on excavation, that the cut containing the burial survived as no more than an ill-defined shallow scoop, 0.6 m in diameter. In the centre of this was the base of a grog-tempered vessel of indeterminate form, associated with a scatter of cremated human bone. The bone, almost certainly originally contained by the vessel, was from an older mature adult of indeterminate sex.

Other features

Within the area enclosed by the ring-ditch were several features other than central burial 120 but none of these can be certainly associated with it. Feature 74, possibly a tree throw hole, has been attributed a Late Neolithic date and a similar shallow scoop, 133, may also have been a tree throw hole (Fig. 32). There were three smaller, shallow, amorphous features (163, 173, and 179) and two groups of possible post-holes — 143 and 145 on the west side, and 76, 78, and 80 to the east. The fills of features 80 and 173 contained burnt flint, but none of these other features, with the exception of 74, produced any dating evidence.

Pit 34 which lay 10 m to the west of the ring-ditch may have been an Early Bronze Age feature but was perhaps unassociated with the bell barrow (Fig. 34). It was oval in plan measuring approximately 1.7 by 0.9 m, was 0.3 m deep and had fairly evenly sloping sides and a rounded bottom. It was filled with yellow gravelly sand and contained a single sherd of grog-tempered pottery.

No other Early Bronze Age features were found, though a single sherd of Beaker pottery came from gully 491, a Late Bronze Age feature.

Middle Bronze Age

A single feature, pit 258, has been assigned a Middle Bronze Age date. This was a shallow, oval pit which measured 1.2 by 0.65 m and was 0.22 m deep. It lay towards the west end of the site (*see* Fig. 35) and contained five sherds of a Deverel-Rimbury cordoned urn. This vessel may have been complete when placed in the pit but the area had been subject to heavy truncation. There were no other finds, apart from a single piece of burnt flint, and no human bone was recovered. There was nothing further to suggest any Middle Bronze Age occupation in the immediate vicinity of the site.

Late Bronze Age

The excavation revealed evidence of a small, unenclosed Late Bronze Age settlement extending over a distance of approximately 150 m along the edge of the floodplain, at a height of between 8 and 8.5 m OD (Fig. 35). This had suffered considerable truncation which had removed the majority of the structural features but two principal and probably related areas of activity were defined. These lay in Areas A and B of the site respectively.

Area A

Structure 1

This lay 35 m to the west of ditch 8/10 and to the south of the majority of the Late Bronze Age features in this area (Fig. 35). Structural evidence was slight, and the principal feature, 443, contained no dating evidence.

Feature 443 comprised a 5.5 m length of curvilinear gully which was 0.3 m wide and up to 0.37 m deep. It sloped up at either end and, if projected, would describe a circle approximately 10 m in diameter (Fig. 36). The fill was a yellowish–brown, slightly loamy gravelly sand. No post-pipes or post-impressions were detected and it is possible that this feature represented a drip gully which had been entirely truncated on the south-west side. Two post-holes, up to 0.35 m in diameter and 0.25 m deep, lay just inside the line of the gully, and one, 468, produced a single sherd of Late Bronze Age pottery.

Ditches

A series of five, shallow, recut ditches at the extreme east end of the site represented two stages in the development of a boundary or field system. The earliest of these formed a right-angled arrangement in the south-east corner of the site, and incorporated the apparently still extant bank of the possible Early Bronze Age barrow (Fig. 35). As many as three ditches (91, 306, and 322) belonged to this earliest stage on the west side of the barrow, with two ditches (519 and 521) to the east. It was impossible to distinguish any sequence in the digging of these ditches. However, these subsequently fell into disuse and became infilled and were replaced by a pair of north-south ditches (8 and 10). These followed the line of the preceding system towards the south edge of the site but continued on a slightly sinuous line northwards beyond the edge of the excavated area. Again, the sequence of digging was unclear. Ditch 8 was the most substantial of the entire group, increasing in width from 0.9 m in the south to 1.5 m in the north, and in depth from 0.45–0.55 m (Fig. 37). At the north end, ditch 8 was sealed by a thin layer of alluvial clay filling the former channel which crossed the north-east corner of the site. All of the ditches (Fig. 37) were filled with undifferentiated gravelly loamy sands and contained varying quantities of Late Bronze Age pottery. The pottery was generally concentrated towards the central sections of the ditches, closest to structure 1 and associated features, with much less towards the north and south ends.

Pits and other features

No Late Bronze Age features were found to the east of the aforementioned ditches but there was a clear concentration immediately to the west, in the vicinity of structure 1, extending over an area of approximately 70 by 70 m (Fig. 35). Situated just above the 8 m contour, this area had been heavily ploughed and the majority of features comprised shallow scoops most of which were probably the bases of pits. A representative range of features is shown in Figure 38.

Two of the most substantial pits were 128 and 149 (Fig. 38). Both were oval in plan, with steeply sloping sides and flattish bottoms. Pit 149, measuring 1.85 by 1.45 m and 0.55 m deep, was slightly larger than pit 128. The fill was a little unusual in that there was a much darker, loamier fill (161) sandwiched between layers of the ubiquitous loamy sands with gravel. Layer 161 contained 31 sherds of pottery, seven quite substantial fragments of perforated clay 'tablet', and a fragment of saddle quern. It was also comparatively rich in cereal grains and weed seeds. Pit 149 produced a total of 63

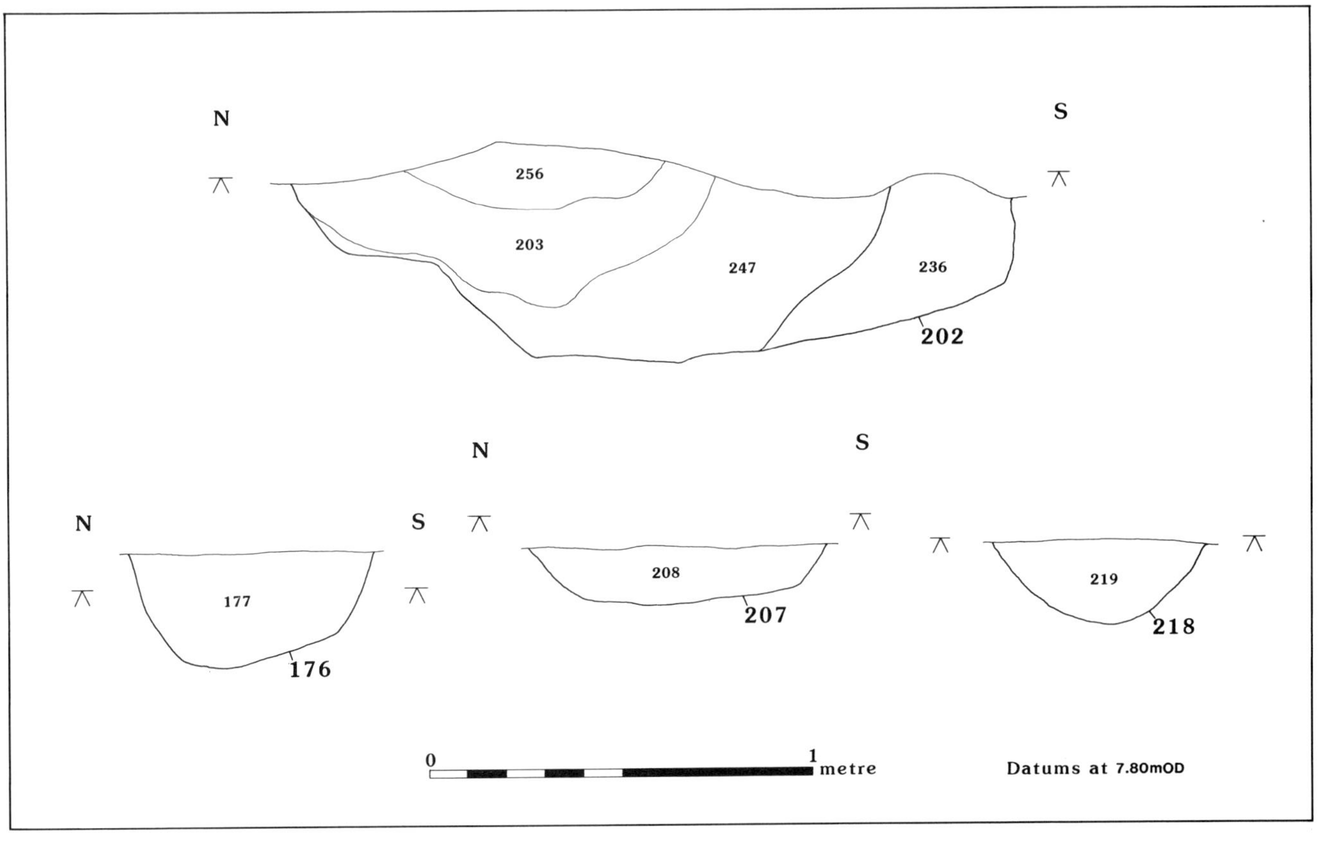

Figure 40 Sections across Late Bronze Age pits in Area B

Plate 10 Pit 239, with deposit of jars 2015 and 2016 (0.2 m and 0.5 m scales). Facing south.

sherds of Late Bronze Age pottery and pit 128, a total of 51 sherds.

Pit 347 may have been similar to pits 128 and 149 but had been heavily truncated. However, the small volume of surviving fill produced 64 sherds of pottery and 16 fragments of perforated clay 'tablet'. Pit 430, which was somewhat larger, measuring 1.9 by 1.2 m, and 0.5 m deep, produced 30 sherds of pottery. Three other pits in this area were also noteworthy: 540 because it contained fragments of two saddle querns, and 153 and 239 because both contained what might be interpreted as 'placed deposits'.

Pit 153, immediately to the north-east of structure 1, survived as no more than a small, shallow scoop 0.07 m deep, but it contained 46 sherds of pottery from a single vessel; whether these came from a complete vessel placed in the pit remains uncertain.

Pit 239 was a sub-oval feature, approximately 2 m long, 1.4 m wide and 0.3 m deep (Fig. 39; Pl. 10). The bottom was covered by a layer varying between 0.05 and 0.15 m thick, perhaps derived from weathering of the sides. Overlying this, at the west end, was approximately 50% of a large, shouldered jar (2016). This was *in situ* but in pieces, with the rim sherds lying up against the edge of the pit. The remains of a large, bucket-shaped jar (2015) lay within the pit but the majority of this vessel had been removed by truncation. No trace of the remainder of jar 2016 was found at the east end of the pit and, while it is possible that this was incomplete when placed in the pit, there was some evidence in the shape and slightly different fill of the pit at this end to suggest that it may have been removed by a later cut. Apart from a small fragment of perforated clay 'tablet' and a few pieces of worked flint, there were no other finds from the pit (a short length of curving iron strip came from the surface, and is assumed to have been intrusive).

Feature 342 was extremely irregular in plan and profile, possibly comprising a complex of shallow scoops, but more closely resembling a group of animal burrows or perhaps a tree-hole (Fig. 38). However, it contained a notable concentration of finds, including 120 sherds of pottery, nine fragments of perforated clay 'tablets' and a piece of quernstone. This feature formed an approximate right-angle measuring *c.* 2x2 m and up to 0.25 m deep, and was filled with a dark greyish–brown sandy loam containing some burnt flint and occasional charcoal flecks.

Feature 489 was a slot or gully, 2.2 m long, 0.85 m wide, and 0.26 m deep (Fig. 38). It was aligned north-west–south-east, filled with brown gravelly sand, and contained 80 sherds of pottery, several fragments of perforated clay 'tablets', and a small fragment of quern.

The remaining features in this area which have been assigned to the Late Bronze Age, were all small and probably heavily truncated. These are most likely to have been pits and all contained varying but small quantities of pottery (<30 sherds) and few other finds.

Area B

Structure 2

This was one of two possible structures identified towards the centre of the site. It and structure 3 lay close together, some 80 m to the west of structure 1 (Fig. 35).

Structure 2 (Fig. 36) comprised an approximate 5 m length of shallow, curvilinear slot or gully, 378. This was up to 0.45 m wide and 0.25 m deep and, if projected, described a circle approximately 12 m in diameter. It was filled with a dark brown sandy loam containing Late Bronze Age pottery. No post-impressions or post-pipes were apparent. Within the area enclosed by gully 378 were several small pits or post-holes, all less than 0.15 m deep. Some contained Late Bronze Age pottery, but it is uncertain if all were contemporaneous and related. One, feature 325, contained a stone which appears to have been used for burnishing copper alloy objects (*see* below).

Structure 3

Structure 3 (Figs 35 and 36) lay immediately to the north of structure 2 and was represented by two substantial post-holes, 338 and 351, which lay 1.5 m apart (centre to centre) and were up to 0.7 m in diameter and

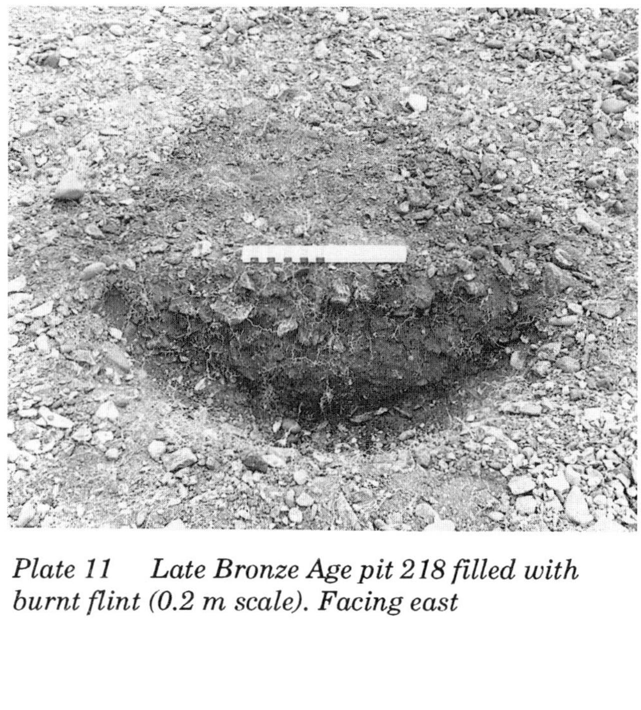

Plate 11 Late Bronze Age pit 218 filled with burnt flint (0.2 m scale). Facing east

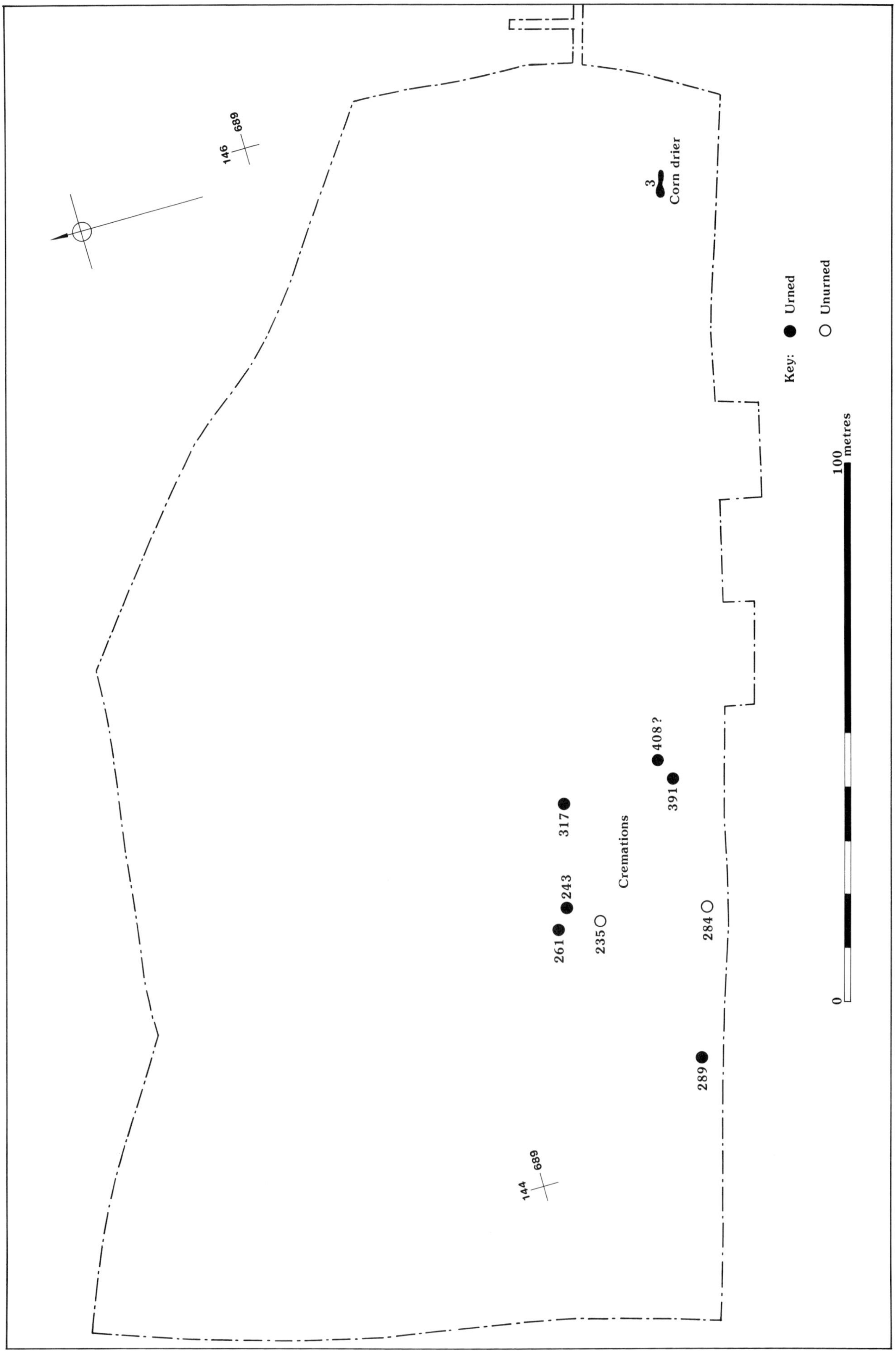

Figure 41 Plan of Romano-British features

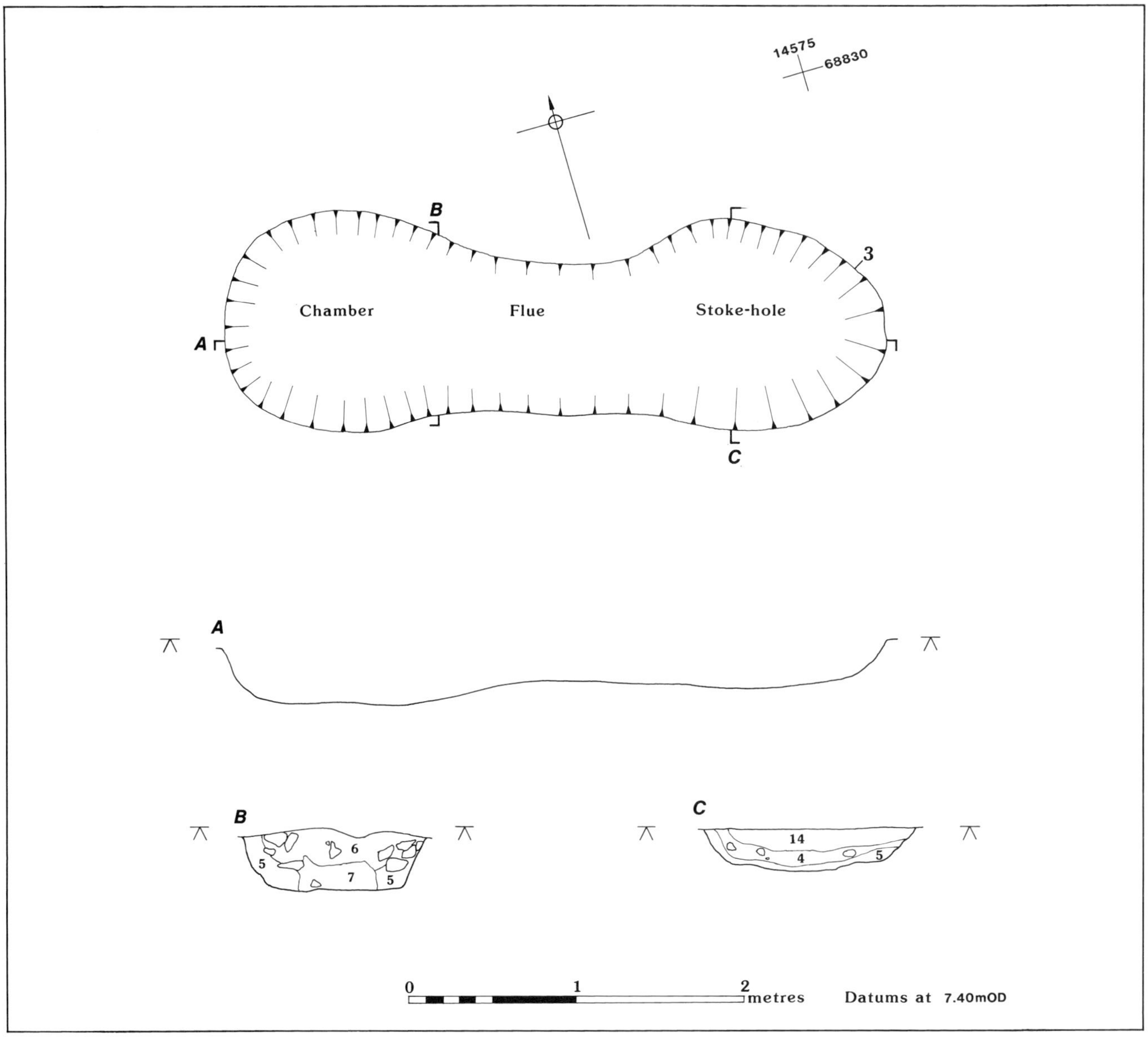

Figure 42 Plan and sections of Romano-British corn drier 3

0.35 m deep. These might be interpreted as representing post-holes marking a south-facing entrance to a circular structure. A complex of three shallow post-holes (365, 367, and 369) lay 1 m within the postulated entrance and all contained small quantities of Late Bronze Age pottery. No other features lay within the area occupied by the structure, except for a very faint, curvilinear soil stain which perhaps marked its extent to the south-east. There was insufficient of this to provide an accurate diameter, but an area approximately 12 m in diameter was defined by this soil stain, post-holes 338 and 351, and an arc of pits on the north and west sides of the postulated structure.

Pits

All but one of the Late Bronze Age pits towards the west end of the site were characterised by fills of burnt flint in an ashy matrix (Pl. 11). The 21 pits comprising this group extended over an area some 50 m square but the majority were concentrated immediately to the north-west of structures 2 and 3. Outlying pits 294 and 307 lay to the south, 309 and 319 to the east, and 413 and 428 to the north-west. All of the pits, with the exception of 202, were generally small, bowl-shaped, with diameters between 0.6 and 0.7 m and depths of up to 0.4 m; allowing for truncation, they may have originally been up to 0.8 m deep. The burnt flint was tightly packed within the pits and there was comparatively little charcoal. A single sherd of Late Bronze Age pottery was found in pit 196.

Pit 202 also contained burnt flint but was larger than the other examples (Fig. 40). It lay just to the north-east of structure 3, on the edge of the concentration of burnt flint filled features (Fig. 35). It was approximately oval in plan, measuring 2.8 by 1.6 m, and up to 0.6 m deep. The bottom was rounded but the sides were irregular and there was no surviving evidence for it having had a timber or clay lining. The fills varied, and there was some indication of a later recut or disturbance. The initial fill, 236, comprised almost entirely burnt flints in an ashy soil similar to that in the other burnt flint filled features. Fills 203, 247, and 256 in contrast were quite ashy but contained very little burnt flint, and 247 comprised a series of near vertically sided lenses of gravel, perhaps indicative of rapid infilling. All but fill 236 might have represented a later feature or recut of pit 202 but no finds were recovered from this feature.

Pit 320 was the only other Late Bronze Age feature in the area. This was a small, shallow feature, 0.5 m in diameter and only 0.15 m deep, filled with gravelly loamy sand. However, it contained 66 sherds from a single vessel (a jar) probably complete when placed in the pit but damaged by subsequent truncation.

Romano-British

Evidence for Romano-British occupation in the area was provided by a corn drier towards the south-east corner of the site, and a small group of cremation burials just over 100 m to the west (Fig. 41). These features have been dated to the 1st or 2nd century AD and a small quantity of residual Roman pottery of the same date was also recovered from early Saxon pit 125 which lay approximately midway between the corn drier and cremation burials. A few sherds of later Roman pottery were recovered but all occurred as residual finds in Saxon features.

Corndrier 3

This was aligned approximately east–west, and comprised a narrow flue just over 1 m long linking a larger, bowl-shaped stoke-hole at the east end with a similar shaped chamber at the west end (Fig. 42; Pl. 12). The chamber survived to a depth of 0.4 m and both this and the flue contained extensive traces of a clay lining (layer 5), lightly burnt in places within the flue. Remnants of a dome were found which had collapsed into the chamber and flue; this dome was made up of clay tempered with a large number of flint nodules (layer 7). On the floor of the chamber was a large fragment of a rotary quern, with a further fragment on the floor of the flue. Layer 4, on the floor of the stoke-hole, contained

Plate 12 Romano-British corn drier 3; chamber in foreground, flue unexcavated (0.2 m and 0.5 m scales). Facing north-east

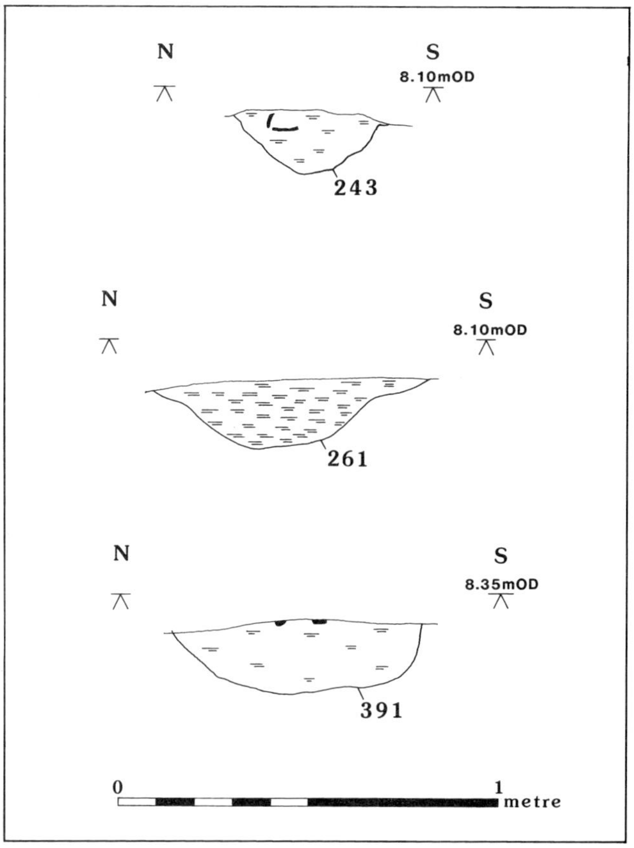

Figure 43 Sections across pits containing Romano-British cremation burials

sherds from at least three greyware jars, including a large storage jar, all dating to the 1st or 2nd century AD. A soil sample taken from this layer produced a notable quantity of carbonised cereal and weed seeds.

Cremation burials

The heavily truncated remains of eight cremation burials were found along the central southern edge of the site. These occupied an area of 50 by at least 30 m on a small, low spur of ground around the 8.5 m OD contour (Fig. 41). Six of the cremation burials were associated with sherds of urns and these vessels probably contained the cremations rather than represented grave goods. Three of the urns were small, handmade, everted rim jars with a likely date range in the 1st or early 2nd centuries AD, and another was a similar but heavier-duty vessel; insufficient of the other two vessels were present to determine their forms. The two remaining cremation burials, 235 and 284, were apparently unurned. All of the surviving cremation pits, except that containing 408, were small, 0.4–0.6 m in diameter and less than 0.2 m deep (Fig. 43). Cremation burial 408 was in a larger pit, 0.95 m in diameter and 0.4 m deep, and may represent a disturbed or redeposited burial; potsherds from a single vessel and only two fragments of human bone were found dispersed throughout the pit.

Variable quantities of cremated human bone were recovered, all subadult or older, and all were of indeterminate sex except for one possible male.

Saxon

Six or possibly seven sunken-featured buildings (SFBs), three pits, and several undated but probably contemporaneous ditches and gullies have been assigned to this period (Fig. 44). All of the features, except one small pit, lay within 100 m of each other in the western half of the site, above the 7.5 m OD contour. The sunken-featured buildings were all aligned approximately east–west. The pottery has proved difficult to date closely and can only be assigned a broad date range encompassing the 5th–7th centuries AD.

Sunken-featured buildings

SFB 16

This lay on the eastern fringe of the excavated group and differed from the others in several respects. It was the largest example, just under 6 m long, 3.5 m wide, and was up to 0.5 m deep (Fig. 45; Pl. 13). It was approximately sub-rectangular in plan but there were several irregularities and the sides sloped at varying angles down to a rounded bottom. At the east end the side sloped gently and evenly forming a 'ramp' in the centre up to 1 m wide. Either side of this, towards the bottom, were two post-holes 3 m apart. Post-holes 42 and 333 were roughly 0.3 m in diameter and 0.3 m deep, though the former was more irregular near the top, perhaps resulting from the removal of the post. No post-holes were found at the west end, though there was a shallow, centrally positioned depression. Two shallow undated 'L'-shaped gullies lay just beyond the north-west and south-west corners of this SFB and may have been associated with it.

The fill of SFB 16 was a generally undifferentiated dark yellowish–brown sandy loam, grading to brown towards the bottom. However, at the east end, there was a markedly darker, charcoal-rich spread confined to the area of the 'ramp', which extended from the edge of the pit down to the bottom and directly overlay natural. This deposit was comparatively rich in charred cereal grain and weed seeds, along with some chaff, and perhaps represented a discrete dump of refuse in the abandoned SFB (this is discussed further below). The main fill in the SFB produced a considerable quantity, though limited range, of finds and was the most prolific of all the excavated SFBs. The finds were fairly evenly distributed throughout the fill and included 195 sherds of pottery, three iron objects comprising a latch lifter, a perforated strap, and a girdle hanger or key, the side link from a ?Roman copper alloy bridle bit, and a fragment of quern.

Plate 13 Sunken-featured building 16 during excavation. Facing north-east

Plate 14 Sunken-featured building 186 (1 m and 2 m scales). Facing north

SFB 69

This lay towards the centre of the group of SFBs (Fig. 45). The sub-rectangular pit measured 3 m by 2.2 m and survived to a maximum depth of 0.2 m. The sides sloped evenly towards a flat bottom, and centrally placed at each end, just outside the pit, were two substantial post-holes, 387 and 388 (Fig. 45). This was the only example where the post-holes lay entirely outside the surviving limits of the pit. The post-holes were 0.4 m in diameter and up to 0.5 m deep; neither contained any evidence of post-pipes or post-impressions.

The fill of the pit was a yellowish–brown loamy gravelly sand, containing relatively few finds. Only 16 sherds of pottery were recovered along with a fragment of an iron steelyard beam.

SFB 137

This lay on the north-east edge of the group of SFBs, just above the 7.5 m contour (Fig. 45). The somewhat irregular, sub-rectangular pit measured 2.9 m by 2.4 m, and survived to a depth of 0.2 m. The sides sloped evenly to a slightly rounded bottom, and two post-holes, 147 and 211, were centrally-placed at either end on the edge of the pit. The post-holes were up to 0.3 m in diameter and 0.5 m deep.

The pit and post-holes were filled with an undifferentiated deposit of dark yellowish–brown sandy loam which contained 37 sherds of pottery and an iron heckle tooth from a weaving or carding comb.

SFB 186

This lay towards the centre of the group of SFBs, was broadly sub-rectangular in plan, and measured 3.2 m by 2.7 m (Fig. 46; Pl. 14). It was 0.2 m deep at the west end increasing to 0.3 m towards the east, with evenly sloping sides and a flat bottom. Two post-holes, 217 and 314,

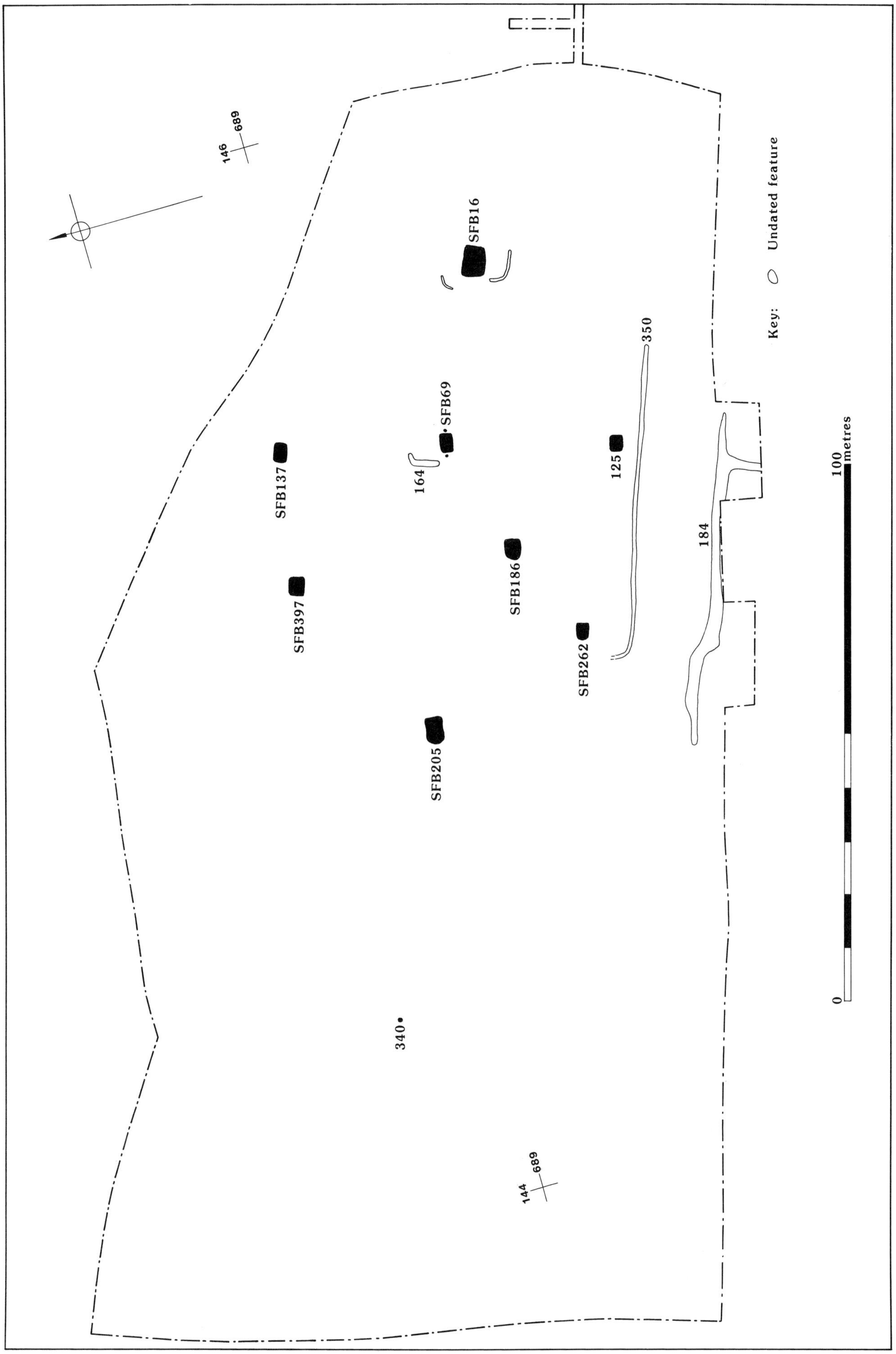

Figure 44 Plan of Saxon features

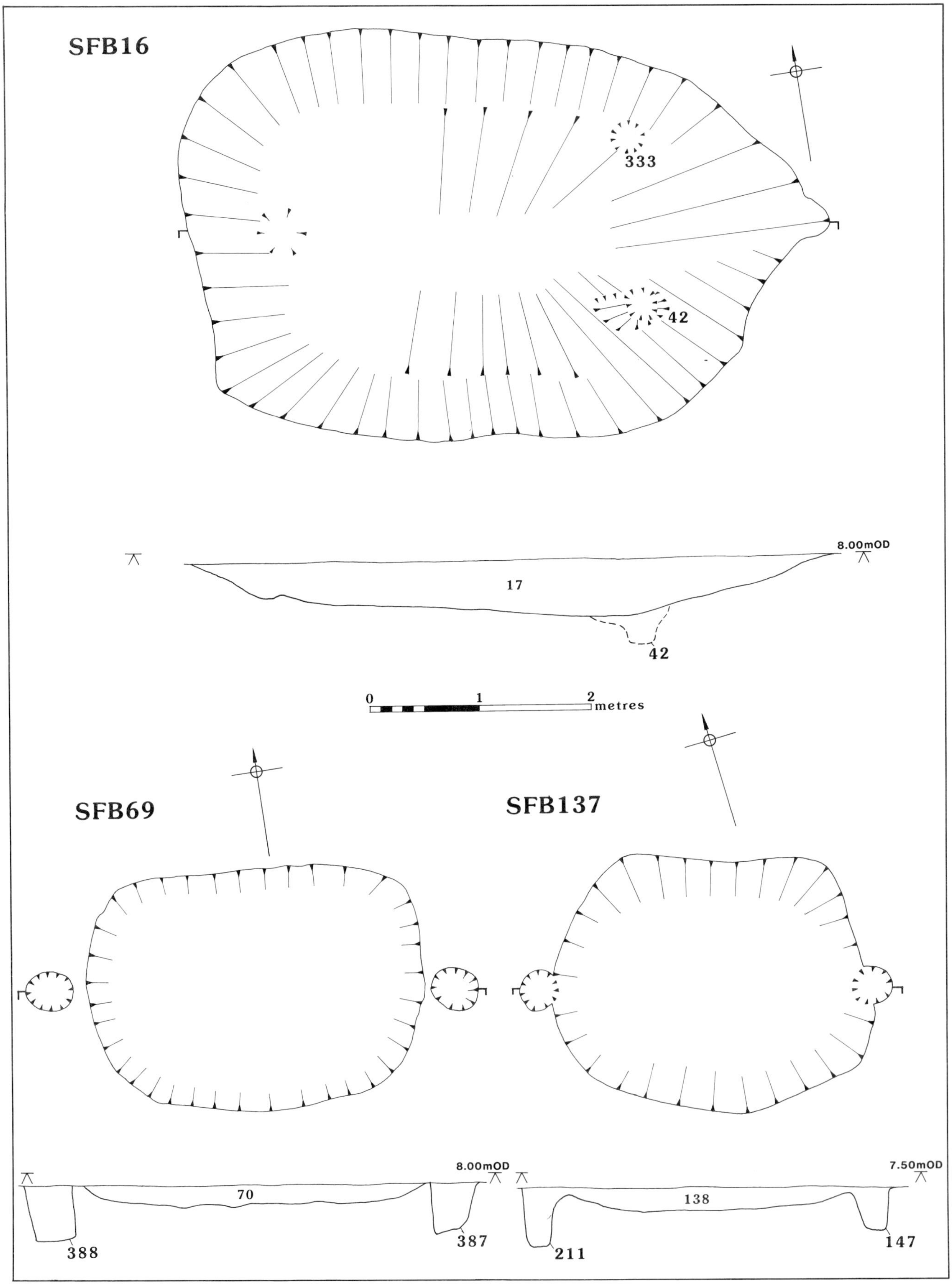

Figure 45 Plans and sections of sunken-featured buildings

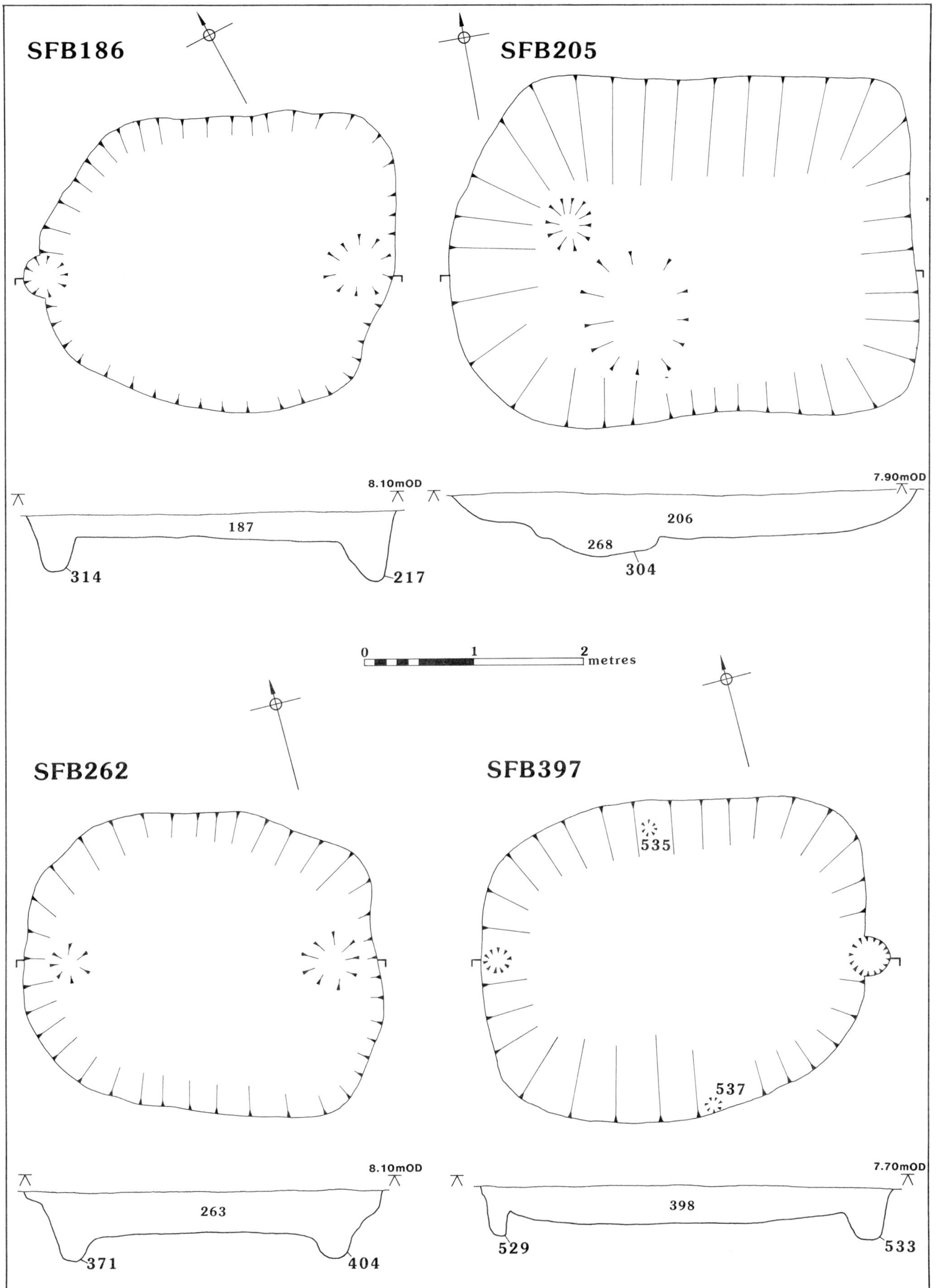

Figure 46 Plans and sections of sunken-featured buildings

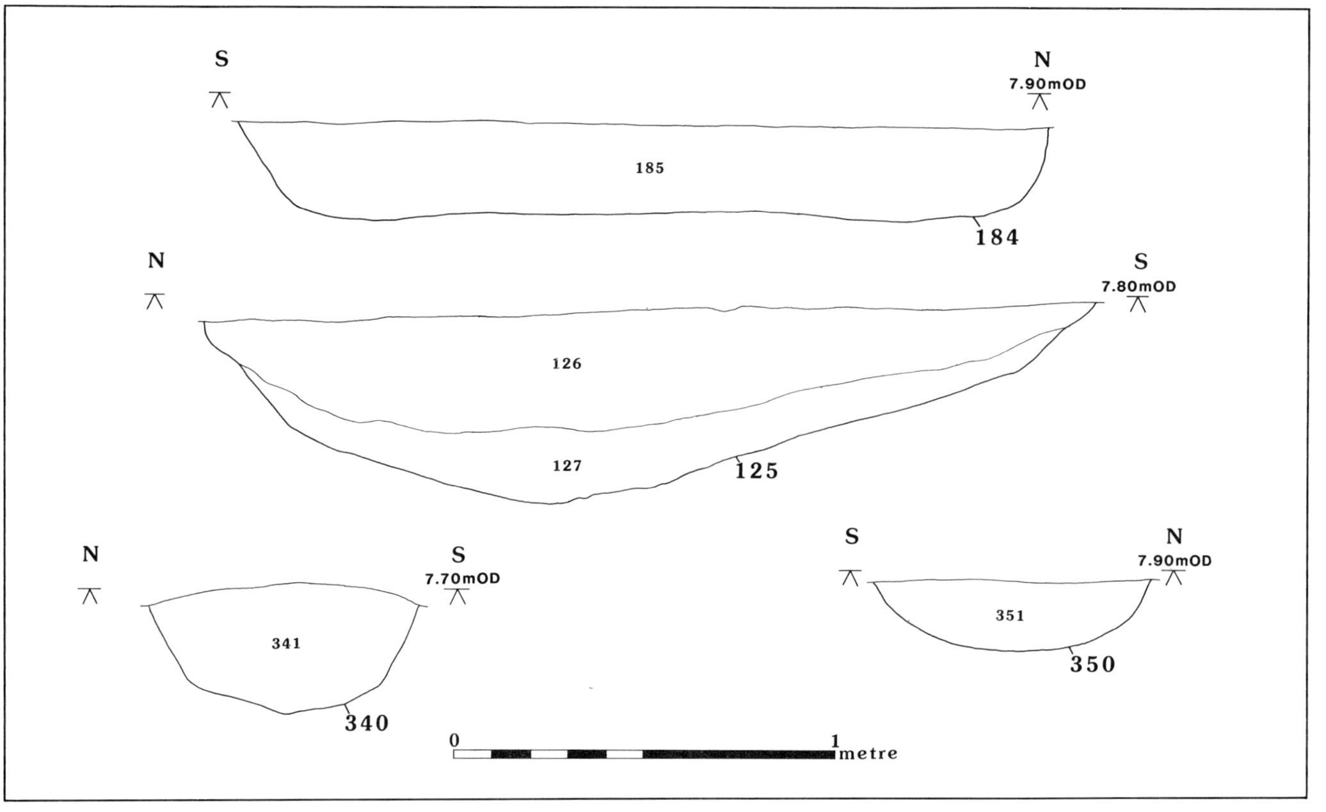

Figure 47 Sections across Saxon ditches and pits

were centrally placed at either end. The larger, 217, was approximately 0.6 m in diameter and 0.7 m deep, and lay just within the edge of the pit. The smaller post-hole, 314, was 0.4 m in diameter and 0.5 m deep, and lay on the edge of the pit.

The homogeneous fill of dark yellowish–brown gravelly sandy loam produced 113 sherds of pottery and a slightly more varied assemblage of finds compared to most of the other SFBs. These include fragments of a whetstone and a quern, and an iron heckle tooth.

SFB 205

Although this has been classified as a SFB, it varied in several respects from the other examples. It lay on the west side of the group, was sub-rectangular in plan with a square east end and a slightly rounded west end (Fig. 46). It was larger than the other SFBs with the exception of SFB16, measuring 4.3 m by approximately 3 m. It was up to 0.4 m deep with irregularly sloping sides and a flat bottom. A sub-rectangular feature, 304, which was 0.6 m deep and lay towards the south-west corner may have been the truncated remains of an earlier pit but it was filled with redeposited sand which contained no finds. A single, somewhat irregular ?post- hole lay in the north-west corner at the bottom of the slope.

The fill of the majority of the pit was difficult to discern from the natural. The fill comprised principally a dark yellowish–brown gravelly loamy sand which, over much of the bottom, overlay a thin layer of reddish, lightly burnt gravelly sand which may have been scorched natural. This burning was concentrated towards the west end of the pit but its limits were ill-defined. SFB 205 produced very few finds; a total of five sherds of pottery comprise three Romano-British (Oxford colour coat) and two Saxon sherds. There are also two rotary quern fragments, a lump of ?sarsen, and a fragment of iron bar. It is suggested below that SFB 205 may have been some form of crop drier, but there is no direct evidence for this.

SFB 262

This lay on the south-west fringe of the group and was sub-rectangular in plan (3.2 m by 2.75 m, up to 0.4 m deep (Fig. 46)). It had steeply sloping sides with a slightly rounded bottom. The centrally placed post-holes at either end were set 0.2 m within the edges of the pit and only 2.4 m apart; this was the closest pair of post-holes in any of the SFBs. Both post-holes were sub-circular in plan and 0.7 m deep, but 404 was the larger with a diameter of 0.5 m, compared to 0.4 m for 371.

The fill of the pit and post-holes was a uniform dark yellowish–brown gravelly loamy sand. Although this was a fairly substantial SFB in terms of its volume, it produced comparatively few finds. These comprised 27 sherds of pottery, including one comb-decorated sherd probably from the same vessel found in SFB 186, and two iron knives.

SFB 397

This and SFB 137 were the most northerly of the group. SFB 397 measured 3.5 m by 3 m and was 0.35 m deep (Fig. 46). It had gently sloping sides, a rounded bottom, and differed from the others in that there were four post-holes, one placed midway along each side. The largest, 529 and 533, lay at the west and east ends respectively, with smaller post-holes 535 and 537 along the north and south sides. Post-hole 529, set just within the west edge of the pit, was 0.25 m in diameter and 0.45 m deep, whereas 533 on the east edge was somewhat larger with a diameter of 0.4 m, but was also 0.45 m deep. Post-holes 535 and 537 were only 0.15 m in diameter and 0.2 m deep and both were set towards the edges of the pit.

The lower part of the fill of SFB 397 was distinctly darker than the remainder, though there was no clear boundary. As with the other SFBs, the fills of the pit and the post-holes were indistinguishable, and no post-impressions or post-pipes were apparent.

Finds were comparatively prolific and include 130 sherds of pottery, a spindlewhorl, small stone ?counter, and a complete hearth bottom from an iron-smithing hearth.

Ditches

Several shallow linear features were identified which have been tentatively ascribed to this period on the basis of their alignments and locations relative to the SFBs (Fig. 44). However, none contained any dating evidence and all had suffered varying degrees of truncation.

Features 184 and 350 lay immediately to the south of the cluster of SFBs and pit 125. They were broadly aligned east–west and ran parallel to each other for more than 50 m, approximately 15 m apart. Gully 350 turned to the north at the west end before petering out and may also have formerly continued further to the east. Ditch 184 may also have originally continued further to the east and west and there was also a branch to the south, at 90° to 184, which extended beyond the limit of excavation. Ditch 184 was broad, with a maximum width of just over 2 m, whereas gully 350 was less than 0.75 m wide (Fig. 47). Both, however, were very shallow; depths rarely exceeded 0.2 m and, in places, the edges were ill-defined. Their fills were undifferentiated, brown very gravelly sandy loams.

A similarly ill-defined, short length of ditch or gully, 164, lay just to the north-west of SFB 69 and may have been contemporaneous and related to the latter (Fig. 44). Two narrower, 'L' shaped gullies just beyond the north-west and south-west corners of SFB 16 may have been associated with this structure.

Pits

Two pits belong to this period. The largest, 125, lay immediately to the south of the SFBs, with a smaller example, 340, 50 m to the west (Fig. 44).

Pit 125 was sub-rectangular, almost 3 m long, 2.3 m wide, and 0.5 m deep (Fig. 47). The lower fill, 127, was loamier and contained more charcoal than the upper fill, 126. Pit 125 produced a total of 70 sherds of pottery comprising 62 Saxon sherds and eight residual Roman sherds.

Pit 340 was a small, sub-circular feature, 0.7 m in diameter and 0.4 m deep (Fig. 47). The fill contained a

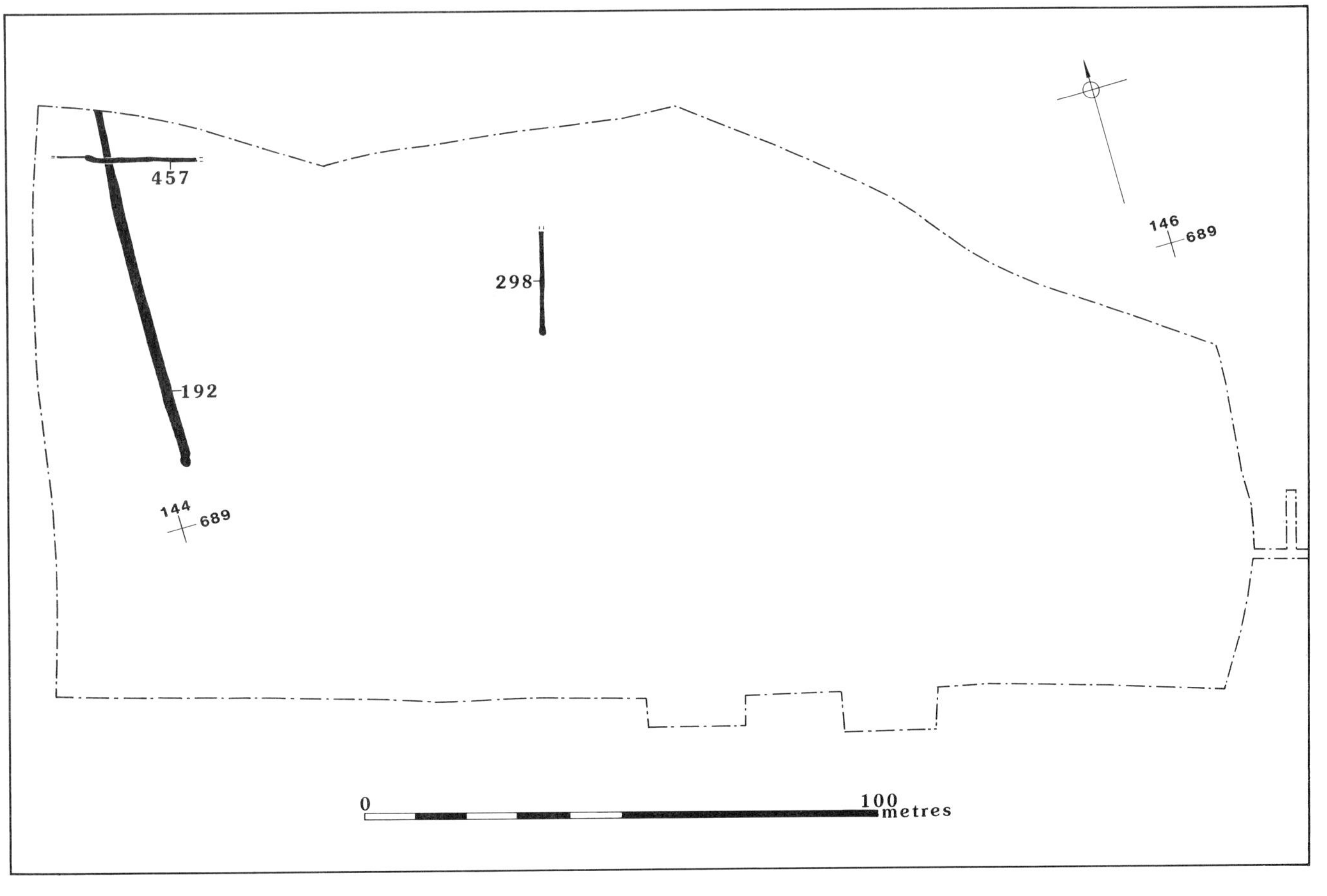

Figure 48 Plan of post-medieval features

sherd of a comb-decorated vessel, similar to those found in SFBs 186 and 262.

Post-Medieval / Early Modern

Three linear features, pre-dating the laying-out of the racecourse, were found in the main area excavation and two further linear features in the small trench excavated some 100 m to the west across the projected line of the parish boundary between East Molesey and West Molesey (*see* Fig. 28 for location).

Ditch 192, aligned north–south, was the largest of these features and extended for a distance of at least 50 m, beyond the limit of excavation to the north (Fig. 48). Here, it could be seen to cut the alluvial deposits in the former river channel. It terminated abruptly to the south, with no evidence of any former continuation having been truncated. The ditch had been recut along its entire length on at least one occasion. The earliest ditch, on the west side, was approximately 1.5 m wide and 0.6 m deep and had a 'V' shaped profile with a pronounced channel along the bottom indicating that it had been cleaned out. A later ditch ran alongside and cut the west side of the earlier ditch; this later ditch was approximately 1.6 m wide and 0.5 m deep, with sloping sides and a flat bottom.

A narrow, shallow gully, 457, ran east–west and cut across ditch 192 in the north-west corner of the excavation (Fig. 48). Two slightly offset lengths were recorded over a distance of at least 30 m but these petered out at either end.

A similar narrow, shallow gully, 298, lay towards the middle of the site. This was aligned approximately north-east–south-west and survived to a length of just over 20 m. It petered out at the north end but terminated to the south in a small bowl-shaped depression.

All of these features were filled with a gravelly dark grey to dark greyish–brown loamy sand, and both 192 and 457 produced quantities of post-medieval/early modern pottery, glass, and ceramic building material.

The two linear features recorded in the trench across the line of the parish boundary were only partially excavated and neither was bottomed. Both were aligned north–south and lay adjacent to each other. They were approximately 2 m and 1 m wide respectively and filled with large quantities of 19th-century pottery, bottle glass, and ceramic building material. It seems likely that both were ditches, probably open at the same time, which served to mark the parish boundary prior to the laying out of the racecourse, at which time they were presumably infilled.

4. Finds

Metalwork, by R. Montague

Three objects of copper alloy and 23 of iron were recovered during the excavation. Of these, two iron objects were retrieved from the surfaces of Late Bronze Age features and are considered to have been intrusive. Of the remainder, two copper alloy objects came from a Romano-British cremation, one copper alloy and 15 iron objects from Saxon features, and six iron objects were recovered from post-medieval, modern, and undated features.

All metalwork was X-radiographed and a selection of 11 objects was chosen for interrogative conservation, which was carried out by Elizabeth Goodman of the Salisbury Conservation Laboratory.

Late Bronze Age

A curving strip and a nail, both of iron, were recovered from the surfaces of pits 239 and 375 respectively. Both are likely to have been intrusive in these features. The strip is undiagnostic and the nail is hand-made and therefore unlikely to be modern. It is of a type (flat, round head and square-sectioned shank) commonly occurring from the Iron Age through to the post- medieval period.

Romano-British cremation burials

Four fragments of a curving copper alloy object (Fig. 49, 1) were retrieved from cremation burial 261, that of an unsexed adult. These fragments are probably part of an undecorated copper alloy bracelet with a circular section. The condition of the fragments strongly suggests that they have been exposed to high temperatures and it seems likely, therefore, that either the bracelet was worn by the deceased on the pyre, or it was a pyre good. Bracelets of this type occur throughout the Romano-British period.

Also from this context are two conjoining fragments of a melted copper alloy object (Obj. No. 2014, not illustrated). The fragments are in a very poor condition, with crazed and pitted surfaces, and are heavily corroded. The lower fragment is dished as if the molten copper alloy formed in a small hollow, although the irregular shape of the upper fragment shows that this could not have been in a crucible. This fact, and the context of the find, mean that this must be a melted object rather than technological waste, and is likely to have been a pyre good. Recent experimental pyre firings have shown that high enough temperatures can be reached to fully melt samples of sand-cast 12% tin bronze, depending on factors such as their position on the pyre, the length of time of firing, and the composition of the alloy (Northover and McDonnell pers. comm.).

Saxon

A total of 16 metal objects was retrieved from Saxon features, one of copper alloy and 15 of iron. Of these, seven came from SFB 16, two from SFB 69, one from SFB 137, two from SFB 186, two from SFB 262, one from pit 125 and one from SFB 205.

Copper alloy object

A single copper alloy object came from SFB 16 (Fig. 49, 2). This has been tentatively identified as a side link from a bridle bit. It has a bead and reel decoration on the shank and grooved decoration on one of the looped terminals. It may be a residual Iron Age or Romano-British object.

Iron objects

The tools, comprising a chisel from pit 125 (Fig. 49, 3), a heckle tooth from SFB 137 (Fig. 49, 4), and another possible heckle tooth from SFB 16 (Obj. No. 2003B, not

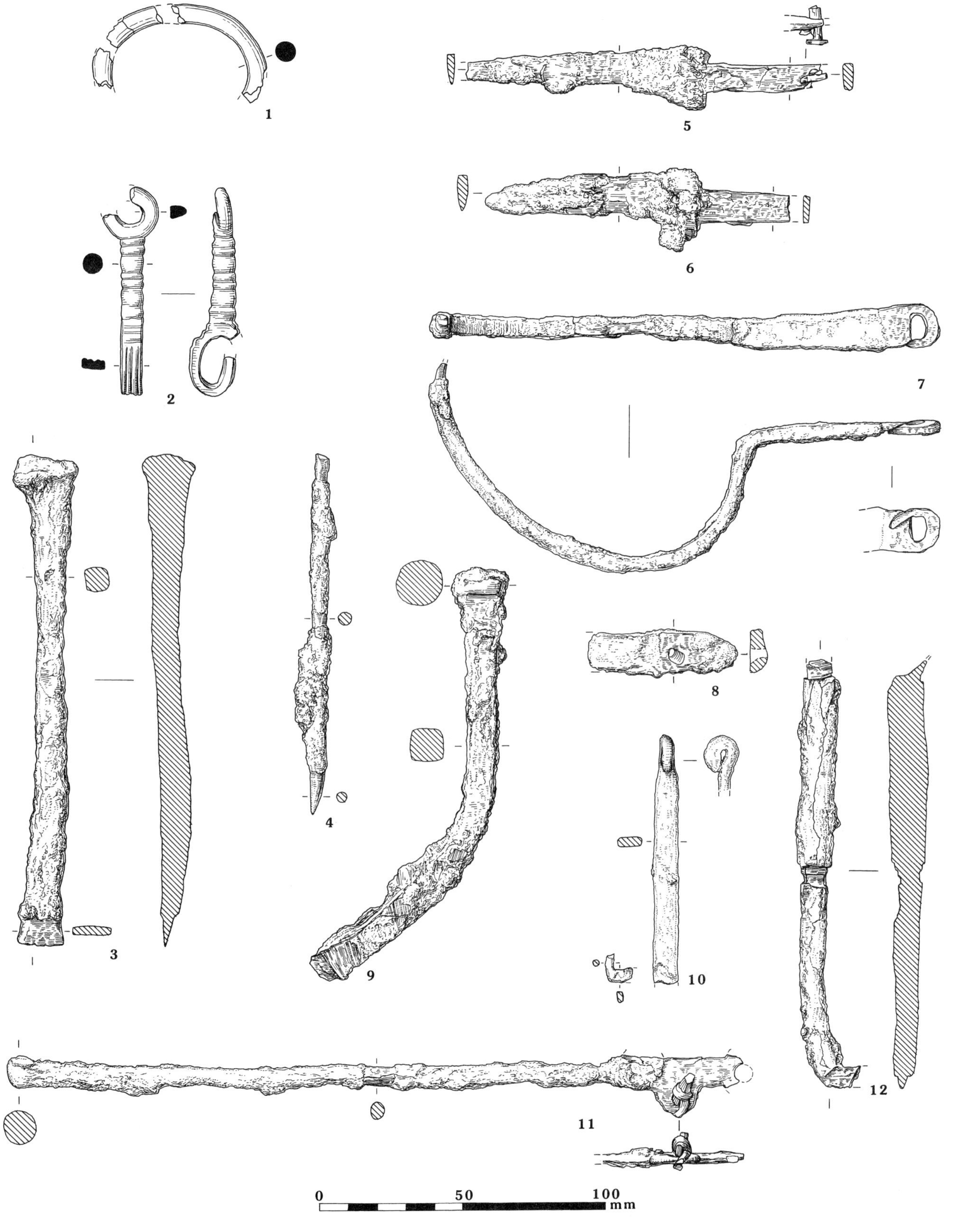

Figure 49 Copper alloy and iron objects

illustrated) provide some evidence that woodworking and textile preparation took place on the site. Three similar chisels were recovered from the excavations of Late Saxon features at Thetford, Norfolk (Goodall 1984, 77, fig. 115, 5–7), and heckle teeth, used in the preparation of fibres prior to spinning, are a common find on Saxon and medieval sites; large numbers were recovered from excavations of early and late Saxon features at West Stow, Suffolk and Thetford respectively (West 1985, 62, fig. 242; Goodall 1984, 79, fig. 119).

Two knives were recovered, both from SFB 262 (Fig. 49, 5, 6). One (Obj. No. 2026) has a 'T' headed rivet through the tang. Not enough of the tang survives to determine if it is a whittle or a scale tang, although the presence of a rivet and the parallel sides suggest the latter. Plate tang knives were common in the Romano-British period but appear to have fallen out of use later, to be reintroduced as scale tang knives in the 13th century (Manning 1985, 108–13; Goodall 1990, 409). Knives with riveted handles are not common in the Anglo-Saxon period, although a single knife with a rivet through the tang (of undescribed type) was recovered at West Stow (from a layer containing Iron Age, Romano-British, and Anglo-Saxon material). (West 1985, 61, fig. 240, 32).

The other knife has a similarly wide, broken tang, although it is tapering and seems to be a whittle tang. Similar knives are common finds on Anglo-Saxon sites, such as West Stow (West 1985, 124, fig. 240) and Thetford (Goodall 1984, 81, figs 122–5).

A typology developed for the knives from the Anglo-Saxon cemetery at Buckland, Dover (which was in use from AD 475–750), uses the shapes of both the back and the cutting edge of the blade (Evison 1987, 113). Both of the Hurst Park knives appear, by visual inspection and with reference to the X-radiographs, to have straight backs along their entire lengths and the cutting edges have been heavily resharpened, thus potentially making the application of the typology problematic. Only Evison's type 2 has a straight back along its entire length. This type is found in graves dating from AD 475–700 and thus does not allow a close date to be suggested for the knives from SFB 262.

Structural ironwork is represented by a latch lifter, a possible strap hinge fragment, and nails. Latch lifters are a common piece of structural ironwork, first appearing in the Late Iron Age and continuing in use throughout the Romano-British period (Manning 1985, 88). The latch lifter from SFB 16 (Fig. 49, 7) is of very similar form, although smaller than a Romano-British example from Borough Hill, near Daventry in Northamptonshire, and other similarly dated objects (Manning 1985, 89, pl. 38–9, especially O13). A possible latch lifter was recovered from SFB 51 at West Stow (West 1985, 42, fig. 173), although this is of a quite different shape from the Hurst Park example. Although it seems reasonable to suppose that latch lifters are a basic functional item and thus may have changed little over the centuries, the close similarity of the Hurst Park example to Romano-British ones might suggest that this is a residual, perhaps reused piece of ironwork.

The iron fragment with a bluntly pointed and perforated terminal (Fig. 49, 8) may be a fragment of a strap hinge. It was recovered from SFB 16. Strap hinge fragments from Late Saxon features at Thetford compare well with this example (Goodall 1984, 89, fig. 129, 146–7).

Four nails or nail shanks were recovered, two from SFB 16, one from SFB 69 and one from SFB 186. Where the head survives, these are all flat and round and the shanks are square or rectangular-sectioned.

Personal ironwork is represented by a possible girdle hanger or key, in two fragments, from SFB 16 (Fig. 49, 10). As the fragments do not join, it is not possible to reconstruct the lower part of the object. There is a looped terminal for suspension at the upper end and the shank is rectangular-sectioned. In these respects it resembles an iron girdle hanger from West Stow (West 1985, 61, fig. 240, 1).

A steelyard fragment from SFB 69 (Fig. 49, 11) is closely comparable to Romano-British examples, especially a ?4th-century AD item from Icklingham, Suffolk (Manning 1985, 107, pl. 52, p. 42). Part of a rather fragile suspension hook is *in situ*. As with the latch lifter, it is unclear whether this is an Anglo-Saxon form of an object which changed little typologically since the Romano-British period, or whether it is a residual Romano-British object. It is not inconceivable that an iron object such as this could remain in use for up to 300 years or so, although the delicacy of some of its constituent parts might argue against this.

Several objects are unidentified. A square-sectioned bar object from SFB 205 (Fig. 49, 12) has one end flattened and turned through 90° and is broken at both ends. A tapering square-sectioned fragment is also part of an object of unknown function (Obj. No. 2025 from SFB 186, not illustrated).

Modern and undated features

Six iron objects were recovered from later and undated features. A large iron object (Fig. 49, 9), probably a nail, came from surface spread 241. However it is very similar in size and general proportions to the Saxon chisel 2005 (Fig. 49, 3), apart from the more splayed blade edge on the chisel and the shape of the heads, and it may therefore represent a similar object. Object 2006 is undoubtedly a nail, given the presence of the mineral-preserved wood on both sides of the shank.

A round, flat-headed nail with a square-sectioned shank was retrieved from post-medieval ditch 192, whilst a possible nail shank fragment came from pit 426. Two modern pits, 362 and 475, rather satisfyingly contained typologically modern objects — a screw in the former and a wire timber nail in the latter, whilst modern pit 475 produced two conjoining fragments of a featureless and undiagnostic iron sheet.

Metalworking debris

A single piece of metalworking slag was recovered from SFB 397. It is a lump of iron smithing slag weighing 700 grams, and represents a complete hearth-bottom which formed in the base of a smithing hearth. No hammer-scale was present in the soil sample taken from SFB 397 and this would suggest that the smithing did not take place in the immediate vicinity. Given the occurrence of residual Roman finds in Saxon features on the site, it is possible that the piece of slag was also residual.

Discussion

The range of artefacts from the Saxon features, although small, is what might be expected from a domestic assemblage and is generally comparable to the range of material excavated from the early Saxon Halls and SFBs at West Stow and a variety of late Saxon features at Thetford.

It is possible that a few of the objects may be residual or reused Romano-British pieces, namely the ?side link from the bridle bit, the latch lifter and the steelyard. This recycling of earlier material by the Anglo-Saxons is well attested on other sites, both settlement and cemetery, and the material at Hurst Park may have come from a 1st–2nd-century Romano-British settlement which, it is suggested, lay immediately to the south of the excavated area.

List of illustrated objects (Fig. 49)

Copper alloy

1. Four fragments of curving, oval to circular-sectioned undecorated copper alloy object, possible bracelet. Largest fragment appears to increase slightly in diameter, although this may be deformation by burning and corrosion. Diameter 62–68 mm; length of largest fragment 44 mm. Obj. No. 2017, cremation burial 261.
2. ?Side link from bridle bit. Cast copper alloy. Terminals set in opposite planes, both broken. One terminal circular, 'D' shaped section, undecorated. Shaft of link has bead and reel decoration. Other terminal broken and distorted, decorated with four ridges running around circumference. Length 75 mm. Obj. No. 2021, context 290, SFB 16.

Iron

3. Chisel, complete. Flat head burred over, shank square-sectioned; blade edge slightly splayed, becoming more rectangular near edge. Length 171 mm. Obj. No. 2005, context 126, pit 125.
4. Heckle tooth, circular-sectioned, complete. Length 127 mm. Obj. No. 2004, context 213, SFB 137.
5. Knife. Tang broken at only surviving rivet hole; 'T' headed rivet *in situ*. Tang parallel-sided and set central to blade, which has distinct sharpening curve and is broken at tip. Traces of unidentified organic material recorded around rivet. Length 127 mm. Obj. No. 2026, context 265, SFB 262.
6. Whittle tang knife. Tang broken and set central to blade. Tang of similar width to that on knife 2026, but tapers slightly, more likely to be a whittle tang. Blade complete, distinct sharpening curve. Length 108 mm. Obj. No. 2027, context 265, SFB 262.
7. Latch lifter. Almost complete. Strongly curved rectangular–square-sectioned blade, broken at tip, flattened handle, loop formed at end of handle. Length 180 mm. Obj. No. 2003 A, context 17, SFB 16.
8. Perforated strap object. One end broken, other curves to point. Perforated by single hole, apparently punched through as hole is *c.* 4 mm diameter on one side and *c.* 1.5 mm on other, with conical profile. ?Strap hinge fragment, probably originally looped. Length 53 mm. Obj. No. 2019, context 257, SFB 16.
9. Large ?nail; round, slightly domed head, square-sectioned shank, 9 x 9 mm. Shank tapers to thin rectangular-sectioned edge. Traces on both sides of mineral-preserved wood on bottom 67 mm of nail, grain running in same direction, slightly obliquely across shank. Indicates nail was partly driven into wood. Nail bent. Length (unbent) 168 mm. Obj. No. 2006, context 241, surface spread.
10. Incomplete girdle hanger or key; two non-joining fragments. Rectangular-sectioned shank. Suspension terminal formed by looping over narrowed shank. Form of lower part of object uncertain as two fragments do not fit. Length of longer fragment, 87 mm. Obj. No. 2022, context 290, SFB 16.
11. Steelyard fragment; sub-square sectioned beam, rounded stop at end. Flattened head; pierced lug for suspension hook, fragment of which *in situ*. Broken pierced lug at end from which load hung. Upper lug missing. Length 257 mm. Obj. No. 2002, context 71, SFB 69.
12. Bar object, sub-square-sectioned, broken at one end, flattened and turned through 90° at other end, also broken. Function unknown. Length 151 mm. Obj. No. 2068, context 206, dryer 205.

Worked Flint, by R. Montague

A total of 130 pieces of worked flint was recovered during the excavations at Hurst Park. In addition, a total of 34 flints, four of which are described as 'burnt lumps' and may not be worked, were recovered during the two stages of evaluation work by Cotswold Archaeological Trust (Cotswold Archaeological Trust 1994a and 1994b). These have not been studied for this report. However, some reference is made to these finds, based on the conclusions reached in the evaluation reports, in the general discussion below.

The source of the flint used on the site is likely to be the local river gravels. From some of the cores it can be seen that the raw material was small rounded nodules, and where present, both on cores and on flakes, the cortex is thin, rolled, and abraded.

The flints vary in condition, from unpatinated through to a heavy grey–blue patina and some are stained. The majority of the flints exhibit edge damage, varying from small nicks, to heavier crushing and snaps. Several of the flints are rolled, suggesting transport in water for some time, though given the location of the site this is perhaps not too surprising.

There appeared to be little difference between material from the Early Bronze Age and the Late Bronze Age features; both contained flake cores which showed little platform preparation (and the absence of core rejuvenation flakes of any kind from the site confirms this). Similarly, many of the flakes are thick and squat, with wide platforms and exhibiting hard hammer percussion. No diagnostic tool types are present. A Late Mesolithic microlith recovered in the evaluation may simply represent a stray loss during hunting. The few recorded blades are essentially undiagnostic but maybe Neolithic or earlier.

Only five flints (3.9% of the total assemblage) were recovered from Late Neolithic features. A total of 28 flints was retrieved from the Early Bronze Age ring-ditch, forming 21.5% of the total assemblage. These include six of the nine cores recovered during the excavation of which all are flake cores. A small scraper, fashioned from a primary flake, also came from the ring-ditch. Generally though, as discussed above, there is little to distinguish this collection from the flints from the Later Bronze Age features. Two flints (1.5%) came from Middle Bronze Age features, and 68 (52.3%) of the flints were recovered from Late Bronze Age features. All flints from Saxon and later features (18, 13.9%) may safely be considered redeposited. A total of nine flints

(6.9%) was retrieved from undated features or subsoil layers.

Burnt Flint, by M. Laidlaw

A total weight of 34,188 g of burnt, unworked flint was recovered during the excavation and the presence of further burnt flint in certain features was noted without collection. This material type is intrinsically undatable but is frequently found in association with prehistoric artefacts. This is certainly the case for at least some of the burnt flint from Hurst Park. The largest quantities of burnt flint (84%), however, were recovered from otherwise undated pits and post-holes, a proportion which would have been much higher if the total quantities of burnt flint observed on site had been collected.

The distribution of features containing the largest quantities of burnt flint shows a striking concentration within the western half of the site, clustered around the Late Bronze Age structures 1 and 2 (Fig. 57). These features are therefore assumed to be of similar date and one (pit 196) produced a single sherd of Late Bronze Age pottery. This distribution is in marked contrast to the distribution of querns and perforated clay tablets (*see* below). The implication is that the two concentrations represent two contrasting and, therefore, spatially separated activities.

Also recovered was 553 g of burnt, unworked stone (greensand), similarly undatable and associated in every case with burnt flint. Half of this material came from Late Bronze Age features (pit 149, post-hole 28, and ditch 378), the remaining fragments deriving from the undated pits and post-holes.

Worked Stone, by M. Laidlaw, with geological identifications by A. Murray

Fourteen quern fragments, two whetstones, and three other miscellaneous objects were recovered.

Querns

Of the 14 quern fragments, six came from Late Bronze Age features, two from the Romano-British corn drier, five from Saxon SFBs, and one from a post-medieval ditch. The majority are of greensand: five of the quern fragments from Late Bronze Age features, two from Saxon SFBs (186 and 397), and one from post-medieval ditch 192. This is a commonly exploited stone type for the area and occurs in a broad arc to the north of the Wessex chalklands and further afield to the Isle of Wight, the Weald of Sussex and Kent. The best known source is the Lodsworth quarries in West Sussex, exploited during the Iron Age and Romano-British period (Peacock 1987). Other stone types identified include red sandstone (pit 540), coarse quartzite (corn drier 3, SFB 205), and quartz grit (SFB 16), all of which have a possible origin in Devon, Wales, or the Welsh borderland.

Three of the fragments from Late Bronze Age features are derived from saddle querns with worn, polished, and slightly concave surfaces. Two other fragments from Late Bronze Age features are likely to be of the same form; the remaining pieces have no diagnostic features. All six of the Late Bronze Age querns came from features which show a marked concentration in the eastern half of the site around structure 1, in four instances coinciding with occurrences of perforated clay tablets, in direct contrast to the distribution of burnt flint (Fig. 57).

Two rotary quern fragments, possibly from the same stone, in a coarse quartzite, were recovered from Romano-British corn drier 3. Both fragments have worn surfaces and quern 2001 has one polished and one slightly grooved surface with a recess around the outer edge.

Two further rotary quernstone fragments, from the Saxon SFB 205 and SFB 16 respectively, have worn surfaces and radial grooves, more characteristic of Romano-British quernstones, as described, for example, at *Verulamium* (St Albans, Hertfordshire, Frere 1984, 80–1). Also recovered was one fragment of quartzite, of unknown form, from the Saxon 'drier' 205.

Whetstones

One definite (Fig. 50, 2) and one possible whetstone were found in SFBs 186 and 69 respectively. These objects are not datable on morphological grounds alone but, given the context, a Saxon date seems likely. The object from SFB 186 is in a red sandstone with a possible south-west England/Welsh origin.

Miscellaneous objects

One unusual object came from pit 325 (an undated feature, but considered most likely to have been Late Bronze Age) in the area of structure 2 (Fig. 50, 1). This is a flattish, sub-rectangular piece of soft, very fine-grained pumice stone of volcanic origin and has a number of worn grooves of varying profiles on the flat faces, with regularly worn, semi-circular hollows at one end and 'waisting', probably through use-wear, on at least two other edges. The object is broken and its original form is unknown. Too soft to function adequately as a whetstone, this object could have been used for polishing or smoothing finished copper alloy objects after casting. One projection has been formed by rotary, abrasive action, and appears to have been used as a reamer, perhaps for removing the casting sprues and seams from narrow-mouthed castings. The stone type has a possible source in Devon or in north Wales (Stuart Needham has kindly commented on this object and drawn our attention to a similar object from Burderop Down, Wiltshire (Gingell 1992, 111 and fig. 80.2)).

In addition, one disc-shaped pebble, with a small chip removed from the centre which may be a bead rough cut or gaming counter, was recovered from SFB 397, and one flattish fragment of oolitic limestone, possibly with some architectural function, came from the otherwise undated but possibly Saxon ditch 459. The presence of a piece of oolitic limestone on the site, from a possible source in the West Country, is interesting, given the occurrence within the Saxon pottery assemblage of one vessel in an oolitic-tempered fabric (below),

List of illustrated objects (Fig. 50)

1. Object of unknown function, possibly for polishing finished metal objects; grooved and worn on both flat faces and

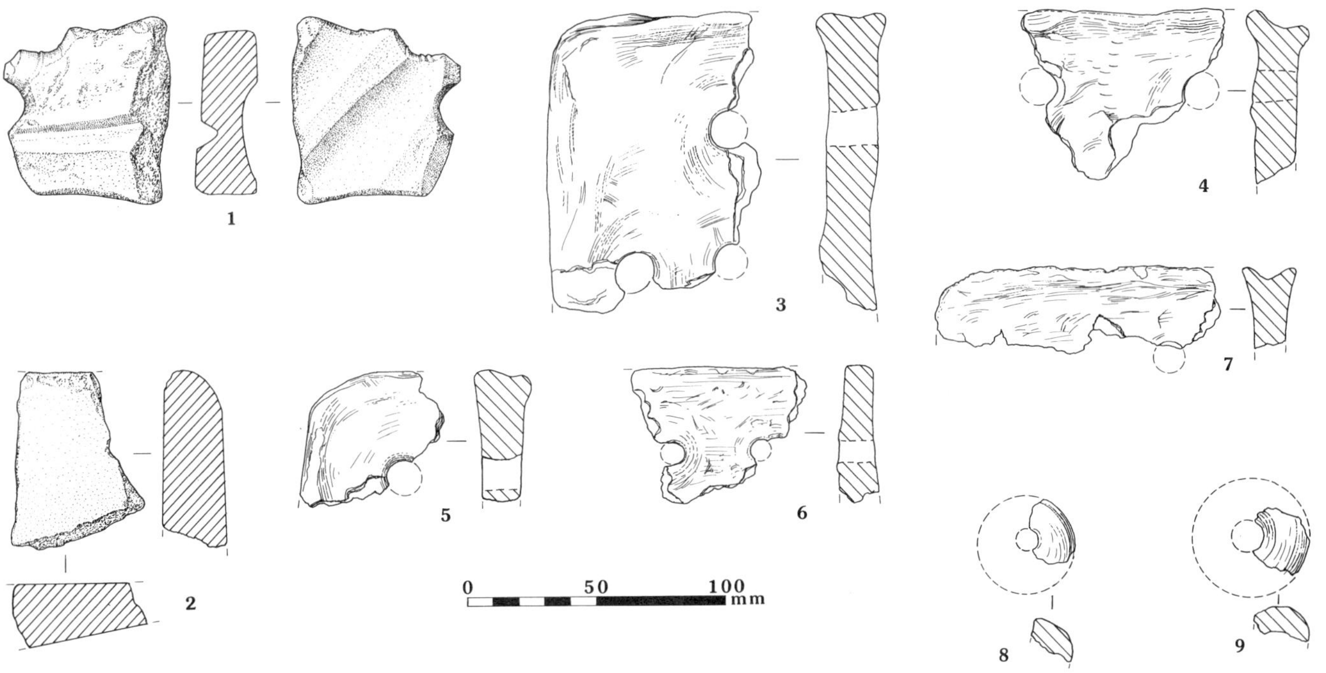

Figure 50 Worked stone and fired clay objects

around edges; soft, fine-grained pumice. Obj. No. 2031, context 326, pit 325.

2. Whetstone, two smooth surfaces, one possible outer edge, in fine-grained red sandstone. Obj. No. 2063. SFB 186.

Pottery, by M. Laidlaw

The pottery assemblage from Hurst Park consists of 1812 sherds (23, 635 g), plus one complete Collared Urn. The majority of the pottery is attributed to the Late Bronze Age period; smaller quantities of earlier prehistoric, Romano-British, Saxon, and post-medieval pottery were also recovered.

Methods

The assemblage was analysed using the standard Wessex Archaeology pottery recording system (Morris 1992). With the exception of the small quantities of Romano-British and post-medieval pottery, the assemblage was divided into fabric types on the basis of the range and coarseness of macroscopic inclusions, using a hand lens (x10 magnification) and a binocular microscope (x20 magnification). These fabric types fall into three broad fabric groups on the basis of the dominant inclusion type: flint-tempered (Group F), grog-tempered (Group G), and sandy (Group Q). An alpha-numeric fabric code has been allocated to each type. Note that these fabric codes are unique to this site, and do not correlate with similarly-coded fabric types from other sites in this volume. Pottery totals by fabric type are listed by chronological period in Table 9.

The pottery was quantified using both number and weight of sherds, by fabric type within each context. A type series was constructed for all diagnostic rim sherds, although in general, the rims were too small to be related to specific vessel forms. Also recorded were details such as surface treatments, decoration, and manufacturing technique. Full records exist in archive.

Terms describing the frequency of the inclusions in the following fabric descriptions and throughout this report are defined as follows: rare (1–3%); sparse (3–10%); moderate (10–20%); common (20–25%); very common (30%); abundant (40–50%). Other percentages throughout are calculated by weight unless otherwise stated. The pottery is discussed by chronological period below.

Late Neolithic

A small quantity of pottery (10 sherds) has been attributed to the Late Neolithic period on the basis of a combination of fabric type and decoration. All the sherds are small and abraded. Two fabric types were identified, one coarsely flint-tempered and one grog-tempered.

F1 Soft, fine-textured matrix; sparse, poorly-sorted, sub-angular flint <4 mm; sparse, rounded quartz grains — <0.25 mm; unoxidised core and internal surface, external surface sometimes oxidised.

G1 Soft, fine matrix; moderate, sub-rounded grog <2 mm; sparse, rounded quartz <0.25 mm; rare, very fine mica; soapy feel; unoxidised core, oxidised surfaces.

The seven flint-tempered sherds (fabric F1) comprise two with twisted cord decoration typical of Mortlake or Ebbsfleet ware (Fig. 51, 2); one with decoration consisting of probable bird bone impressions, possibly Mortlake ware (Fig. 51, 3), and four plain body sherds, ascribed to this period on the basis of similarity of fabric type.

The three joining sherds in fabric G1 have decoration characteristic of the Grooved Ware tradition (Fig. 51, 1). The decoration on these three sherds is interesting, apparently combining elements of more than one Grooved Ware sub-style. The motifs include incised grooves, impressions and a crudely-executed 'knot'. While the impressed motifs are characteristic of the Clacton sub-style, the 'knot', acting as a 'stop' between roughly

Table 9 Pottery fabric totals

Fabric	*No. sherds*	*Weight (g)*	*% of phase*	*% of total*
Late Neolithic				
F1	7	21	–	–
G1	3	22	–	–
Total	10	43	–	0.2
Early Bronze Age				
G2	1	2	–	–
G3	15	370	–	–
G4	1	3	–	–
G5	1	12	–	–
Total	18	387	–	1.6
Middle Bronze Age				
F10	5	496	–	2.1
Late Bronze Age				
F2	147	7652	53.6	–
F3	497	4162	29.1	–
F4	74	394	2.7	–
F6	73	711	5.0	–
F7	25	203	1.4	–
F8	66	335	2.4	–
F9	78	469	3.3	–
Q1	35	351	2.5	–
Total	995	14277	–	60.5
Romano-British				
Greywares	16	191	–	–
Grog-tempered	93	401	–	–
Oxidised sandy	77	357	–	–
Colour-coated	8	67	–	–
Total	194	1016	–	4.3
Saxon				
C400	4	244	3.3	–
Q401	61	438	6.0	–
Q402	213	2915	40.0	–
Q403	26	457	6.2	–
Q404	73	786	10.7	–
Q405	171	2023	27.7	–
Q406	3	31	0.4	–
V401	19	287	3.9	–
V400	7	131	1.8	–
Total	577	7312	–	30.9
Post-Medieval				
	13	104	–	0.4
OVERALL TOTAL	1812	23635	–	–

converging grooves, is more reminiscent of the Woodlands sub-style, where grooved 'knots' occur between converging cordons. This example appears to be a crude imitation of the latter technique, a phenomenon which has also been observed amongst the Grooved Ware pottery from Hunstanton, Norfolk (Cleal 1993, 50–1 and fig. 42).

The Mortlake/Ebbsfleet and Mortlake ware sherds derived from pit 278 also contained the plain body sherd. The three Grooved Ware sherds came from ?treehole 74, within ring-ditch 23.

Later Neolithic pottery is not a particularly common find within Surrey and most of the findspots have so far been within the northern part of the county (Field and Cotton 1987, fig. 4.14). Mortlake ware has been found at Kingston (Serjeantson *et al.* 1992). Grooved Ware is particularly scarce in the area and all finds so far have come from the Thames, although a large group of sherds, all of the Durrington Walls sub-style, is known from Harmondsworth in Middlesex (Field and Cotton 1987, 89; *see* also Chapter 2). The sherds from Hurst Park, therefore, despite the very small quantity involved, are a significant addition to the known distribution.

Early Bronze Age

In addition to the complete Collared Urn, a small proportion of the pottery assemblage (18 sherds) can be dated to the Early Bronze Age period. Five fabrics are identified, all grog-tempered. As well as the complete vessel in fabric G6, this includes base sherds in fabric G3 belonging to one vessel and small body sherds in the fabrics G2, G4, and G5.

G2 Soft, fine matrix; sparse, sub-rounded grog <2 mm; rare, sub-angular flint <1 mm; sparse, rounded quartz <0.25 mm; sparse, very fine mica; unoxidised core, oxidised surfaces.

G3 Hard fabric; moderate sub-rounded grog <7 mm; moderate rounded quartz grains <0.25 mm; irregularly fired, generally unoxidised core, oxidised external surfaces.

G4 Fine, soapy fabric; moderate sub-rounded grog <3 mm; sparse rounded quartz grains <0.25 mm; sparse very fine mica; irregularly fired, oxidised external surface.

G5 Fine, soapy fabric; moderate sub-rounded grog <2 mm; sparse rounded quartz grains <0.25 mm; sparse very fine mica; oxidised core and external surface, internal surface unoxidised.

G6 Soft, moderately fine, poorly-wedged matrix; moderate, poorly-sorted, sub-angular grog <3 mm; rare sub-rounded

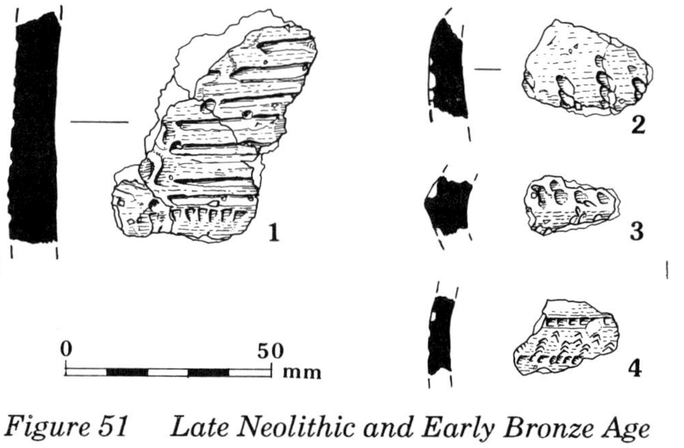

Figure 51 Late Neolithic and Early Bronze Age pottery

quartz <0.5 mm; rare, sub-angular, patinated flint <4 mm; soapy feel; oxidised.

The single sherd of fabric G2 has comb-impressed decoration (Fig. 51, 4) and almost certainly derives from a Beaker vessel; this sherd was found redeposited in the Late Bronze Age ditch 489.

The Collared Urn (fabric G6), although apparently complete, is very fragmentary and, therefore, the overall form cannot be identified. The surviving rim sherds indicate a simple rim form with a straight sided collar and a peaked collar base (Fig. 52, 1). The bold, horizontal, twisted cord decoration which is confined to the collar is a decorative trait characteristic of the South Eastern Style within the Secondary Series as identified by Longworth (1984, 35), and the decoration and collar form would also place the vessel within Burgess's 'Late' style (1986).

This vessel, containing a cremation burial and three faience beads, was recovered from pit 120 within the central area defined by ring-ditch 23 at the eastern end of the site.

The remaining sherds in this group are less diagnostic and have been tentatively assigned to this chronological period on the basis of fabric alone, although it should be noted that grog-tempered fabrics also occur in the Late Neolithic period. All were derived from features in or around ring-ditch 23 (*see* Fig. 30). Fifteen sherds from pit 93 represent the base of a single vessel, containing a cremation, situated just outside the ring-ditch. These are plain base and body sherds, but the funerary association of this vessel and its similarity in fabric to the complete Collared Urn, is sufficient to identify this vessel as a second Collared Urn of unknown form. There is also one fingernail impressed body sherd in fabric G5 from pit 34. None of these sherds were associated with later material and are assumed to be *in situ*, but one further plain body sherd came from the fill of the ring-ditch itself, in the same context as two Late Bronze Age sherds.

The funerary associations of both the complete Collared Urn (cremation burial 120) and the second, partial Collared Urn (cremation burial 93) are demonstrated, and the other potential vessels of this type may have a similar association, although an alternative domestic origin cannot be discounted.

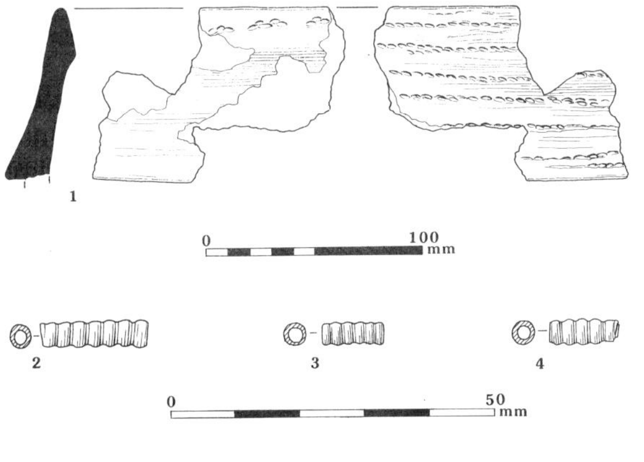

Figure 52 Collared Urn and faience beads (from cremation burial 120)

Middle Bronze Age

One partial vessel, in the coarse flint-tempered fabric F10, was attributed to the Middle Bronze Age on the basis of vessel form.

F10 Hard, coarse fabric; common moderately well-sorted, sub-angular flint <3 mm; moderate rounded quartz grains <0.5 mm; thick walled; unoxidised core, oxidised external surfaces.

Only five sherds survive, two of which have an applied, finger impressed cordon. All sherds apparently represent a single, thick-walled vessel, probably bucket-shaped, of Deverel-Rimbury type, comparable, for example, to urns from the nearby site at Ashford Common, Sunbury (Barrett 1973) and a vessel from Kingston (Serjeantson *et al.* 1992, fig. 10f). The urn was found in pit 258 towards the west side of the excavated area (*see* Fig. 35). As for the Collared Urns, a funerary association is not certain; no human remains were recovered with this vessel, although later disturbance and redeposition of a funerary vessel is a possibility.

Late Bronze Age

A total of eight fabric types, ranging from very coarse to moderately fine, have been identified as Late Bronze Age. These comprise seven flint-tempered fabrics and one sandy fabric. The term 'flint-tempered' is used advisedly here; all seven fabrics contain flint which appears to have been deliberately added to the clay matrix, generally in a calcined, crushed form, as a tempering agent, rather than occurring naturally within the clay. All eight fabrics may be described as 'coarsewares', using Barrett's classification (1980).

Fabrics

F2 Hard, fine fabric; common, moderately well-sorted, sub-angular flint <2 mm; sparse, rounded quartz grains <1 mm; irregularly fired, generally unoxidised core and oxidised external surface.

F3 Moderately fine fabric; moderate, well-sorted, sub-angular, calcined flint <2 mm; sparse, rounded quartz grains <0.25 mm; sparse, very fine mica; unoxidised core and internal surface, oxidised external surface.

F4 Hard, fine fabric; moderate, poorly-sorted, sub-angular calcined flint <3 mm; sparse, rounded quartz grains—<0.25 mm; sparse, very fine mica; unoxidised core and internal surface, oxidised external surface.

F6 Hard, moderately coarse fabric; common, poorly-sorted, sub-angular calcined flint <2 mm; moderate rounded quartz grains <0.25 mm; sparse, very fine mica; unoxidised core and internal surface, irregularly fired external surface.

F7 Hard fabric with soapy feel; sparse, well-sorted, sub-angular flint <2 mm; sparse, rounded quartz grains <0.25 mm; unoxidised core, irregularly fired surfaces.

F8 Hard, coarse textured-fabric; common, moderately-sorted, sub-angular calcined flint <2 mm; moderate rounded quartz grains <0.5 mm; unoxidised core and internal surface, oxidised external surface.

F9 Hard sandy fabric; moderate, poorly-sorted, sub-angular flint <2 mm; moderate iron ore <4 mm; sparse rounded quartz grains <0.25 mm; unoxidised core, oxidised external surface.

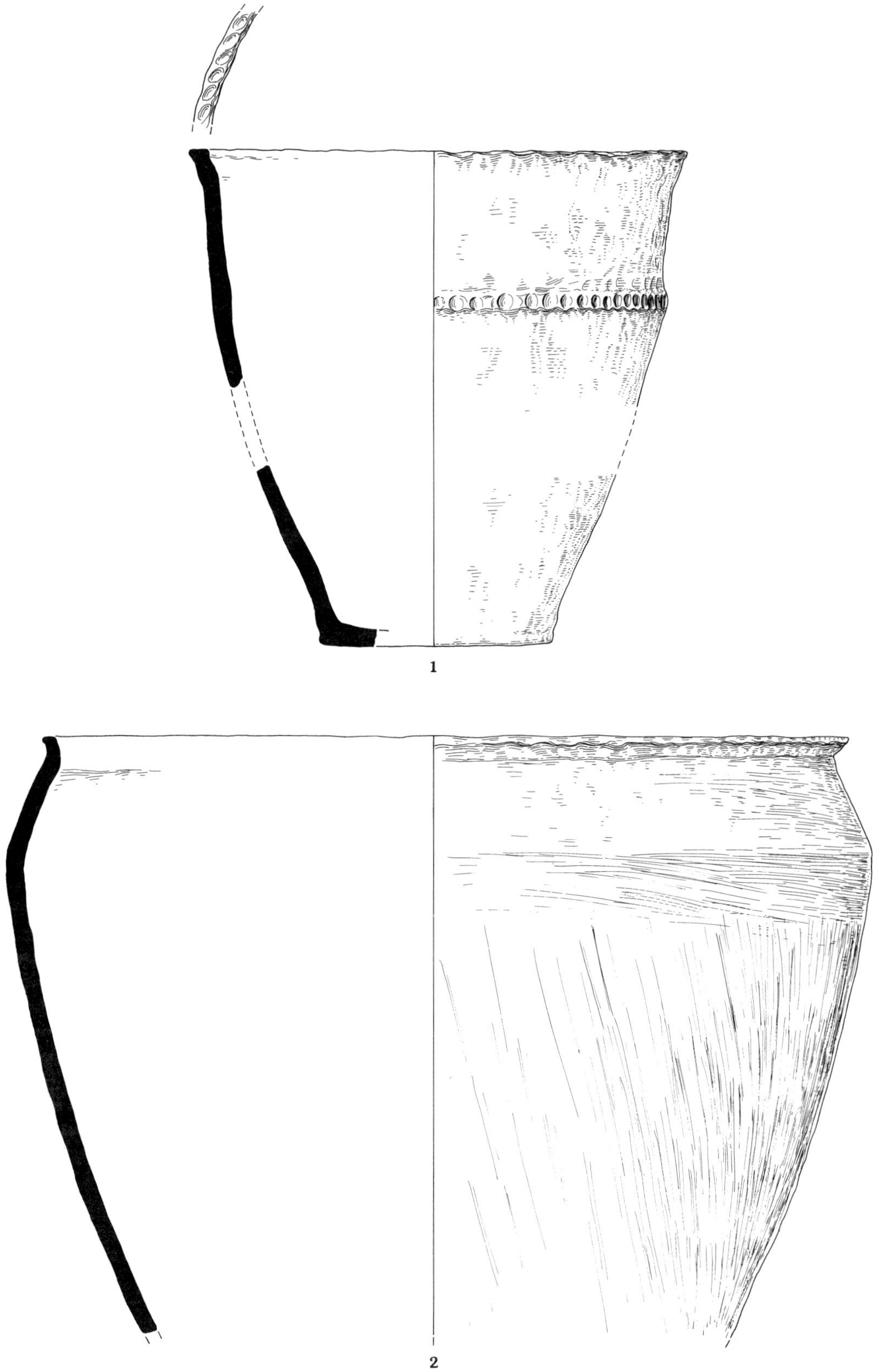

Figure 53 Late Bronze Age pottery

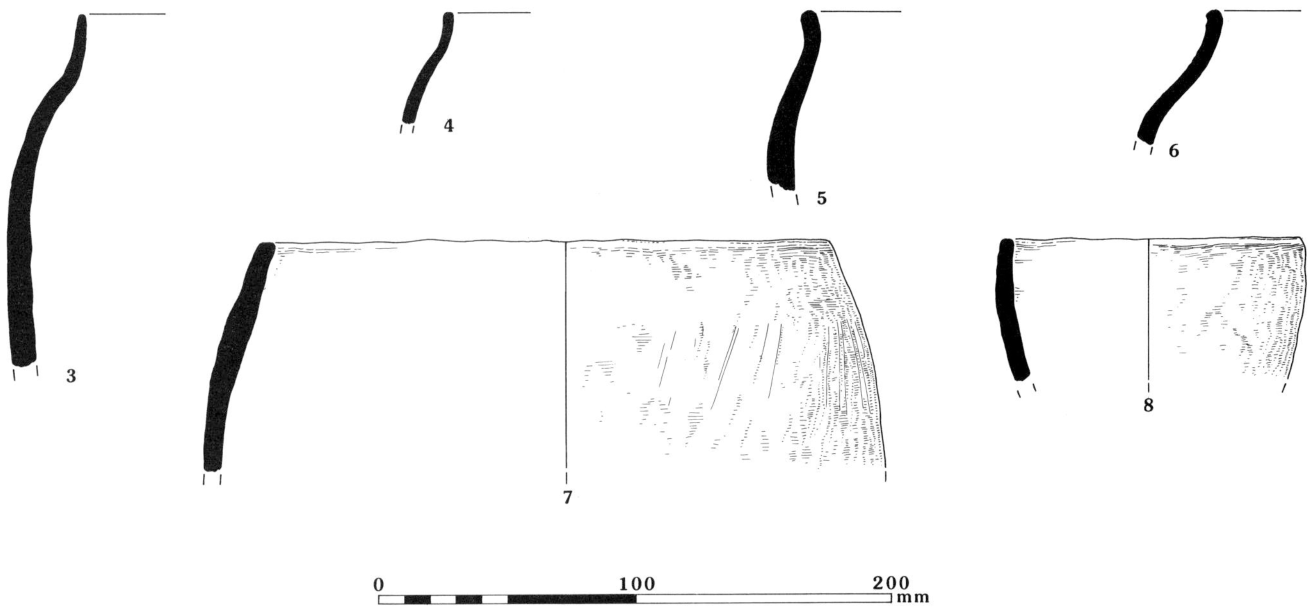

Figure 54 Late Bronze Age pottery

Q1 Hard, moderately coarse fabric; moderate rounded quartz grains <0.5 mm; sparse, poorly-sorted, sub-angular calcined flint <4 mm; sparse, very fine mica; unoxidised core and internal surface, irregularly fired external surface.

Distinctions between the flint-tempered fabrics were not always discrete, as several fabrics covered a wide range of variation. This is only to be expected within an assemblage for which a largely *ad hoc* domestic production is postulated using locally available resources (*see* below). The majority of the sherds occurred in the coarse fabrics F2 and F3 (*see* Table 9). This, however, included three almost complete vessels, two in fabric F2 and the third in fabric F3. The remaining sherds are divided fairly evenly amongst the other fabrics.

There is nothing to suggest anything other than purely local production for any of these fabrics, although slight variations in the clay matrices (eg the obtrusive iron particles in fabric F9 and the varying presence of mica) might suggest the exploitation of more than one clay source. All tempering materials would have been easily accessible. None of the fabrics show evidence of much effort expended in the preparation of the clay and tempering materials, although it may be noted that the crushed flint in fabrics F6 and F8 are moderately well sorted.

Table 10 Late Bronze Age pottery: vessel forms by fabric type (no. of vessels)

	F2	*F3*	*F4*	*F5*	*F6*	*F7*	*Total*
Jars							
Type 1	–	1	–	–	–	–	1
Type 2	1	1	–	–	–	–	2
Type 3	1	4	–	1	2	5	13
Type 4	–	3	1	–	–	–	4
Bowls							
Type 5	–	–	–	1	–	–	1
TOTAL	2	9	1	2	2	5	21

Similarities in the range of fabric types present may be noted with the Late Bronze Age assemblage from Prospect Park (Laidlaw and Mepham, this volume), although the latter site does have a 'fineware' component which is not represented here. No attempt, however, has been made here to correlate the fabric types from the two sites directly.

Forms

The sherds are mainly small, often abraded, and reconstructable profiles are lacking, with very few diagnostic sherds present, apart from the three partial vessels noted above. Only 32 other rim sherds were recovered, 14 of which were too small to attribute to specific forms. The remaining 18 rims were assigned to vessel Types 2–5, described below. The correlation of vessel forms to fabrics is given in Table 10.

Type 1: Large, bucket-shaped jar (Class I), finger-impressed rim and shoulder (Fig. 53, 1).
Type 2: Bipartite jar (Class I), small everted rim (Fig. 53, 2).
Type 3: Slack-shouldered jar (Class I), plain, slightly everted rim (Fig. 54, 3–6).
Type 4: Large, convex jar or bowl (Class I/III), plain, inturned rim (Fig. 54, 7)
Type 5: Convex bowl (Class III), plain rim (Fig. 54, 8).

Three almost complete vessels were recovered, two in the same deposit. These two vessels comprise one large, bucket-shaped jar (Type 1) with a finger-impressed rim and shoulder (Fig. 53, 1), in fabric F3, and a thinner-walled, bipartite jar (Type 2) with a small, everted rim (Fig. 53, 2), crudely wiped on the exterior, in fabric F2. These two jars appeared to have been deliberately deposited in pit 239 (*see* below). The third vessel came from pit 320 (a Late Bronze Age feature): a slack-

Table 11 Late Bronze Age pottery: decoration and surface treatment by fabric type (no. of sherds)

	F3	F4	F6	F8	Total
Surface treatment					
Wiped	29	–	7	3	39
Burnished	5	1	–	7	13
Decoration					
Impressed	2	–	–	–	2
TOTAL	36	1	7	10	54

shouldered jar (Type 3) with a plain upright rim (Fig. 54, 3) in fabric F2. Other vessels were much more fragmentary.

As far as can be ascertained, all the vessel forms identified can be assigned, using Barrett's classification (1980), as either Class I jars or Class III bowls; these forms represent the coarseware elements within assemblages of the later Bronze Age, occurring in coarser fabrics and showing little evidence of labour investment in the form of vessel forming or surface treatment. Class I jars form the major proportion of domestic assemblages, while Class III bowls are generally outnumbered by their finer counterparts (Class IV bowls). There is no evidence at Hurst Park, however, for the presence of anything which could be interpreted as a 'fineware' component.

Surface treatment and decoration
Evidence for surface treatment is very scarce, consisting of 39 sherds in coarse flint-tempered fabrics which have been crudely wiped on the exterior, including 25 sherds from one vessel in the flint-tempered fabric F3 and a further 13 sherds in both coarse and slightly finer flint-tempered fabrics, particularly fabric F8, which have been burnished (*see* Table 11).

Decoration is even scarcer, restricted to finger impressions on the rim and applied cordon of one of the almost complete vessels (Fig. 53, 1) and impressed decoration on one other jar rim.

Chronology and affinities
The emphasis on coarseware attributes such as coarse, flint-tempered fabrics in heavy-duty jar and bowl forms, together with the lack of decoration and surface treatment and the relative scarcity of sandy fabrics, places this assemblage fairly firmly within the earlier, 'plainware' tradition of the later Bronze Age post-Deverel-Rimbury ceramic tradition, which Barrett dates in the lower Thames to between the 11th and 9th centuries BC (1980). There are now a number of such plainware assemblages known from the middle and lower Thames valley, from both north and south of the river (*see* Barrett 1980, fig. 1; Needham 1987, fig. 5.13), including Prospect Park, Harmondsworth (Laidlaw and Mepham, this volume), and most notably the large assemblage at Runnymede Bridge (Longley 1980, 1991), which provide a good framework within which to date the Hurst Park assemblage.

Comparable forms have been identified within other Late Bronze Age assemblages in the area such as Carshalton (Adkins and Needham 1985) and Weston Wood, Albury, area 2 (Russell 1989), two similar plainware assemblages with an emphasis on coarse, flint-tempered fabrics, although both sites also produced a small proportion of sherds in finer sandy fabrics. The Carshalton assemblage is dated to the 10th–8th century BC and Weston Wood to the 10th–9th century BC, both on the basis of ceramic style. A plainware assemblage from Kingston Hill, nearly all flint-tempered, may be more or less contemporaneous but is unusual in being heavily biased towards small 'tableware' vessels (Field and Needham 1986), although this is thought to be more likely to be due to the circumstances of survival.

It seems likely that the Hurst Park assemblage can be placed towards the earlier part of the post-Deverel-Rimbury sequence, contemporary with, or slightly earlier than, the sites mentioned above, perhaps as early as the 11th–10th centuries BC. For example, the assemblage from Prospect Park, published here, is dated to the 10th–9th centuries BC on the basis of the fineware component (Laidlaw and Mepham, this volume). Support for this date range comes from Runnymede Bridge, where the Late Bronze Age occupation has been radiocarbon dated to the 9th–8th centuries BC (Needham 1991, 352–3). The ceramic assemblage from Runnymede contains a significant proportion of fineware bowls and a relatively high level of decoration (about 10% at the beginning of the sequence), which would certainly place it later in the ceramic sequence than Hurst Park (Longley 1991).

Distribution
Late Bronze Age sherds were recovered from various features, particularly those concentrated towards the eastern part of the site around structure 1 in Area B (Fig. 35). This concentration included pit 239 (*see* Fig. 39), which contained what appeared to be a deliberate deposit of two vessels: part of a large, bucket-shaped jar (Fig. 53, 1), which had been carefully placed on top of sherds of a smaller, bipartite jar (Fig. 53, 2). The lower vessel certainly appeared to have been broken *in situ*, the component sherds all in place but flattened out across the base of the feature. This vessel was more or less complete, while the upper vessel had been truncated and was more fragmentary and it is uncertain whether it was deposited as a complete vessel or as already broken sherds. The latter interpretation would seem more likely, as joining sherds from the same vessel were found in pit 128, *c.* 15 m to the south-west. Pit 320 containing another partial vessel, a large jar (Fig. 54, 3), came from the opposite end of the site. Such deposits might be considered to have some kind of funerary interpretation, yet no human remains were associated with either of these examples. Other sizeable collections of sherds came from pits 128, 149, 342, and 347, and slot 489.

Features in the western half of the site, in Area B around structures 2 and 3, produced much less pottery. It may be noted that, with the exception of pit 320, and one pit (196) which produced a single sherd, the only features producing pottery in this area appear to be within, or directly associated with, the structures themselves (post-holes 311, 336, 338, 351, 365, 367, and 369, and gully 378; *see* Fig. 36); the features around the structures, frequently containing large quantities of burnt flint, were markedly devoid of pottery.

Romano-British

Four vessels containing cremated human remains were recovered from cremation pits 243, 261, 289, and 317 respectively, which form a cluster in the south-western corner of the site (*see* Fig. 41). One further vessel came from cremation pit 391, whether as a cinerary container or grave good is uncertain, and a group of sherds, which appear to represent a single vessel, came from the ?redeposited cremation burial 408. Two of the vessels are small, handmade, everted rim jars, one from cremation pit 243 in a grog-tempered fabric (Fig. 55, 1) and one from cremation pit 391 in a fine sandy fabric (Fig. 55, 2). The vessel from cremation burial 408, in a grog-tempered fabric, appears to be of similar form, although only one rim sherd survives. The two sherds from cremation pit 317, in a coarse sandy fabric, are both rim sherds, apparently from a heavier-duty jar. Only plain body sherds in a similar grog-tempered fabric survive from cremation pits 261 and 289.

These vessels could be either latest pre-Romano-British, Iron Age, or early Romano-British; a date range in the 1st or early 2nd century AD is likely. Four of the vessels show evidence of having been subjected to overfiring or burning in the form of variable leaching of the fabric and patchy refiring (reducing) of the surfaces (cremation burials 243, 317, 391, and 408).

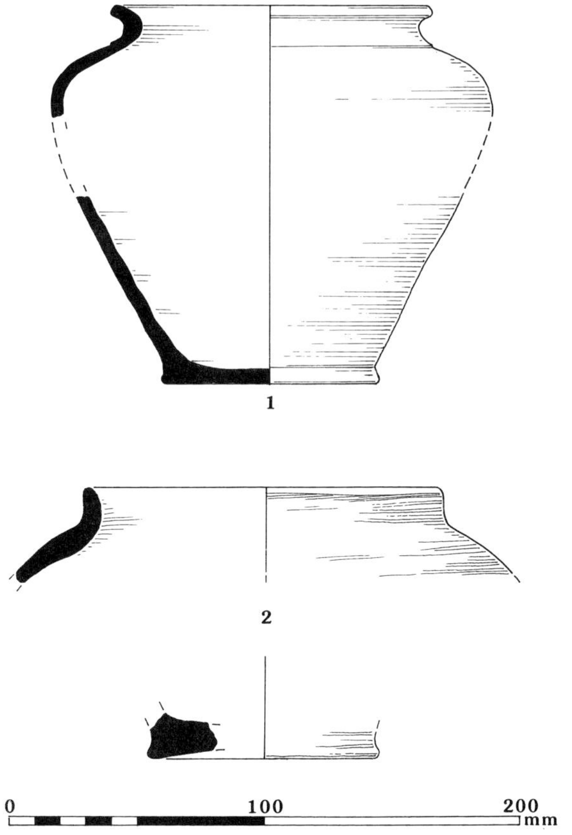

Figure 55 Romano-British pottery

The two rim sherds from cremation pit 317, in particular, are quite badly warped. This may have resulted from these vessels being placed on or close to the pyre during firing and the variation in the traces of burning would be consistent with the wide range of variability in temperatures operating within the pyre (as at Westhampnett, Chichester Bypass: McKinley forthcoming b). The sherds from cremation burial 408 may represent pyre debris rather than a cinerary container, since this cremation seems to have been redeposited (*see* below). The other two vessels, from cremation burials 261 and 289, show no signs of burning (but note the presence of burnt metal objects in cremation burial 261 — *see* above).

In addition, a small quantity of Romano-British pottery (33 sherds) was present within the ceramic assemblage, which has been divided into broad fabric groups, comprising coarse greywares, grog-tempered fabrics, oxidised sandy fabrics, and fine colour-coated wares, the latter mainly from the Oxfordshire production area. The only identifiable vessel forms are one greyware everted rim jar and two grog-tempered cordoned jars, all 1st or 2nd-century AD forms. These three vessels derived from corn drier 3, in the south-eastern corner of the site. The remaining sherds were all redeposited in Saxon contexts and this included all the diagnostically late Roman pottery, comprising the Oxfordshire colour-coated wares. This may be no coincidence, as the deliberate collection of Romano-British pottery, particularly oxidised finewares, has been noted previously in Saxon contexts (Plouviez 1985).

Early Saxon

Almost a third of the total ceramic assemblage by weight can be dated to the Saxon period and is generally in a good condition, including large unabraded sherds. Nine fabric types were identified, comprising one calcareous, two organic-tempered and six sandy fabrics.

Limestone-tempered fabrics

C400 Soft fabric; abundant, fairly well-sorted fragments of oolitic limestone <1 mm; common, well-sorted, rounded quartz grains <0.5 mm; rare pebble <10 mm; unoxidised core and surfaces.

Sandy fabrics

Q401 Hard, fine fabric; moderate, well-sorted, rounded quartz grains <0.5 mm; sparse, very fine mica; unoxidised core and surfaces.

Q402 Hard, fine fabric; moderate, poorly-sorted, rounded quartz grains <1 mm; sparse black iron ore <1 mm; sparse very fine mica; sparse irregular voids <0.5 mm; rare organic material <2 mm; unoxidised core and surfaces.

Q403 Hard, fine fabric; common, poorly-sorted, sub-rounded/sub-angular quartzite <1 mm; sparse, very fine mica; unoxidised core, oxidised surfaces.

Q404 Hard fabric; common, poorly-sorted, rounded quartz grains <2 mm; sparse, very fine mica; unoxidised core and internal surface, oxidised surfaces.

Q405 Hard fabric; common, well-sorted, rounded quartz grains <1 mm; sparse, very fine mica; unoxidised core and surfaces.

Q406 Sparse, rounded quartz <0.25 mm; sparse, sub-angular flint <1 mm; rare iron ore; rare fine mica; unoxidised, oxidised margins.

Organic-tempered fabrics

V401 Hard fabric; moderate, poorly-sorted, rounded quartz grains <0.5 mm; moderate organic temper; sparse, very fine mica; unoxidised core and surfaces.

V402 Hard fabric; common, well-sorted, rounded quartz grains <0.25 mm; common organic temper; unoxidised core and internal surface, oxidised external surface.

The fabric types are predominantly sandy and micaceous but the quartz inclusions varied in the degree of coarseness from fine to very coarse and in abundance from sparse to common. Distinctions between the fabric types were sometimes rather arbitrary, particularly the division between moderately fine and coarse fabrics such as Q402 and Q405, to which the majority of sherds were in fact assigned (*see* Table 9). Only a small proportion of sherds were tempered with the distinctive coarse vegetable matter generally considered to be characteristic of the early to middle Saxon period (fabrics V401 and V402).

This relatively homogeneous group of fabrics, lacking clear-cut divisions, would be expected from an assemblage deriving essentially from localised, domestic production and there is little evidence from Hurst Park to indicate that this was not the case here. The use of bonfire or clamp kilns is reflected in the inconsistent and irregular firing of the fabrics. The normal mode of production for early and middle Saxon domestic pottery in the south of England would appear to be a household level of manufacture (eg Timby 1988, 110), in which many individuals were making vessels for their own use. It is interesting to compare this range of fabrics with those from Prospect Park (Laidlaw and Mepham, this volume), which show a much wider diversity and a correspondingly more complex picture of production and distribution. Of the fabric types described here, only the organic-tempered fabrics are closely paralleled at Prospect Park.

Most of the fabrics could have been locally produced, particularly the vegetable-tempered fabrics although, as for the Late Bronze Age fabrics, variations in the composition of the clay matrices are apparent, suggesting that different clay sources were exploited. Perhaps most notable is the rather obtrusive mica in fabrics Q403, Q404, and Q405; this is not apparent in any of the prehistoric fabrics but this need not rule out a local source.

There is, however, at least one indication of possible non-local production. Fabric C400 contains oolitic limestone, the nearest source for which is in the West Country. The four sherds in this fabric may only represent a single vessel but, nonetheless, their occurrence so far from their potential source area is significant and it may be worth noting here the presence on the site, in the undated but possible Saxon ditch 459, of a piece of oolitic limestone possibly of architectural origin (*see* above).

One other suggestion of non-local production comes in the form of a single sherd from a decorated, very highly-burnished carinated bowl in fabric Q401 (Fig. 56, 20), which stands out as being particularly well-made and well-finished, although the fabric type is matched elsewhere on the site in less well-finished vessel forms. This vessel might represent a second, more specialised mode of production, operating alongside household manufacture, where a few specialists served a local area.

Vessel forms

Diagnostic vessel forms were scarce, even though a substantial quantity of rim sherds were recovered. In total, 49 rim sherds were identified but there were no complete profiles and a number of these sherds represented less than 5% of the total rim diameter. It was, therefore, difficult in many cases to assign rim forms to particular vessel forms. Forty rims were therefore used to create a type series which was linked, as far as possible, to vessel forms. Ten rim/vessel forms were defined and the correlation to fabric type is given in Table 12.

It was felt appropriate to use the term 'vessel' throughout the description of Types 1–8, rather than attempt to define 'jars' and 'bowls', since the distinction between 'closed' and 'open' forms cannot always be made. Moreover, the functional interpretation implied by the terms 'jar' and 'bowl' may be meaningless within an unstandardised assemblage such as this, where many vessels are likely to have been multi-functional.

Type 1: Shouldered vessels, upright or everted plain rims (Fig. 56: 1–2).

Type 2: Globular vessels, upright or slightly everted plain or thickened rims (Fig. 56: 3–8).

Type 3: Globular vessels, long necks and upright or slightly inturned plain rims (Fig. 56: 9, 10).

Type 4: Slack-shouldered vessels, upright or slightly inturned rims (Fig. 56: 11).

Type 5: Slack-shouldered vessels, upright and externally thickened and flattened rims (Fig. 56: 12–15).

Type 6: Slack-shouldered vessels, 'baggy' profiles, everted rims (Fig. 56: 16, 17).

Table 12 Saxon pottery: vessel form by fabric type (no. of vessels)

Vessel form	*Q401*	*Q402*	*Q404*	*Q405*	*V401*	*Total*
Type 1	1	2	1	6	1	11
Type 2	1	–	1	6	–	8
Type 3	–	–	–	2	–	2
Type 4	–	–	–	1	–	1
Type 5	1	1	1	3	1	7
Type 6	–	–	–	2	–	2
Type 7	–	–	–	1	–	1
Type 8	1	–	1	–	–	2
Type 9	3	1	–	1	–	5
Type 10	–	–	–	–	1	1
TOTAL	7	4	4	22	3	40

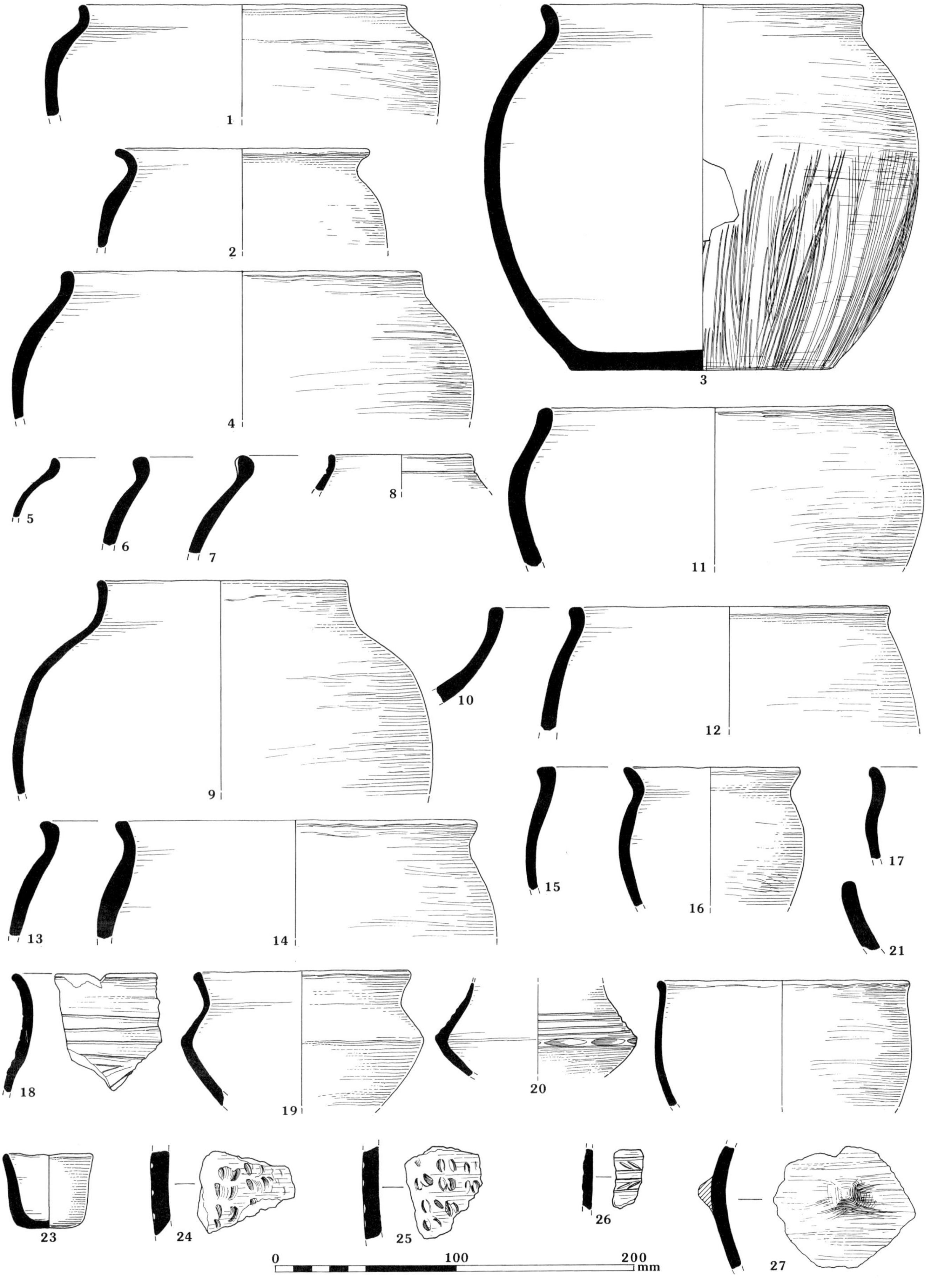

Figure 56 Early Saxon pottery

Type 7: Necked vessels, rounded profiles, everted rims (Fig. 56: 18).
Type 8: Sharply biconical vessels, plain everted or upright rims (Fig. 56: 19, 20).
Type 9: Bowls with straight or convex sides, plain or beaded rims (Fig. 56: 21, 22).
Type 10: Small thumb pot (Fig. 56: 23).

The paucity of complete profiles means that overall vessel shape is difficult to assess. There are definite examples of biconical (Type 8) and globular forms (Types 2 and 3) and there are obvious open forms with 'baggy' profiles (Type 6). Other forms are likely to fill a wide spectrum of variation between these. There is an obvious lack of standardisation, either in shape or in size, and what is apparent is that this represents a range of vessels of which the overwhelming majority are of purely domestic, utilitarian type, a fact which is underlined by the concentration of these vessels on the site in the sunken-featured buildings. A small proportion of vessels which show a higher degree of finishing and/or the presence of decoration (*see* below) might fulfil a more specialised function, but still within the overall domestic assemblage; there is no evidence of non-domestic activities on the site (eg burials).

Decoration and surface treatment
Many of the sherds are burnished, often externally and internally, and these tend to occur in the finer fabrics Q401 and Q405 (*see* Table 13). Other fabrics are occasionally crudely wiped (eg Fig. 56, 1).

Decoration, which is also restricted to the finer fabrics, comprises 20 sherds, including examples of vertical combing (Fig. 56, 3), finger 'pinching' (Fig. 56, 24–25), one slashed cordon (Fig. 56, 26), and one pinched boss (Fig. 56, 27).

Distribution
The Saxon pottery is largely derived from the sunken-featured buildings, particularly 16, 397, and 186; these three features contained almost three-quarters (by weight) of the whole Saxon assemblage. A further substantial group (62 sherds) was recovered from the large pit 125. With the exception of single sherds from pit 340 and ditch 449 respectively, all the remaining pottery derived from sunken-featured buildings.

Chronology and affinities
Given the lack of fine decorated vessels and the conservative nature of simple vessel forms present, the Saxon pottery appears to constitute a standard domestic assemblage with functional considerations paramount. This assemblage has proved difficult to date because of the general lack of well-dated comparable assemblages and the undiagnostic nature of the vessel forms, nor are the fabric types chronologically significant. Organic-tempered fabrics were in use from at least the 5th century until the 8th century and possibly beyond; there is evidence for their use at Wraysbury in Berkshire, for example, well into the late Saxon period (Astill and Lobb 1989). The sandy wares are even less distinctive and were equally long-lived.

The dating of vessel forms cannot be considered to be reliable, given the purely domestic, unstandardised nature of the assemblage. Myres' typology (1977, 8) offers conflicting evidence; sharply biconical and globular forms are among his 'early' groups (5th and early 6th century) — Types 2, 3, and 8 fall within this range of forms — while the wide-mouthed forms (Type 9) are considered to be later: 6th or 7th century. A later date, in the 6th or 7th century, would seem most likely, given the settlement morphology. The almost complete absence of non-local fabric types, in contrast with the assemblage from Prospect Park, Harmondsworth (Laidlaw and Mepham, this volume), which is dated to the 5th or 6th century, may also be noted.

List of illustrated vessels
Fig. 51: Late Neolithic and Early Bronze Age

1. Grooved Ware, 3 conjoining sherds, parallel incised lines, impressions and 'knot'. Fabric G1. Context 66, ?treehole 74.
2. ?Mortlake or Ebbsfleet ware; body sherds, twisted cord decoration. Fabric F1. Context 279, pit 278.
3. ?Mortlake ware body sherd, impressed decoration. Unoxidised. Fabric F1. Context 297, pit 278.
4. ?Beaker body sherd, impressed decoration. Unoxidised. Fabric G2. Context 490, slot 489.

Table 13 Saxon pottery: decoration and surface treatment by fabric type (no. of sherds)

	Q401	*Q402*	*Q404*	*Q405*	*V401*	*Total*
SURFACE TREATMENT						
Burnished	12	4	4	11	1	32
DECORATION						
Vertical combing	4	11	3	2	–	20
Incised lines	–	–	–	1	–	1
Finger-pinching	–	2	3	–	–	5
Finger impression	–	–	1	–	–	1
Slashed cordon	1	–	–	–	–	1
Pinched boss	–	–	–	1	–	1
Corrugated shoulder	1	–	–	–	–	1
TOTAL	18	17	11	15	1	62

Fig. 52: Collared Urn grave group
1. Collared Urn; simple rim form, straight sided collar, horizontal impressed twisted cord decoration; plain body. Fabric G6. Cremation pit 120.
2–4. Three faience beads. Cremation pit 120.

Fig. 53: Late Bronze Age
1. Bucket-shaped jar, finger impressed rim and cordon (Type 1), slight cord impressions below rim. Fabric F3. Obj. No. 2015. Context 129/240; pits 128/239.
2. Thin-walled, shouldered jar, small everted rim; crudely wiped vertically on exterior (Type 2). Fabric F2. Obj. No. 2016. Context 240, pit 239.

Fig. 54
3. Slack-shouldered jar, plain rim (Type 3). Fabric F2. Context 321; cremation pit 320.
4. Slack-shouldered jar, plain rim (Type 3). Fabric F7. Context 11, ditch 10.
5. Slack-shouldered jar, plain rim (Type 3). Fabric F6. Context 431, pit 430.
6. Slack-shouldered jar, plain rim (Type 3). Fabric F3. Context 390, pit 389.
7. Convex jar or bowl, plain inturned rim (Type 4). Fabric F3. Context 129, pit 128.
8. Convex bowl, plain inturned rim (Type 5). Fabric F5. Context 366, pit 365.

Fig. 55: Romano-British Cremation Vessels
1. Small cordoned jar; grog-tempered. Obj. No. 2012; cremation burial 243.
2. Small everted rim jar; sandy fabric. Obj. No. 2036; cremation burial 391.

Fig. 56: Early Saxon
1. Shouldered vessel (Type 1), plain upright rim. Burnished externally on the neck and crudely wiped horizontally below shoulder. Fabric V401. Context 17, SFB 16.
2. Shouldered vessel (Type 1), everted rim. Fabric Q405. Context 213, SFB 137.
3. Rounded vessel (Type 2), slightly everted rim. Vertical scoring on lower part of body. Fabric Q405. Context 398, SFB 397.
4. Rounded vessel (Type 2), plain upright rim. Traces of burnishing externally. Fabric Q405. Context 364 and 357, SFB 69.
5. Small, rounded vessel (Type 2), upright, internally thickened rim. Traces of burnishing externally. Fabric Q405. Context 187, SFB 186.
6. Rounded vessel (Type 2), short everted rim. Fabric Q405. Context 222, SFB 186.
7. Rounded vessel (Form 2), short everted rim. Fabric Q405. Context 266, SFB 262.
8. Small rounded vessel (Type 2), upright rim, horizontal groove around neck. Fabric Q402. Context 511, SFB 397.
9. Necked, globular vessel (Type 3), upright rim. Possibly burnished externally. Fabric Q405. Context 17, SFB 16.
10. Necked, globular vessel (Type 3), upright rim. Fabric Q405. Context 272, SFB 16.
11. Biconical vessel (Type 4), plain upright rim. Burnished over rim. Fabric Q405. Context 291, SFB 16.
12. Slack-shouldered vessel (Type 5), short, plain upright rim. Traces of burnishing externally. Fabric Q402. Context 17, SFB 16.
13. Slack-shouldered vessel (Type 5), everted, internally expanded rim. Fabric Q405. Context 222, SFB 186.
14. Slack-shouldered vessel (Type 5), thickened shoulder and everted rim. Burnished inside and out. Fabric V401. Context 290, SFB 16.
15. Slack shouldered vessel (Type 5), thickened, flattened rim. Possibly burnished externally. Fabric Q405. Context 264, SFB 262.
16. Small, slack-shouldered vessel (Type 6), everted rim. Fabric Q405. Context 398, SFB 397.
17. Slack-shouldered vessel (Type 6), slightly everted rim. Burnished internally. Fabric Q405. Context 511, SFB 397.
18. Necked, rounded vessel (Type 7), everted rim; horizontal incised lines around neck. Burnished inside and out. Fabric Q405. Context 127, pit 125.
19. Sharply biconical vessel (Type 8), flaring rim. Fabric Q404. Context 272, SFB 16.
20. Sharply biconical vessel (Type 8), horizontally furrowed on shoulder, impressed on carination; burnished internally, very highly-burnished externally. Fabric Q401. Context 290, SFB 16.
21. Convex bowl (Type 9), plain rim. Fabric Q402. Context 511, SFB 397.
22. Convex bowl (Type 9), slightly thickened rim; burnished inside and out. Fabric Q401. Context 272, SFB 16.
23. Small, pinched thumb pot (Type 10). Fabric V401. Context 511, SFB 397.
24. Body sherd, finger-pinched decoration. Fabric Q404. Context 17, SFB 16.
25. Body sherd, finger-pinched decoration. Fabric Q404. Context 17, SFB 16.
26. Small body sherd, slashed-cordon decoration; well-burnished. Fabric Q401. Context 398, SFB 397.
27. Body sherd, pinched boss; crudely burnished externally. Fabric Q405. Context 127, pit 125.

Faience Beads, by M. Laidlaw

Three faience beads were found within the fill of the Collared Urn containing the Early Bronze Age cremation burial 120 (Fig. 52, 2–4). The beads are all of segmented form and range in length from 12–22 mm. All are pierced with a single central perforation, diameters ranging from 2–3 mm. The colouring of all three is mid-turquoise, but all have been burnt along one side, resulting in each case in a leaching of colour from that part of the bead.

Grave goods, particularly trinkets of exotic materials such as faience, are not commonly found either within or associated with Collared Urns. Longworth (1984, 73) lists 12 examples of Collared Urn/faience bead associations, of which nine include segmented forms. The burning on the Hurst Park beads indicates that the three were strung together, perhaps on a necklace or bracelet, and burnt with the body.

List of illustrated beads (Fig. 52)
2. Segmented faience bead, burnt along one side. Obj. No. 2065. Context 119. Cremation burial 120.
3. Segmented faience bead, burnt along one side. Obj. No. 2066. Context 119. Cremation burial 120.
4. Segmented faience bead, burnt along one side. Obj. No. 2067. Context 119. Cremation burial 120.

Ceramic Building Material, by M. Laidlaw

A total of 56 fragments of ceramic building material (2463 g) was recovered during the excavation, the majority of which comprised post-medieval or modern tile and brick fragments. These fragments were quantified by context but no further analysis was undertaken and the material was discarded.

Six tile fragments (292 g), however, were attributed to the Romano-British period on morphological grounds, including fragments of one *tegula* and one *imbrex*. These fragments were found in SFBs 16, 186, and 262, along with a few sherds of Romano-British pottery (*see* above), and again are likely to represent deliberate collection. The presence of ceramic building material provides some evidence that substantial buildings may have lain in the vicinity of the site in the Romano-British period.

Fired Clay, by M. Laidlaw

Overall, a total of 136 fragments (277 g) of fired clay was recovered. This can be divided into two categories: featureless fragments and recognisable objects. The featureless fragments make up about half of the fired clay assemblage (71 fragments weighing 1105 g). These fragments are all undiagnostic with only a small number of irregular surfaces visible. The latter suggest that some fragments were structural in origin, either from pit or hearth linings, or from wattle and daub structures, although no definite wattle impressions were observed apart from on two joining fragments from corndrier 3. The featureless fragments were found dispersed in small quantities in features of prehistoric, Roman, and Saxon date; no concentrations were noted.

The recognisable objects comprise fragments from two spindle whorls and a quantity of perforated 'tablets'. The perforated clay 'tablets' (Fig. 50, 3–7) are flat, sub-rectangular, possibly with one rounded end, and have multiple circular pre-firing perforations. A number of fragments have particularly regular dimensions: circular perforations which measure 10 mm or 15 mm in diameter and a slab thickness of 11–15 mm and 20 mm respectively. With the exception of one distinctive organic-tempered 'tablet' (Fig. 50, 6 and 7), the remainder are all in coarsely flint-tempered fabrics which range in the frequency of flint inclusions from moderate (10–15%) to abundant (40%). A number of surfaces have been roughly smoothed, with finger and fingernail impressions also evident, and many outer edge fragments are grooved.

These objects were recovered from Late Bronze Age features with concentrations in pits 149, 342, and 347, ditch 489, and cut 200. The remaining fragments were dispersed in small quantities within other Late Bronze Age pits. With very few exceptions, these features show a marked concentration around structure 1 in the western half of the site, coinciding in several instances with occurrences of quern fragments, and contrasting with the distribution of burnt flint around structures 2 and 3 (*see* Fig. 57); the implication is that the two spatially distinct distributions of tablets and burnt flint have some functional significance, representing two different activities or processes.

Perforated clay tablets have been accepted as characteristic of Late Bronze Age sites in the Thames Valley; for example at the Kingston Hill settlement (Field and Needham 1986, fig. 5), Runnymede (Longley 1980, fig. 17), and Carshalton (Adkins and Needham 1985, figs 12 and 13). Their function, however, remains obscure, although various suggestions have been made, such as a use in salt-making, pottery manufacture, or cooking. In this instance, an interpretation involving pottery manufacture or any other industrial process seems unlikely, since none of the tablets show signs of having been subjected to the high temperatures which these processes would involve. Salt-making seems equally unlikely in this context and it seems more probable that they were used in cooking, perhaps as parts of baking ovens.

The two spindle whorls (Fig. 50, 8 and 9), both recovered from SFB 397, are of similar biconical form. One is in a fine, micaceous sandy fabric and the second in an organic-tempered fabric. Although these objects are not datable on morphology alone, their context would indicate a Saxon date and it may be noted that spindle whorls and other artefacts associated with spinning and weaving are common finds in sunken-featured buildings of this date (eg West 1985).

List of illustrated objects (Fig. 50)

3. Perforated clay tablet corner fragment; one roughly smoothed surface, grooved along one outer edge, three perforations. Oxidised, flint-gritted fabric. Obj. No. 2008, context 161, pit 149.
4. Perforated clay tablet fragment; one roughly smoothed surface, grooved along one outer edge, two perforations. Oxidised, flint-gritted fabric. Obj. No. 2009, context 161, pit 149.
5. Perforated clay tablet corner fragment; one roughly smoothed surface, grooved along one outer edge, one perforation. Oxidised, flint-gritted fabric. Obj. No. 2011, context 161, pit 149.
6. Perforated clay tablet edge fragment; one roughly smoothed surface, three perforations. Oxidised, organic-tempered fabric. Obj. No. 2047, context 343, pit 342.
7. Perforated clay tablet edge fragment; 'grooved' edge; one roughly smoothed surface; organic-tempered fabric. Obj. No. 2047, context 343, pit 342.
8. Biconical spindle whorl fragment, 25% survives, one surface missing. Fine sandy, micaceous fabric, unoxidised, outer surface polished. Obj. No. 2041, context 419, SFB 397.
9. Biconical spindle whorl fragment, 25% survives. Fine sandy, micaceous grass-tempered fabric. Obj. No. 2043, context 511, SFB 397.

5. Environmental Evidence

Cremated Human Bone, by Jacqueline I. McKinley.

Introduction

Bone from 14 contexts was received for examination, comprising two Early Bronze Age and seven

Romano-British burials, one redeposited and four unphased miscellaneous contexts. Details of recovery methods and osteological procedure followed are described in Chapter 3 of Prospect Park.

Results

A summary of the results is presented in Table 14, with the exception of the miscellaneous contexts which proved either non human or not to be cremation-related. Weights of bone from all contexts containing bone are presented in the archive. All weights are given in grams (g) to one decimal place. All measurements are given in millimetres (mm). Unless stated as otherwise, all bone, human and animal, is cremated/burnt.

Disturbance and condition of bone

With the exception of the central burial within ring-ditch 23 (120), all the cremation-related contexts were cropped to some extent. Additional disturbance had subsequently occurred to all contexts as a result of the racecourse passing directly over the cemeteries, which had only a shallow depth of soil as protection.

Most of the bone appeared in fairly good condition. Bone from two of the most disturbed, adjacent urned burials (243 and 261), was worn and had a chalky texture, that from one unurned burial (284) was worn. One unurned burial (235) appeared unworn, as did other fairly disturbed burials. The lack of consistency suggests localised variations in the degree of soil acidity, or may indicate different episodes of disturbance.

Demography

Demographic comment is limited both by the small size of the cemeteries and by the high level of disturbance affecting the quantity and quality of information it was possible to retrieve from the bone.

Three individuals were identified from the two Early Bronze Age burials, the central primary burial being dual. Seven individuals, all adult, were identified from the Romano-British burials. The cremated bone in context 408 represented redeposited material and may have originated from a burial or pyre debris. In view of the very shallow depth of some of the Romano-British burials, it is possible that further burials may have been totally obliterated.

Pyre technology and ritual

Efficiency of cremation

With a single exception, the bone was universally buff–white, indicative of full oxidation. One fragment of temporal vault in burial 391 was slightly blue, the variation being of little significance.

Collection

Since almost all the burials were disturbed to some extent and an unknown quantity of bone has probably been lost, little significance may be attributed to the weights of bone which will no longer represent the quantities originally present.

The one exception is the central Early Bronze Age burial 120, which included 2017.8 g of bone from two individuals, representing *c.* 62% of the expected bone weight from an adult cremation for each individual (McKinley 1993a). It has been noted elsewhere by the writer that consistently high bone weights are recorded from Bronze Age central barrow burials, both in comparison with other types of cremation burial of the same date and burials from other periods (McKinley forthcoming a). Other similar burials at Portsdown, Hampshire (Nicholls 1987) and Ashey Down, Isle of Wight (Drewett 1970), also show high weights of bone at 1190 g and 1077 g respectively (but note that the majority of these comparative figures are from single burials or multiples, including an adult and immature individual). As with other aspects of the cremation ritual, it may be that the time expended on collecting bone for burial in some way reflected the status of the deceased, in whatever terms that may have been calculated by the mourners.

The damage incurred by disturbance of many of the features will have affected the size of bone fragments (McKinley 1994b). The percentage of bone in the 10 mm fraction varied between 43–62% in the Bronze Age burials and 13–57% in the Romano-British, with an average of *c.* 44%. The size of the maximum fragment in each context ranged from 32–52 mm in the Bronze Age contexts and 11–56 mm in the Romano-British. There was no evidence which would indicate deliberate fragmentation of bone prior to burial.

Comment on the skeletal elements included in the burial is precluded by the severe truncation in most of the burials. In the central Bronze Age burial 120 there is no evidence to suggest that bone from a particular skeletal area was deliberately selected for burial.

Dual cremation / burial

The central Early Bronze Age burial 120 comprises two adults, a female and a probable male. Multiple cremation burials most commonly include a subadult or adult, of either sex, with an immature individual, although two adults together are not unknown. The list of multiple cremation burials presented by Petersen (1981) shows 68% to be of adults with immature individuals, 28% of two adults, and 4% of two immature individuals.

Various alternative interpretations of these multiple burials have been discussed in detail elsewhere by the writer (McKinley 1994a; McKinley forthcoming a), where it was concluded, that in most instances, the implication was that the individuals were cremated together on the same pyre. However, evidence for an alternative explanation in some cases is provided by both archaeology and literature. One of the Bronze Age urned burials from Twyford Down, Hampshire (Mckinley forthcoming a) had been emptied by the writer in 20 mm spits and analysis of the distribution of bone within the vessel suggested that the remains of the two adults identified were added as separate deposits, one above the other. The retention of bone from one cremation until the bone from a second can be included prior to burial is supported by a passage in Homer's *Odyssey*, in which the spirit of Agamemnon addresses that of Achilles '...In this [golden amphora] your white bones lie, my lord Achilles, and mingled with them the bones of Menoetius' son Patroclus, dead before you, and

Table 14 Cremated bone: summary results

Context	*Period*	*Type*	*Total wt*	*No. ind.*	*Age*	*Sex*	*Pathology/morphological variation*	*Animal*	*Pyre/grave good*
93	EBA	u	132.8	1	older mature adult	?	abscesses–maxilla	?	–
120	EBA	u	2017.8	2	1)older mature adult 2) adult	female & ?male	–	–	–
235	RB	un	133.9	1	older subadult/adult	?	hypercementosis	–	–
243	RB	u	28.7	1	adult	?	m.v. – ?metopic suture	–	–
261	RB	u	20.7	1	adult	?	–	p/s size	cu-alloy
284	RB	?un	191.9	1	older mature/older adult	??male	ddd– C; exo – femur shaft	–	–
289	RB	u	18.6	1	older subadult/adult	?	–	–	–
317	RB	u	240.1	1	mature/older adult	?	abscess – mandible; erosive lesion – vault; m.v. – ?retention deciduous molar	–	–
391	RB	?cb	264.8	1	older mature/older adult	?	o.a. – T	imm.	–
407	RB	r	6.4	–	adult	?	–	–	–

Key:

Period

RB Romano-British
EBA Early Bronze Age

Animal

imm. immature
p/s pig/sheep size

Type

u urned cremation burial
un unurned cremation burial
cb cremation burial; mode of deposition unknown
r redeposited

Pathological/morphological variation

C cervical
ddd degenerative disc disease
exo exostoses
m.v. morphological variation
o.a. osteoarthritis
T thoracic

separately those of Antilochus, who was your closest friend after Patroclus' death...' (1972 trans. Rieu; 24, 73–76).

Cremated animal bone
Fragments of cremated animal bone were recovered from two of the Romano-British burials (29%), with a further fragment from the Early Bronze Age satellite burial (93). Most of the material is unidentified, but several ribs, probably from a lamb or piglet, came from Romano-British burial 391. The presence of cremated animal bone in burials from both periods is not unusual, eg *c.* 48% of the Romano-British burials from St Stephen's cemetery, Verulamium (McKinley 1992) and 13.5% of burials from Baldock 15 (McKinley 1991 unpublished) contained cremated animal bone. Animal bone is also known from Bronze Age burials, for example from the Middle Bronze Age urned cremations at Prospect Park discussed above.

Pyre debris
Varying quantities of pyre debris, charcoal and/or burnt flint, was recovered in the backfills of both Early Bronze Age and three of the Romano-British graves. The presence of such debris suggests that the pyre sites were in the general vicinity of the burials. That no pyre sites were recovered is not surprising in view of the ephemeral nature of these features and the severe truncation suffered by the site. Experimental pyres conducted by Dr Alistair Marshall and the writer have shown that the effects of a pyre penetrate only *c.* 0.10 m below ground surface (Marshall and McKinley in prep.). Such a feature would be totally obliterated by the level of disturbance noted here.

Evidence for the location of pyre sites close to the place of burial has been noted elsewhere on both Bronze Age and Romano-British sites, for instance at Prospect Park discussed above.

Score-marks
A small fragment of skull vault (*c.* 7 mm) recovered from burial 243 has two parallel score-marks, *c.* 1 mm apart, across the length of the outer plate. The marks are not recent, and the possible cause is at present unknown.

Pathology
Minor pathological lesions were noted in one Early Bronze Age and four Romano-British burials, and morphological variations were noted in two Romano-British burials (summary in Table 14).

Burial 93 had dental abscesses in three right maxillary sockets (premolar and molar). Abscesses were also noted in the mandibular incisor sockets in burial 317. Other minor lesions and degenerative conditions were most probably the result of age-related wear-and-tear. The aetiology of the erosive lesions in an exocranial vault fragment from burial 317 is unclear. There was no indication of any new bone formation and the full extent of the lesion could not be ascertained.

Animal Bone, by Michael J. Allen

The faunal assemblage recovered from 14 contexts comprises only 117 small, weathered, and eroded bone fragments. The number of fragments is over-representative as many are possibly from the same bone. The majority are teeth fragments (cattle) and small fragments of long bone which testifies to the very poor preservation of the assemblage. Most (112 fragments) are from Saxon contexts and are predominantly cattle and large mammal, but some small mammal (presumably sheep/goat) is present. The only identified pig bone is from a post-medieval context.

The poor preservation of the assemblage with no measurable bones, and the fragmentary nature of the teeth precluding the measurement of wear patterns, does not allow any palaeo-environmental conclusions. All that can be said is that the material provides evidence that cattle and possibly sheep/goats were a component of the Saxon farming economy.

Charred Plant Remains, by Pat Hinton

Methods

Samples were processed as described for Prospect Park in Chapter 3.

Results

All samples include modern seeds and roots and most have few charred remains. Three samples, however, one from each of three periods contain more significant amounts of cereals and other plant seeds. Preservation is poor, mostly, and all samples include very small fragments of cereal grains which have been recorded simply in terms of volume. A few samples have lumps of shiny, tar-like material some of which look like parts of agglomerates of charred vegetable material. The results are presented in Table 15.

Early Bronze Age
The sample from the satellite cremation burial 93 produced only some indeterminate cereal fragments, a single grass seed, and some pieces of the amorphous charred material.

Late Bronze Age
Two of the three pit samples contained very few charred seeds but that from pit 149 (161), includes more. *Hordeum vulgare* (hulled barley) is the major cereal represented and, among the few wheats, are probably both *Triticum dicoccum* (emmer) and *Triticum spelta* (spelt). Most of the wild plants have only general requirements for disturbed lighter soils and were probably weeds of the crops. In addition, there are fragments equivalent to two basal internodes ('tubers') of *Arrhenatherum elatius* (onion couch). The 'tubers' have been associated with Bronze Age cremation burials, where the charred remains indicate fuel. It is possible

Table 15 Charred plant remains

		Early Bronze Age	*Late Bronze Age*			*Romano-British*		*Early Saxon*			
	Feature	Urn burial	Pits			Corn drier	Cremation	Pit	SFBs		
	Context no.	93	149	129	321	4	243	127	315	266	419
	Sample no.	1100	1004	1010	1112	1000	1104	1002	1012	1014	1015
	Sample vol. (litres)	10	12	13	10	7	10	10	11	10	10
CULTIVATED											
Hordeum vulgare L.	hulled barley	–	6(7)	–	2	>7	–	(1)	6	–	1
Triticum cf *dicoccum* Schubl	emmer wheat	–	1	–	–	–	–	–	2	–	–
Triticum dicoccum glume bases		–	1	–	–	–	–	–	2	–	–
Triticum cf *spelta*	spelt wheat	–	1	–	–	54	–	–	91	–	–
Triticum cf *spelta* glume bases		–	–	–	–	13	–	–	74	–	–
Triticum dicoccum / spelta glume bases		–	–	1	–	11	–	–	35	–	–
Triticum cf *aestivum* s.l.	bread wheat	–	–	–	–	5	–	2	4	–	–
Triticum spp.	undiff'd wheat	–	>7	–	3	>30	–	2	>50	–	–
Secale cereale L.	rye	–	–	–	–	–	–	1	(1)	–	–
Avena sp.	oats	–	–	–	–	–	–	2	(4)	–	–
Avena awn fragment		–	–	–	–	–	–	–	1	–	–
Cerealia indet.	unid'd cereals	1 ml	1 ml	1.5 ml	0.6 ml	2.3 ml	0.5 ml	0.7 ml	2.5 ml	0.25 ml	0.5 ml
ARABLE AND GRASSLAND						–	–	–	–	–	–
Chenopodium album l.	fat hen	–	1	–	–	2	–	–	–	–	–
*Chenopodium*sp.	goose foots	–	–	–	–	10	–	–	4	–	–
Atriplex prostrata / patula	orache	–	1	–	–	3	–	–	3(2)	–	–
Stellaria media / neglecta	chickweed	–	2	1	–	–	–	–	–	–	–
Spergula arvensis L.	corn spurrey	–	–	–	–	1	–	–	–	–	–
Persicaria lapathifolia (L.) Gray	pale persicaria	–	–	–	–	1	–	–	–	–	–
Polygonum aviculare s.l.		–	–	–	–	1	–	–	–	–	–
Fallopia convolvuulus (L.) Á. Löve	black bindweed	–	5	–	–	1	–	–	1	(1)	–
Rumex acetosella L.	sheep's sorrel	–	–	–	–	9	–	–	1	–	–
Rumex cf *acetosa* L.	common sorrel	–	–	–	–	2	–	–	9	–	–

Table 15 Continued

		Early Bronze Age	Late Bronze Age			Romano-British		Early Saxon			
	Feature	Urn burial	Pits			Corn drier	Cremation	Pit	SFBs		
	Context no.	93	149	129	321	4	243	127	315	266	419
	Sample no.	1100	1004	1010	1112	1000	1104	1002	1012	1014	1015
	Sample vol. (litres)	10	12	13	10	7	10	10	11	10	10
ARABLE AND GRASSLAND contd.											
Rumex cf *crispus*	curled dock	–	1	–	–	3	–	–	16	–	–
Rumex sp.	undiff'd docks	–	–	–	–	5	–	–	4	–	–
Viola sp.	violet/ pansy	–	–	–	–	–	–	–	1	–	–
Vicia cf *hirsuta* (L.) Gray	hairy tare	–	2	–	–	–	–	–		–	–
Vicia cf *tetrasperma* (L.) Schreber	smooth tare	–	–	–	–	–	–	–	3	–	–
Vicia / Lathyrus sp.	vetch/vetchling	–	>2	–	–	–	(1)	–	2	–	–
Trifolium cf *dubium* Sibth.	lesser trefoil	–	–	–	–	–	–	–	1	–	–
cf *Trifolium* sp.	trefoil/clover	–	3	–	–	–	–	–	1	–	–
Trifolium / Medicago sp.	clover/medick	–	–	–	–	–	16	–	–	–	–
Plantago media L.	hoary plantain	–	–	–	–	–	–	–	1	–	–
Prunella vulgaris L.	selfheal	–	–	–	–	1	–	–	–	–	–
Plantago lanceolata L.	ribwort plantain	–	–	–	–	1	–	–	–	–	–
Velerianella locusta (L.) Laterr	common cornsalad	–	–	–	–	–	–	–	1	–	–
Anthemis cotula L.	stinking mayweed	–	–	–	–	3	–	–	13	–	–
Tripleurospermum inodorum (L.) Schultz-Bip	scentless mayweed	–	–	–	–	5	–	–	12	–	–
Asteraceae indet.	daisy family	–	–	–	–	1	–	–	36	–	–
Poa annua L.	annual grass	–	–	–	–	1	–	–	–	–	–
Arrhenatherum elatius (L.) Beav. var *bulbosum*. 'tubers'	onion couch	–	2	–	–	–	–	–	–	–	–
Bromus cf *secalinus* L.	rye brome	–	–	–	–	>35	–	–	>180	–	–
Poaceae indet.	grass family	1	–	–	–	1	–	–	–	–	–
WOODLAND, WOOD MARGINS, CLEARINGS											
cf *Carpinus betulus* L. – nut shell fragment	hornbeam	–	–	–	–	–	–	–	1	–	–
Corylus avellana L. – nut shell fragment	hazel	–	–	–	21	–	–	–	1	–	–
Crataegus monogyna– inner fruit fragment	hawthorn	–	–	–	–	–	–	–	1	–	–

–Key: ( ) = identification uncertain

that this grass, whose dried stems persist for some time, may have been pulled up as tinder but perhaps in an attempt to remove an invasive weed. Robinson (1988) has described it as growing in neutral or calcareous grassland on which grazing is absent or irregular and these conditions might be met in field borders.

Romano-British

The sample from the corn drier, not surprisingly, includes more cereals, chaff, and seeds of probable crop weeds than any of the other samples. Spelt wheat is dominant but the presence of emmer cannot be ruled out as not all the chaff fragments can be safely differentiated. Also present are several grains which have a shorter, more rounded form and steeper radicle depression and are probably *Triticum aestivum* s.l. (a free-threshing bread wheat). These make up a lesser proportion, as does hulled barley. In this sample it is possible, from two slightly twisted grains, to recognise the presence of six-row barley.

Most of the crop weeds, as before, are common to the disturbed soil and open conditions of arable fields and *Spergula arvensis* (corn spurrey) and *Rumex acetosella* (sheep's sorrel) are indicators of acid, sandy soil. *Tripleurospermum inodorum* (scentless mayweed) is also characteristic of light soils, but the presence in the same sample of *Anthemis cotula* (stinking mayweed) and *Prunella vulgaris* (self-heal), typical of heavier damp clay soils, suggests that more than one soil type or area was being cultivated. *Bromus secalinus* (rye brome) forms a considerable proportion (35:51) of the non-cereal seeds. This grass is often closely associated with spelt and whether the seeds were tolerated, or the plant even actively encouraged, is uncertain.

The sample from cremation burial 243 includes only very few cereal fragments and seeds of small *Medicago* (medicks) and/or *Trifolium* species (clovers) and one possible *Vicia* or *Lathyrus* (vetch or vetchling). Poor preservation prevents closer identification. When dealing with a total of only 17 seeds, too much significance should perhaps not be given to this instance of exclusively Fabaceae (leguminous plants) and, if any sort of ritual meaning is discounted, then the seeds probably originated with the fuel. The medicks, clovers, and vetches are plants of open grassy places and, like onion couch in the Late Bronze Age sample, might have been included when dried grasses were gathered as tinder. Alternatively, these seeds may have been originally associated with the very few cereal remains. In other cases, with a high proportion of seeds of this family, it has been questioned whether, because of their nitrogen-fixing capability and consequent independence of other nutrients, they indicated soil impoverishment and were tolerated or even encouraged as a means of improving soil fertility (Monk 1991).

Early Saxon

There were only a few cereals from pit 125 (127) but these include oats and one grain of *Secale cereale* (rye) in addition to wheat and barley. Sample 1012 from the lowest fill of SFB 16 was more rewarding. Hulled barley is again present and spelt wheat is the dominant cereal but there are also small numbers of probable emmer, free-threshing wheat, and oats; rye is uncertainly identified. The emmer or spelt glume bases, in almost equal numbers to emmer or spelt grains (111:93), may mean grain stored in the ear or, with the weed seeds, a product of cereal processing. Rye brome, as before, accompanies the wheats, but in higher proportions. Interpretation of these figures can only be conjectural on account of the poor preservation and the undoubted loss of many seeds or elements of chaff.

A few spelt grains showed signs of germination. These were somewhat shrunken examples and, in two, the flat coleoptile (sprout) had emerged and reached approximately half way along the dorsal surface, lying in a shallow groove. Several other similar but shrivelled grains retained only a trace of the groove and there were two examples of detached sprouts. The presence of this groove indicates that germination began while the grains were still enclosed in their spikelets. Modern spelt spikelets exposed on wet paper showed that the sprouts, appressed to the grains by the glumes, reached this length in 48 hours. Naked grains began germinating much earlier and the sprout was more rounded and grew away from the grain at an angle. More evidence is necessary to say whether the Saxon grains sprouted because of accidental wetting or deliberate malting.

Although many of the crop weed seeds are non-specific in their requirements, indications of lighter soils are provided by the presence of sheep's sorrel and scentless mayweed. However, as in the sample from the Roman corn drier, stinking mayweed is also present in significant numbers, typical of heavier, damp clay conditions. The sample from SFB 16 also has a considerable number of seeds listed only as Asteraceae which appear to be the inner or true seeds which have emerged after the cypselas, or outer casings, have split. From their size these are probably *Anthemis* species but it has not been possible to identify them more closely.

Summary

The cereals from the Bronze Age, Romano-British, and Saxon phases, although in some cases rather meagre, reflect the probable agricultural regimes of the times. The Early Bronze Age yielded very little; the later Bronze Age was characteristic in that barley was a major, if not the most important, cereal. By the Romano-British period spelt is dominant and there is some bread wheat and barley. In the Saxon period spelt is still dominant, with some indication of germination; bread wheat and barley are minor components and emmer continues, probably as a relic. Rye is present in one sample but uncertainly identified in another.

Other seeds, mainly commonly reported weeds of crop fields, include a few which indicate lighter, acid, sandy soils, although the seeds of stinking mayweed in the Romano-British and Saxon periods show that heavier clay soils were also utilised. Rye brome is present in interestingly high proportions in two Romano-British and Saxon samples, but whether these result from differential preservation or reflect its status is unclear. Hazel and hawthorn reflect scrub or woodland edges and clearings. Hornbeam (*Carpinus betulus*), only uncertainly identified from a small fragment of nut shell in one Saxon SFB, typically grows in clay soils.

Charcoal, by Rowena Gale

Materials and methods

The charcoal fragments were mainly small and poorly preserved. Some were vitrified/tarry and presented few diagnostic features. Fragments measuring >2± mm in the transverse surface were selected for identification. These were fractured to expose fresh transverse surfaces and sorted into groups based on the anatomical features observed using a x20 hand lens. Representative fragments from each group were selected for detailed examination at high magnification. These were fractures to expose clean surfaces in the tangential and radial longitudinal orientations and supported in sand. The fragments were examined using an incident-light microscope at magnifications of up to x400 and the diagnostic features matched to prepared reference material.

Results

The taxa identified are:

- *Acer* sp., maple
- *Betula* sp., birch
- *Corylus* sp., hazel
- ?Ericaceae, heathers
- Pomoideae, a subfamily of Rosaceae which includes *Crateagus* sp., hawthorn, *Malus* sp., apple, *Pyrus* sp., pear, *Sorbus* spp., rowan, whitebeam and wild service. These genera are anatomically similar.
- *Prunus* spp., which includes *P. avium,* wild cherry, *P. padus,* bird cherry, *P spinosa,* blackthorn.
- *Quercus* sp., oak
- Salicaceae which includes *Salix* sp., willow and *Populus* sp., poplar. These genera cannot be distinguished using anatomical methods.
- ?Rosaceae which includes Pomoideae (*see* above), Prunoideae (*see Prunus*) and Rosoideae (*Rosa* sp., rose and *Rubus* sp., bramble)
- *Ulex* sp., gorse/*Cytisus* sp., broom. The genera are anatomically similar.

Early Bronze Age

The central urned burial (120) within the ring-ditch contained cremated bone and poorly preserved charcoal. Some pieces of charcoal were vitrified but the remaining identifiable fragments included blackthorn or cherry and possibly oak.

Late Bronze Age

Pit 149 contained burnt flint, potsherds, and charcoal. The charcoal consisted of oak (stem), hazel, gorse/broom, *Prunus,* and Pomoideae. Feature 232, which was filled with burnt flint, included rather vitrified/tarry fragments of charcoal, some of which were identified as *Prunus.* Pit 320 contained sherds from a single pot but there is no evidence that this was a cremation burial. The associated charcoal comprised small fragments of oak, maple, *Prunus,* and Pomoideae.

Romano British

Charcoal from the fill of corndrier 3 includes stem material from oak and hazel. Charcoal associated with cremation burial 284 includes oak (heartwood and stem) and willow and/or poplar. Cremation burial 317 includes fragments of oak (?juvenile) and some vitrified/tarry pieces lacking any recognisable structure.

Early Saxon

A charcoal sample from SFB 262 includes oak, birch, and a poorly preserved fragment tentatively identified as heather or a member of the Rosaceae. If these remains represented part of the structure of the building one could argue that the combination of birch and heather indicated the use of brushwood for thatching and flooring.

Discussion

Woodland trees were represented on site mainly by oak which occurred consistently in samples from the Early Bronze Age to the Saxon. Other trees included maple and birch. Oak and birch woodlands are characteristic of acidic and sandy soils, which typified the contemporaneous landscapes. The damp or seasonally wet soils of the river banks and floodplain would have provided the ideal habitat for willows and poplars. The remaining genera identified, which form small trees and shrubs, probably grew in marginal woodland or more open areas. The taxa identified includes trees and shrubs characteristic of similar riverine sites today. Other species such as elm (*Ulmus*) and ash (*Fraxinus*) may also have been present but were not represented in the charcoal.

The shrubs and trees growing at or near the site provided a good range of woods suited to various uses. The samples examined suggested that most originated from some type of fuel and, as such, all the woods identified (with the possible exception of willow and poplar) would have burnt well and generated a good heat. The interpretation of the remains from the Saxon structure (based on a single sample) was speculative and inconclusive.

6. Discussion

Neolithic

A single microlith provides the only indication for Mesolithic activity on or in the vicinity of the site. The first evidence for probable settlement occurs in the Late Neolithic period. Two small pits, one possibly a tree hole, which lay towards the east end of the site produced small quantities of Late Neolithic pottery, including Grooved Ware which is rare in Surrey. There were no traces of any associated structural remains but evidence for these may have been removed by the extensive subsequent damage which has taken place on the site.

It is suggested that the settlement lay on the edge of the gravel terrace immediately to the south of a channel, now infilled, one of several in this area through which the River Thames may have formerly flowed. No cult-

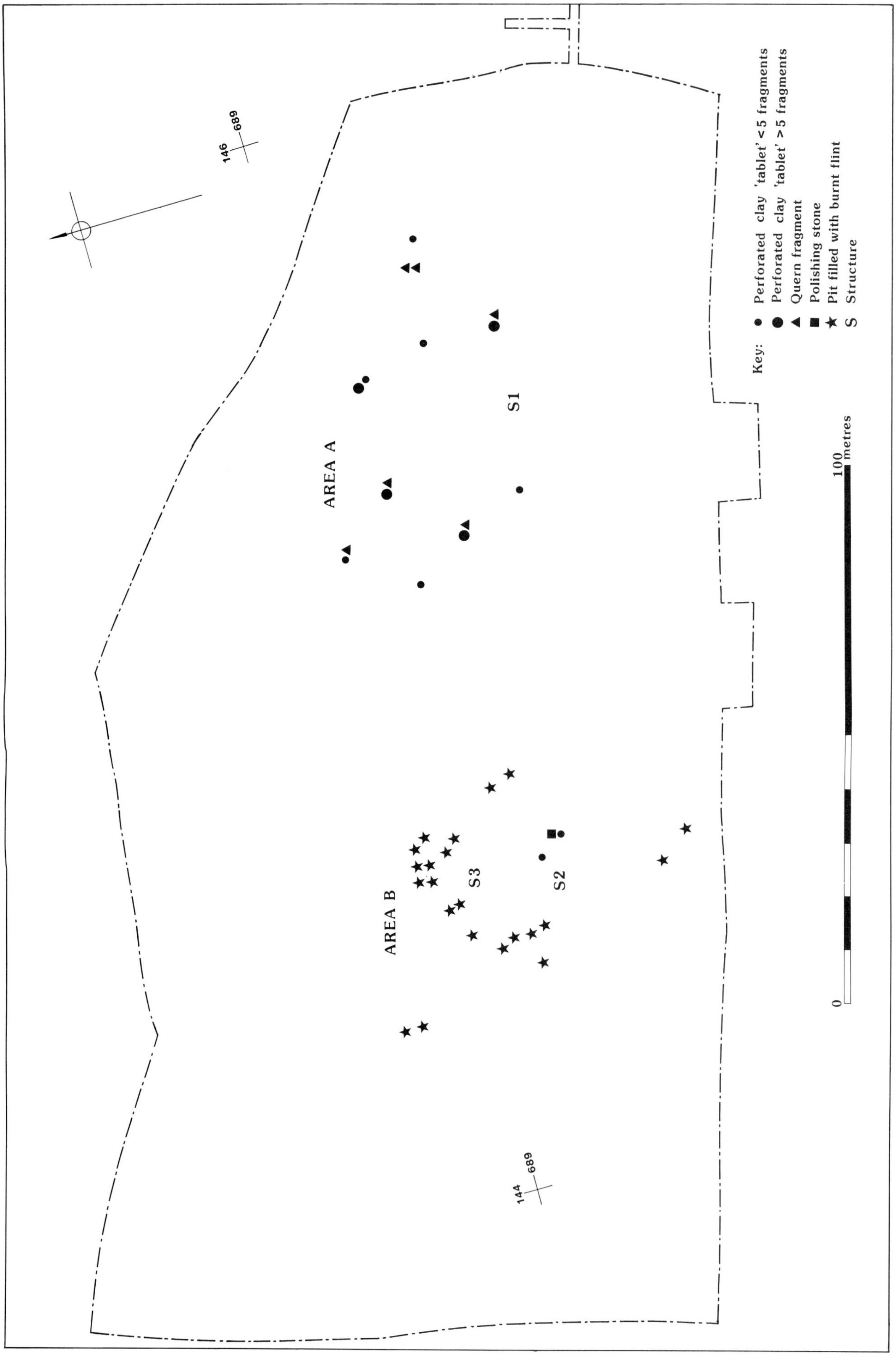

Figure 57 Distribution of selected Late Bronze Age finds

ural material, waterlogged deposits or other environmental material were noted in any of the sections exposed through the channel; these revealed undifferentiated silty clays perhaps deriving from a combination of gradual silting followed by overbank alluviation.

The archaeological evaluation indicated that there may also have been (Late Neolithic) occupation on what appears to have been an eyot or island between two of the river channels but this area was not investigated during the main phase of excavation.

A group of possible tree-holes lay towards the north-west corner of the site and may represent tree clearance alongside the river during the Late Neolithic period. Similar features which date broadly to the same period have been excavated on other sites (eg Petters Sports Field, Egham; O'Connell 1986, 20). These clearances would have provided small, open areas for settlement. This remains conjectural in the absence of more certain evidence and it is possible that more extensive clearance did not begin until later, during the Bronze Age. However, the notable concentration of Neolithic axes from the River Thames in this area, 37 from between Kingston and Hampton being recorded by 1978 (Adkins and Jackson 1978; see also Field and Cotton 1987, fig. 4.7) would support an earlier, Neolithic date for the beginning of extensive tree clearance in this area.

Early–Middle Bronze Age

Some tree clearance had certainly taken place by the Early Bronze Age when a bell barrow was constructed on what would have been marginal land on the edge of the gravel terrace. An oval ring-ditch enclosed a central pit containing a double adult cremation in an inverted Collared Urn. A single, satellite cremation burial, also of an adult, lay just outside the ring-ditch in the incomplete remains of an upright ?Collared Urn. No other burials were found and, although the ring-ditch was not fully excavated, it is considered unlikely that any others lay undetected within the fill of the ditch. It is possible, however, that some burials may have been entirely cropped by disturbance. Trenching at the east end of the site failed to reveal evidence for any further ring-ditches and it would appear that ring-ditch 23 was an isolated example.

The uncommon occurrence of two adults in multiple cremation burials (in *c.* 25% of those recorded) and the rarity of Collared Urn / faience bead associations have been noted above. These facts, coupled with the high weight of cremated bone from the central burial might reflect a comparatively high status for the deceased.

There is only sparse evidence for Early Bronze Age occupation in the area, comprising one small pit and a very few sherds of pottery, including a single Beaker sherd. The small quantity of worked flint from the site is largely undiagnostic, though some can probably be assigned to this period. Some indeterminate cereal fragments provide slight evidence for crop cultivation in the vicinity at this time.

The Middle Bronze Age is represented by an isolated small pit which contained part of a Deverel-Rimbury cordoned urn. This was possibly complete when placed in the pit and, although no human bone was present, it may have been the remains of a burial. The presence of Deverel-Rimbury burials in close proximity to Collared Urn burials is a relatively common occurrence (see for instance Bradley 1982).

Late Bronze Age

Settlement on the site is first clearly attested in the Late Bronze Age, perhaps as early as the 11th century BC. Although many of the features had been truncated and only ephemeral traces of three structures survived, it would appear that virtually the entire settlement was exposed within the excavated area. This comprised two, probably contemporaneous areas of activity (Areas A and B), approximately 75 m apart, on the edge of the highest part of the gravel terrace above the 8 m OD contour.

Immediately to the east of the structures were two phases of shallow ditches which probably formed part of an associated field system. The first phase probably demarcated a square or rectangular enclosure to the south-east and incorporated the still upstanding bank of the Early Bronze Age bell barrow. This lay in the north-west corner of the suggested enclosure and may have been the principal marker used in laying out the system of ditches. The second phase of ditches (ditches 8 and 10) which extended to the north, clearly continued beneath the alluvial deposits which filled the channel. How far these ditches continued to the north could not be ascertained but this relationship clearly demonstrated that silting of the channel, at least along the southern edge, did not begin any earlier than the Late Bronze Age.

Although three hut sites have been defined, little can be deduced about them from the slight structural remains that survived. It is suggested that they were all contemporary, as there was no evidence for rebuilding or replacement, and thus the Late Bronze Age remains probably represent a fairly short-lived and essentially single phase of occupation. All three structures were apparently circular, with estimated diameters in the order of 10–12 m; this is in keeping with Bronze Age round-houses excavated elsewhere (eg at Reading Business Park (Moore 1992) and Petters Sports Field, Egham (O'Connell 1986)). The surviving lengths of gullies could have been eaves-drip gullies, though they may have been shallow foundation trenches which held wattle walls. Whether or not all of these structures were roofed is unknown. The function of the various post-holes is similarly unclear, with the possible exception of the pair in structure 3 interpreted as marking a doorway in the south-west side. No post-rings were apparent, nor any other internal features.

What seems clearer is that Area A, along with structure 1, and Area B with structures 2 and 3, were the foci of two different but perhaps related activities: baking and boiling respectively (*see* Fig. 57).

In Area A, structure 1 was associated with a series of shallow pits and scoops, several of which contained fragments of perforated clay 'tablets'. The six fragments of querns, probably all from saddle querns, also came from this area and one of the pits (149) was comparatively rich in cereal remains; barley predominated, with smaller quantities of wheat. From this assemblage of artefacts and ecofacts it might be suggested that, in Area A, cereals were ground and the flour used in baking. The perforated clay 'tablets' were perhaps the floors in the ovens, separating the flue from the chamber above, with the grooves noted along the outer edges enabling them to be supported within the oven. Various functions have been suggested for these objects in the past, such as a use in cooking, salt-making, or pottery production but in this context, cooking and, more specifically, baking seems likely, particularly since salt-making is improbable and none of the fragments has been subject to high temperatures.

The function of most of the pits and scoops in Area A remains obscure. The possible 'placed deposit' in pit 239 is discussed further (*see* below) but the small size and domestic nature of the contents of the remainder would suggest that they had no specific function other than for casual, household rubbish disposal. None appears to have been dug for storage, even allowing for up to *c.* 0.4 m of truncation of the deposits. Because of this truncation, it is possible that substantial quantities of material which was disposed of on middens has not survived.

In Area B, structures 2 and 3 were associated with more than 20 small pits containing burnt flint and one larger feature (202) also containing burnt flint, but in lesser quantity. Dating of these features rests on a single sherd of Late Bronze Age pottery and it is suggested that the burnt flint derives from the heating of water. Whether this was for cooking or perhaps for some form of sauna remains uncertain, as does the reason for disposing of the debris in this way. Pit 202 may have been a boiling pit but no trace of clay lining survived and there was no evidence of it having had a wood lining. No exact parallels are known for the arrangement of burnt flint filled features at Hurst Park, but cooking or boiling pits associated with dumps of burnt flint are a relatively common occurrence on Bronze Age and Iron Age sites in the British Isles. Sites at Wickhams Field (this volume) and Bermondsey (Merriman 1990, 25; Bowsher 1991) provide recently excavated examples and Bradley *et al.* (1994, 121 and 163) discuss this type of feature further. Spreads of burnt flint assigned a Late Bronze Age date have also been found on other riverside sites nearby at Kingston (Serjeantson *et al.* 1992, 87–8) and Runnymede (Needham 1987).

Comparatively few finds came from Area B but there were a few fragments of perforated clay 'tablets', a small assemblage of pottery and a stone object which it is suggested was used for burnishing or polishing copper alloy objects. Although no copper alloy objects or metalworking debris was recovered from any of the Late Bronze Age contexts on the site, there is evidence of metalworking nearby at Kingston Hill (Field and Needham 1986). The stone came from a small pit which was otherwise undated but, given its location, a Late Bronze Age date is considered most probable. It appeared to have been placed on the bottom of the pit, in the centre, and may represent a 'placed deposit'. The same is also suggested for two groups of pottery: the two vessels in pit 239 in Area A and the single vessel in pit 320 in Area B. All of these were jars and it would appear that the lower vessel in pit 239 may have been broken *in situ* and the rim sherds arranged around the edge of the pit (*see* Fig. 39). It is tempting to interpret the vessels in both pits as funerary deposits but in neither case were they associated with human remains, nor any other finds.

The Late Bronze Age ceramic assemblage is characterised by heavy duty jar and bowl forms, almost all in flint-tempered fabrics, which lack decoration and surface treatment. This assemblage can be placed in the earlier 'plainware' tradition of the later Bronze Age post-Deverel-Rimbury ceramic tradition and has been assigned to perhaps as early as the 11th–10th centuries BC. 'Finewares' were conspicuous by their absence.

It would appear, therefore, that the Late Bronze Age features and finds at Hurst Park represent a small, probably short-lived, riverside settlement centred around two contemporaneous and related hut sites. Finds are interpreted as evidence for domestic occupation, including baking and boiling on mutually exclusive sites. The polishing/burnishing stone may indicate that copper alloy objects were 'finished' on site, though no other copper alloy objects or metalworking debris was found. An adjacent area to the east was given over to fields or enclosures defined by ditches. The nature of the agricultural use of the area is uncertain, partly because animal bone has not survived in the acidic soil conditions. However, taking into account the available environmental evidence and the local topography, it would seem reasonable to postulate a mixture of arable and pastoral use. The acidic, light, well-drained sandy soils on the terrace would have been suitable for cereal production, mainly barley, and would have supported tracts of oak and birch woodland. The heavier clay, damp or seasonally wet soils of the floodplain and river bank would have been more suited to grazing livestock. These soils would have supported grass and woodland comprising willows and poplars. In addition to these genera, there is evidence for a variety of other trees and shrubs characteristic of marginal woodland and more open spaces.

Romano-British

The Late Bronze Age settlement appears to have been abandoned before or during the 9th century BC and there is no evidence for any further activity on the site until the 1st or 2nd century AD. A corndrier and a small group of cremation burials have been interpreted as evidence for a Romano-British settlement of unknown size and status which lay a short distance to the southeast, in an area now covered by part of East Molesey. The corndrier and cremation burials would have lain on the periphery of this settlement, in what appears to have been an open area with no evidence for any contemporary ditched enclosures or field boundaries.

The soil sample from the corndrier was dominated by spelt wheat and this contrasts with the Late Bronze Age contexts where barley was predominant, albeit in small quantities. Bread wheat, possibly emmer wheat, and barley were also present in the sample from the corndrier, along with crop weeds common to arable fields. Some of the latter indicate light, acidic sandy soils, but others are typical of heavy, damp, clay soils, and together these might indicate that both the terrace and the floodplain soils were being cultivated. The two fragments of rotary quern and sherds from three jars in the corndrier would suggest that the grain, having been dried, was then ground at the site and the flour stored or transported in jars.

The cremation burials were concentrated on the highest part of the site, on a small, low promontory of ground defined approximately by the 8.5 m OD contour. The southern limit of the cremation cemetery lay outside the excavated area and thus it may have been considerably more extensive than appears. Truncation of deposits was greatest in the area of the cemetery and it is probable that the eight cremation burials were the survivors of a once larger number. The degree of loss and disturbance means that comparatively little can be deduced from the remaining cremation burials. However, all were adults and six of the eight appear to have been placed in or with pottery vessels of 1st or 2nd century date. One unurned cremation was accompanied by two copper alloy objects, a bracelet and an object which had melted to a state precluding identification.

Although a very small quantity of later (3rd–4th century AD) Roman pottery was recovered, this was all residual in Saxon features and provides no certain evidence that the postulated 1st–2nd century AD settlement continued to be occupied until this time, or that there was any other late Roman occupation in the immediate vicinity. It is more likely that this material, comprising colour-coated wares, was deliberately collected during the Saxon period and brought into the settlement from elsewhere.

Early Saxon

The Saxon settlement is considered from the structural remains and finds to belong to the early Saxon period. More exact dating is difficult in the absence of closely datable finds but it is tentatively suggested that this occupation might be assigned to the 6th or 7th century AD.

It appears likely that all of the structures which comprised this settlement were exposed in the excavation and these, like the Late Bronze Age structures, may represent a small, comparatively short-lived and possibly single phase of occupation.

The structures are all sunken-featured buildings and there is no evidence for any timber halls. Although it is possible that all traces of the latter may have been lost, this seems improbable. Furthermore, the regular close spacing of the SFBs, approximately 30 m apart, might also indicate that there were no associated timber halls. This regularity in the spacing, with no closely-spaced or intercutting SFBs, provides the principal evidence that this was a single phase settlement and there is no evidence that it shifted over time. If there were other SFBs, then they can only have lain to the south beyond the limit of excavation.

Six SFBs have certainly been identified, with a further possible example (SFB 205) on the western edge of the group. Four of the six SFBs were of the most commonly occurring, two-post type, with a single substantial post-hole centrally placed at either end. The post-holes were all set on or just inside the edge of the pit, except in the case of SFB 69 where they lay just outside. SFB 397 differed slightly in that, in addition to the two principal post-holes, there were smaller post-holes midway along each of the other two sides. However, SFB 397 cannot be classified as a true four-post type as the latter have four equal sized post-holes, usually set in the corners of the pit. SFB 16, which was substantially larger than the other examples, may have been a variation of the two-post type, but the post arrangement remains somewhat uncertain with possibly two post-holes at one end and one at the other. SFB 16 also had a sloping 'ramp' at the east end which may have been created for a specific purpose but no other example for this is known.

It is uncertain whether these SFBs had revetted pit walls and raised floors, or if the bottoms of the pits were the floors; a raised, planked floor would have had an open air space below to maintain a relatively dry atmosphere within the hut. However, no trace of any floor surfaces, occupation deposits, or hearths were found on the bottoms of any of the pits, with the possible exception of SFB 16, and this might provide slender evidence in favour of the existence of raised floors. The areas of the pits (mostly m2) would also seem rather small for them to represent the entire floor spaces.

The SFBs generally had homogeneous fills and no post-impressions or post-pipes were detected. In SFB 16, the lower fill of the pit was markedly darker than the remainder but this may simply have reflected the deposition of domestic rubbish in the pit after the SFB had been abandoned and dismantled, rather than an occupation layer which accumulated whilst it was still in use. If the finds in the other SFB pits are similarly interpreted, then their relative numbers might be used to deduce a sequence of abandonment, with the one containing the fewest representing the last to be abandoned. On this basis, SFB 27 would have been the last occupied and subsequently abandoned.

The SFBs produced varying assemblages of finds, principally pottery. Few vessel forms could be identified but these included a range of types, mostly undecorated, which cannot be closely dated. There is nothing to indicate that this is anything other than a domestic assemblage, a conclusion supported by the limited range of other finds. These include several items of metalwork which may have been residual Roman items, perhaps deliberately collected by the Saxons, most notably the possible side link from a bridle bit (Fig. 49:2), the latch lifter (Fig. 49:7), the steelyard fragment (Fig. 49:11) and perhaps the scale tang knife (Fig. 49:5). These represent a notable proportion of the metalwork assemblage and, if all are Roman objects, then they must either have been collected as curiosities or scrap, assuming that they were no longer functional.

The chisel, heckle tooth, and spindle whorl fragments provide some evidence for woodworking and textile production but, perhaps surprisingly, there were no loomweights or other equipment which would indicate weaving. A single hearth bottom derives from iron-smithing but no hammer-scale was recovered from the soil samples. Iron-smithing slag is not an unusual find on early Saxon sites but a residual, Romano-British source for this piece cannot be entirely ruled out.

The environmental remains suggest a similar pattern of arable exploitation as in the Romano-British period, with both the sandy terrace soils and the clay floodplain soils being utilised. Spelt wheat is again dominant, with some slight evidence for malting, and bread wheat, barley, and possibly rye were also present in smaller numbers. The virtual absence of animal bone, which has not survived in the acidic soil conditions means, that again we have no information on the animal economy of the site.

The feature designated SFB 205 has been interpreted as a possible 'drier' for crops but there remains some uncertainty concerning this. Although similar in shape and size to the other SFBs, there was only one possible post-hole. The fill of redeposited sandy gravel contained very few finds, the majority of which were residual Roman. Two fragments of rotary quern and the scorching on the bottom provide some evidence for suggesting that this feature may have been used as a drier, but the absence of charred plant remains unfortunately provides no support for this interpretation.

All of the SFBs, with the possible exception of 205, may have been used for occupation. However, it cannot be shown with certainty that some did not have other functions, such as for storage or weaving, although no loomweights were found.

There were two small pits but any function other than for rubbish disposal is unclear; most domestic refuse is likely to have been disposed of on middens or in abandoned SFBs and perhaps subsequently used for manuring fields.

The short lengths of shallow gullies around SFBs 16 and 69 may represent small enclosures, possibly fenced, around the buildings. Similar features have been noted at Old Down Farm, Andover, but the dating there is equivocal and it is suggested that they may have been Roman (Davies 1980, 163).

The existence of fields in the immediate vicinity is suggested by the undated but apparently related shallow ditches along the southern edge of the site. Features 184 and 350 may have defined a track or drove which was on the same east–west alignment and appears to have respected the SFBs, with a field system to the south. If these features have been correctly attributed to the early Saxon period, then it would provide a shred of evidence in support of a 'late' (6th or 7th century AD) date for the settlement, for the development of boundaries has been considered to be characteristic of the later part of this period (West 1985, 151).

Post-Medieval

There is no evidence for any occupation on the site after the early Saxon period. Late Saxon and medieval settlement is likely to have developed to the south, on the marginally higher ground where East Molesey church now stands. The earliest documentary reference to (East) Molesey occurs in the grants of land made to Chertsey Abbey in the 7th century, which include estates at 'Mulesey' — Mul's Island or meadow; there are two later, 10th century references, to 'Muleseige' and 'Muleseye' respectively, all recorded in Birch's *Cartularium Saxonicum* (see Gover *et al.* 1982, 94–5). In the Domesday Survey, three manors are recorded at Molesey, tenanted by knights who had come over from Normandy. Prior to the beginning of the 13th century, the only settlement was at East Molesey and it was only after this date that the prefix East was added to differentiate it from the village which developed later at West Molesey.

With the development of settlement on a new site at East Molesey, Hurst Park is likely to have reverted to agricultural use and, during Henry VIII's residence at Hampton Court, became part of one of his deer parks.

Several post-medieval ditches provide evidence for the subsequent laying out of fields, with ditch 192, which had been recut several times, probably representing a more substantial and longer-lived boundary. The parish boundary between East and West Molesey was also defined by a series of recut ditches but the date of the establishment of this boundary could not be determined.

3. Prospect Park and Hurst Park: the Settlements and the Landscape

by Phil Andrews

The excavations at Prospect Park and Hurst Park have provided two chronologically similar sequences of activity which can be fitted into a broader pattern of settlement development in the middle part of the Thames Valley. The sites, less than 15 km apart, occupy similar positions on the edges of gravel terraces, close to the River Thames or its tributaries.

Neolithic

There is increasing evidence for the utilisation of this part of the Thames Valley from the Early Neolithic period onwards in an area where a large number of Neolithic sites are now known (Fig. 58).

No long barrows have been identified, but Neolithic causewayed enclosures have been excavated at Yeovney Lodge, Staines (Robertson-Mackay 1987) and Eton Wick (Ford 1986), and another may exist at Dorney Reach. Smaller, Neolithic interrupted ditch enclosures, which probably served a funerary function, have also been found at Heathrow, Shepperton and Mayfield Farm (Merriman 1990, 23–4), and more recently at Manor Farm, Horton (Ford in prep.). The Stanwell Cursus, which may terminate by Bigley Ditch, a short distance to the south-west of Prospect Park, is another major monument in the area (O'Connell 1990). Although not all of these monuments were contemporary in their construction and use, they nevertheless constitute a remarkable complex. An area of special importance for Neolithic communities is suggested, perhaps even an organised landscape, on the fertile gravel terraces close to the River Thames.

Evidence for possible settlement is widely scattered but would appear to favour riverine sites where various resources could be utilised. River confluences, such as those between the River Thames and its tributaries the Mole, the Wey, and the Colne, would have been particularly favoured because they allowed access to 'inland' areas and were in a position to control river traffic.

Neolithic structures have generally proved elusive, with Runnymede Bridge being the most notable exception (Needham and Trott 1987). This is the only site where Neolithic houses have certainly been identified, although recent excavations at Cranford Lane, Hillingdon, to the west of Prospect Park, have uncovered an arrangement of Middle Neolithic post-holes interpreted by the excavator as a house, and some associated pits (Mark Birley, pers. comm.). At Prospect Park, the possible structure represented by a 'hollow' and associated features is considered more likely to have had a domestic rather than ceremonial use, although the associated Grooved Ware assemblage might favour the latter function and a similar interpretation has been made for the deposits of Grooved Ware in pits at Holloway Lane, Harmondsworth (Merriman 1990, 24), and also at Horton (Ford in prep.).

Most sites interpreted as settlements, like those at Prospect Park and Hurst Park, remain ill-defined and comprise isolated features containing small quantities of struck flint and pottery (eg sites at Harmondsworth and at Sipson (Cotton *et al.* 1986)). It is unclear at present what they consisted of and what form they took.

The presence of these various monuments and sites suggests that extensive woodland clearance had begun to take place in the area during the Neolithic period and this is supported by concentrations of broken and fragmented stone axes which have been found in the River Thames near Kingston (Adkins and Jackson 1978; see also Field and Cotton 1987, fig. 4.7) and in the Sipson/Harmondsworth area (Cotton *et al.* 1986). The pollen sequence obtained from Eden Walk, Kingston also indicates open areas, possibly man-made, nearby at this time (Penn *et al.* 1984, 18–19). As noted above, riverside sites were favoured for settlement and the slight evidence from Hurst Park, along with more substantial evidence from Kingston (Penn *et al.* 1984, 11; Serjeantson *et al.* 1992) and in particular Runnymede Bridge (Needham 1992), demonstrates this. All lay within, or adjacent to, a system of braided river channels which were subject to various patterns of shifting, silting, and overbank alluviation and, at Kingston and Runnymede Bridge, varying quantities of domestic debris had been disposed of in the channels. Unfortunately, no such debris was encountered at Hurst Park, possibly because organic materials had not survived, because deposits were present but were not revealed in the excavations, or because little material was disposed of in the channel. At Hurst Park, it is not clear by what date the channel had become infilled, though this was certainly after the Late Bronze Age and whether the infill was a result of gradual silting or overbank alluviation, or perhaps both at different times as the sea level continued to rise.

Early–Middle Bronze Age

The bell barrow at Hurst Park is an important discovery and has provided a rare opportunity to excavate a type of funerary monument which is likely to have been a much more common feature in the area. Other examples, destroyed by gravel extraction or development, are likely to have existed close by, with probable

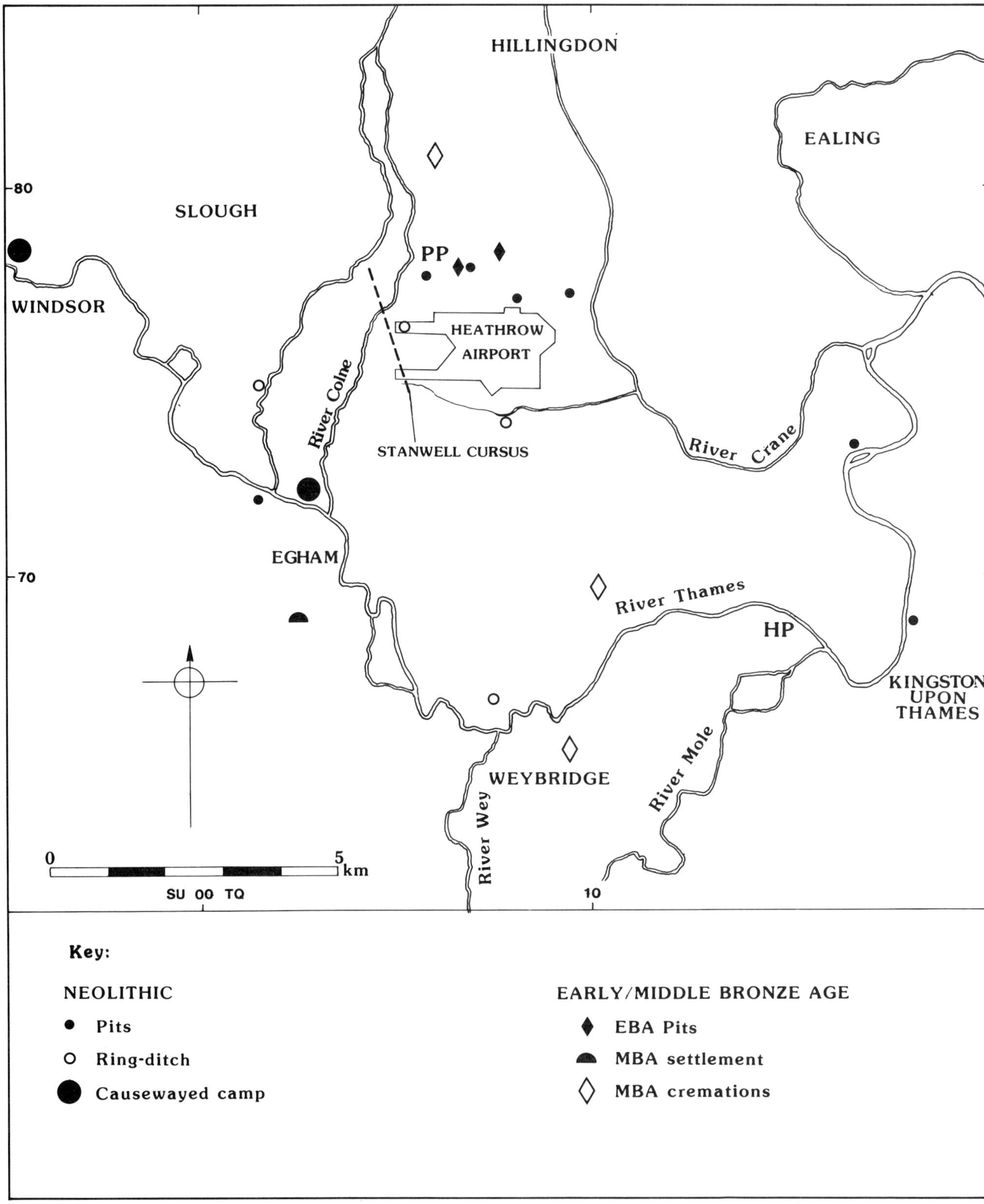

Figure 58 Neolithic and Early / Middle Bronze Age sites in the area of Prospect Park and Hurst Park

examples at Kingston Hill (Field and Needham 1986, 148) and Teddington (Akerman 1855). The latter seems to have been quite substantial and a bronze dagger, recovered during antiquarian investigations, suggests that it may have contained at least one richly furnished burial. The apparently isolated example at Hurst Park is generally typical of other Surrey barrows in that they rarely occur in large groups but is unusual in that all the known bell barrows lie in the south-west of the county. This form, generally associated with the 'Wessex culture', is rarely found outside Wessex, but the Hurst Park example, with its central grave containing a double cremation placed within a Collared Urn and accompanied by faience beads, may provide a link with this group. Although insufficient material was obtained from the Hurst Park cremation burials to enable a radiocarbon determination to be made, the urn can be broadly dated to around the middle of the 2nd millennium BC and this is compatible with the dating accepted for this form of barrow.

The former existence of a barrow is also indicated at Prospect Park but this is of unknown form and is probably, though not certainly, of Bronze Age date. This also seems to have been an isolated example but others appear to have existed in the vicinity, most impressively at Stanwell where a line of nine ring-ditches is recorded (Longley 1976, 33, fig. 12). The concentration of Neolithic monuments in this landscape may have provided a focus for subsequent Bronze Age funerary activity.

Excavated evidence for Early Bronze Age settlement has proved elusive and the single pit and few sherds of pottery found at Hurst Park is in keeping with what has been found elsewhere in the area. A few pits, some containing loomweights, have been excavated at Sipson (Merriman 1990, 24–5) but no structures have been identified here or elsewhere.

Two Middle Bronze Age bucket urns, associated with cremated remains, were found at Prospect Park and a single example without any cremated remains at Hurst Park. The former lay quite close to and may have been associated with the ring-ditch but at Hurst Park the vessel was in a pit some distance away from the Early Bronze Age barrow which would still have been visible.

In north-west Surrey Needham (1987, 108) has noted the apparent exclusion between users of Deverel-Rimbury pottery and earlier, collared and biconical funerary urn styles which probably continued in use into the Middle Bronze Age. This is particularly apparent on the Heathrow Terraces, on which Prospect Park lies, where there is extensive evidence of Neolithic activity and several Deverel-Rimbury sites but comparatively little indication of any Early Bronze Age presence. Most of the Deverel-Rimbury sites, like that at Prospect Park and possibly also Hurst Park, are cemeteries (eg Barrett 1973; Gardner 1924, 23–6) but limited settlement evidence has been excavated in the area at Staines (Needham 1987, 133) and Petters Sports Field, Egham (O'Connell 1986, 8–9), and more substantial remains at Muckhatch Farm, Thorpe (Johnson 1975, 19–23) and Bray (Barnes *et al.* 1995, 1–51). In the latter report, attention has been drawn to the fact that Middle Bronze Age settlement remains in this area might, like those of any Early Bronze Age settlements, be relatively insubstantial and therefore difficult to recognise; the apparent absence is not likely to be a real absence given the common occurrence of metalwork and cremation vessels (Cleal 1995, 49).

Late Bronze Age

The settlements at Prospect Park and Hurst Park are chronologically and perhaps functionally different, and this is reflected to some extent in the respective finds assemblages. The settlement at Hurst Park has been assigned, on ceramic evidence, to the earlier part of the Late Bronze Age, in the 11th and 10th centuries BC, whereas that at Prospect Park was slightly later and spanned the 10th and 9th centuries BC.

The Late Bronze Age is likely to have witnessed greater agricultural production, increased population, and denser settlement which probably concentrated in the fertile river valleys and adjacent terraces. The appearance of field and enclosure ditches at Hurst Park and Prospect Park are likely to have been a result of this increased pressure on available land.

The small settlement at Hurst Park fills a lacuna in the lower Mole Valley which, before now, had been unexpectedly devoid of Late Bronze Age material and can be placed into a hierarchy of settlements in the area which lie on or close to the Thames and its tributaries (*see* Fig. 59). The largest, such as those at Carshalton (Adkins and Needham 1985) and the recently reinterpreted site at Mayfield Farm near Heathrow (Cotton 1991, 153), were large, circular, defended settlements. These may have been regional centres which supported metalworking and other craft activities and provided places to meet and barter. A now largely destroyed site at Kingston Hill may have been a similar but smaller version of these sites. It too might have been enclosed by an earthwork and there is considerable evidence that bronze-working was carried out there (Field and Needham 1986).

Smaller, strategically located and perhaps stockaded waterside sites, such as at Runnymede (Needham 1991), would have been important in being involved in and controlling local and long distance trade.

The smallest settlements, like that at Hurst Park, were small farmsteads comprising a cluster of unenclosed, circular huts. The arrangement at Hurst Park shows clear evidence of different activities, suggested to have been baking and boiling, in mutually exclusive parts of the site. Similar patterns of activity have been noted elsewhere, at Black Patch and Itford Hill, Sussex (Drewett 1982) and Aldermaston Wharf, Berkshire (Bradley *et al.* 1980), but at these sites the division has been drawn between food preparation and consumption and this distinction is highlighted by the relative concentrations of coarsewares (in areas of preparation) and finewares (in areas of consumption). Distinguishing between the relatively small assemblages in the two areas at Hurst Park has not been possible because they comprise entirely of 'plainwares' with no finewares or decorated sherds. The absence of finewares is considered to reflect an earlier date for this assemblage rather than any socio-economic difference between the sites. Two noteworthy features of the finds assemblage from Hurst Park are the stone possibly used for burnishing copper alloy objects, particularly significant given the evidence for metalworking at nearby Kingston Hill (Field and Needham 1986, 141–8) and the perforated clay 'tablets' which now seem to be a common component of finds assemblages from Late Bronze Age sites in the Thames Valley (Champion 1980, 223–6). However, metalwork and evidence for leather and textile working were absent at Hurst Park, the former perhaps a reflection of the 'low status' of the site.

The Late Bronze Age features at Prospect Park clearly belonged to a more extensive, open and, it is suggested, longer-lived settlement than that at Hurst Park. More of probably the same settlement has been exposed on the adjacent, larger-scale excavations at Holloway Lane and perhaps also at Cranford Lane, further to the east, where three phases of field systems and circular huts have been identified spanning some

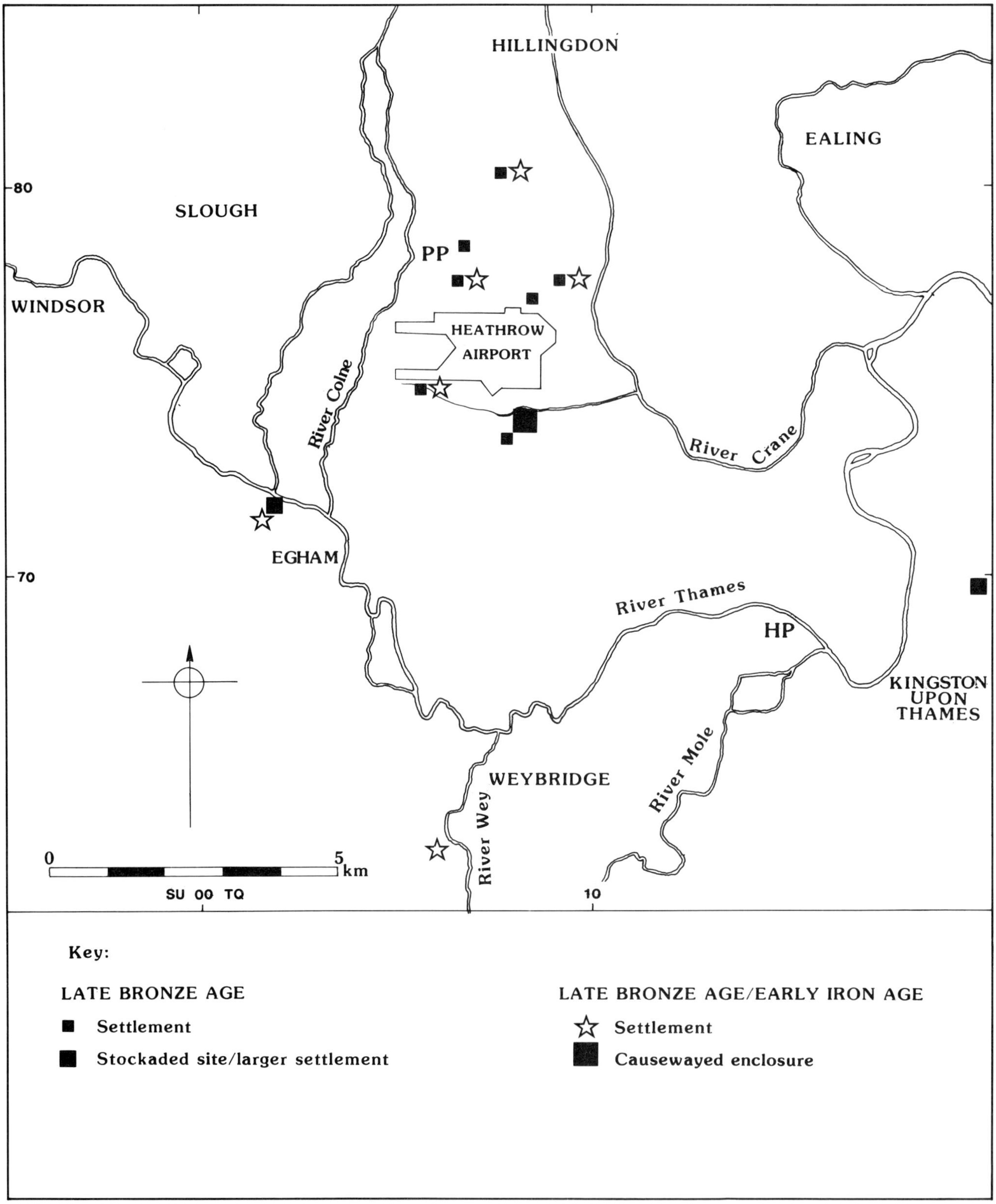

Figure 59 Late Bronze Age sites in the area of Prospect Park and Hurst Park

750 years, from *c.* 1250–500 BC (Mark Birley pers. comm.). It seems likely, therefore, that the features at Prospect Park can be linked to the middle phases at Cranford Lane. The layout, including a droveway at Holloway Lane defined by two substantial ditches, and the finds suggest that this was a farming settlement. At Prospect Park there was no evidence for any other activities; there was no metalwork, no spindle-whorls or loomweights, and no perforated clay 'tablets'. However, this and the absence of querns may reflect the peripheral location of the excavation on the western edge of the settlement.

The poor survival of animal bone has undoubtedly biased the picture in favour of the arable element, as is also the case at Hurst Park. Amongst the cereal remains are the glumed wheats (emmer and spelt), bread wheat, and six-row barley, which are generally the most commonly represented grains recovered from British Bronze Age sites (Greig 1991b). The four-post and possible two-post structures, types not apparently present at Hurst Park but recognised on Late Bronze Age sites elsewhere (eg Mucking; Bond 1988, 13), provide further evidence for cereal production and storage.

Recently excavated evidence for similar settlements to that at Prospect Park/Holloway Lane/Cranford Lane has come from several other sites in the vicinity. At Stanwell (O'Connell 1990, 35–54) an extensive field system established *c.* 1000 BC went out of use and was followed by a period of dispersed occupation towards the end of the Late Bronze Age in the 7th or 6th century BC. More limited excavations at Petters Sports Field, Egham revealed the terminal to a substantial Late Bronze Age ditch and a scatter of later post-holes interpreted as defining huts of Late Bronze Age/Early Iron Age date (O'Connell 1986).

Romano-British

Both sites produced Romano-British cremation burials — one at Prospect Park and eight at Hurst Park, all probably of 1st or 2nd century AD date. A corn drier at the latter site was the only other feature of this period and this slender evidence has been taken to indicate the presence of a hitherto unrecognised settlement, perhaps a farmstead, at East Molesey. This would have lain approximately midway between the Roman settlements at Staines and Ewell, in an area where surprisingly few Roman remains have been found (Bird 1987, 179, fig. 7.7). However, recent work has revealed some evidence for Romano-British farmsteads on sites at Hampton Wick, Twickenham, and Richmond upon Thames (Jonathan Nowell, pers. comm.), suggesting that this absence may simply reflect a lack of opportunities for fieldwork. It may be significant that a short length of Roman road has been traced extending in a north-westerly direction from Stane Street, between Dorking and Ewell (Bird 1987, 167, fig. 7.1), which if projected less than 10 km would run very close to the postulated settlement at East Molesey.

Little can be deduced from the single cremation burial at Prospect Park. However, during the watching brief several other burials were discovered to the south-west of the excavated areas. These have not yet been fully analysed at the time of writing. In addition, Romano-British pits, post-holes, and other finds have been recorded some 400 m to the south at Harmondsworth and several other sites, 2 km or more to the east, have revealed pits, wells, and ovens set within small, ditched enclosures (Cotton *et al.* 1986). These features, along with a variety of finds, provide evidence for one or more late Roman (3rd–4th century AD) settlements but no earlier sites have yet been discovered.

In both areas, relatively few non-villa sites have been studied in detail and, until further sites are discovered and investigated, it is difficult to put the slight remains at both Prospect Park and Hurst Park in a wider context (*see* Fig. 60 for the extent of Romano-British settlement activity in the area).

Saxon

The discovery of Anglo-Saxon settlements at Prospect Park and Hurst Park has added considerably to our knowledge of the area where sites of this period are comparatively scarce (*see* Fig. 60). The two settlements differed from each other in several respects and are considered to have possibly been occupied at different times — Prospect Park earlier, in the 5th or 6th century AD and Hurst Park later, in the 6th or 7th century AD.

At Prospect Park it would appear that only part of an extensive, dispersed settlement was exposed. This settlement was probably 'strung out' along the edge of the river terrace, around the 30 m contour. Earlier work to the north, during widening of the M4, revealed part of a sunken-featured building and at least one further example was found during excavations in Harmondsworth to the south. If these all belonged to the same settlement, then it would appear to have extended over a distance of at least 0.5 km.

Although no sequence of settlement could be deduced, either from the layout of sunken-featured buildings or from the finds at Prospect Park, it is conceivable that the various SFBs which have been found in this area all belonged to a small settlement which shifted over time, along the edge of the terrace, rather than a single, large settlement which was occupied for only a comparatively short period. Settlement shift, as may have occurred at Prospect Park, has been recorded elsewhere, most notably at Mucking (Hamerow 1991).

This contrasts with the sunken-featured buildings at Hurst Park which appear to represent a small, nucleated, single phase settlement which may have been completely exposed within the excavated area. No other features or finds have been reported in the immediate vicinity of Hurst Park, although this may simply reflect a lack of excavation. The nearest excavated evidence for settlement lies approximately 5 km downstream at Kingston-upon-Thames; sunken-featured buildings have been found here, and also at Ham just beyond (Poulton 1987a, 207; Bob Cowie, pers. comm.). However, these sites may not all have been contemporaneous and this is discussed further below.

Besides the variations in extent and density of the sunken-featured buildings, two other differences are apparent in the nature and layout of the settlements at Prospect Park and Hurst Park. First, Prospect Park is the only site in the area which has produced evidence for post-built timber halls, contemporary and apparently associated with the sunken-featured buildings. At Hurst Park it seems fairly certain that there were no timber halls and that the sunken-featured buildings were used for occupation as well as for storage and craft activities. However, it is possible that evidence for timber halls was not recognised on the less extensive excavations elsewhere in the area. The significance of the presence or absence of timber halls is not clear; the proximity of the sites at Prospect Park and Hurst Park suggests that it was not a reflection of geography and the sequence identified at West Stow, Suffolk (West 1985) indicates that it is not a matter of chronology as timber halls were present in both earlier (5th–6th century) and later (6th–7th century) phases of the settle-

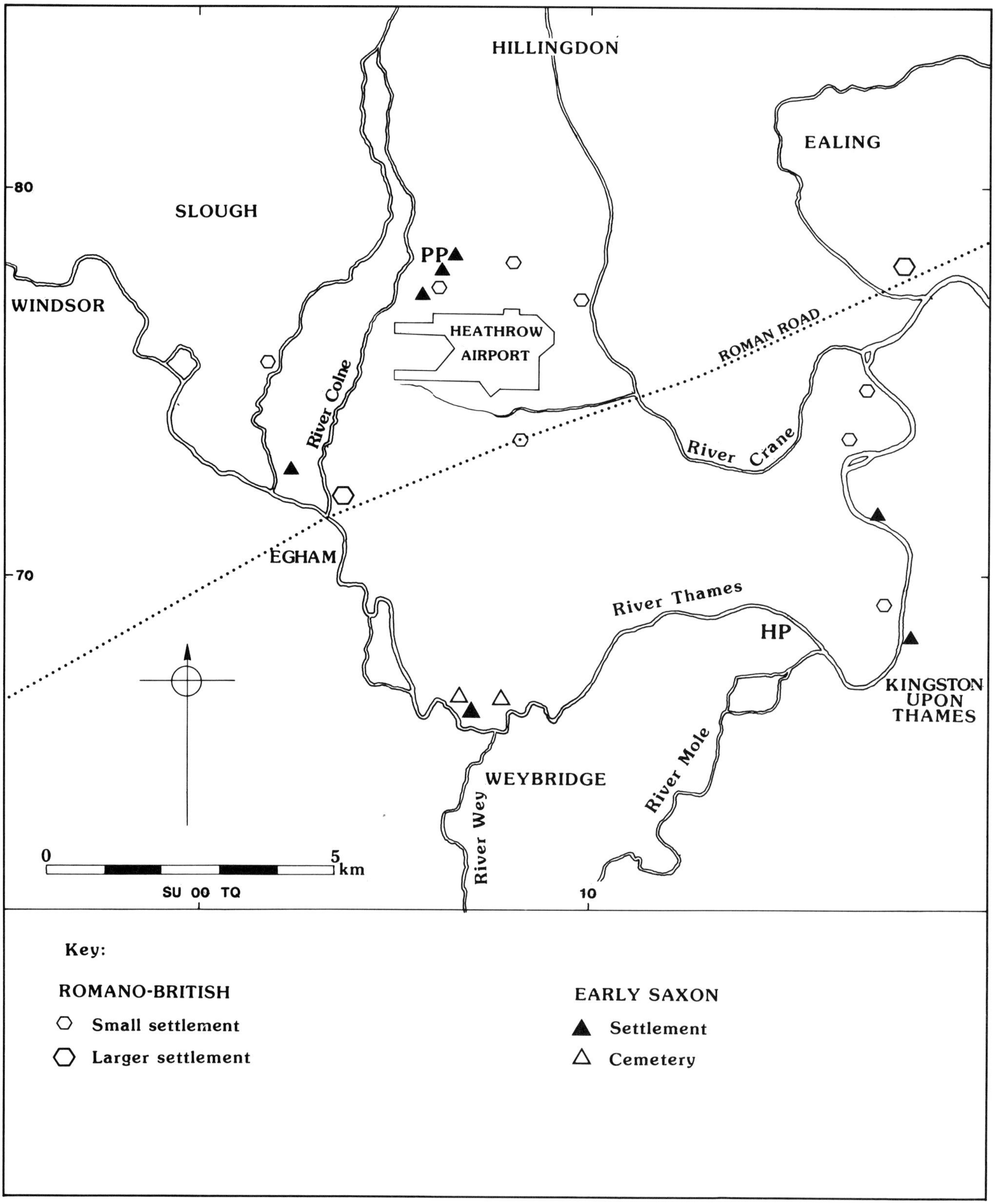

Figure 60 Romano-British and Early Saxon sites in the area of Prospect Park and Hurst Park

ment. Perhaps a combination of factors, which might also include the size, status, and function of the settlement, determined whether or not timber halls were built.

The second difference between Prospect Park and Hurst Park is the presence at the latter of several linear features which have been interpreted as part of a field system contemporary with the settlement. It has been suggested (West 1985, 151) that the presence of such field systems is a reflection of chronology, but characteristic of later (6th–7th century) settlement when more formal land divisions began to be established. Unfortunately, the linear features at Hurst Park are undated and the finds are of little help in closely dating the settlement as a whole; all that can be said is that there is nothing in the ceramic assemblage from the site which is clearly early.

If the settlement at Hurst Park was 'late' (6th–7th century), then it contrasts with those at Kingston-upon-Thames, Ham, and Hammersmith, as well as Prospect Park, which are all considered to be early (Bob Cowie, pers. comm.). These sites have all produced early pottery and the assemblages from Prospect Park and Hammersmith contain unusual groups of non-local wares, possibly from the Midlands, or perhaps of continental (North Germany) origin, which may date to as early as the 5th century. The presence of this non-local pottery might suggest an involvement in early trade for some settlements in the lower Thames Valley, all of which lay close to the River Thames or its tributaries, with Prospect Park being the furthest west of this group yet discovered. The suggested early dating and possible continental origin of the pottery might also reflect early migration into the lower Thames valley from the continent in the 5th century, and clearly further work is required on this and similar early, non-local ceramic assemblages in the London area before the full implications of its presence there can be properly considered.

At Prospect Park, the presence of non-local pottery and timber halls, including the unique example 721 with the semi-circular arrangement of post-holes at its west end, might be indicative of a higher status settlement, although there is nothing else which would support this suggestion. Alternatively, their presence may be a function of chronology, and reflect the suggested earlier date of the settlement at Prospect Park compared to that at Hurst Park.

No Anglo-Saxon burial sites have been found near Prospect Park but a burial complex, including cremation, inhumation, and barrow burials, along with an associated settlement site, is known at Shepperton Green less than 10 km to the west of Hurst Park; this site has been dated to between the 6th and 12th centuries AD (Canham 1979; Poulton 1987b). Another cemetery, about a kilometre away, known as Upper West Field, Shepperton, was found in the 19th century and has been dated to the late 5th or early 6th century (Longley and Poulton 1982). Much of this latter cemetery was destroyed during the 19th century but the two sites at Shepperton serve to indicate the presence of one or more settlements in the vicinity during the early Saxon period and again emphasises the concentration of activity in the river valleys.

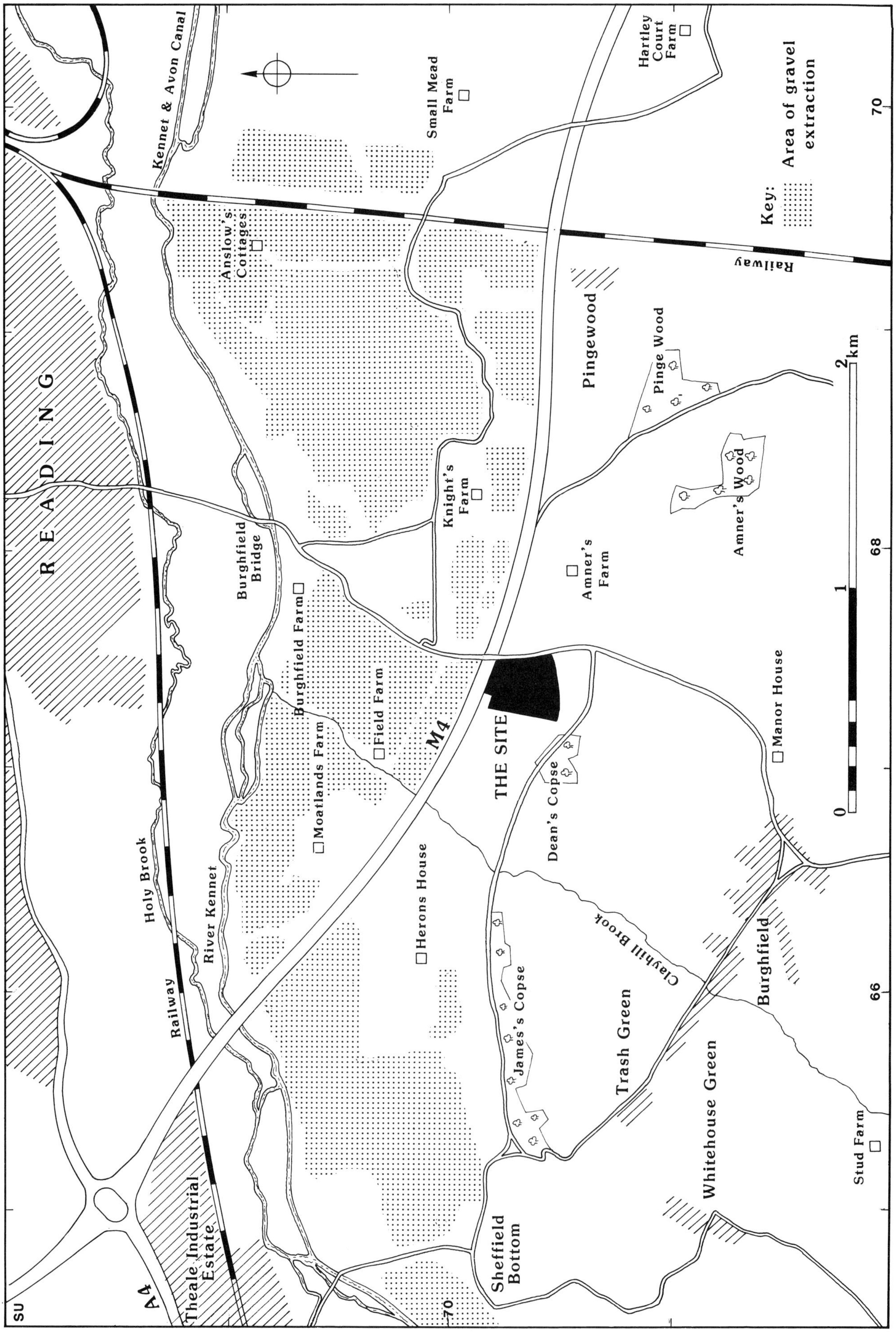

Figure 61 Location plan of Wickhams Field

4. Iron Age to Saxon Settlement at Wickhams Field, near Reading, Berkshire: Excavations on the Site of the M4 Granada Reading Motorway Service Area

by Andrew Crockett

With contributions from Michael J. Allen, Rowena Gale, P.A. Harding, M. Laidlaw, Jacqueline I. McKinley, Lorraine Mepham, and Nicholas A. Wells

1. Introduction

Project Background

Between February and April 1994 Wessex Archaeology undertook excavations in advance of the construction, by Granada Hospitality Ltd, of a new motorway service area (MSA) on the M4 (south side of the carriageway) near Reading. The site (centred on SU 6750 6970) lies 3.5 km to the south-east of Theale village and 5 km south-west of Reading town centre (Fig. 61). The site lies in an area currently devoid of suitable place names and has been called 'Wickhams Field' by reference to the name which was formerly applied to the local fields (Burghfield tithe map of 1844; Berkshire Record Office m.f. no. 97066/B7). The placename Wickham (such as Wickham Bushes, Easthampstead) derives from the Old English *Wicham*, and is believed to relate to the presence of Roman roads and settlements (Gelling 1973, 24).

Planning permission for the development included a Section 106 legal agreement between Mobil Oil Company Ltd, Englefield Estate Trust Corporation Ltd, and Newbury District Council. This agreement included a scheme of archaeological works to be implemented prior to development (*M4 Service Area, Reading; Archaeological Scheme,* dated 22.12.92). The Scheme outlined the methods proposed to examine and record the anticipated archaeological resource within the development area. The known archaeological background to the site had previously been reviewed in a desk-based study undertaken by Wessex Archaeology on behalf of Mobil Oil Company Ltd (Wessex Archaeology 1992).

Archaeological Background

The site lies within an area which has been the focus of much archaeological work in recent years. The construction of the M4 motorway and, more recently, the demand for gravel by the construction industry, have provided the impetus for many of the changes that the area has undergone, leading to a number of important excavations in the immediate vicinity. In addition, the site lies within an area investigated as part of the Kennet Valley Survey (Lobb and Rose forthcoming). For the most part the Kennet Valley Survey comprised an extensive fieldwalking programme but the project also included the excavation of threatened sites in advance of gravel extraction and the undertaking of watching briefs as such sites were being worked.

The river gravels of the Kennet Valley and their associated alluvial cover have provided an excellent base for the formation and observation of cropmarks (Gates 1975). In many instances cropmark complexes have provided the focus for archaeological excavation. Within the immediate vicinity of the development site, the following cropmark sites have been excavated (Fig. 61):

- Knight's Farm — Middle and Late Bronze Age (Bradley *et al.* 1980).
- Field Farm — Neolithic, Late Bronze Age, Anglo-Saxon, and later (Butterworth and Lobb 1992).
- Herons House — prehistoric, possibly Bronze Age (Bradley and Richards 1979–80).

In the local area other primarily Bronze Age settlement sites have been excavated at Pingewood and Anslow's Cottages, to the east and north-east respectively (Fig. 61). The important site at Anslow's Cottages, which included well-preserved timber structures associated with a Bronze Age waterfront, was not known from cropmarks but was found as the result of an archaeological field evaluation (Butterworth and Lobb 1992).

A detailed and extensive account of the archaeological and historical development within the region is not included in this report; reference should be made to recently published literature, in particular Butterworth and Lobb (1992). However, to place the area into a broad chronological framework, short summaries are provided for the major chronological periods represented.

Palaeolithic (before 8500 BC)

Evidence for Palaeolithic activity in the immediate area is scarce. A Levallois flake was found during fieldwalking north-east of Dean's Farm (Lobb and Rose forthcoming), with handaxes also recovered from Holy Brook to the north-west and from gravel pits at Sulhamstead to the south-west (Wessex Archaeology 1993, 64).

Mesolithic and Neolithic (8500–2400 BC)
A small amount of earlier prehistoric flint was recovered during fieldwalking at Field Farm (*op. cit.*). A few pieces of Mesolithic flint and a hearth and pottery vessel (Mortlake Ware) of the Neolithic period were found during excavations at Field Farm (Butterworth and Lobb 1992).

Bronze Age (2400–700 BC)
There is much evidence for Bronze Age activity in the immediate vicinity of the site. Occupation sites have been recorded at Knight's Farm and to a lesser degree, Field Farm which represents part of the same extensive settlement (Bradley *et al.* 1980; Butterworth and Lobb 1992; Lobb 1983–85). One large and several smaller ring-ditches at the latter site, probably the encircling ditches of ploughed-out round barrows, appear to have been parts of a cremation cemetery. Other ring-ditches and cremations, probably, although not certainly, of Bronze Age date, have been excavated west of the application site at Herons House (Bradley and Richards 1979–80).

Iron Age and Roman (700 BC–AD 410)
There is no structural evidence of Iron Age or Roman activity in the immediate vicinity and finds of this period are not prolific. Isolated Middle to Late Iron Age cremation burials are recorded in the vicinity of Anslow's Cottage and Pingewood (Butterworth and Lobb 1992), and a small cluster of Romano-British pottery was found during fieldwalking at Green Farm (Lobb and Rose forthcoming).

Saxon and Medieval (AD 410–1500)
Saxon activity within the area is represented by a 7th-century AD inhumation cemetery which reused (and extended beyond) the largest Bronze Age ring-ditch at Field Farm (Butterworth and Lobb 1992). No associated settlement has, as yet, been found, although documentary references indicate late Saxon settlement at Burghfield and possibly Sheffield Bottom (*ibid.*). Little direct archaeological evidence exists for the medieval period within the study area, although a small cluster of medieval pottery has been found during fieldwalking at Green Farm (centred on the same area as the cluster of Romano-British pottery; Lobb and Rose forthcoming).

Overall, prior to the start of archaeological excavation, the site was known to lie within a rich archaeological landscape, with evidence of human activity, intermittently, from earlier prehistoric times through to the present day. The potential of the site was, therefore, deemed to be high, especially since it was surrounded on three sides by extensive areas of former cropmarks, many of which no longer survive.

Excavation Methods

The methods implemented were in accordance with those outlined in the *Archaeological Scheme* document, part of the Section 106 legal agreement relating to the development, as discussed above.

Stage 1 of the archaeological works concerned the removal of approximately 5 ha (50200 m^2) of topsoil from the site, using tracked hydraulic excavators and 25 tonne dump trucks. This work was carried out under constant archaeological supervision, and took place during atrocious weather over a three week period in February and March 1994 (Pl. 15).

In accordance with the Section 106 agreement, on completion of Stage 1, a review meeting was held between MACE Ltd (acting on behalf of Granada Hospitality Ltd), the Principal Archaeologist, Babtie Group (as Consultants to Berkshire County Council), and Wessex Archaeology. The preliminary assessment of the results of the topsoil strip was(*see* Fig. 62):

- the presence of considerable numbers of pits, postholes, and ditches providing evidence for a probable prehistoric settlement on the higher ground formed by the Reading Beds in the south-west corner of the stripped area;
- numerous undated isolated features, including several large (*c.* 4 m diameter) pits, identified on the valley gravel across the lower, north-east part of the site, and;
- an area of colluvium (hillwash) covering approximately 20,000 m^2 at the base of the slope around the probable prehistoric settlement. In plan the zone of colluvium formed an arc across the central part of the excavation, reflecting the contours of the south-west corner of the site.

The review resulted in a document, drawn up by Wessex Archaeology (*Theale MSA, Berkshire — Archaeology: Strategy and Programme for Archaeological Excavation (Stage 2 Works)*, dated 14.03.94), formalising the agreements reached for the main excavation. This document included a detailed strategy to be implemented for assessing the colluvial deposits across the site. Stage 2

Plate 15 Foul weather conditions during topsoil stripping, looking south-west to Deans Copse

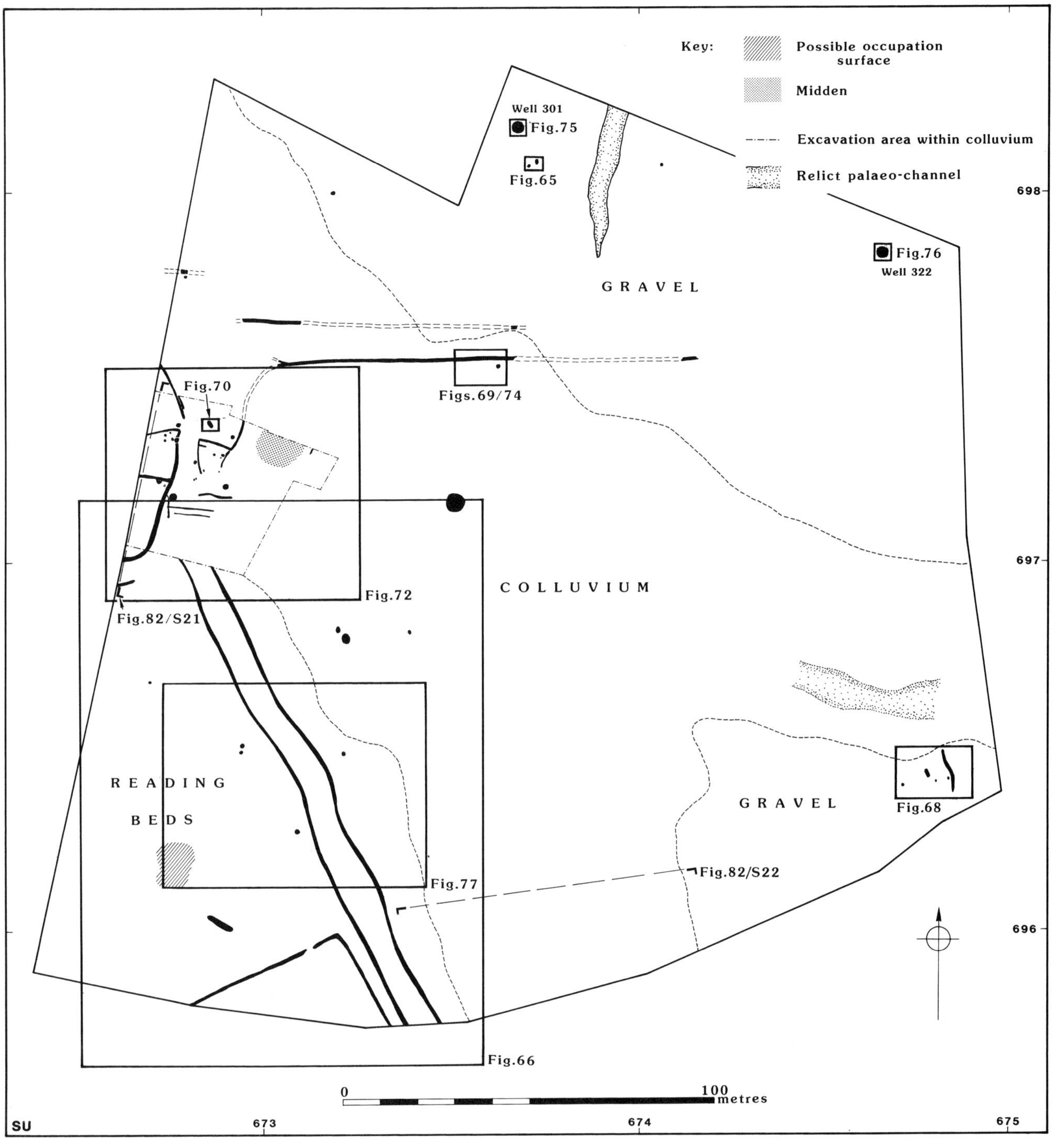

Figure 62 Overall feature location plan, showing the limits of the detailed plans

of the excavation commenced almost immediately and comprised the following:

- the examination of 15% of the colluvium by means of radiating trenches approximately perpendicular to the curve of the slope against which the colluvium was situated
- the excavation of several machine trenches across a linear band of alluvial material; this proved to represent the route of a relict channel which formerly crossed the site on an approximately west–east alignment
- the hand-excavation of all visible features, in accordance with the methodology outlined below

The colluvium assessment (details in archive) revealed a concentration of features of probable Romano-British date identified against the western limit of the excavation area, coinciding with the proposed location for the MSA fuel filling station. On the basis of these discoveries it was deemed necessary to remove a larger area of colluvium, extending across the main development zone of the fuel filling station (*see* Fig. 62, Pl. 16). A number of smaller trenches were also excavated adjacent to

Plate 16 Colluvium excavation area during stripping, looking north-east towards the M4

isolated features uncovered in evaluation trenches containing colluvium further to the east.

The excavation and recording methods, as detailed in the Section 106 agreement, involved a minimum of 10% excavation of linear features, such as ditches, gullies etc. and a minimum 50% excavation of discrete features such as pits, post-holes etc. A comprehensive set of sealed and/or dated environmental samples were taken from these features. All recording was carried out using Wessex Archaeology *pro forma* recording sheets and all features were recorded both by illustration and photographically. All fieldwork was completed on 29 April 1994, the Stage 2 excavation period lasting seven weeks in total.

Geology and Topography

Available geological data (Mobil Oil Company Ltd. 1991; Ordnance Survey 1971) indicates recent valley gravel, deposited by the River Kennet and its main tributaries, covering the north-eastern portion of the site. This gravel is comprised of chalk-derived flints and flint pebbles originating from the Eocene strata (Reading Beds), combined with sandstone and quartzite fragments in a sandy matrix. Borehole data indicates the valley gravel to reach a maximum thickness of *c.* 12 m.

At Wickhams Field the gravel overlies solid geology comprising Eocene Reading Beds, which rise up to form part of the southern edge of the River Kennet floodplain. In addition, a cap of London Clay originally existed to the south-west of the site, adjacent to Dean's Copse. However, although formal records do not exist, it is known that the London Clay was removed during construction work associated with the M4 motorway in 1970.

Within the Reading district in general, the Reading Beds are believed to comprise fluviatile mottled plastic clays and light-coloured sand strata forming up to 27 m of deposits, incorporating an upper mantle of clay-rich deposits, overlying more sandy material. From this evidence it is clear that the material identified at Wickhams Field represents the lower sandy portion of the Reading Beds. Bedrock in the area comprises Cretaceous Upper Chalk, the upper surface of which dips gently to the south. On geological and topographical grounds, therefore, the site can be divided into three broad zones, as outlined below and delimited on Figure 62:

- features identified cutting into the surface of the Reading Beds on the high ground in the south-west corner of the site
- features cutting through and/or sealed by the colluvium
- features cutting through the valley gravel along the north and east edges of the site

2. Site Description

The dating of features is based on a combination of stratigraphy, ceramic analysis and radiocarbon dating. With regard to the former, very limited horizontal stratigraphy was recorded and it was almost wholly confined to the area of excavation within the colluvium (*see* Fig. 72). Vertical stratigraphy was observed in the sequence of colluvial deposits (as discussed below). A group of features was essentially undatable. Some of these have been assigned a date with a fair degree of confidence, based on their association with other, datable, features. Those features which cannot be dated with any degree of confidence have been assigned 'undated' and are briefly summarised here; fuller details on this group is held in the project archive. The chronological sequence of activity may be summarised as follows:

- Late Neolithic–Early Bronze Age
- Early Iron Age
- Earlier Romano-British
- Later Romano-British
- Saxon
- Post-medieval and modern

Prehistoric

Although features attributable to this period were recorded throughout the excavation area, they were concentrated within the south-west portion, primarily on the higher Reading Beds (Fig. 63).

Late Neolithic–Early Bronze Age (c. 3000–1500 BC)

The only feature containing earlier prehistoric pottery, Fengate style Peterborough Ware (Fig. 80, 1), was pit 9 (Fig. 65), recorded on the Valley Gravel towards the northern limit of the excavation area. This was elliptical in plan, measuring 0.6 x 0.38 m and 0.05 m deep, with fairly steep sides and a flat base, and filled with dark greyish–brown silt loam containing quantities of burnt material including quartz, flint, and charcoal (Fig. 65, S1). Pit 501, a similarly shaped but undated feature, was considered to be possibly contemporaneous and was situated approximately 1.2 m to the west-south-west. This measured 0.5 x 0.4 m and 0.05 m deep, with a similar fill also containing burnt flint. The long axis for

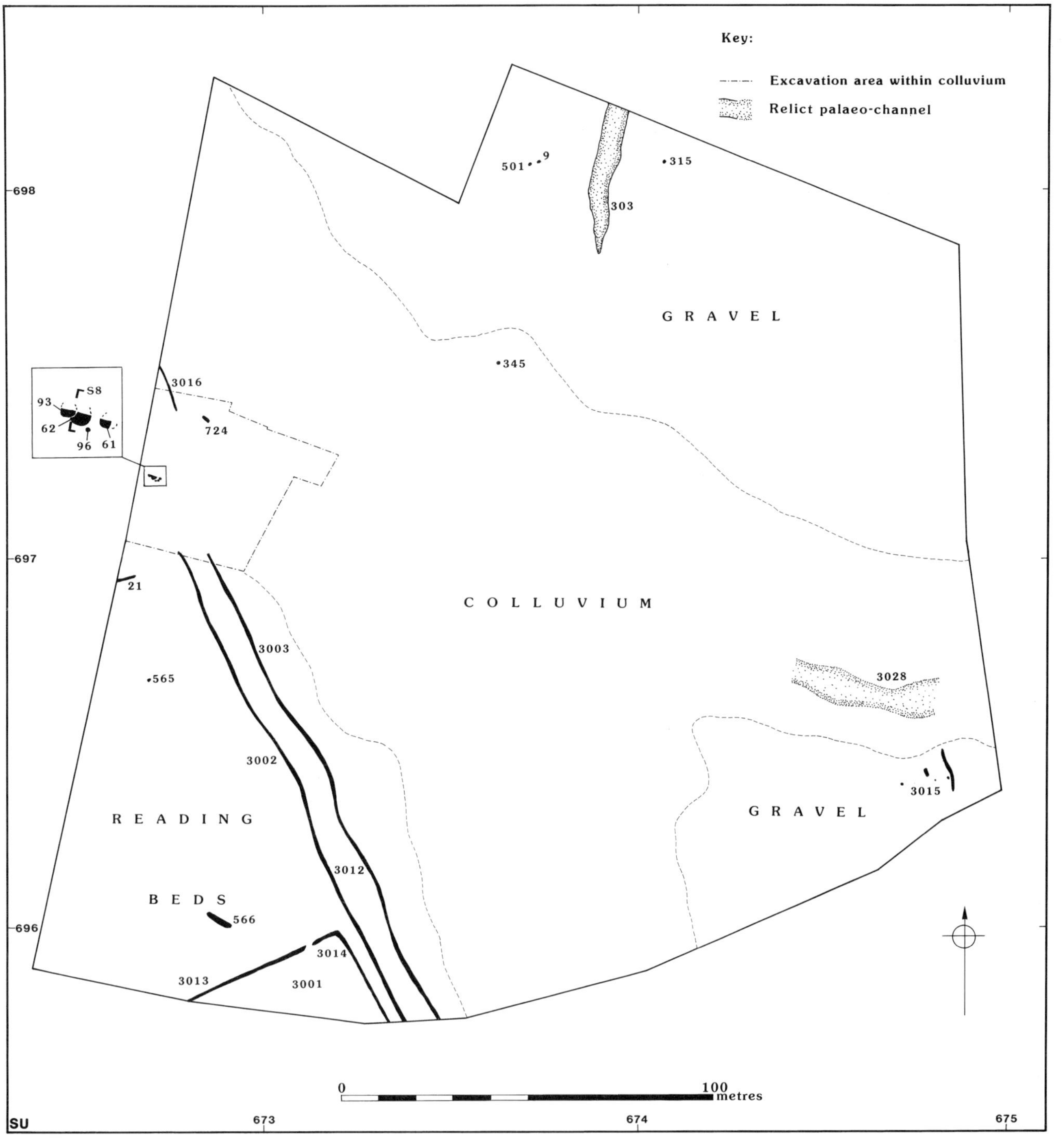

Figure 63 Overall plan of prehistoric features

both features was aligned approximately south-west to north-east.

Early Iron Age (*c.* 700–400 BC)

Trackway 3012

The principal feature associated with this phase was trackway 3012 (Fig. 63 and 66), comprising a pair of parallel ditches: 3002 to the west and 3003 to the east. Although meandering very slightly, the trackway was aligned generally south-south-east to north-north-west across the brow of the higher ground in the south-west, and continued beyond the southern excavation limit.

The trackway extended across the excavation area for at least 145 m. The average internal width was *c.* 7 m, ranging between *c.* 5.5 m and 9 m. Limited evidence for recutting was recorded, with isolated segments (259 and 591) within both ditches revealing firm evidence for steeper, deeper recuts (262 and 594; Fig. 67, S3 and S4 respectively). No evidence, such as tip lines or slumping, was recorded for the presence or absence of upcast banks associated with either ditch.

Possible terminals were identified at the northern ends of both ditches, recorded within segments 615 (ditch 3002; Fig. 67, S6) and 269 (ditch 3003). However, the shallow ephemeral nature of these segments does

Plate 17 Early Iron Age clay-lined pit 416, group 3015 (2 m scale)

not preclude the possibility that the trackway originally continued to the north and has been removed and/or eroded by later activity.

In summary, the westernmost ditch 3002 was generally narrower and deeper than ditch 3003, with proportionately steeper sides, as indicated by the smaller depth to width ratio.

Stratigraphic sequences recorded through ditch 3002 were relatively simple, with a maximum of three definable layers present in any one segment, and more often only two or one. The soil matrices can be summarised as predominantly charcoal flecked greyish/yellowish–brown silty clays to silty loams, with occasional primary fills of mottled dark yellowish–brown sandy loam.

The stratigraphic sequences recorded through ditch 3003 were similarly relatively simple, again with a maximum of three definable layers present in any one segment, and often only two or one. The soil matrices can be summarised as predominantly yellowish–brown to greyish–brown silty clays, with occasional primary fills of dark yellowish–brown clay loam and mottled grey clay. Other than charcoal-flecking within most layers, concentrated lenses of charcoal were also present within the secondary fills of two segments (591 and 613; Fig. 67, S4 and S5 respectively).

Enclosure 3001

Enclosure 3001 was represented by ditches 3013 and 3014, these features combining to form the north-east corner of a probable rectilinear area (Figs 63 and 66). One side of this enclosure was parallel to trackway 3012, and *c.* 3.5 m to the west of the trackway. Ditch 3014 was at least 36 m long overall, including a 90° turn to form the corner of the enclosure, whilst ditch 3013 was at least 35 m long.

An interval between the western terminal of ditch 3014 and the eastern terminal of ditch 3013, measuring *c.* 3 m, probably represents an entrance into the enclosure. Although terminal features, such as post-holes, could not be positively identified, the irregular shape in plan of the ditch terminal to the west of the probable entrance suggests the presence of such a feature. No features were identified within the enclosure.

As with trackway 3012 (above), a number of segments were excavated through the enclosure ditches. In summary, although ditch 3013 was generally both narrower and shallower than ditch 3014, both ditches exhibited similar profiles in terms of their depth to width ratios. None of the excavated segments through either ditch revealed more than a single homogeneous fill, the soil matrices can be summarised as predominantly greyish–brown clay loams and silty clays.

Feature group 3015

This group of features was recorded on the valley gravel in the south-east corner of the excavation area and comprised pits 416 and 430, post-holes 412 and 414, and layer 409 (Figs 63 and 68). Of these features, only pit 416 produced dating evidence other than charcoal, but all are considered to be contemporaneous. This interpretation is based partly on the similar fills, including frequent to profuse fragments of burnt flint, and partly on their proximity to each other in an area that is otherwise virtually devoid of features. A further pair of post-holes (Fig. 68, S10), one of which also contained Early Iron Age pottery, were cut into the upper fill of pit 416, and as such are not considered as part of this group.

Pit 416 was a sub-rectangular feature on an approximate north–south alignment, up to 3.3 m long, 1.75 m wide, and 0.4 m deep, with very steep, slightly concave north and west sides and moderate south and east sides (Fig. 68, S10). The base was generally flat, with a shallow rounded depression filled with a mixture of sand (427) and redeposited valley gravel (429) within the south-west corner. Excavation indicated the presence of

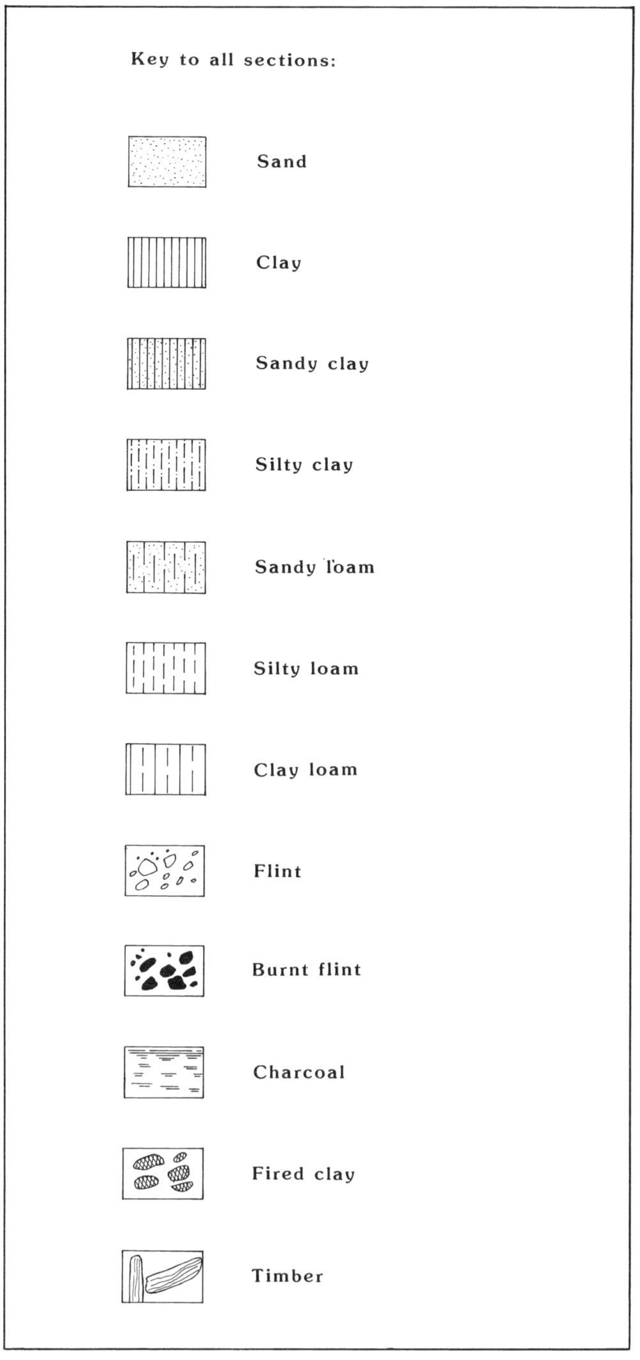

Figure 64 Key to all section conventions

a heat-affected clay lining (426) on the base and sides (Pl. 17). This lining sealed the fill of the shallow depression noted above (Fig. 68, S10). It is not clear, therefore, whether this depression represents the truncated remains of an earlier feature, or merely an uneven base that required levelling prior to lining the pit with clay.

The internal dimensions for the area defined by the clay lining were 1.9 m long and 0.8 m wide, with very steep almost vertical sides and a flat base. Lining 416 survived as a thin intermittent layer forming the base, up to 0.06 m thick, with short clay walls on all four sides surviving to a maximum height of 0.17 m. There was no evidence to suggest that any other materials, such as stonework, were used in the construction of this lining. The almost vertical interface between layers 415 and 417 continued beyond the upper limit of the clay-lining to ground surface (Fig. 68, S10). Its presence suggests that the upper portion of the clay-lining had been deliberately removed after fill 415 had been deposited, to be backfilled with layer 417. However, it was not possible to positively identify any 'robber' cuts.

The feature was filled almost entirely with layer 415, a single deposit of very dark brown silt containing in excess of *c.* 86 kgs of burnt flint, with layer 425, a small primary deposit of similar composition situated in the north-west corner. Dating evidence was restricted to a small sherd of undiagnostic later prehistoric pottery recovered from layer 415. Although it is reasonable to assume that this clay-lined feature was used to contain water, which could be warmed by adding heated flints, the function of the feature (ie cooking, sauna, industrial, etc.) is unclear.

Pit 430 was situated *c.* 7 m to the west-south-west of pit 416 and was a sub-circular feature, 0.85 m long, 0.7 m wide, and 0.24 m deep, with vertical sides and a slightly rounded base. Two fills were identified, both comprising very heavily charcoal-flecked black silts containing profuse quantities of slag, as well as burnt flint and fired clay. It is possible that the quantities of iron slag within this feature and burnt flint within pit 416 represent by-products of the same process.

Post-holes 412 and 414 were *c.* 4 m apart on a west-south-west to east-north-east line, with the westernmost post-hole (414) adjacent to the south-east corner of pit 416. Both post-holes were sub-circular, measuring *c.* 0.18 m and 0.11 m in diameter respectively, and steep sided, with a flat base to post-hole 412 and a narrow rounded base to post-hole 414.

Layer 409 was a linear spread of burnt flint, aligned roughly north–south and *c.* 5 m to the east of pit 416. The spread passed to the east of, and appeared to respect, post-hole 412. Overall, it covered an area of *c.* 8.5 x 0.5 m, with excavation revealing a depth of no more than 0.03 m. It is possible that this feature represents the remains of a larger spread of burnt flint inadvertently removed during topsoil stripping, and preserved in its recorded shape due to compaction by 25 tonne dump truck wheels subsiding through the topsoil.

Ditches

Other than the ditches recorded as sub-divisions of either trackway 3012 or enclosure 3001 (above), at least three additional linear features are attributed to this phase.

Ditch 566 (Figs 63 and 66) was aligned south-east–north-west, and was 7.5 m long, 1.8 m wide, and only 0.2 m deep. This broad shallow feature was recorded *c.* 13 m to the north-west of enclosure 3001, and filled with dark yellowish–brown slightly sandy clay loam. Although both terminals were identified, no terminal features were identified.

Ditch 21 (Figs 63 and 67) was a 'V' profiled feature, aligned west-south-west–east-north-east, and at least 6 m long, 0.56 m wide, and 0.18 m deep. This was recorded to the west of the northern limit of trackway 3012, and continued beyond the western limit of the excavation. All segments examined revealed identical sequences of primary and upper fills, comprising dark yellowish–

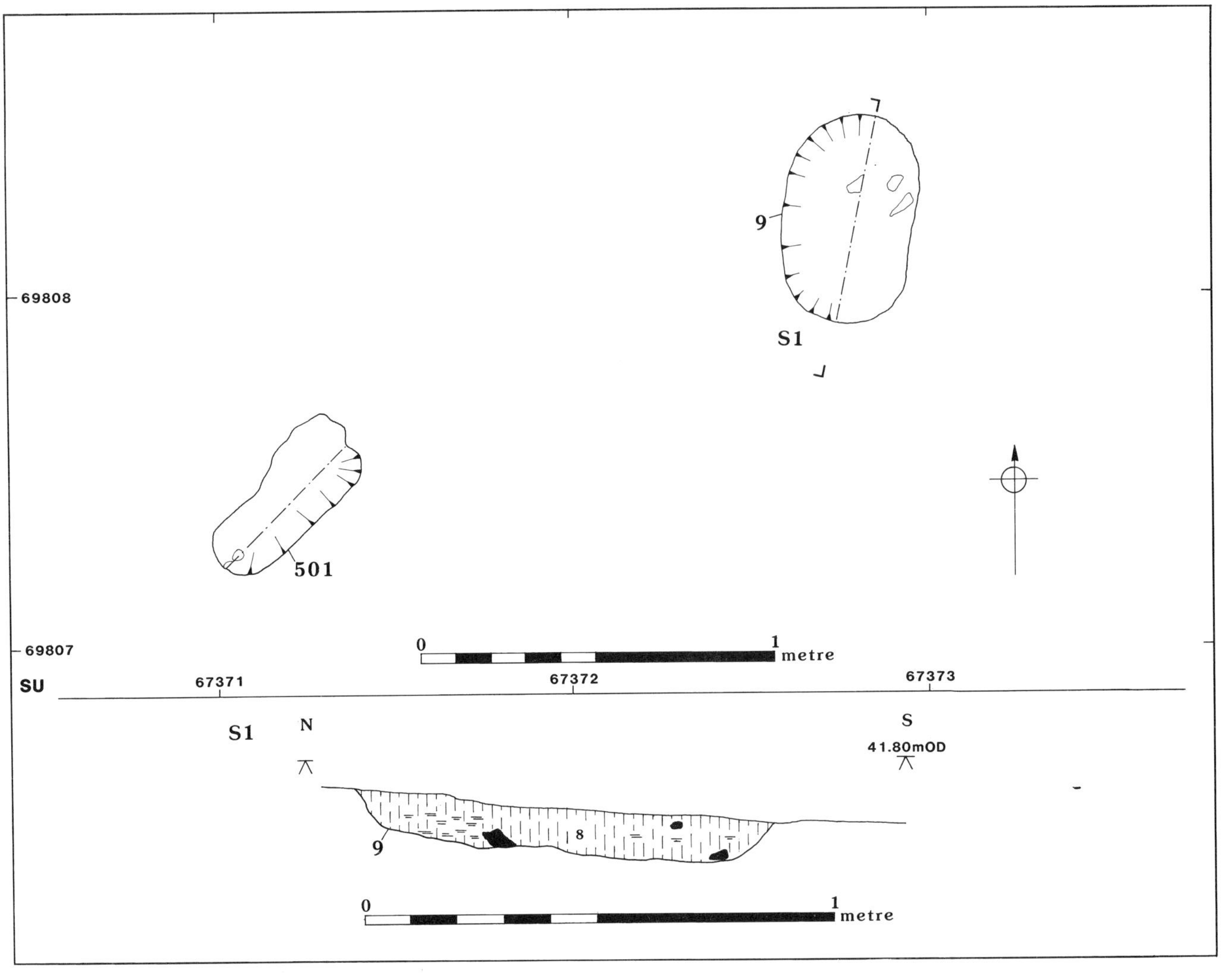

Figure 65 Detailed plan of Late Neolithic–Early Bronze Age pits 9 and 501, with section of pit 9

brown clay loam sealed by greyish–brown clay loam. Examination of the apparent eastern 'terminal' appeared to indicate that the feature had been reduced by subsequent disturbance and probably originally continued further eastwards towards trackway 3012.

Ditch 3016 (Fig. 63) was aligned south- south-east to north-north-west, and at least 13 m long, 0.64 m wide, and up to 0.24 m deep with moderately sloping sides and a slightly irregular pointed base. This was within the area of colluvium, following approximately the same line as ditch 3003 (trackway 3012) to the south and continued beyond the western limit of the excavation. Although a southern 'terminal' for this feature was recorded, its shallow tapering nature and the absence of a terminal feature suggest that it originally continued to the south and had been truncated by subsequent disturbance.

The east edge of ditch 3016 had been recut by ditch 3017, a similarly aligned feature for which a southern terminal was also recorded, *c.* 2 m to the north of the southern terminal of ditch 3016. However, despite the apparent association between these two features, ditch 3017 produced both Romano-British and late prehistoric pottery, and it is therefore phased as Romano-British, although the possibility of intrusive finds should not be discounted.

Although there was an interval of *c.* 40 m between ditches 3016 and 3003, it is possible that they represent parts of the same trackway ditch. If so, the gap between these two features could be deliberate, but is perhaps more likely to be the result of subsequent disturbance related to Romano-British activity in the area. This argument is supported by the distribution of late prehistoric pottery within Romano-British features in the vicinity which is restricted to those features and ditch segments that are situated on the projected line of the ditch. It therefore appears that trackway 3012 originally continued to the north, incorporating ditch 3016.

Pits and post-holes

Securely dated discrete Early Iron Age features, although few on the ground, were present throughout the excavation area. There did not appear to be a concentration in the vicinity of trackway 3012 and enclosure 3001, although at least six of the features identified in this area could not be dated (see below). The dated features are discussed individually below.

Pit 345 (Figs 63 and 69; Pl. 18) was a sub-circular feature towards the northern limit of the colluvium, and had partially been disturbed by recent activity. The pit was *c.* 1.3 m in diameter and 0.37 m deep, with a shallow sloping concave south side, a steep sloping concave north

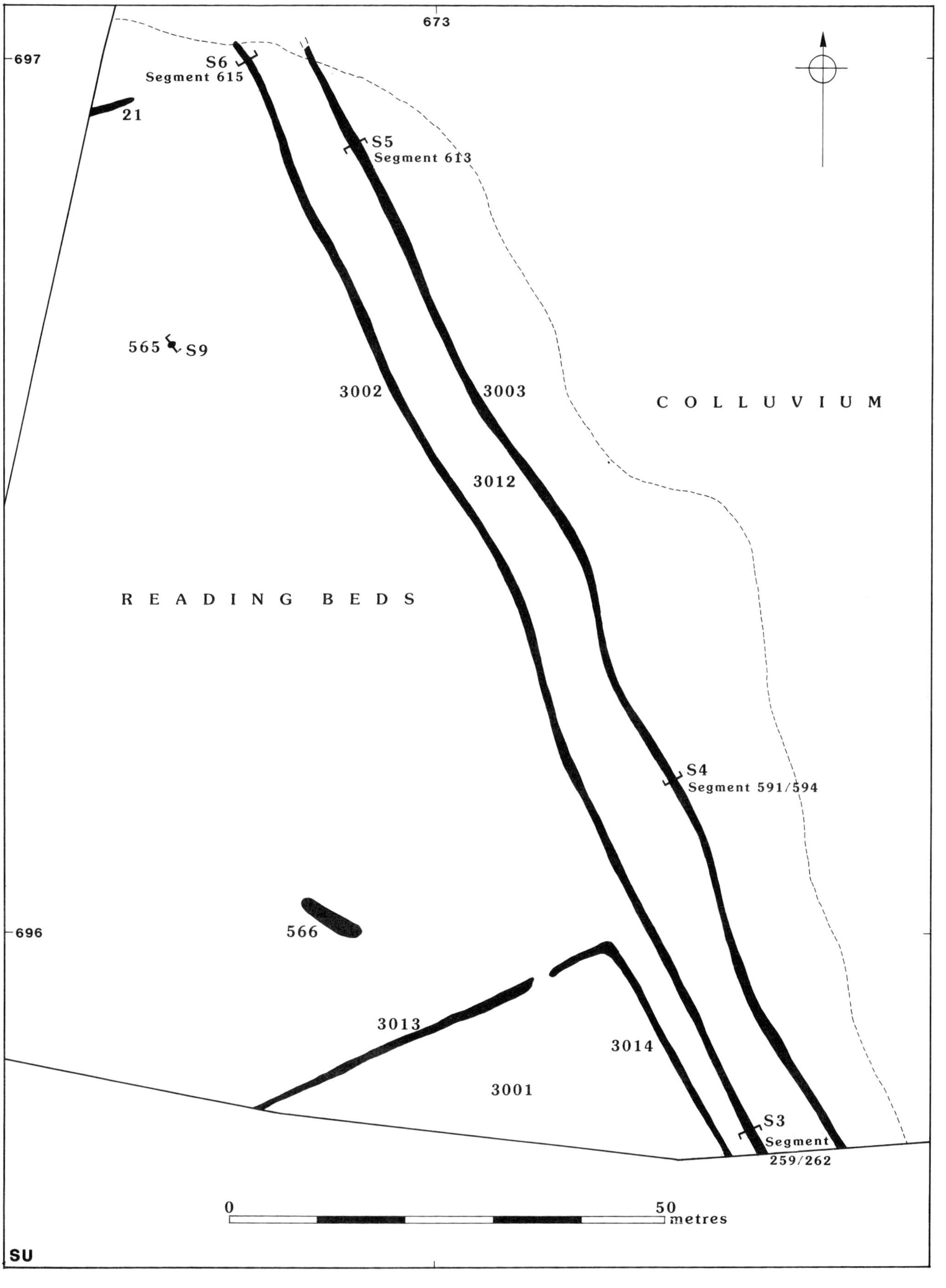

Figure 66 *Plan of prehistoric features in south-west corner of excavation area*

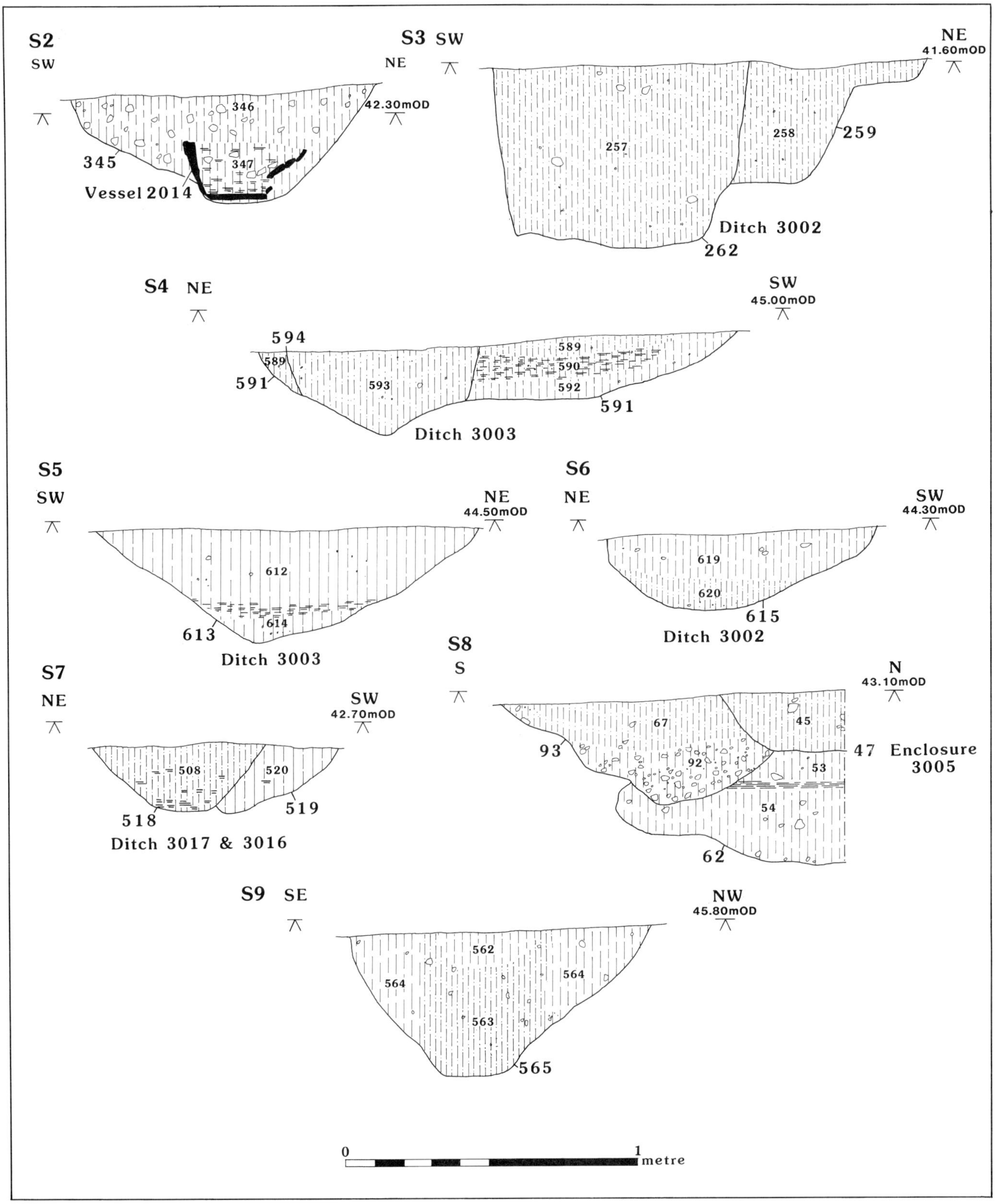

Figure 67 Sections across prehistoric ditches, pits, and post-holes

side, and a small, circular flat base offset towards the north edge. Seated on the base was Object No. 2014, the fragmented remains of a large pottery vessel containing charcoal flecked yellowish–brown silty clay, the main body of the pit containing yellowish–brown sandy loam (Fig. 67, S2). Although this feature resembled a funerary deposit, no finds were recovered to support such an interpretation.

Pits 61 and 62 were adjacent to each other (Fig. 63), both being substantially disturbed by the later Romano-British enclosure ditches 3004 and 3005 (*see* below). This disturbance may explain the presence of

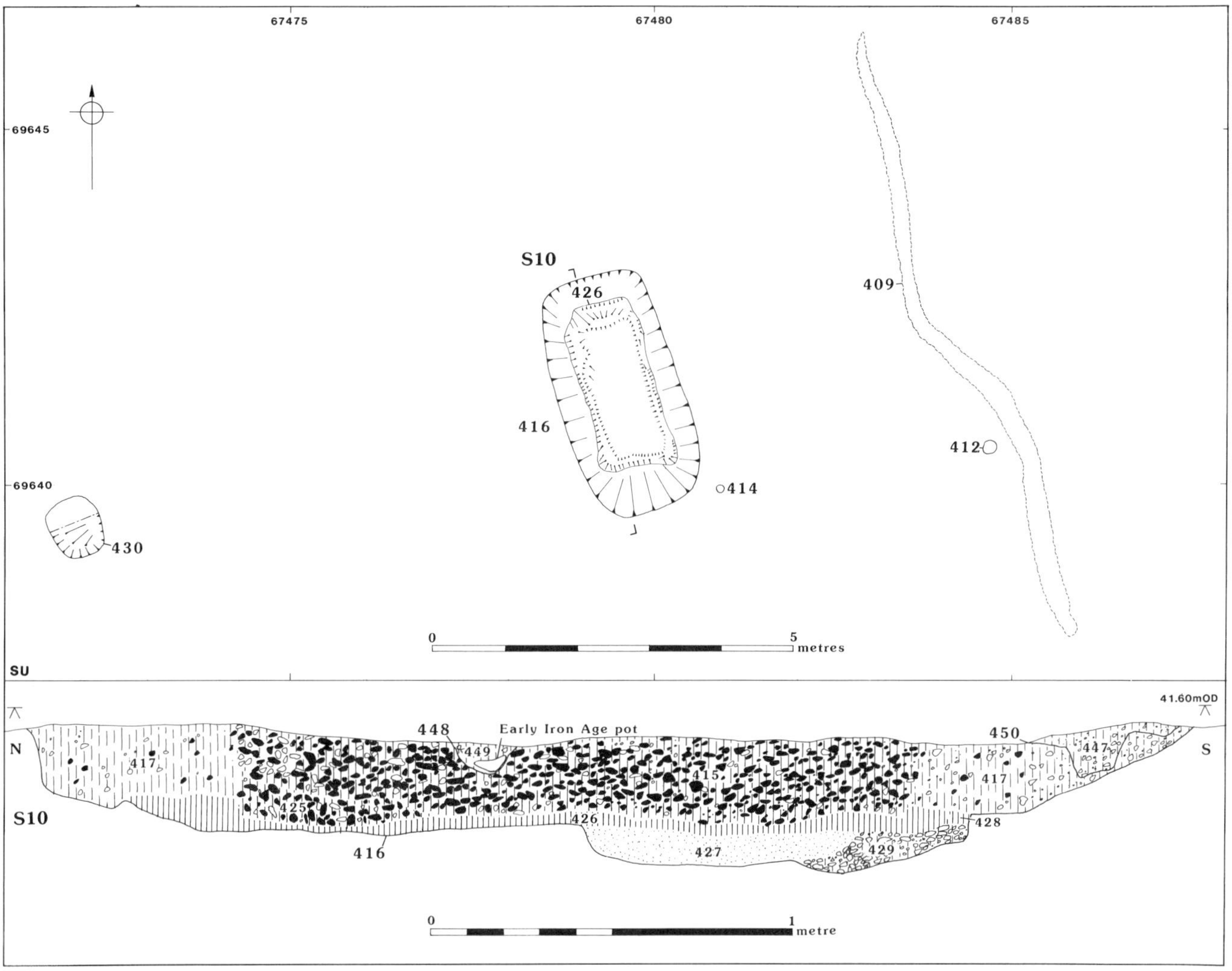

Figure 68 Detailed plan of group 3015, with section of pit 416

isolated Romano-British sherds within the larger late prehistoric pottery assemblages recovered from each pit. The pits were sub-circular, though slightly irregular, in plan with pit 61 at least 1 x 0.8 m and pit 62 (Fig. 67, S8) at least 1.2 x 1.3 m. Both had generally moderate sloping sides and flat bases, although pit 62 exhibited a slightly overhanging edge on its southern side and was filled with grey silty clay. Post-hole 96 (Fig. 63), immediately to the south of pit 62, was an extremely shallow flat bottomed feature, 0.26 m in diameter and 0.03 deep, filled with yellowish–brown silty clay.

In addition to the group of features noted above, pit 93 (Fig. 63) was situated slightly to the west, cutting through the western edge of pit 62 and also cut by Romano-British enclosure ditch 3005 (Fig. 67, S8). Although stratigraphically later than pit 62, finds from this feature include a substantial quantity of late prehistoric pottery with no other diagnostic pottery present. The surviving portion of the feature was sub-circular, at least 0.92 m in diameter and 0.36 m deep, with irregular stepped sides and a small flat base, and filled with brownish–grey silty clay above greyish–brown clay loam.

Pit 724 (Figs 63 and 70) was a shallow sub-rectangular feature aligned south-east–north-west, and

Plate 18 Excavation of Early Iron Age vessel 2014, pit 345

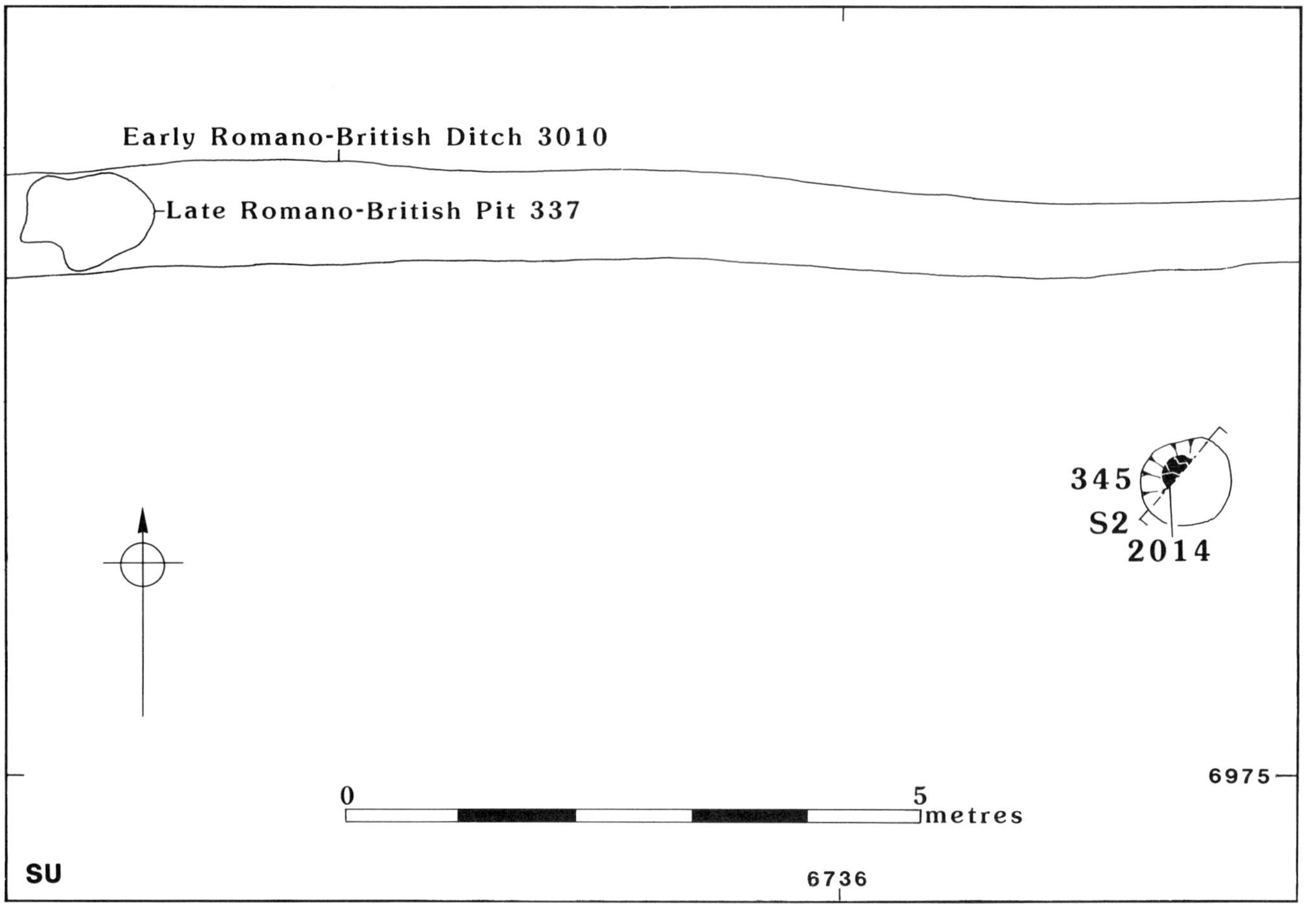

Figure 69 Detailed plan of Early Iron Age pit 345

situated *c.* 20 m to the north-east of pit 61. This feature was 2.1 m long, 0.6 m wide, and 0.2 m deep, with moderate sloping sides and a flat base, and filled with dark yellowish–brown silty clay. Finds recovered include two distinct concentrations of Iron Age pottery towards either end of the feature, identified as representing the fragmented remains of two vessels (*see* Fig. 70). Although this feature resembles a grave cut, complete with possible votive offerings, no human remains were recovered to support such an interpretation.

Post-hole 565 (Figs 63 and 66) was an isolated elliptical feature, recorded *c.* 20 m to the west of trackway 3012. It measured 1 x 0.8 m, the long axis aligned east-south-east to west-north-west, and had moderate concave sides. The main body of this feature was 0.39 m deep, at the base of which was a 0.11 m deep, sub-circular, steep sided and flat bottomed depression measuring 0.35 x 0.24 m. The section (Fig. 67, S9) clearly demonstrated a vertical column of greyish–brown silty clay above the depression, almost certainly representing a post-pipe. The upper 0.11 m of this post-pipe contained dark greyish–brown silty clay with common charcoal flecks, possibly representing the remains of a post burnt *in situ*. Packing material to either side of the post-pipe comprised relatively stone-free yellowish–brown silty loam.

Pit 315 (Fig. 63) was a very shallow circular feature situated on the valley gravel towards the northern limit of the excavation area. It was 0.4 m in diameter and only 0.06 m deep, with moderate concave sides and a rounded base, and filled with dark grey silty clay containing very common charcoal flecking and probably grass-tempered Early Iron Age pottery.

Post-holes 448 and 450 were *c.* 1.7 m apart on a north–south line, and identified in the south-east corner of the excavation, cutting through the backfilled remains of pit 416 (feature group 3015; Fig. 68, S10). Both were sub-circular in plan and steep sided, *c.* 0.16 m in diameter and 0.1 m deep, post-hole 448 having an even sloping base, and post-hole 450 a slightly rounded base. Although Early Iron Age pottery was only recovered from post-hole 448, post-hole 450 is considered as contemporaneous on the basis of its similarity and proximity. Insufficient evidence was recovered to interpret the function of these features.

Romano-British

On the basis of diagnostic sherds and stratigraphic evidence, the majority of the features attributable to this period are early Romano-British (ie 1st or 2nd century AD). These were primarily concentrated towards the western limit of the excavation area and sealed by more recent colluvial deposits (Fig. 71), with a west–east aligned trackway partially on the valley gravel to the north-east. Isolated features within the main concentration to the west produced later Romano-British (ie 3rd–4th century) pottery, including a small enclosure ditch and pit. However, most of this material was recov-

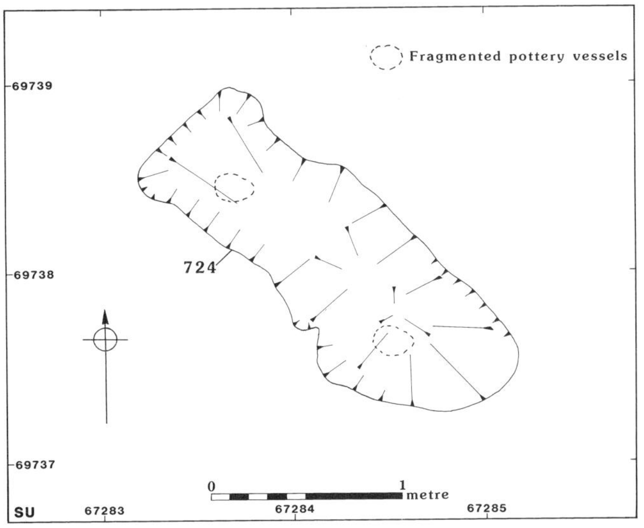

Figure 70 Detailed plan of Early Iron Age pit 724

ered from a midden deposit towards the eastern limit of the main concentration of general Romano-British activity.

Earlier Romano-British (*c.* 1st–2nd century AD)

The stratigraphically earliest features attributable to this phase were trackway 3018 (Fig. 71) and ditch 3019 (Fig. 72). Both contained 1st–2nd century AD pottery and both have been cut by features also containing 1st–2nd century AD pottery. As such, these features are discussed first, although it is not considered that they represented a separate phase of activity, but merely a sub-phase for the general early Romano-British period.

Trackway 3018

This east–west aligned linear feature comprised a pair of parallel ditches: ditch 3011 to the north and ditch 3010 to the south (Fig. 71). These ditches passed from the northern edge of the colluvium onto the valley gravel to the north-east. Sections examined, particularly towards the western limit of the trackway (segments 274 and 735, ditch 3011; segments 745 and 657, ditch 3010), indicated that this feature had cut through the earliest layers of colluvium and were sealed by more recent material. As a result, apart from the colluvium evaluation trenches, the western extent of the ditches were not recorded in plan view.

In addition, the route of the trackway eastwards across the valley gravel had also been lost, probably by plough damage, in all but a few isolated places. These locations corresponded to apparent slight depressions in the upper surface of the valley gravels that were filled with small outlying patches of colluvium. Overall, the recorded length of the trackway was at least 125 m, with an internal width of *c.* 8 m, but ranging between *c.* 7 and 10 m. No evidence was recovered for either recutting or ditch terminals.

Feature 328 was an elongated very shallow discrete feature on the line of ditch 3011 that probably represents the truncated remains of the ditch. In summary, although ditch 3010 appears to have been generally broader and deeper than ditch 3011, the latter does appear to have had consistently steeper sloping sides, as indicated by its lower depth to width ratio.

Apart from one segment (438, *see* below), stratigraphic sequences through both ditches were relatively simple, with only one or two definable layers present in a segment, but more often than not only a single fill recorded. The soil matrices for ditch 3010 can be characterised as predominantly dark yellowish–brown to yellowish–brown silty clays, with primary fills evident as greyish–brown silty clays. Those for ditch 3011 appeared to be predominantly darker and slightly sandier, comprising dark yellowish–brown to greyish–brown silty clays to silty loams.

Segment 438 (Fig. 73, S11) through ditch 3011 contained at least three fills, with the primary and secondary fills laid against the north side of the feature and sloping down to the south. These comprised stonefree, yellowish–brown silt below dark yellowish–brown silty flint gravel and sealed by an upper fill of yellowish–brown silty clay with occasional flint gravel. The presence of apparent tip or slumping lines originating from the north edge of the segment suggests that these layers represent eroded material from an upcast bank to the north.

Ditch 3019

This north–south aligned, slightly irregular feature was within the area of Romano-British activity towards the western limit of the excavation area (Fig. 72). Overall, the feature was *c.* 6.5 m long, 0.6 m wide, and 0.17 m deep with moderate concave sides and a shallow rounded base, although the middle section, measuring 1.3 m, was both narrower and shallower. Terminal features were evident immediately to the west of both the north and south ends of this ditch, comprising shallow, sub-circular post-holes, *c.* 0.25–0.3 m in diameter, with a pair at the north and one at the south. The northern end of this feature appeared to respect the east edge of enclosure 3004, whilst the central shallower portion had been cut by part of structure 3022.

Enclosure 3004

This comprised a single curving ditch forming the south-eastern corner of a possible sub-rectangular enclosure, recorded at the southern limit of the colluvium and

Plate 19 Romano-British enclosure ditch 3004 (larger scale 1 m)

continuing beyond the west side of the excavation area (Fig. 72, Pl. 19). The area enclosed by this ditch was probably *c.* 35 m north–south and at least 6 m east–west, although the northernmost *c.* 13 m of this enclosure had been recut by later enclosure 3005 (*see* below).

On average the ditch was *c.* 1.2 m wide and between 0.2 m and 0.48 m deep, its upper edges following a convex slope and lower edges a concave slope, with a generally rounded base (eg segment 91; Fig. 73, S13). A maximum of five layers was recorded within the ditch, these comprising alternating layers of inclusion free and gravelly silty clays, the majority being yellowish–brown, with primary fills of slightly greyish, darker material. No direct evidence was recorded for the presence of an associated upcast bank, although the presence of a group of similarly dated pits (feature group 3006 below) within the north-east corner of this enclosure suggests an external bank if any.

Structure 3007 and ditch 3008

These features were situated to the east of enclosure 3004 and comprised at least five post-holes and a hearth (structure 3007) surrounded by a discontinuous ditch forming a sub-rectangular area (ditch 3008). This ditch also continued northwards from the north-east corner of this area to beyond the limit of excavation. Dating evidence was only recovered from several segments excavated through ditch 3008 and one of the post-holes forming structure 3007. However, these features are all considered as contemporaneous on the basis of their general layout in relation to each other.

Structure 3007

This structure comprised post-holes 278, 274, 394, and 678, forming the south-west, south-east, north-east, and north-west corners respectively of a trapezoidal area covering *c.* 16 m^2 (Fig. 72). They were all shallow sub-circular features, 0.22 x 0.45 m in diameter, filled with grey to greyish–brown silty clay. Their truncated nature suggests that additional features may have originally existed that have been completely removed by later activity. It is unclear whether these features formed the remains of either a system of internal roof supports or external wall posts. However, the position of hearth 377 (below) may suggest that the former is perhaps more likely.

In addition, post-hole 214 (Fig. 72; Pl. 20) was identified on the northern side of this trapezoid, *c.* 2.1 m from the north-east corner (post-hole 394). It was 0.75 m in diameter and 0.25 m deep with steep sides and a rounded base and contained a primary fill of compact flint gravel, lining both the base and sides, sealed by a secondary fill of greyish–brown clay loam. The lower deposit of flint gravel probably represents the remains of a post-pad/packing for a substantial upright timber. The position of this post-hole, approximately central to the entire group comprising 3007 and 3008, perhaps indicates the location of the principal supporting member for the structure.

Hearth 377 (Fig. 72), immediately to the north- east of post-hole 394, was an approximately circular feature, *c.* 0.9 m in diameter and 0.16 m deep, with very steep, partially overhanging sides and a broad flat base. This was filled with dark grey sandy silt containing burnt flint, and frequent charcoal flecking which was concentrated to the south on the base of the feature. Although interpreted as a hearth, there was no evidence for burning on the surface of the natural subsoil at the base of the feature, suggesting the use of hearth-stones that have since been removed.

Plate 20 Romano-British post-hole 214, structure 3007 (1 m scale)

Ditch 3008

This feature surrounded structure 3007 to the west, north, and east (Fig. 72), although insufficient evidence was recovered to confirm whether this represented an associated drainage ditch or part of the foundations for structure 3007. On the basis of dimensions, it is possible that different lengths of the ditch performed different functions. Overall, the feature covered an area *c.* 8 m long and 7 m wide, narrowing to *c.* 5.5 m at its southern limit. In addition, a short length of ditch extended eastwards from the north-west corner into the area formed, whilst another length continued from the north-east corner due north-north-east beyond the limit of the excavation.

The west ditch of this feature, including the short length of ditch projecting into the area, was *c.* 0.4 m wide and 0.13 m deep with a rounded profile, and filled with brownish–grey silty clay. Towards the southern limit of this feature it curved slightly towards the east, although it was not possible to identify a southern terminal.

The east ditch was up to *c.* 0.17 m deep with very shallow sides and a slightly rounded base, narrowing from *c.* 1.1 m wide at its northern end to *c.* 0.3 m to the south. The ditch was filled with material ranging from greyish–brown silty clay at its southern end, to a primary fill of greyish–brown sandy silt sealed by light brown silt at its northern extent. Examination of the apparent southern terminal indicated that the feature had probably been damaged by later activity and had originally continued further to the south. Although a drainage function cannot be excluded, these relatively insubstantial east and west features may possibly be

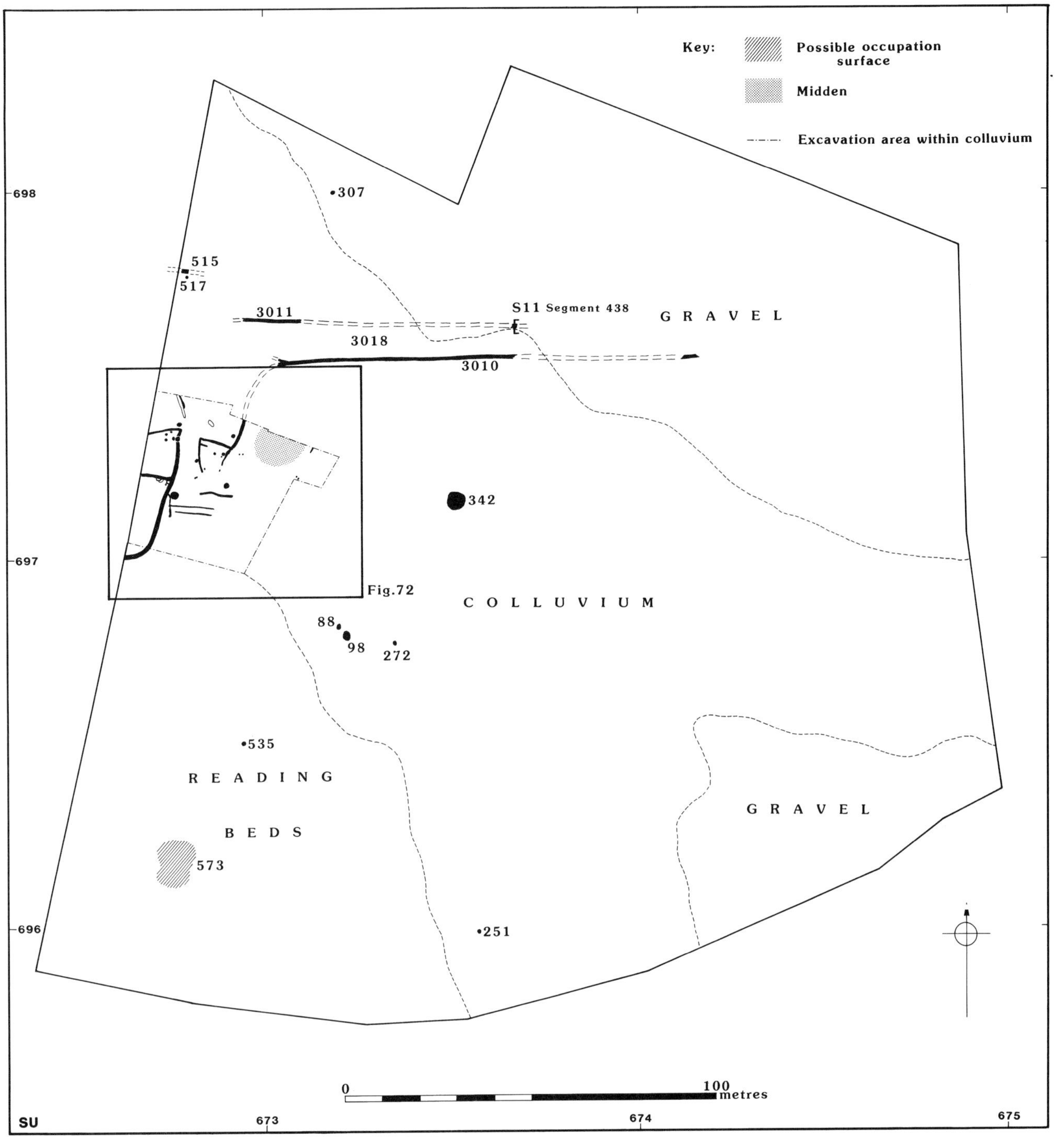

Figure 71 Overall plan of Romano-British features

beam slots, representing part of the foundations for structure 3007.

The northern ditch was generally more substantial than the east and west ditches, up to *c.* 0.8 m wide and 0.32 m deep, with moderate to steep sides and a flat base. This was filled with greyish–brown silty clay, tending to silt and sandy silt towards the east, and is interpreted as a drainage feature. At its east end, this ditch turned to the north-north-east and continued beyond the limits of the excavation area to the north. Although this ditch is considered contemporaneous with the west ditch for the structure, their relationship was obscured by a later pit (pit 390; Fig. 72).

The extension of the northern ditch beyond the excavation area appeared to continue to the north as ditch 745, cutting through ditch 3010 (trackway 3018; Fig. 71) and forming a second phase of activity associated with the aforementioned trackway.

Structure 3022

This east–west aligned feature was situated to the east of enclosure 3004, and comprised a pair of parallel narrow slots (Fig. 72), 3020 to the north and 3021 to the south. Overall, the structure covered an area at least 12.5 m long and 2 m wide, with each slot up to 0.12 m wide and 0.07 m deep, and filled with grey to dark grey

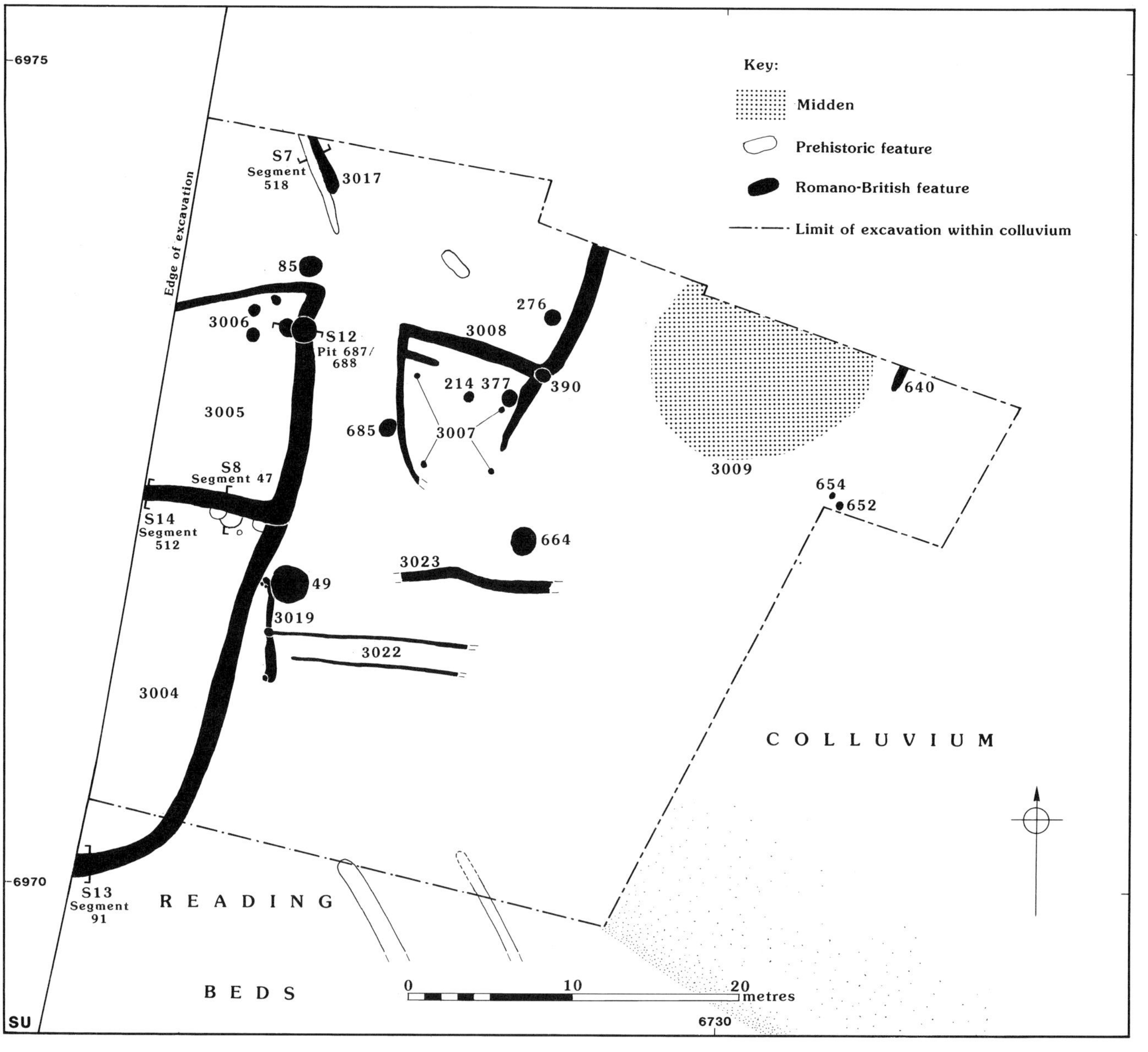

Figure 72 Plan of Romano-British features within colluvium excavation

clayey sand. A post-hole, cutting through ditch 3019 (above), was recorded at the western terminal for slot 3020. This post-hole was 0.5 m in diameter and 0.12 m deep, containing a primary fill of compacted gravel below grey clayey sand. No other terminals were identified, the eastern continuations of these slots probably removed by modern disturbance resulting from the construction of structure 3027 (below). The function of these narrow insubstantial slots is uncertain, though they are unlikely to be drainage features. The presence of a terminal post possibly indicates they represent foundation trenches for timber walls or fences.

Feature group 3006

This comprised four pits in a group, covering an area of c. 6 m^2 to the north of enclosure 3004 (Fig. 72). These consisted of three similar smaller pits, with a larger pit to the the south-east which had been disturbed by later activity. The smaller pits (397, 751, and 674) were either sub-circular or slightly elliptical in plan, measuring c. 0.8 m in diameter, and with similar 'U' shaped profiles. They all produced 1st–2nd century AD material and were filled with mottled grey, green, and yellow sandy and silty clay, with upper fills identified in pits 674 and 751 comprising greyish–brown silty loam.

The larger circular pit (687; Fig. 73, S12) was at least 1.1 m in diameter, cut by a later pit to the east, and had moderately sloping, slightly concave sides and a narrow rounded base. It was filled by three distinct layers comprising bluish–grey silty clay, sealed by greyish–brown loam, with an upper fill of greyish–brown silty loam. Although the bulk of the dating evidence

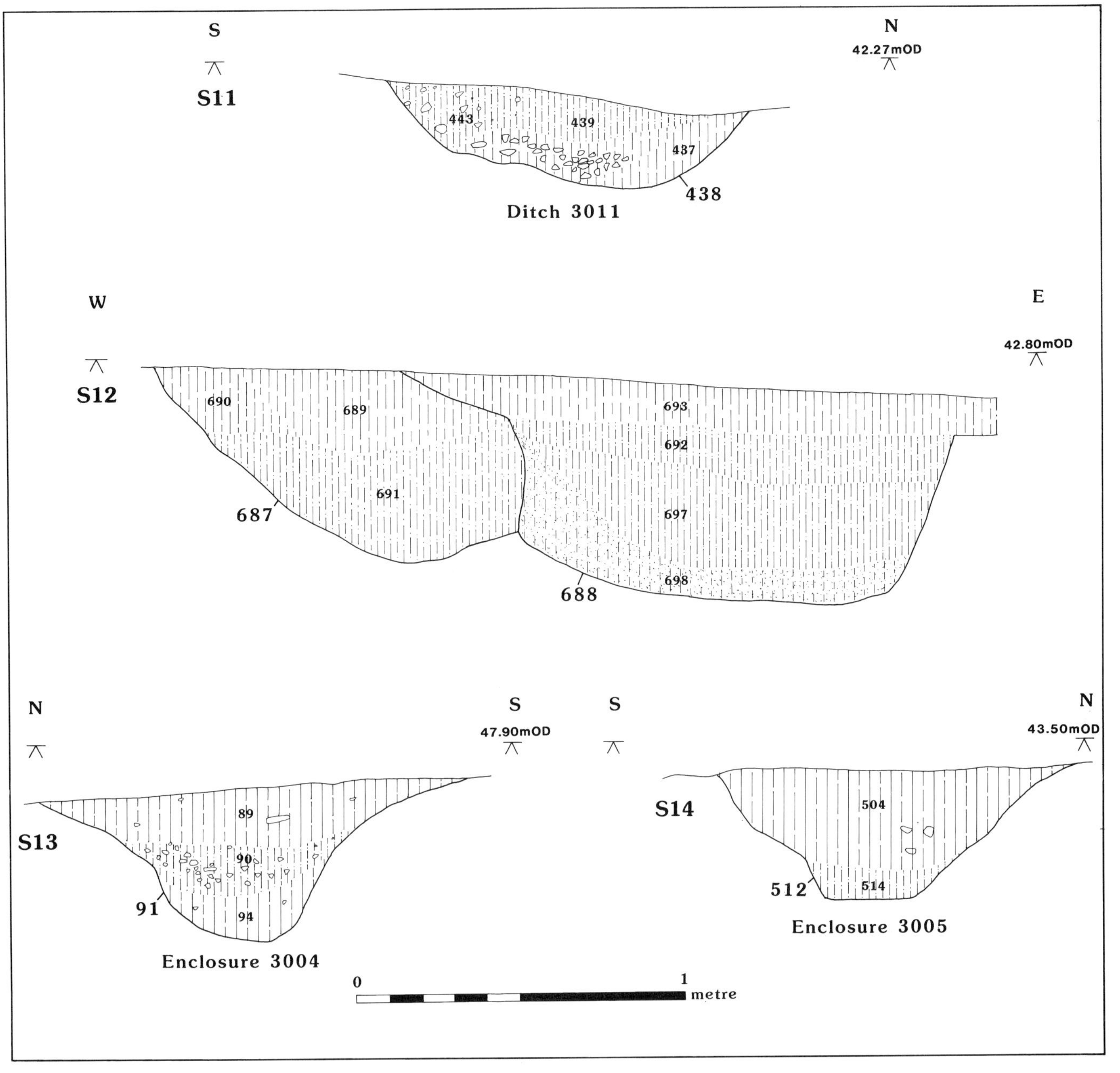

Figure 73 Sections across Romano-British ditches and pits

recovered from this feature was of 1st–2nd century AD date (and earlier), the assemblage included two sherds of later Roman pottery from the upper fill. However, in view of the later pit disturbance, these sherds are considered to be intrusive finds.

No evidence was recovered to identify these features as post-holes, it is therefore likely that they represent a group of pits, possibly for refuse, in the corner of enclosure 3004.

Ditches

Ditch 3017 (Fig. 72) was a north-north-west to south-south-east aligned feature, at least 11 m long, *c.* 0.57 m wide, and up to 0.22 m deep with moderate sloping sides and a flat base, filled with grey to yellowish–brown silty clay. This feature was situated adjacent to, and partially cutting, the east edge of Early Iron Age ditch 3016 (Fig. 67, S7), and produced both 1st–2nd century and undiagnostic prehistoric pottery. A southern terminal was recorded for this feature, although no terminal features were visible. It is possible that the interval between this terminal and the north-east corner of enclosure 3004, *c.* 5.5 m to the south, represents an entranceway into the western area beyond.

Ditch 3023 (Fig. 72) was an east–west aligned slightly meandering feature, *c.* 4 m to the north of slot 3020 (structure 3022). Although neither terminal could be identified, the ditch was at least 8 m long, up to 0.6 m wide and 0.14 m wide, with steep sides and a flat base towards the west, tending to fairly moderate concave sides and a rounded base to the east. The fill also varied from west to east, comprising yellowish–brown silty

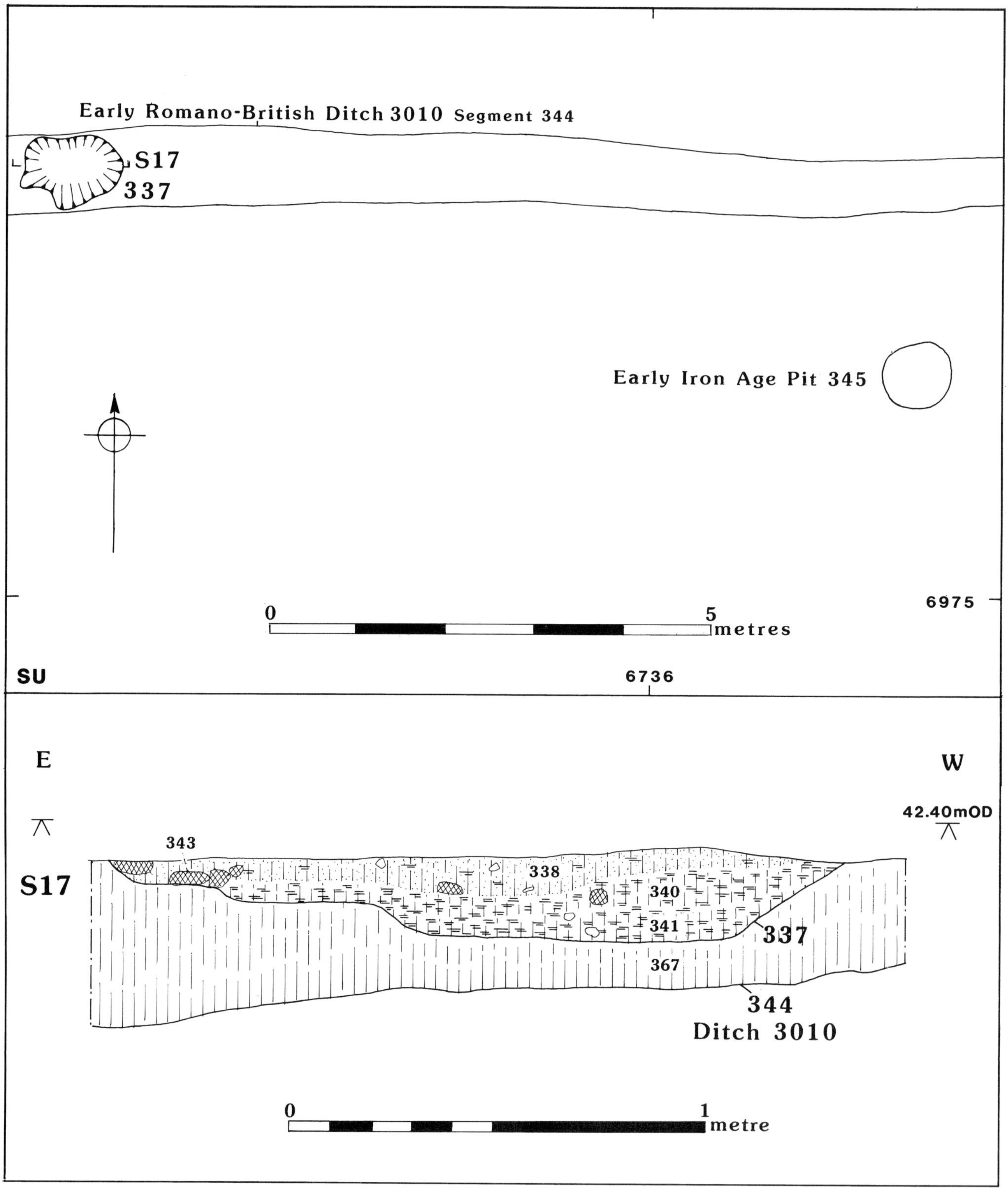

Figure 74 *Detailed plan and section of Romano-British pit 337*

Plate 21 Colluvium excavation area, with midden 3009 'chequerboard' excavation in foreground, looking south-west to Dean's Copse

loam and greyish–brown clayey loam respectively. Although it is difficult to identify a function for this feature, it is roughly parallel to structure 3022, and may possibly be the truncated remains of an associated drainage feature.

Pits and post-holes
Pit 685 (Fig. 72) was situated adjacent to the west side of ditch 3008 and consisted of a shallow elliptical feature, 1.35 m long, 1.2 m wide, and 0.1 m deep with shallow slightly concave sides and an irregular, though generally level base. The shallow nature of this feature probably indicates considerable truncation by later activity in the area.

Later Romano-British (*c.* AD 200–AD 400)

Enclosure 3005
This comprised a continuous ditch, excavated as segments 512 (Figs 72, 73, S14), 47 (Fig. 68, S8), 288, 451, 399, 696, and 670, and forming the south, east, and north sides of what appeared to be a sub-rectangular enclosure. This enclosure continued to the west beyond the limit of the excavation area. The dimensions and profiles of the various segments excavated through this ditch can be divided into two distinct groups; the south and east sides; and the north side.

The south and east sections of the enclosure ditch (segments 512, 47, 288, 451, and 399) were at least 1.1 m wide and 0.45 m deep, with moderately sloping, concave sides and gently rounded bases. In addition, two segments examined (512 and 288) revealed shallow, flat bottomed slots at the very base of the feature. In general, two to three fills were recorded in each segment, comprising grey to greyish–brown clay loams and silty clays, with a deposit of coarse grey sand filling one of the base slots noted above. No evidence was recorded to indicate the position of an upcast bank associated with these sections of the ditch.

The north section of the enclosure ditch (segments 696 and 670) was less substantial being *c.* 0.53 m wide and 0.25–0.3 m deep, with steep convex sides and a flat base to the west, tending to a more concave rounded profile to the east. This contained two fills, with a primary deposit partially slumped against the north side of the ditch comprising a mixed deposit of clay loam, sealed by an upper layer of dark yellowish–brown to greyish–brown silty clay. The slumped nature of the primary deposit may indicate eroded material originating from an associated bank to the north of this section of ditch. It is possible that this section of ditch represents part of that for early Romano-British enclosure 3004, utilised in the construction of enclosure 3005. No features considered as contemporaneous were recorded within enclosure 3005.

Midden 3009
This was a sub-circular spread of predominantly dark grey sandy silt to clay loam, situated *c.* 20 m to the east of enclosure 3005, and extending to the north beyond the limit of investigations within the colluvium (Fig. 72; Pl. 21). This deposit covered an area *c.* 15 m east–west and at least 10 m north–south, to a maximum thickness of 0.33 m, and averaging *c.* 0.17 m. Finds recovered include large quantities of pottery, as well as animal bone, burnt flint, brick and tile, fired clay, slag, stone, copper alloy, and iron. Although some of the diagnostic pieces of pottery were 1st–2nd century, the vast majority were 3rd–4th century in date. As a result of the range and quantity of finds recovered from this deposit, it is interpreted as a midden, probably associated with the late Romano-British settlement in the adjacent area to the west. No features were identified either within or beneath this deposit.

Ditches
Ditch 515 (Fig. 71) was an east–west aligned feature recorded *c.* 50 m to the north of the main centre of Romano-British activity against the west edge of the excavation area. It was 1.5 m wide and 0.43 m deep, with moderately sloping, slightly concave sides and a rounded base, and filled with a primary fill of greyish–brown clay loam, sealed by a layer of charcoal-rich grey silty clay. The primary fill was banked against the south side of the feature, suggesting the presence of eroded material originating from an associated upcast bank to the south.

Pits
Pit 49 (Fig. 72) was situated *c.* 3 m south of the south-east corner of enclosure 3005, and had cut through earlier ditch 3019. It was circular in plan (2.5 m in diameter and 0.93 m deep), with moderate slightly convex sides and a slightly irregular flat base. This was filled with a single deposit of greyish–brown silty clay containing large quantities of finds, including animal bone and pottery.

Pit 85 (Fig. 72) was situated *c.* 0.5 m north of the north-east corner of enclosure 3005. It was elliptical in plan, measuring 1.7 by 1.4 m, and aligned roughly east–west with slightly irregular concave sides and a rounded base. This was filled with a primary fill of grey clay, sealed by slightly brownish–grey silty clay.

Unphased Romano-British

A number of features only produced undiagnostic Romano-British finds. However, features of note are discussed below, including a pit interpreted as a pyre base that produced cremated human bone. Although the majority of the undiagnostic Romano-British features were concentrated within the area of early and late Romano-British activity to the west, the pyre base was situated approximately centrally within the excavation area.

Ditches

Ditch 640 (Fig. 72) comprised the southern terminal for a north-north-east to south-south-west aligned linear feature, situated to the east of midden 3009 and continuing northwards beyond the limit of the colluvium excavation. It was at least 0.9 m long, 0.6 m wide, and 0.16 m deep, with shallow concave sides and a gently rounded base, and filled with dark grey clay loam above a primary deposit of greyish–brown clay loam. Although no pottery was recovered from this feature, the upper fill did produce cremated human bone, possibly *in situ*, in association with a fragment of copper alloy twisted wire bracelet.

Pits

Pit 337 (Figs 69 and 74) was situated towards the northern limit of the colluvium, cutting through the fill of ditch 3010 (trackway 3018). This was roughly elliptical in plan, measuring *c.* 1.8 x 0.9 m and 0.2 m deep, with shallow concave sides, and a slightly uneven flat base. This feature appeared to be sporadically lined with partially fired fragments of clay or daub, and contained three fills comprising a primary deposit of heavily charcoal flecked reddish–brown silty clay, sealed by a charcoal rich layer of black fine silty clay, and then by charcoal and fired clay flecked by dark brown sandy loam (Fig. 74, S17). Fragments of cremated human bone were recovered from all fills, the majority from the upper deposit. This feature probably represents a truncated pyre base and, whilst the dating evidence recovered includes both 1st century AD and prehistoric pottery sherds, the stratigraphic relationship with earlier ditch 3010 implies that these sherds are residual and a late Romano-British date is more likely.

Layers

Layer 573 (Fig. 71) was situated towards the south-west corner of the excavation area, on the higher Reading Beds. The layer comprised an irregular 'guitar' shaped thin spread of mottled greyish–brown silty clay measuring *c.* 11 x 10 m and up to 0.05 m deep. No features were recorded at either the limits of the layer or beneath it, although a few pieces of undiagnostic worked flint and Romano-British pottery were recovered during excavation. It is possible that this layer represents part of an occupation surface.

Saxon (c. AD 410–AD 1066)

Other than an isolated sherd of Saxon pottery considered as intrusive within an earlier feature (pit 98), the features dated to this phase are grouped together on the basis of pottery, radiocarbon dating, and similarities in morphology, and comprise a group of three pits and a pair of large timber-lined wells. The pits, on the higher ground formed by the Reading Beds within the south-west corner of the excavation area, lie to either side of the Early Iron Age trackway 3012 (Fig. 77; pit 536 and pit 542 to the west, pit 557 to the east), whilst the wells are situated on the lower valley gravel to the north (Fig. 62; well 301 to the north-west, well 322 to the north-east).

Wells

Two large pits were positively identified as wells (Fig. 62; well 301 and well 322). Very little ceramic dating evidence was recovered from these features, comprising a small undiagnostic Romano-British pottery sherd from the upper fill of well 301; and an undiagnostic Romano-British pottery sherd, and a sherd of Saxon pottery from the upper fill of well 322, as well as a small sherd of 3rd–4th century pottery from the penultimate fill of the same feature. However, radiocarbon dating of an *in situ* timber within well 322 has produced a mid Saxon date (GU-4362, 1290±50 BP; cal AD 650–870), and as such well 301 is considered, on morphological grounds, to be of a similar date.

Well 301

This was situated on the valley gravel within the north-west corner of the excavation area and was sub-circular in plan, measuring 3.6 m east–west by 3.4 m north–south, and 1.73 m deep (Figs 62 and 74; Pl. 22). The eroded upper portion of the well, to a depth of *c.* 1.1 m, had a convex sloping edge merging into a concave sloping base. The surviving uneroded well shaft below this portion was *c.* 1.3 m in diameter and 0.63 m deep, with fairly steep convex sides and a rounded base (Fig. 75, S15). The position of the shaft was offset in relation to the centre of the main body, resulting in a slight 'platform' to the east.

The main body of the well was filled with a massive deposit of dark yellowish–brown silty loam, sealing a greyish–brown silty clay. Below this, the subcircular shaft contained three layers of greyish–black clays and slightly silty clays, the secondary fill included a compacted mass of brushwood, twigs, small branches etc. The anaerobic waterlogged conditions within the shaft had also preserved the remains of a timber lining at the base, comprising at least nine upright oak planks and posts, between 0.3 m and 0.56 m in length (Object nos 2003–2011)

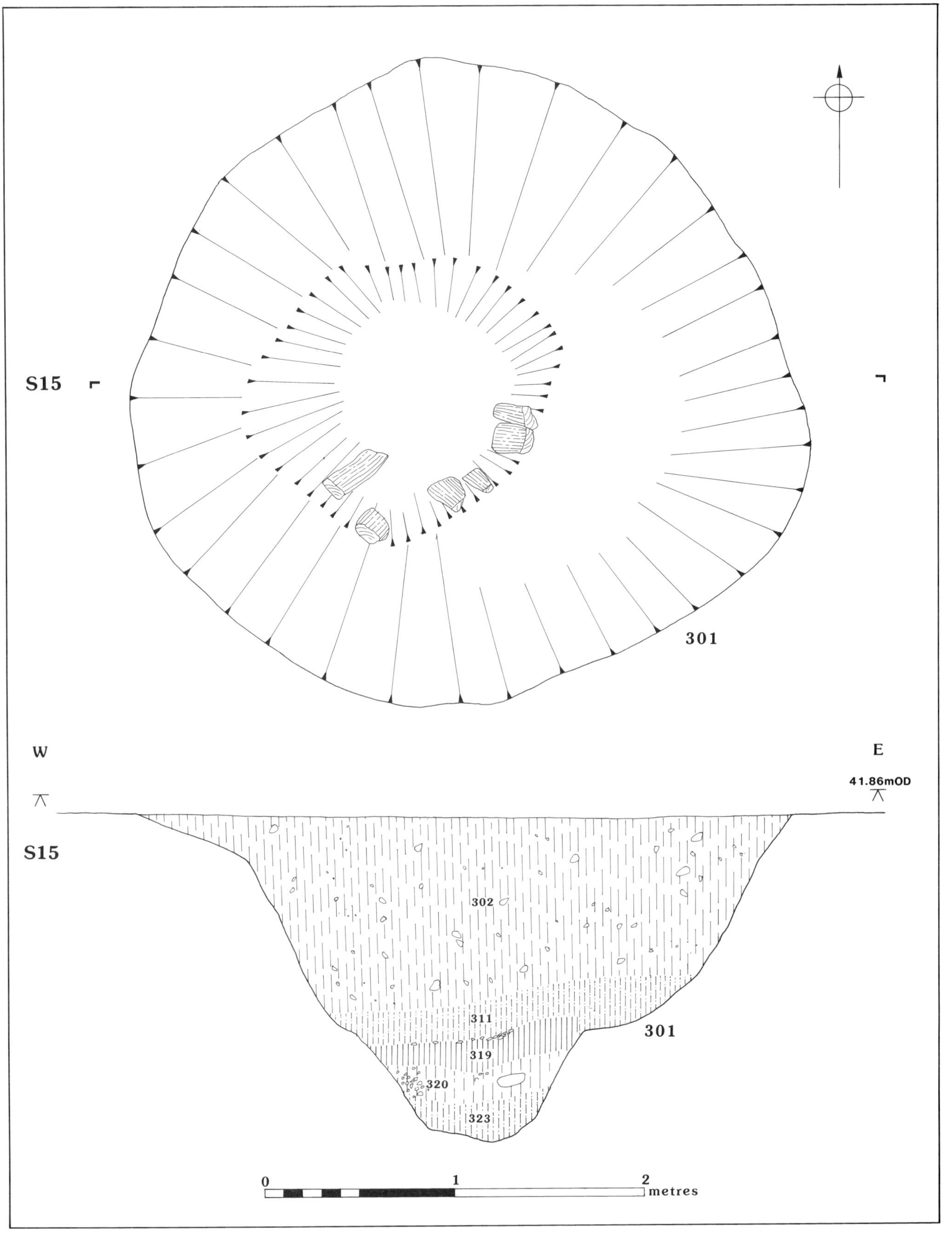

Figure 75 Detailed plan and section of Saxon well 301

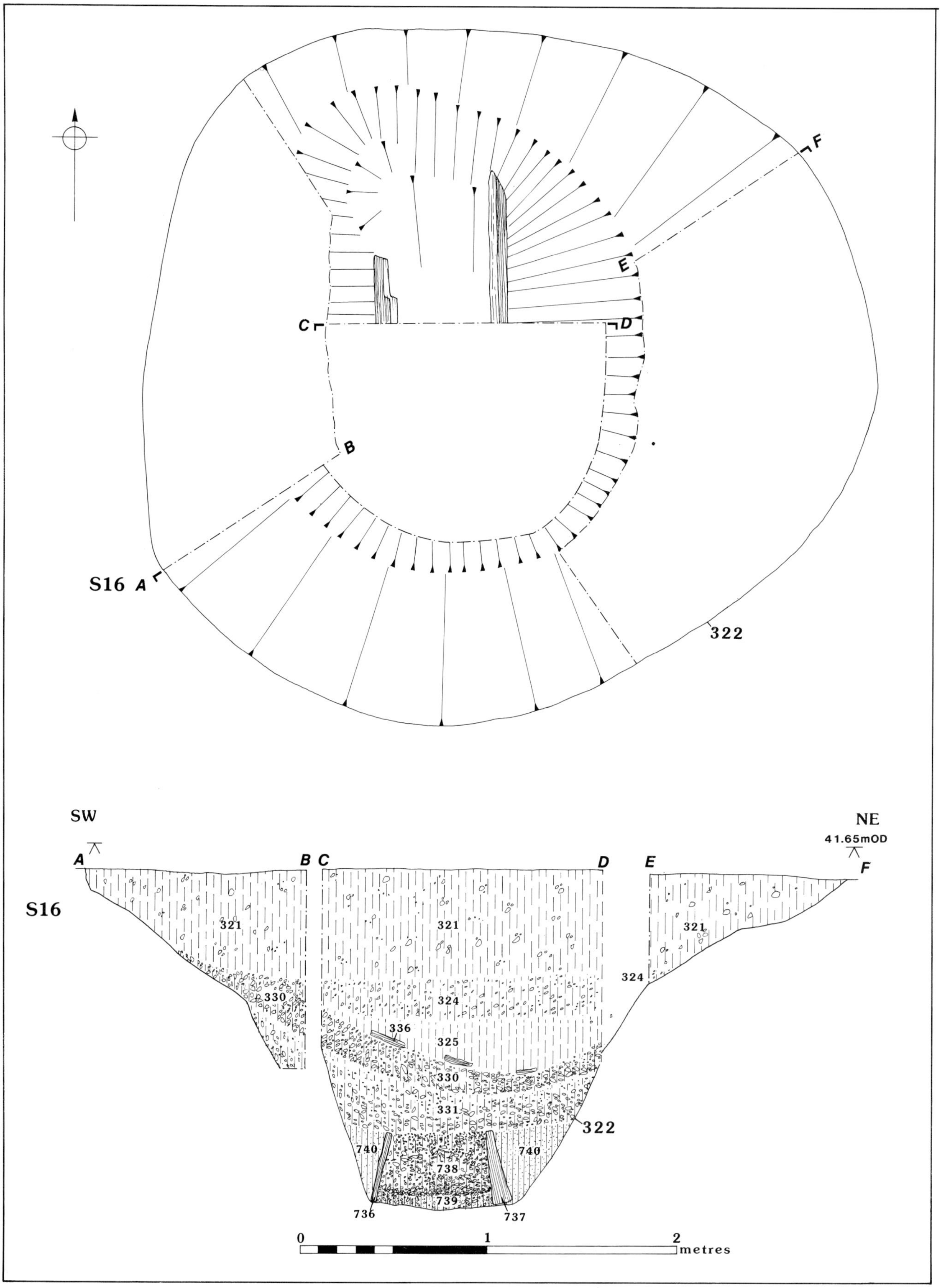

Figure 76 Detailed plan and section of Saxon well 322

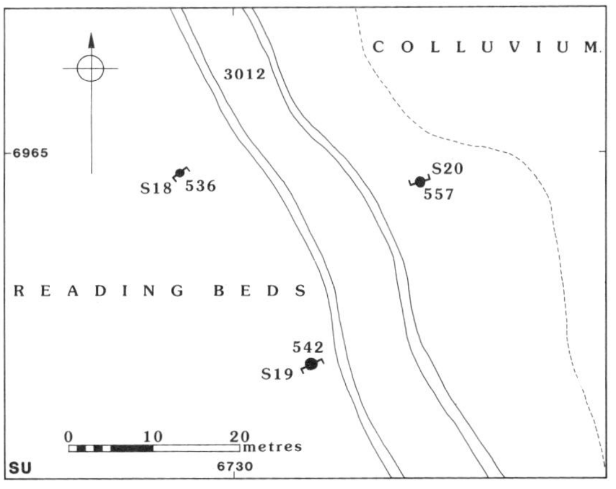

Figure 77 Overall plan of Saxon pits

The surviving timbers were all situated against the south side of the subcircular well shaft and, whilst insufficient information was recovered to positively identify the construction techniques for the well lining, it is likely to have comprised closely spaced uprights. This style of construction is reminiscent of urban Saxon wells, for which open-ended barrels were often used as well linings, although this comparison cannot be confirmed at Wickhams Field. The missing timbers are unlikely to be the result of differential preservation conditions and were possibly removed when the well fell into disuse.

Well 322
This was also situated on the valley gravel, within the north-east corner of the excavation area (Figs 62 and 76). It was circular in plan, measuring *c.* 3.8 m in diameter, and 1.8 m deep, with moderate to steep convex sloping sides and a very slightly rounded base. The upper three fills of the well comprised dark brown to dark greyish–brown sandy silts, and sealed a thin layer of twigs and brushwood, above two layers of light brown, loose, silty gravel, possibly representing the collapsed sides of the original feature. Below these was a layer of dark greyish–brown clay sealing the preserved remains of the timber lining for the well (Fig. 76, S16).

The lining comprised a pair of wide oak planks (Object nos 2025 and 2026), set on edge to form the opposing sides of a rectangular box aligned north–south, the internal dimensions of which were at least 0.8 m long, 0.55 m wide, and 0.4 m deep. It is probable that either a framework of horizontal members or internal upright corner posts would have originally held the sides of the timber box in place. Unfortunately, unstable ground conditions at the time of investigations only allowed excavation of the northern half of this timber box, its full length was possibly *c.* 1.6 m. No evidence was recovered for timbers forming the north side of the box in the section examined, these possibly having been removed when the well fell into disuse. The fill, both within and outside the timber box, comprised grey sandy gravel, although a thin primary layer of dark grey sandy clay and gravel was recorded between the timbers.

Pits

Pit group 3025
Pit 536 (Fig. 78, S18; Pl. 23) was a sub-circular feature, *c.* 0.9 m in diameter and 0.65 m deep, with vertical south and north sides and undercut east and west sides, and a slightly uneven flat base. This was filled with a primary fill of brownish–grey silty clay, overlain to the east and west by slumped layers of mottled redeposited natural. The upper fills comprised heavily charcoal flecked dark grey silty clay and a greyish–brown silty loam. The 'bell-shaped' sides of this feature are possibly not deliberate and may have been caused by collapsing sides, as indicated by the slumped layers of redeposited natural towards the base of the pit.

Pit 542 (Fig. 78, S19) was an elliptical feature, measuring 1.7 m east to west and 1.4 m north to south in plan, and 1 m deep, with a slightly uneven flat base.

Plate 22 Excavation of Saxon well 301, showing timbers in situ

Plate 23 Saxon pit 536, group 3025 (larger scale 1 m)

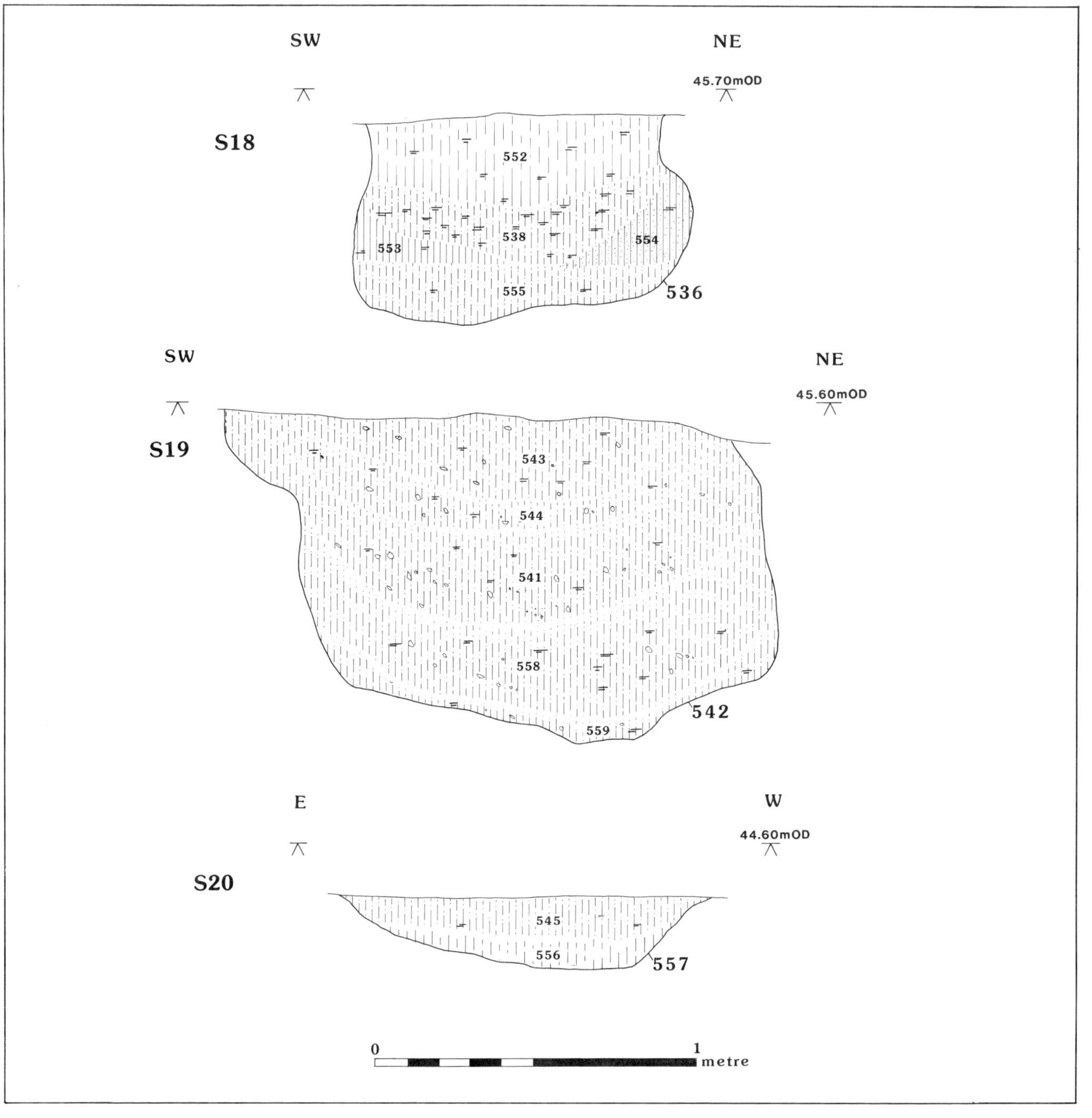

Figure 78 Sections of Saxon pit group 3025 (pits 536, 542, and 557)

The upper edge on the east side of this pit was slightly undercut, whilst the upper west edge, although disturbed by modern activity, appeared to have a moderately concave slope. Below these upper edges the main body of the pit, measuring 1.5 m east to west, had vertical sides. This was filled with a sequence of five layers comprising grey to greyish–yellow silty clay.

Pit 557 (Fig. 78, S20) was an elliptical feature, measuring 1.34 m north–south and 1.2 m east–west, and 0.23 m deep, with a small circular flat base. This base was offset to the south-east side of this feature to such a degree that the edge on this side was undercut, whilst the opposing north-west side had a shallow concave slope. This was filled with a primary fill of yellowish–brown clayey silt and an upper fill of dark brownish–grey silty clay.

Post-medieval and Modern (c. AD 1500 onwards)

Other than numerous land drains recorded across the excavation area, two features are attributed to this phase, structure 3027 and ditch 3026. Post-hole 254, although producing a small fragment of probable post-medieval brick or tile, is more likely to be prehistoric on the basis of the quantities of worked and burnt flint also recovered. The fragment of brick or tile is therefore likely to be intrusive and, in the absence of any diagnostic worked flint, post-hole 254 is considered as unphased.

Structure 3027

This was represented by the south-east corner of a rectangular building platform, cutting into the north-facing slope to the south-east of the centre of Romano-British activity, within the colluvium excavation. The remains comprised the south side of a flat bottomed east–west aligned terrace, up to 8 m long and 0.3 m deep, and filled with black ashy loam containing modern material (plastic, barbed wire, etc — not collected). The eastern end of this terrace was delineated by a 5 m long north–south aligned 0.1–0.2 m wide trench. The trench was filled with unconsolidated slag and clinker, its vacuous nature suggesting that this was an associated drainage feature. The north and west sides to the building platform were removed during machine stripping prior to the colluvium excavation.

Ditch 3026

This was up to 1.5 m wide, crossing the entire excavation area from west to east, and was the only feature clearly visible in the upper surface of the colluvium. As with structure 3027, this feature contained obviously modern material (not collected) and as such was not excavated. This ditch is indicated as a field boundary on the 1st edition 6 inch Ordnance Survey map for the area (Berkshire Record Office, sheet XXXVII).

Undated

A number of features did not produce diagnostic finds, these are summarised in the archive, with a provisional date provided where possible.

3. Finds

Roman Coins, by Nicholas A. Wells

A total of 27 coins, all of copper alloy, was found. All were discovered in the main colluvial layer (context 10) using a metal detector. The majority (20) are incomplete, two more are heavily corroded making further identification impossible. It was only possible to identify three of the coins with any degree of confidence, although a further 12 have some recognisable markings. These have been catalogued below. Full records can be found in the site archive.

1 Carausius, Æ Antoninianus
AD 287–293
Ob IMPCCAR [AVSIVSPFAVG]
Radiate and draped bust facing right
Rev PA / X [AVG]
Pax standing, facing left with vertical sceptre.
Mint S/ P in field, exergue unclear.
Worn on both faces and incomplete. Striations on the face of the bust may indicate defacing of the coin. Object No. 2100.

2 Æ 3
Mid to late 4th Century
Ob Diademed bust facing right. Inscription illegible.
Rev [GLORIA] RO / [MANORVM]
Victory standing facing left and holding wreath and palm
Mint Not clear.
Worn on both faces and incomplete. Object No. 2101.

3 Æ 3
Mid to late 4th Century
Ob ....AVG
Diademed bust facing right.
Rev Inscription illegible. Possibly GLORIA ROMANORVM.
Draped emperor with right hand dragging captive to the right and holding *labarum* in left hand.
Mint Not clear.
Worn on both faces and incomplete. Object No. 2102.

4 Æ 3
Mid to late 4th Century
Ob Bust facing right. Inscription illegible.
Rev Inscription illegible. Possibly GLORIA ROMANORVM.
Victory standing, facing left and holding wreath and palm
Mint Not clear
Worn on both faces and incomplete. Object No. 2103.

5 Æ 3
Mid to late 4th Century
Ob Bust facing right with pearl diadem. Inscription illegible.
Rev GLORIARO / MANORVM
Draped emperor with right hand dragging captive to the right, and holding labarum in left hand.
Mint OF/II in field. Exergue unclear. Possibly minted at *Lugdunum* (Lyon), second *Officina*.
Slightly worn on both faces and incomplete. Object No. 2104.

6 Æ 4
Mid 4th Century onwards
Ob Bust facing right. Inscription illegible
Rev Virtus facing left, with shield on the left arm spearing fallen horseman who is sitting on the ground beside the horse. Inscription illegible.

Mint Not clear
Very worn on both faces. Copy of FEL TEMP REPARATIO (Fallen Horseman) type. Object No. 2106.

7 Æ 3/4
Early to mid 4th Century
Ob Diademed bust facing right. Inscription illegible.
Rev Inscription illegible. Possibly GLORIA EXERCITVS.
Two soldiers standing with spear and shield. Between them two standards.
Mint Not clear.
Worn on both faces and incomplete. Object No. 2107.

8 Constans, Æ 2/3
AD 337–350
Ob DNCONSTA/NSPFAVG
Draped bust facing right, pearl and rosetted diadem.
Rev FELTEM/PREPARATIO
Phoenix facing right on an orb.
Mint Not clear.
Worn on both faces. Object No. 2108.

9 Valens, Æ 3
AD 364–378
Ob DNVALEN / SPFAVG
Draped bust facing right, pearl diadem,
Rev GLORIARO / MANORVM
Victory standing, facing left, holding a wreath and palm
Mint * in field, TRP in exergue; minted in First *Officina* of *Treveri* (Trier) mint.
Slightly worn on both faces and incomplete. Object No. 2109.

10 Æ 3
Mid to late 4th Century
Ob ....PFAVG
Draped bust facing right with pearl diadem,
Rev SECVRITAS / REIPVBLICAE
Victory standing facing left and holding a wreath and palm.
Mint * in field, exergue not clear. Possibly minted at *Lugdunum* (Lyons).
Slightly worn on both faces and incomplete. Object No. 2113.

11 Æ 3
Early to mid 4th Century
Ob ....AVG
Diademed bust facing right.
Rev Inscription illegible but almost certainly GLORIA EXERCITVS.
Two soldiers vis-á-vis with spear and shield. One standard between them.
Mint X in standard, exergue unclear. Possibly minted at *Constantia* (Arles).
Worn on both faces and incomplete. Object No. 2116.

12 Æ 3
Mid to late 4th Century
Ob Bust facing right. Inscription illegible.
Rev SECVRITAS/REIPVBLICAE
Victory standing, facing left, and holding wreath and palm.
Mint OF / I in field, exergue not clear. Possibly from the *Lugdunum* (Lyon) mint, First *Officina*.
Slightly worn on both faces and incomplete. Object No. 2118.

13 Æ 3
Mid to late 4th Century
Ob Diademed bust facing right. Inscription illegible.
Rev SECVRITAS/REIPVBLICAE
Victory standing, facing left, and holding wreath and palm.
Mint OF / II in filed, exergue not clear. Possibly from *Lugdunum* (Lyon) mint, Second *Officina*.
Slightly worn on both faces and incomplete. Object No. 2119.

14 Æ 3
Mid to late 4th Century
Ob Pearl diademed bust facing right. Inscription illegible.
Rev SECVRITAS/REIPVBLICAE
Victory standing, facing left, and holding wreath and palm.
Mint Not clear.
Worn on both faces and incomplete. Object No. 2122.

15 Æ 3
Mid 4th Century
Ob Diademed bust facing right, with cuirass and in paludamentum. Inscription illegible.
Rev VICTORIAEDDAVGGQNN
Two victories, vis-á-vis, each holding wreath.
Mint ♥ in Field, exergue not clear.
Slightly worn on both faces and incomplete. Object No. 2123.

All identifiable coins apart from one, are 4th-century AD Æ coins, the exception being a very late 3rd-century Æ Antoninianus of the usurper Carausius (AD 287–293). In general, from those coins that have been dated, it can be seen that coin dates are spread fairly evenly throughout the 4th century with GLORIA ROMANORVM and SECVRITAS REIPVBLICAE types dominating.

Metalwork, by R. Montague

A total of 22 pieces of metalwork was recovered during the excavations, 10 of copper alloy, one of lead, one of an unidentified metal (possibly gunmetal), and 10 of iron. All the objects were X-radiographed and the identifications below have been made from a combination of the unconserved objects and the X-radiograph plates. All items are discussed below, but only those items which have been illustrated are fully catalogued. Further details of all metalwork are held in the archive.

Eleven objects were retrieved from four Romano-British features — midden 3009 (eight objects), ditches 640 and 515, and pit 85 (one object each). Ten objects came from the main colluvial layer (context 10), and one from the topsoil. All the non-ferrous metalwork from the colluvium was found by a metal detector suggesting that the signals from the ferrous material were masked out, rather than there being a true absence of iron objects in this deposit.

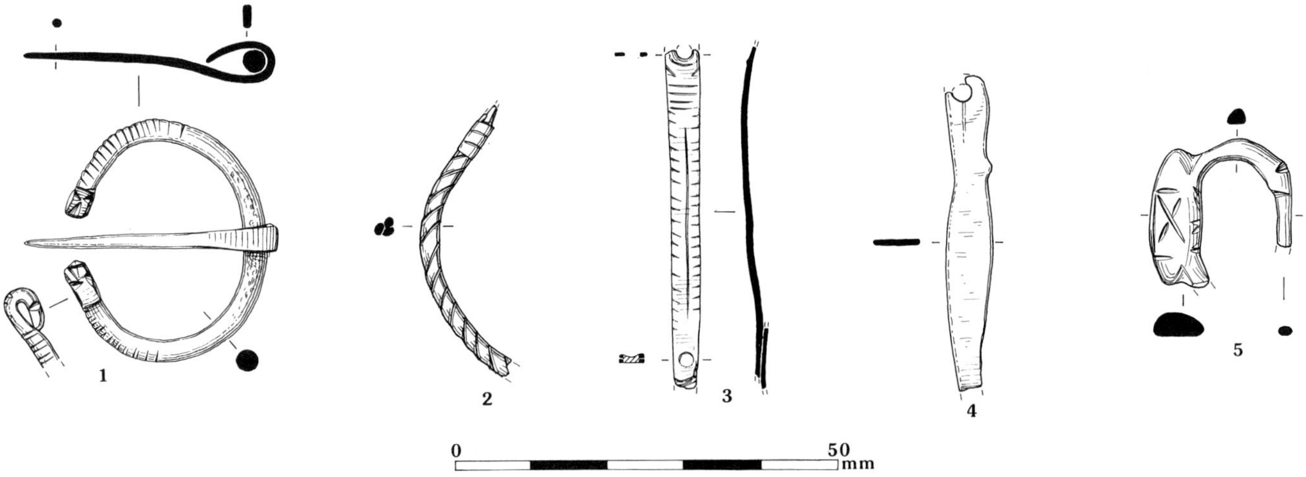

Figure 79 Copper alloy objects (1–5)

Romano-British

The copper alloy penannular brooch from midden 3009 (Fig. 79, 1) is of Fowler's type D or a sub-type thereof (1960, 152). It is a penannular brooch with the terminals bent back on themselves at right-angles to the plane of the ring and with a straight pin. The presence of zoomorphic terminals is hinted at, but uncertain as the brooch has not been conserved. Ribbing is visible, both on the object itself and on the X-ray, but again it is unclear whether this continues around the entire circumference of the brooch. If these decorative motifs are present, it would prove possible to place the brooch in a sub-type, which might have implications for refinement of the dating of this artefact. Type D brooches first appeared in the late 1st century BC or early 1st century AD, with sub-types developing through the 1st and 2nd centuries AD (Fowler 1960, 169–70). A copper alloy bracelet fragment (Fig. 79, 2) was retrieved from ditch 640, but this is not closely datable as twisted cable bracelets were very common from the late 1st–4th centuries AD (Cool 1993, 89).

The other seven objects from midden 3009 are all of iron, and include a possible small chisel (Obj. No. 2024), a small wedge or nail (Obj. No. 2020), two other nails, both with round, flat heads and square or rectangular-sectioned shanks (Obj. Nos. 2023 and 2205), and three nail shanks (Obj. Nos. 2021, 2022 and 2212). A single iron nail of indeterminate type was recovered from pit 85 (Obj. No. 2012), and a possible iron strap object, which may be perforated, came from ditch 515, although due to its corroded state, this identification is tentative (Obj. No. 2204).

In addition to the metal artefacts from Romano-British features, one object which is typologically Romano-British, and another which may possibly date from this period were retrieved from the main colluvial layer. A fragment of copper alloy strip bracelet (Fig. 79, 3) is almost identical in decoration to one from a 4th-century AD context at Cirencester, Gloucestershire (Viner 1986, 106, fig. 78.17); and another from a context dated *c.* AD 320–*c.* 450 at Colchester, Essex (Crummy 1983, 45, fig. 47.1725). It is possible that the thinner end of the fragment is the terminal complete with rivet *in situ,* and the perforation at the other broken end is unintentional, perhaps accidentally formed by punching right through the strip at the first zone of punched circular decoration. It seems less likely that the perforation at the wider end represents the eye for a hook and eye fastening, as bracelets usually widen out from the terminal, and also this makes the presence of the rivet somewhat problematic — although it could be a simple repair. However, the decoration places this bracelet in the later Romano-British period, probably the 4th or 5th century AD. A sheet copper alloy object (Fig. 79, 4) is possibly a cosmetic implement such as a scoop or a nail cleaner. There is a perforation at one end and below this the body swells in width and then thins out again. It resembles the general outline of a nail cleaner from a late 4th century context at Greyhound Yard, Dorchester, Dorset, although this example is somewhat thicker (Henig 1993, 123, fig. 64.58).

Medieval and post-medieval

Three copper alloy objects, all retrieved from the main colluvial layer, may be attributed on typological grounds to these periods.

A broken buckle frame which is typologically late 12th–late 14th century in date (Fig. 79, 5) can be compared with examples of a similar date from London, with oval frames, an offset and narrowed bar, and an ornate outside edge (Egan and Pritchard 1991, 72–8, figs 44 and 46). As there is no other evidence for medieval activity on the site, this probably represents a casual loss. A sexfoil button with integral loop (Obj. No. 2129) is almost identical in size and decoration to a belt mount (ie with two holes for attachment by rivets rather than with an integral loop) from St Peter's Street, Northampton, from contexts dating to the late 15th and early 16th centuries (Oakley and Webster 1979, 253, Cu. alloy fig. 3.39). A small rectangular buckle with a central bar and with white metal plating on one surface (Obj. No. 2131) is of a popular and long-lived type, and cannot be more closely dated than the late medieval/post-medieval periods.

Modern and indeterminate

Of the six modern or indeterminate objects one is a modern cast copper alloy object of unknown function

(Obj. No. 2133), and another an unidentified modern metal tube (Obj. No. 2136). A lead token with illegible text in upper case letters and with a blank reverse was also recovered (Obj. No. 2135). This may be post-medieval or modern. All three objects came from the colluvium.

Two copper alloy rings, also from the colluvium, are of similar dimensions (diameters 18 mm and 20 mm), roughly made and finished (Obj. Nos 2127 and 2128), of irregular widths with flattened upper and lower surfaces, and one has a distinct bevel on its inner edge. They compare well with Romano-British copper alloy harness rings from Chichester, Sussex (Down 1989, 196, fig. 27.1/17–8), although as similar rings are commonly found in most periods it is not possible to date them with any certainty. A single iron nail was recovered from the topsoil (Obj. No. 2206). This is hand-made, but could belong to any period.

List of illustrated objects (Fig. 79)

1. Copper alloy penannular brooch. Terminals, possibly zoomorphic, bent back on themselves at right angles to plane of brooch; pin extends beyond body of brooch. Ribbing visible on object near terminals, X-ray suggests that ribbing continues from both terminals for c. of circumference. Obj. No. 2019, context 809, midden 3009, test pit 158.
2. Fragment of copper alloy twisted cable bracelet. Two cables, broken at both ends. Bracelet slightly flattened on two faces. Obj. No. 2018, context 641, ditch 640.
3. Fragment of copper alloy strip ?bracelet. Tapering strip, wider end broken at perforation; other end also broken, pierced by copper alloy rivet, which holds another small fragment of copper alloy strip in place on underside of object. Upper surface decorated with notch on either side of perforation, then zone of four parallel lines incised across body just above perforation, then zone (the greater part of the fragment) with incised central line with short diagonal lines along either edge. Obj. No. 2132, context 10, colluvium.
4. Copper alloy strip object, broken at both ends. One end slightly perforated and expanded, broken at perforation; below this body swells gently and then narrows again. Obj. No. 2130, context 10, colluvium.
5. Copper alloy buckle frame, broken. Bar is offset and narrowed; frame opposite this expanded with ornate outer edge, protruding at either side and decorated with incised lines. Obj. No. 2134, context 10, colluvium.

Slag, by Phil Andrews and Lorraine Mepham

Metalworking debris, principally ironworking slag, totalling 77 pieces (1798 g) was recovered from later prehistoric and Romano-British features, as well as from topsoil and unstratified contexts. Of this total, 60 pieces (1488 g) came from the probable Early Iron Age pit 430. The material from this feature comprises smithing slag, including fragments of vitrified hearth lining, and hearth bottoms. The quantity of such slag within one feature suggests that this represents the by-products from ironworking in the vicinity, although possibly only reflecting a single episode of such activity. Pit 430 produced no dating evidence, but is possibly associated with pit 416 which contained large quantities of burnt flint, and raises the possibility that the activities represented by the two pits may be connected in some way. Pit 416 is dated on the basis of a single non-diagnostic sherd to the later prehistoric (Early Iron Age) period; if this dating is also accepted for pit 430, the presence of such a quantity of ironworking slag at such an early date is very significant.

Two further pieces of slag came from Early Iron Age contexts, again both smithing slag: one piece from ditch 3013 (enclosure 3001) and one from ditch 3002 (trackway 3012). These could have originated from the same episode of ironworking which produced the deposit in pit 430.

Much smaller quantities of slag were derived from Romano-British and Saxon contexts:three pieces (42 g) from midden 3009 and nine pieces (172 g) from Saxon well 322. These again represent smithing slag. The quantities are too small to suggest ironworking on site at this period and these pieces could represent either redeposited pre- historic material or more recent intrusive finds.

Stone Objects, by M. Laidlaw

Five stone objects were recovered consisting of three possible quernstone fragments, one whetstone fragment, and one possible counter. In addition, a number of small and featureless pieces of lava (total weight 408 g) almost certainly derive from at least one quernstone. With the exception of the lava, all the quernstone fragments were identified on the basis of surviving surfaces but identification as either upper or lower stones was not possible. The majority of the quernstone fragments were recovered from topsoil and Romano-British features (midden 3009, pit 88, and pit 98). One fragment of lava quern from Saxon pit 542 and fragments from Saxon well 301 may demonstrate that lava querns were a common import during the Saxon period as illustrated at excavations elsewhere (ie Hamwic, Southampton; Morton 1992).

The three more complete quern fragments are in greensand, sarsen, and gritstone respectively. Greensand occurs in a broad arc to the north of the Wessex chalklands and further afield to the Isle of Wight, the Weald of Sussex, and Kent. The Lodsworth quarry in West Sussex was exploiting greensand in the Iron Age and into the early Romano-British period (Peacock 1987), and this is a likely source for the Wickhams Field example. The source for the sarsen fragment may have been south-central England and the possible gritstone fragment may have been obtained from the Mendips, Derbyshire/Yorkshire, or the Hampshire Basin (Brown 1984). The lava quern(s) have a continental origin.

The whetstone fragment, recovered from pit 542, is of fine-grained sandstone, characteristically smooth, with rounded edges and worn surfaces. Whetstones are rarely datable on morphological grounds, occurring in very similar forms from the prehistoric period onwards; pit 542 is dated on pottery grounds to the Saxon period. A possible stone counter, diameter 18 mm and 1 mm thick, was also recovered from midden 3009. This appears to be a naturally disc-shaped pebble, but could have been utilised as a counter. Discs or counters in a variety of material types, including stone, are well

Table 16 Quantification of worked flint by date and feature

Date	*Provenance*	*Flint category*								*Total*
		1	2	3	4	5	6	7	8	
Late Neolithic –Early Bronze Age	Pits	–	–	1	4	3	–	1	–	9
	TOTAL	–	–	1	4	3	–	1	–	9
Early Iron Age	Trackway 3012	–	1	4	4	1	2	2	1 leaf a/head	15
	Enclosure 3001	–	–	1	–	–	–	–	–	1
	Ditches	1	–	2	3	–	–	–	–	6
	Post-holes	–	–	1	–	–	–	–	–	1
	Layers	1	–	–	1	–	–	–	–	2
	TOTAL	2	1	8	8	1	2	2	1	25
Romano-British	Enclosures 3004 & 3005	–	–	1	2	–	–	–	–	3
	Midden 3009	2	–	5	8	–	2	1	–	18
	Ditches	1	2	10	12	–	–	1	1 PTD	27
	Pits	1	1	5	5	–	–	1	–	13
	TOTAL	4	3	21	27	–	2	3	1	61
Saxon	Pits	–	–	7	7	–	1	–	1 obl. a/head	16
	TOTAL	–	–	7	7	–	1	–	1	16
Med / post-med.	Ditches	–	1	3	4	–	–	–	–	8
	TOTAL	–	1	3	4	–	–	–	–	8
Undated	Ditches	–	1	22	11	–	2	–	–	36
	Pits	2	–	17	8	3	–	–	–	30
	Post-holes	–	–	1	–	–	–	–	–	1
	Layers	–	–	3	3	–	–	–	–	6
	TOTAL	2	1	43	22	3	2	–	–	73
Unstratified	Colluvium	3	2	7	9	–	–	2	–	23
	Topsoil	12	–	42	33	3	2	2	1PTD	95
	TOTAL	15	2	49	42	3	2	4	1	118
	OVERALL TOTAL	23	8	132	114	10	9	10	4	310

Key to flint categories:
1. cores; 2. broken cores; 3. complete flakes; 4. broken flakes; 5. burnt, worked flint; 6. retouched flakes; 7.

known from the Romano-British period (Crummy 1983, 96).

Worked Flint, by P.A. Harding

The total quantity of flint is shown by chronological phase and by grouped contexts in Table 16. Flint was found in features of all types and periods at the site and is therefore likely to be predominantly residual.

Approximately two-thirds of the assemblage exhibits some form of post-depositional edge damage ranging from isolated nicks on otherwise undamaged edges, to snaps and scars characteristic of plough damage. The material is generally unpatinated, although isolated pieces, including an unstratified end scraper, have surfaces similar to those from alkaline soils. These pieces may have been introduced with manure from elsewhere.

The 23 cores recovered indicate that raw material from the valley gravel was used for blank production. Nodules used are small and sub-spherical with heavily weathered cortex. They include those of Bullhead flint from the Reading Beds which have a green cortex over an orange rind. Most of the cores are undiagnostic and include single platform, biconical, and miscellaneous examples. These are heavily damaged by repeated percussion.

There are insufficient quantities of flakes from individual contexts to warrant detailed analysis. A visual assessment has shown that flakes with well-prepared striking platforms and occasional deliberate blades are present on the site. The tools consist principally of end scrapers made on flakes including a thumb-nail scraper. Most are well-made and some exhibit retouch which was probably undertaken using pressure. However, some of the retouched pieces have individual notches, lengths of denticulate retouch, or coarse truncations which are much cruder in their application.

The diagnostic implements from the site comprise a well-made, bifacially-flaked leaf arrowhead, two chisel arrowheads, and an oblique arrowhead.

Discussion

The flint assemblage is too small to provide detailed conclusions about activity which predates the Middle Bronze Age ceramic evidence. However, the technology and tool typology indicate activity for which there are few obvious associated features. The earliest activity, both Early and Late Neolithic, is indicated from arrowheads which may represent casual hunting losses rather than settled activity. The diagnostic Early Neolithic leaf arrowhead may also be associated with the isolated blades, as there is nothing to indicate that they are of Mesolithic date. Most of the end scrapers may best be regarded as 'earlier prehistoric'.

The flintwork, recovered from features on the higher Reading Beds (*see* Fig. 66), is also likely to include quantities of residual material. The main evidence for knapping contemporary with the occupation lies with the coarsely retouched flakes which are commonly associated with Late Bronze Age/Early Iron Age sites.

Burnt Flint, by M. Laidlaw

A large quantity of burnt, unworked flint was recovered from the site, comprising 590 fragments (9872 g), plus an estimated 86 kg within pit 416. Apart from the latter feature, the fragments were dispersed in small quantities in various features with only one slight concentration occurring within undated pit 254.

Burnt, unworked flint is intrinsically undatable, but is frequently found in association with other prehistoric artefacts. This seems to be the case in most instances here, where burnt and worked flint occur in the same contexts. However, the burnt flint also occurs in Romano-British and Saxon features.

The low-level background scatter of burnt flint over the rest of the site serves to emphasise the significance of the very large deposit from pit 416, the fill of which contained up to 25% (by volume) burnt flint. This feature, sub-rectangular with a clay lining, was assigned an Early Iron Age date on the basis of one flint-tempered sherd. Its function is uncertain, but it falls within the range of similarly enigmatic features containing large quantities of burnt flint, generally dated to the prehistoric period, and for which a variety of possible functions have been suggested, such as domestic use, for warming water in the cooking process (Barfield and Hodder 1987), or for saunas (O'Drisceoil 1988). A burnt flint concentration dated to the Late Bronze Age, although lacking associated pits, was excavated at nearby Anslows Cottages (Butterworth and Lobb 1992, 90 and 166–7).

Pottery, by M. Laidlaw

Introduction

The ceramic assemblage from Wickhams Field consists of 1930 sherds (20, 321 g) plus two almost complete vessels, and ranges in date from the later prehistoric to the post-medieval period. The bulk of the assemblage was attributed to the Romano-British period, a large proportion to the later prehistoric period, and small quantities to the early prehistoric, Saxon, and post-medieval periods.

Methods

The assemblage was analysed using the standard Wessex pottery recording system (Morris 1992) as described for Prospect Park and Hurst Park. However, in view of the distance between this and the other two sites, the fabrics from Wickhams are discussed separately. The quantification of fabric types is listed in Table 17, and by feature in Tables 18 and 20. Percent- ages throughout this report have been calculated by weight unless otherwise stated.

Early prehistoric

Two conjoining sherds have been assigned to the early prehistoric period, on the basis of fabric type and vessel form. The unusual bone-tempered fabric is described below.

V1 Soft, soapy fabric, common, poorly sorted calcined bone — <9 mm; moderate, rounded quartz grains <0.25 mm; rare, very fine mica; uneven firing (buff–orange).

These two conjoining rim sherds have been tentatively dated to the Late Neolithic/Early Bronze Age period. The rim sherds probably derive from a form of collared vessel, with a concave neck and internal moulding beneath the rim (Fig. 80, 1); an alternative interpretation as a bowl rim is unlikely given the surviving profile. Although no decoration is present, the fabric suggests a Peterborough Ware vessel in Fengate style. The sherds were recovered from pit 9 on the valley gravel towards the northern limit of the excavation.

The use of a bone temper is very unusual but not unknown in early prehistoric ceramics. It has been identified in fabrics of both Neolithic and Bronze Age date. The existing evidence is summarised by Smith and Darvill who list three examples from England, including two from Wiltshire (1990, 152), and two further examples from Wiltshire have recently been identified (Cleal in prep).

Later prehistoric

The 13 fabric types attributed broadly to the later prehistoric period can be divided into two main fabric groups: flint-tempered/flint-gritted fabrics, ranging from fine to coarse, and sandy fabrics, often with some vegetable temper. Using Barrett's (1980) classification the assemblage may be divided into coarsewares (all flint-tempered/flint-gritted fabrics with the possible exceptions of F4 and F9) and finewares (all sandy fabrics except Q10); fabrics F4, F9 and Q10 are not readily assigned to either group.

Flint-tempered and flint-gritted fabrics
Nine fabric types were identified altogether in this group. The terms 'flint-tempered' and 'flint-gritted' are used in a specific sense to describe, respectively, fabrics to which flint has been added deliberately, usually in a crushed form; and fabrics in which the flint inclusions are likely to be naturally occurring in the clay matrix. In this case, the two fabrics F5 and F9 have been identified as 'flint-gritted' while the remaining seven may be considered 'flint-tempered', although the distinction between deliberate and accidental inclusions is not always clearcut.

F1 Hard, moderately fine fabric; moderate, well-sorted, sub-angular flint <1 mm; moderate rounded quartz grains <0.5 mm; sparse very fine mica; unoxidised, some oxidisation on surfaces.
F2 Hard, moderately fine fabric; common, poorly-sorted, sub-angular flint <4 mm; moderate rounded quartz grains <1 mm; moderate glauconite; sparse very fine mica; sparse sub-rounded iron ore <1 mm; unoxidised core, some oxidisation on exterior surface.
F3 Hard, moderately fine fabric; moderate, well-sorted, sub-angular flint <2 mm; moderate rounded quartz grains <1 mm; sparse very fine mica; sparse sub-rounded iron ore <4 mm; unoxidised, oxidised surfaces.
F4 Hard, moderately fine fabric; moderate, well-sorted, sub-angular flint <2 mm; moderate rounded quartz grains <1 mm; sparse, very fine mica; sparse, sub-rounded iron ore <4 mm; unoxidised, oxidised surfaces.
F5 Hard, moderately fine fabric; moderate, poorly-sorted, sub-angular flint <2 mm (naturally occurring?); moderate rounded quartz grains <0.5 mm; sparse very fine mica; moderate sub-rounded iron ore <3 mm; unoxidised core, oxidised surfaces.
F6 Hard, moderately fine fabric; moderate, well-sorted, sub-angular flint <4 mm; sparse rounded quartz grains <0.25 mm; sparse very fine mica; sparse sub-rounded iron ore <0.25 mm; unoxidised, oxidised surfaces.
F7 Hard, fine fabric; common, well-sorted, sub-angular flint <2 mm; sparse rounded quartz <0.25 mm; sparse very fine mica; unoxidised, internal surface oxidised.
F8 Hard, moderately coarse fabric; common, poorly-sorted, sub-angular flint <4 mm; moderate rounded quartz — <0.25 mm; unoxidised core, oxidised surfaces.
F9 Hard, fine fabric; sparse, poorly-sorted, sub-angular flint <3 mm (naturally occurring?); sparse rounded quartz grains <0.25 mm; sparse very fine mica; sparse sub-rounded iron ore <1 mm; unoxidised.

Sandy fabrics
Four fabric types were identified, ranging from coarse (Q10) to moderately fine (Q11 and Q13).

Q10 Hard, coarse fabric; moderate, well-sorted, rounded quartz <1 mm; sparse moderately-sorted, sub-angular flint <5 mm; unoxidised, oxidised external surface.
Q11 Hard, moderately fine fabric; moderate, well-sorted, rounded quartz <0.25 mm; sparse vegetable matter; rare poorly-sorted, sub-angular flint <1 mm; unoxidised.
Q12 Soft, moderately coarse fabric; moderate, well-sorted, rounded quartz <0.25 mm; moderate poorly-sorted iron ore <2 mm; sparse very fine mica; unoxidised, some oxidisation on surfaces.
Q13 Soft, moderately fine fabric; moderate, well-sorted, rounded quartz <0.25 mm; sparse vegetable matter; sparse sub-rounded iron ore <1 mm; sparse, very fine mica; unoxidised, some oxidisation on surfaces.

Approximately two-thirds of the later prehistoric assemblage is flint-tempered/flint-gritted, of which 74% of the sherds occur in the coarsely flint-tempered fabric F2. The next largest groups occur in the finer fabrics F5, F1, and F4 (11%, 4% and 4%) respectively. The remaining one-third of the prehistoric assemblage consists of sandy fabrics, 53% of which consist of the moderately fine, organic-tempered fabric Q13 (Table 18).

Distinguishing between different fabric types proved difficult in some cases, especially within the coarse flint-tempered group, as several fabrics covered a wide variation of inclusion size and concentration. Another problem encountered was differentiating between the prehistoric and possible Saxon organic-tempered fabrics, both of which use micaceous, moderately fine clay matrices. In this case, distinctions were made both on the frequency of vegetable temper, which could be broadly defined as ranging from sparse in the prehistoric fabrics to common in the Saxon fabrics, creating a very laminated appearance in the latter examples, and also on the associated pottery within each feature.

The similarities in the clay matrix and inclusion types for the majority of the fabrics suggest a relatively restricted source area for the raw materials, all of which would have been locally accessible within the geology of the area, from the London Clay and Reading Beds. The presence within the distinctive fabric F3 of well-rounded, reddish–brown grains of glauconite/limonite may, however, be indicative of a separate source area for this fabric. Glauconite is often associated with Greensand formations which occur in north Hampshire and Oxfordshire, although glauconitic sand is also found in some locations of the local Reading Beds (White 1907). Similar glauconitic fabrics have been identified at Dunston Park, Thatcham (Morris and Mepham 1995, fabric F6, Q3) and Thames Valley Park, Reading (Mepham forthcoming, fabrics B8, B9). If these glauconitic fabrics were derived from a non-local source, it could suggest a level of regional exchange above what appears to be fairly *ad hoc* domestic production for the majority of the ceramics of this period.

Vessel forms
Two almost complete vessels were recovered. The first, from the upper fill of ditch 3002 (trackway 3012) is in fabric F2 and very fragmentary with no diagnostic sherds. The second vessel, from pit 345, within the colluvium, is more complete: a large, slack-shouldered jar in fabric F3 with an incised bead rim, a moderately straight-sided profile, and a slightly concave base with a large concentration of crushed flint on the underside (Fig. 80, 2; Pl. 4).

In general, the later prehistoric sherds are small and abraded (mean sherd weight 6.4 g), with an almost complete lack of diagnostic material. Apart from the two vessels noted above, only one rim form was recognised, a flattened, finger-impressed rim in fabric F1, probably from a medium to large-sized jar (Fig. 80, 3). In addition, horizontally incised sherds from one vessel (Fig. 80, 4) in the fine sandy fabric Q13 may derive from a furrowed bowl, although it should be noted that the fabric, form

Table 17 Pottery fabric totals

Fabric date	*Fabric type*	*No. of sherds*	*Weight (g)*	*% of total assemblage (by wt)*
Early prehistoric	V1	2	12	
Total early prehistoric		2	12	0.06
Later prehistoric	F1	39	207	
	F2	248	3695	
	F3	11	95	
	F4	52	210	
	F5	62	533	
	F6	5	48	
	F7	9	72	
	F8	5	105	
	F9	15	43	
Total flint-tempered		446	5008	
	Q10	7	57	
	Q11	32	202	
	Q12	22	126	
	Q13	149	433	
Total sandy		210	818	
Total later prehistoric		656	5826	26.90
Romano-British	samian	7	46	
	Central Gaulish	1	2	
	Oxfordshire	70	725	
	New Forest	9	77	
Total finewares		87	850	
	G100	10	262	
	G101	22	493	
	G102	25	561	
	G103	29	166	
	G104	73	1006	
	Total grog-tempered	159	2488	
	Silchester ware	193	2625	
	Black burnished	83	787	
	Q101	56	1000	
	Q102	238	1638	
	Q103	145	1755	
	Q104	27	380	
	Q105	58	1602	
	Q106	113	952	
	Q107	56	790	
	Q108	26	273	
	Q110	7	82	
	Q111	29	438	
	Total coarse sandy	838	9697	
Total Romano-British		1277	15660	72.32
Saxon	Q401	4	36	
	Q402	9	80	
Total Saxon		13	116	0.54
Post-medieval		6	40	0.18
OVERALL TOTAL	all	1954	21654	

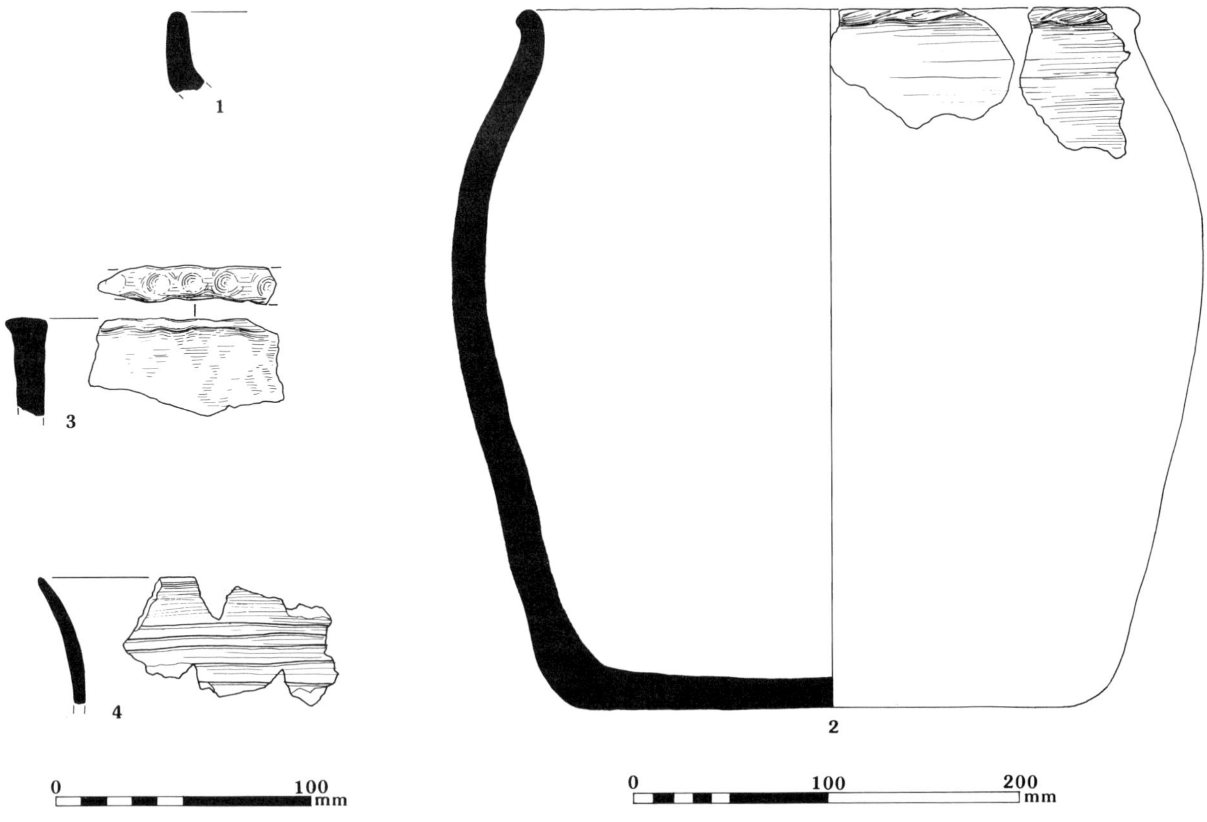

Figure 80 Prehistoric pottery (1–4)

and linear decoration could just as well be attributed to the Saxon period (compare, for example, Myres 1977, fig. 90). On the basis of associated pottery within the same feature (pit 724) this vessel has been assigned to the later prehistoric phase. Four body sherds in the coarse flint-tempered fabric F8, recovered from ditch segment 591, may possibly derive from Middle Bronze Age Deverel-Rimbury type urns (eg Woodward 1992); these sherds are distinctive by their coarseness and thick body walls, but conclusive diagnostic evidence is lacking.

Decoration and surface treatment

Decoration is very scarce in the later prehistoric assemblage, consisting of only five incised body sherds, sherds from a possible furrowed bowl, and one finger-impressed rim. These occur in the finer flint-tempered fabric F1 and sandy fabrics Q12 and Q13 respectively. Surface treatment is also very rare; only four body sherds were identified as having smoothed surfaces, and one body sherd, presumably from an open form, is burnished internally. Surface treatment is restricted to the flint-tempered/flint-gritted fabrics F1, F7 and F9, and the sandy fabric Q12.

Chronology and affinities

With the possible exception of the thick-walled sherds in the coarse flint-tempered fabric F8, which could be derived from urns of Deverel-Rimbury type, the later prehistoric group as a whole belongs to the post-Deverel-Rimbury tradition of southern England (Barrett 1980) and finds similarities in material from nearby sites in the Kennet Valley, such as Aldermaston, Dunston Park, the Field Farm/Knight's Farm complex, and Anslow's Cottages (Bradley *et al.* 1980; Morris and Mepham 1995; Mepham 1992a; 1992b). The relatively small size of the assemblage, and the lack of diagnostic material, makes closer dating within this sequence problematic, but there are some chronological indicators in the presence of a relatively high proportion of sandy fabrics, and the identification of a possible furrowed bowl; a form which is dated elsewhere to the 8th–7th centuries BC (Cunliffe 1984, 254). The increased use of sandy fabrics at the expense of flint-tempered fabrics has been noted elsewhere as a late phenomenon within this post-Deverel-Rimbury phase, for example at Runnymede Bridge (Longley 1980, 65), and this later date is supported by the presence of decorated sherds and fine bowl forms, albeit in very small quantities. Altogether, the evidence suggests a date towards the beginning of the Early Iron Age, broadly contemporary with the assemblage at Knight's Farm, dated to the 8th–7th century BC (Bradley *et al.* 1980), which has a larger proportion of decoration and fineware vessel forms.

Distribution

Small, non-diagnostic body sherds were recovered, mainly from the higher ground (Reading Beds) in the south-west corner of the excavation, and also further dispersed in smaller quantities within the colluvium and the valley gravels.

The largest quantities originated from ditches Early Iron Age 3002 and 3003 (trackway 3012). These features

Table 18 Prehistoric pottery by fabric type and feature

Feature date	Provenance	Fabric Tempers				
		Organic no. / wt (g)	Flint no / wt (g)	Sandy no. / wt (g)	Intrusive no. / wt (g)	Total no. / wt (g)
Late Neolithic–Early Bronze Age	Pit 9	2/12	–	–	–	2/12
Early Iron Age	Trackway 3012 (ditch 3002)	–	542/945	7/27	1/8 p-med.	550/980
	Trackway 3012 (ditch 3003)	–	79/464	124/381	–	203/845
	Enclosure 3001 (ditch 3013)	–	10/36	2/9	–	12/45
	Enclosure 3001 (ditch 3014)	–	–	–	1/2 R-B	1/2
	Group 3015 (pit 416)	–	1/3	–	–	1/3
	Ditch 566	–	15/45	–	–	15/45
	Ditch 3016	–	1/1	–	2/12 R-B	3/13
	Ditch 21	–	1/3	–	–	1/3
	Pit 61	–	5/79	–	1/21 R-B	6/100
	Pit 62	–	3/30	3/31	–	6/61
	Pit 93	–	5/93	3/27	3/36 R-B	11/156
	Pit 315	–	–	1/2	–	1/2
	Pit 345	–	102/2644	–	–	102/2644
	Pit 724	–	–	34/163	–	34/163
	Post-hole 96	–	1/3	–	–	1/3
	Post-hole 448	–	1/23	–	–	1/23
	Post-hole 565	–	1/4	–	–	1/4
Romano-British	Ditch 3017	–	3/9	–	2/28 R-B	5/37
TOTAL		2/12	770/4382	174/640	10/107	956/5141

produced an almost equal proportion of flint-tempered and sandy fabrics (Table 18), but the majority of the latter comprised sherds of what appeared to be a single vessel in fabric Q13. Parts of single vessels were also recovered from ditch 3002 (fabric F2; unreconstructable) and from pit 345 within the colluvium (fabric F3: Fig. 80, 2). Early Iron Age pit 724 in the colluvium excavation area yielded sherds of what seemed to be at least two vessels in two groups of sherds, one from each end of the feature. All sherds were in sandy fabrics and include one reconstructable profile, part of a furrowed bowl in fabric Q13 (Fig. 80, 4).

Small quantities came from other scattered features on the valley gravel and within the colluvium. Pits 61 and 93 also contained stray sherds of Romano-British pottery, possibly resulting from later disturbance, since these features were in an area of subsequent Romano-British activity.

Very little later prehistoric pottery was recovered from features on the valley gravel, consisting of one small flint-tempered body sherd from the upper layer of the clay-lined pit 416, a second flint-tempered sherd from a post-hole cutting pit 416, and one sandy sherd from pit 315 at the northern limit of excavation.

Romano-British

Romano-British pottery formed the bulk of the Wickhams Field ceramic assemblage and ranged in date from the 1st–4th centuries AD. The majority of sherds are in good condition, moderately large and unabraded (mean sherd weight 12.0 g). The fabrics can be divided broadly into four groups: finewares; grog-tempered fabrics; flint-tempered, and coarse sandy wares. Quantification of pottery by fabric type is given in Table 17.

Finewares

The finewares can be further divided into imported wares and British finewares. A very small range of imported wares are identified within the assemblage, represented by seven small, abraded sherds of samian, with a possible Central Gaulish source, including sherds from Drag 18/31 platters, and one possible Drag 37 bowl. There are also two possible Central Gaulish colour-coated body sherds in a fine, buff fabric with a dark brown colour coat, dated to AD 70–150 (Greene 1978).

British finewares include Oxfordshire colour-coated and white wares and New Forest colour-coated wares. The Oxfordshire red/brown colour-coated fabric is hard and micaceous, varying in colour from brownish–orange to reddish–brown and often with a grey core (Young 1977). At Wickhams Field the sherds were very abraded and only small traces of the reddish–orange colour coat survived. The forms identified consist of jars or bowls with beaded rims copying samian bowl forms Drag 31, Drag 37 and Drag 38 (*ibid.*, types 44; 55–63, 51–3 respectively). It is likely that the sherds are datable to

Table 19 Romano-British pottery — vessel form by fabric type

Vessel form	*Sandy fabrics (E100, Q101–Q11)*	*Grog-tempered (G100–G104)*	*Silchester ware (E151)*
Large storage jar	3	2	2
Everted rim jar: 1st/2nd centuries AD	26	4	3
Everted rim jar: 3rd/4th centuries AD	9	–	–
Bead rim jar	10	3	5
Hemispherical bowl	5	–	–
Drop-flanged bowl	15	–	–
Bead rim bowl	3	–	–
Dog dish	8	–	–
TOTAL NUMBERS	79	9	10

the main production phase of the Oxfordshire industry in the 3rd and 4th centuries AD, when colour-coated wares were widely distributed across southern England (*ibid.*, 133). This date range would also apply to the possible Oxfordshire white wares, including two body sherds and one flagon/bottle spout. The remaining nine plain colour-coated body sherds are all small and abraded, in a fine-grained grey fabric with traces of darker grey colour coat, comparable to New Forest colour-coated wares produced from AD 270–400 (Fulford 1975).

Grog tempered fabrics
Five grog-tempered fabrics were identified:

G100 Hard, coarse fabric; moderate well-sorted, sub-rounded grog <5 mm; moderate iron ore <0.5 mm; moderate rounded quartz <0.5 mm; sparse very fine mica; unoxidised, external surface oxidised.

G101 Hard, coarse fabric; moderate well-sorted, sub-rounded grog <4 mm; moderate black iron ore <2 mm; sparse rounded quartz <1 mm; unoxidised, oxidised margins.

G102 Hard, coarse fabric; moderate well-sorted, sub-rounded grog <2 mm; sparse iron ore <1 mm; sparse rounded quartz <0.25 mm; oxidised.

G103 Hard, fine fabric; moderate well-sorted, sub-rounded grog <2 mm; sparse iron ore — <0.25 mm; sparse rounded quartz <0.25 mm; sparse very fine mica; oxidised.

G104 Hard, coarse fabric; moderate well-sorted, sub-rounded grog <1 mm; sparse rounded quartz <0.25 mm; sparse very fine mica; unoxidised.

A small percentage (16%) of the Romano-British assemblage consist of the five grog-tempered fabrics listed above, which range from soft, fine fabrics to hard, coarse fabrics. The vessel forms identified are plain utilitarian jars, including two large storage jars with beaded rims, four smaller everted rim jars (Fig. 81, 9), and three finer bead rim jars. Grog-tempered fabric types are more likely to be of local origins, continuing a well-attested Late Iron Age potting tradition in the area into the early Romano-British period. There is, for example, evidence of a possible 1st-century AD kiln producing wheel-thrown, grog-tempered vessels in a restricted range of forms at Thames Valley Park, Reading, although this is likely to have been supplying only that settlement and its immediate vicinity (Mepham forthcoming).

Flint-tempered fabrics
One flint-tempered fabric was identified, which corresponds to the coarse fabric defined as 'Silchester ware' (Charles 1979).

E151 Silchester ware: hard, coarse fabric; common poorly-sorted, sub-angular flint <4 mm; moderate rounded quartz <0.25 mm; sparse iron ore; either unoxidised or oxidised.

This fabric made up 17% of the Romano-British assemblage. In some cases it was difficult to distinguish this fabric from Late Bronze Age flint-tempered fabrics in the absence of diagnostic forms (eg fabric F7). The forms identified consist of three jars with upright rims, two jars with inturned rims, which were expanded internally, three beaded rims, and two large everted rim storage jars (Fig. 81, 6–8).

'Silchester ware' was produced from the latest pre-Conquest period until at least AD 70 and probably to the end of the 1st century AD; one possible kiln has been excavated at Oakfield Park, *c.* 5 km from Silchester (Charles 1979). It is rarely found more than about 30 km from this centre.

Coarse sandy fabrics

E100 Black Burnished ware (BB1); see Seager Smith and Davies 1993, 249, for a full fabric description.

Q101 Hard, coarse-textured fabric; abundant, well-sorted, rounded quartz <1 mm; sparse iron ore; rare sub-angular flint <2 mm; unoxidised (grey).

Q102 Hard, fine fabric; common, well-sorted, rounded quartz <0.25 mm; unoxidised (grey surfaces pale core).

Q103 Hard, coarse-textured fabric; abundant, well-sorted, rounded quartz <1 mm; unoxidisd (grey with pale core).

Q104 Hard, fine fabric; moderate, poorly-sorted, rounded quartz <0.25 mm; sparse very fine mica; unoxidised, generally oxidised core or internal surface.

Q105 Moderately coarse-textured fabric; common, moderately-sorted, rounded quartz <0.5 mm; unoxidised (grey).

Q106 Hard, fine fabric; common, well-sorted, rounded quartz <0.25 mm; unoxidised (grey).

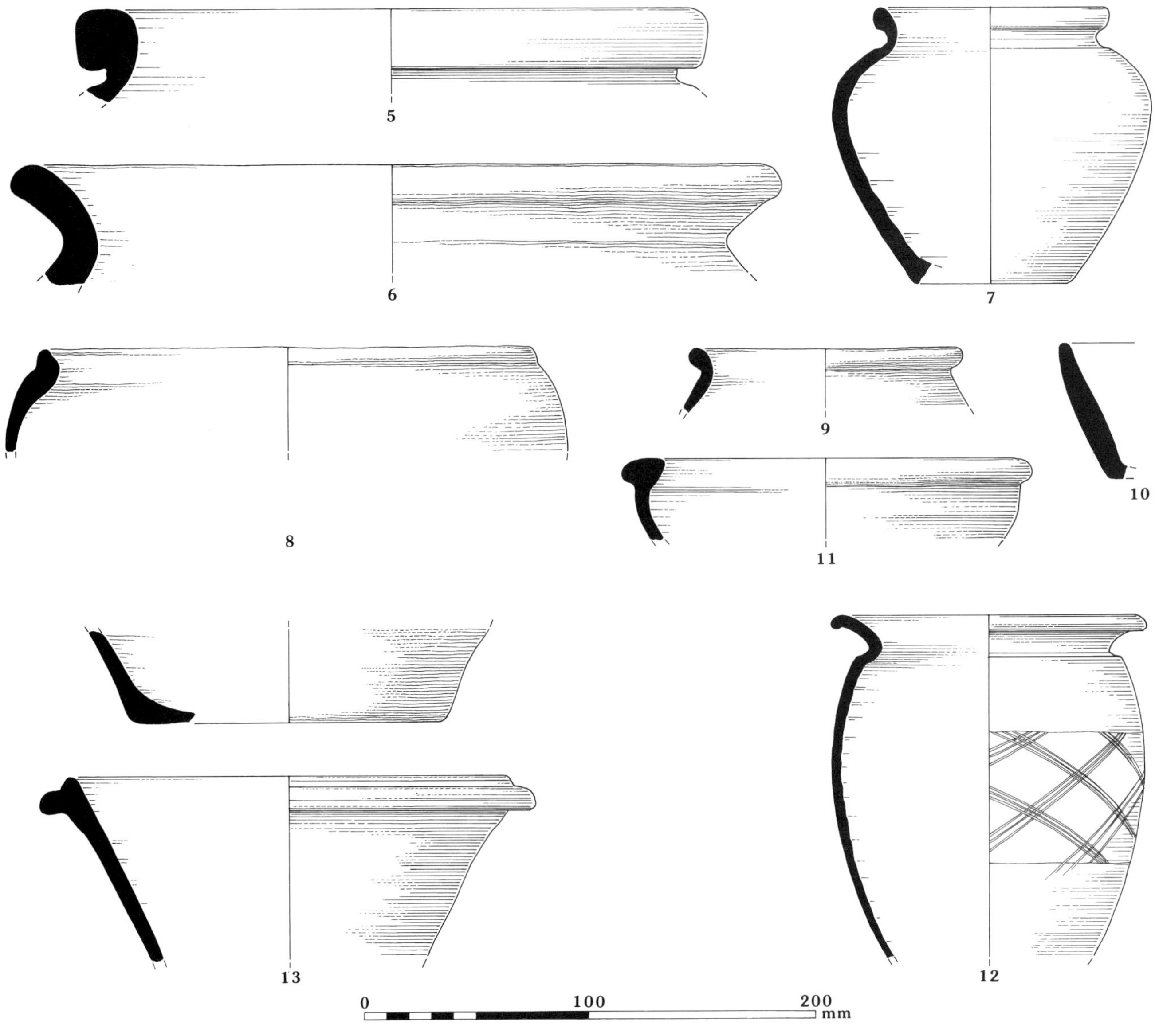

Figure 81 Romano-British pottery (5–13)

Q107 Hard, coarse sandy fabric; abundant, well-sorted, rounded quartz <1 mm; unoxidised, oxidised margins (grey with orange sandwich core).

Q108 Hard, fine fabric; abundant, well-sorted, rounded quartz <0.25 mm; sparse, very fine mica; unoxidised (dark grey surfaces, pale core).

Q110 Hard, coarse fabric; common, moderately-sorted, rounded quartz <0.5 mm; oxidised (pale orange).

Q111 Hard, coarse sandy fabric; common, poorly-sorted, rounded quartz <2 mm; sparse iron ore <1 mm; oxidised (pale orange).

Coarse sandy wares make up the largest group within the assemblage (62% by weight). The only fabric of known source identified was E100, Black Burnished ware (BB1) from south-east Dorset (Poole Harbour area). A moderate quantity of Black Burnished ware sherds was identified (83 sherds). Vessel forms identified spanned both the earlier (later 1st–2nd centuries AD) and later (3rd–4th centuries AD). Earlier forms include bead rim jars and flat-rimmed bowls; later forms include everted rim jars and flanged bowls.

A further large amount of the course sandy wares (57%) consists of grey wares of uncertain source (fabrics Q101 to Q111), which probably have a number of potential sources, eg the Alice Holt and Oxfordshire production centres. Another possible source for grey wares is the group of kilns excavated at Hamstead Marshall near Newbury, Berkshire, which were in operation from the mid 2nd to the 4th centuries AD, producing a range of plain jars and bowls (Rashbrook 1983).

The forms identified within the coarse grey ware assemblage (Table 19) consist of a large quantity of utilitarian everted rim jars, bowls with rims ranging from plain flat-topped to drop-flanged and reeded, jars with beaded and flat-topped rims, plain-rimmed dishes, and large storage jars (Fig. 81, 5, 10–13).

Burnishing was the predominant surface treatment identified for the coarse wares, particularly on Black Burnished fabrics and the fine fabric Q108. In some cases fabric Q108 may be imitating Black Burnished

Table 20 Romano-British pottery by fabric type and feature

Provenance	*Sandy fabrics no. / wt (g)*	*Grog-tempered no. / wt (g)*	*Silchester ware no. / wt (g)*	*Samian imports no. / wt (g)*	*British finewares no / wt (g)*	*Total*
Trackway 3018 (ditch 3011)	–	16/195	–	–	–	16/195
Trackway 3018 (ditch 3010)	–	–	37/478	–	–	37/478
Enclosure 3004	11/222	–	4/167	–	–	15/389
Enclosure 3005	54/725	43/1075	29/503	1/37	11/171	138/2511
Structure 3007	4/38	–	–	–	–	4/38
Structure 3022	–	21/142	11/73	–	–	32/215
Group 3006	26/253	25/272	13/111	2/10	2/6	68/652
Midden 3009	562/6522	12/123	2/220	1/5	73/652	650/7522
Ditch 515	27/259	1/11	–	–	–	28/270
Ditch 3008	22/373	18/238	7/37	2/4	–	49/652
Ditch 3019	1/8	–	41/386	–	–	42/394
Ditch 3023	1/4	–	2/10	–	–	3/14
Well 301	1/3	–	–	–	–	1/3
Well 322	2/9	–	–	–	1/2	3/11
Pit 49	15/152	4/91	7/53	2/20	–	28/316
Pit 85	7/99	1/4	–	–	–	8/103
Pit 98	3/22	–	–	–	–	3/22
Pit 251	1/3	–	–	–	–	1/3
Pit 307	6/129	–	–	–	1/9	7/138
Pit 337	1/4	–	1/4	–	–	2/8
Pit 342	3/84	–	–	–	–	3/84
Pit 517	2/9	–	–	–	–	2/9
Pit 685	1/17	1/64	–	–	–	2/81
Post-hole 652	1/3	–	–	–	–	1/3
Post-hole 654	3/19	–	–	–	–	3/19
Colluvium	42/444	–	28/716	–	–	70/1160
TOTAL	796/9401	142/2215	182/2758	8/76	88/840	1216/15290

ware. Incised radiating lines were observed on one base sherd, and incised decoration was also identified on a small number of body sherds, including the obtuse lattice pattern on a 3rd–4th century everted rim jar in the fine fabric Q106 (Fig. 81, 12).

Chronology and affinities

The Romano-British assemblage is typical of a small rural site, with predominantly coarse fabrics and only a small quantity of finewares. The assemblage can be broadly divided into mainly early 1st–2nd century AD forms and fabrics, characterised by a substantial proportion of coarse, locally-produced, flint-tempered and grog-tempered wares, with smaller proportions of grey-wares; and a slightly smaller quantity of later 3rd–4th century AD forms, including Oxfordshire and New Forest finewares.

It would appear that there was a bias in the early Roman period towards locally produced pottery, such as Silchester ware and grog-tempered fabrics, illustrating the conservative nature of local potting traditions with the continuity of use of Iron Age fabrics and forms. There is a scarcity in this period of any finewares which further emphasises the lack of more regional contacts. A similar range of material has been identified at other early Romano-British sites in the Kennet Valley, including Aldermaston (Cowell *et al.* 1978), Ufton Nervet (Manning 1974), and Pingewood (Johnston 1985).

The coarse grey wares which occur throughout the Romano-British period may possibly indicate a shift in sources from the Alice Holt production centre in the early Roman period to Oxfordshire, or even the New Forest in the later Roman period, in parallel with the introduction of finewares from the latter centres. The

Black Burnished ware (BB1) includes vessel forms dated to both early and later Roman periods.

Distribution

The early Romano-British fabrics, such as Silchester ware and grog-tempered fabrics, were concentrated in a number of features within the colluvium; pit group 3006, ditches 3008, 3010, 3011, 3019, and structure 3022 all produced large enough quantities to make their attribution to this period fairly secure (Fig. 81, 8–9). Enclosure 3004, ditch 3023, and pit 49 yielded smaller quantities of early material (Fig. 81, 7). The high proportion of Silchester ware deriving from the colluvium and the absence of definitely later Romano-British material is at odds with the other artefactual dating for this deposit.

Approximately one half of the Romano-British assemblage from Wickhams Field was retrieved from midden 3009 (Table 20). Although early Romano-British fabrics are present within this group, including sherds of Silchester ware and grog-tempered fabrics, as well as two sherds of samian, the emphasis is firmly on the later Romano-British period, with a large proportion of the British finewares, particularly Oxfordshire colour-coated wares, deriving from this deposit (Fig. 81, 5, 6, 10, 11, 13).

Enclosure 3005 is also dated to the late Romano-British period on the basis of stratigraphic relationships and the small quantity of Oxfordshire finewares found in the ditch fills, although 1st–2nd century material was also present in some quantity.

The remaining features associated with the Romano-British activity on the site are not closely datable and produced mainly undiagnostic sherds of coarse sandy wares.

Saxon

A small component of the assemblage has been ascribed a Saxon date (14 sherds/116 g). Two fabrics were identified, both containing organic temper:

Q401 Hard, laminated fabric; moderate, well-sorted, rounded quartz <0.25 mm; common organic matter; unoxidised, oxidised external surface.

Q402 Hard, laminated fabric; moderate, well-sorted, rounded quartz <0.5 mm; common organic matter; moderate very fine mica; unoxidised.

These two fabrics have been tentatively assigned to the early to middle Saxon period on the basis of the frequency of organic temper; the difficulties in distinguishing between Saxon and later prehistoric organic-tempered sandy fabrics have already been noted. The rim forms recovered were also non-diagnostic in that they could have occurred in either period. Two small, nondescript rim forms occur in these two fabrics. Seven conjoining base sherd fragments in fabric Q402 have a smoothed exterior surface and burnished internal surface indicative of a bowl or other open form. The remaining body sherds are plain and non-diagnostic.

Distribution

In total, 14 sherds of this period were recovered, most of which (11 sherds) were found in the three pits: 536, 542, and 557 (pit group 3025), situated within the south-west corner of the excavation area. Another sherd was recovered from the Saxon well 322, with an intrusive sherd from Romano-British pit 98, and one sherd from the topsoil.

Post-medieval

Only a very small quantity of post-medieval sherds was recovered and consisted of four red earthenware sherds, one glazed cream earthenware probably from the Surrey/Hampshire Border Ware, industry and one English stoneware of 18th/19th century type. These were recovered from the recut section of ditch 3002 (trackway 3012), topsoil and colluvium respectively.

List of illustrated pottery

(Fig. 80) Earlier prehistoric

1. Small rim, concave neck and internal moulding; fabric V1; possibly Fengate Ware; light brown, irregularly fired. Context 8. Pit 9.

Later prehistoric

2. Slack-shouldered jar, obliquely-slashed bead rim; fabric F3; unoxidised core and oxidised surfaces. Context 346; pit 345.
3. Jar with expanded, finger-impressed rim; fabric F1; unoxidised, traces of oxidisation on surfaces. Context 575; segment 582, ditch 3003, trackway 3012.
4. Furrowed bowl; fabric Q13; unoxidised core, oxidised surfaces. Context 723; pit 724.

(Fig. 81) Romano-British

5. Large storage jar, squared rim; coarse greyware Q105; wheelthrown; unoxidised. Context 358; midden 3009.
6. Large storage jar, everted rim; Silchester ware E151; handmade; unoxidised core, oxidised surfaces. Context 358; midden 3009.
7. Bead rim jar; Silchester ware, E151, unoxidised, some oxidisation on interior surface. Context 48; pit 49.
8. Bead rim jar; Silchester ware E151; handmade; unoxidised core and external surface, oxidised internal surface. Context 350; segment 349, ditch 3010, trackway 3018.
9. Everted rim jar; grog-tempered fabric G104; handmade; unoxidised core and surfaces. Context 273; segment 274, ditch 3011, trackway 3018.
10. 'Dog dish'; coarse greyware Q104; wheelthrown; unoxidised, oxidised margins. Context 827; midden 3009.
11. Hemispherical bowl, thickened, flattened rim; coarse greyware Q105; wheelthrown; unoxidised. Context 827; midden 3009.
12. Jar with flaring everted rim, incised obtuse lattice decoration; fine greyware Q106; wheelthrown; unoxidised. Context 513; main colluvial layer.
13. Drop-flanged bowl; coarse greyware Q101; wheelthrown; unoxidised. Context 821; midden 3009.

Ceramic Building Material, by M. Laidlaw

A total of 97 fragments (4719 g) of ceramic building material was recovered. The bulk of the collection has been attributed to the Romano-British period on the basis of surviving dimensions, fabric, and associated pottery. This Romano-British assemblage consists of mainly moderately sized, featureless fragments of tile and brick, some of which are abraded. Only two diagnostic *tegula* fragments and one incised flue tile fragment were identified. The mean thicknesses for the tile and brick fragments are 20 mm and 40 mm respectively.

No detailed fabric analysis was undertaken but a brief visual examination of the assemblage indicated three distinct, broadly defined fabric types. All are oxidised, often with an unoxidised core, have moderate iron ore (<2 mm) and very fine mica inclusions; quartz grain ranges in size from moderately fine (<0.25 mm) to very coarse (<1 mm), and rare large flint inclusions are present.

The largest concentration of ceramic building material was recovered from midden 3009 (23 fragments) with smaller quantities dispersed in various pits and ditches throughout the colluvium. Structure 3007 may represent the original source for the clay roof tile fragments. The remaining fragments occurred in small quantities in dispersed features over the site, including 22 pieces from the topsoil and main colluvial layer.

Fired Clay, by M. Laidlaw

Eighty-two fragments of fired clay were recovered, the bulk of which comprise small featureless fragments, probably structural in origin, from wattle and daub structures or from hearth linings, a small number of surfaces and possible wattle impressions are visible. Most fragments were oxidised in a fine to coarse quartz sand fabric, occasionally containing flint inclusions.

Also present are identifiable pieces of at least five triangular loomweights. The loomweights are in a fairly hard, fine, micaceous, slightly sandy fabric and perforated through one, two, or all three corners, although no complete dimensions survive to attribute them to a type. The loomweights are of a type widely distributed in southern England from the Middle Iron Age into the Romano-British period (Champion 1975, fig. 2). From their context, the examples from Wickhams Field would seem to be Romano-British in date.
The loomweight fragments were recovered from the main colluvial layer and enclosures 3004 and 3005 within the colluvium excavation area. The remaining fired clay fragments occurred in small quantities dispersed in various features across the site.

Worked Timbers, by Rowena Gale and Lorraine Mepham

Eleven timbers were examined, all from well linings, nine from well 301 and two from well 322. All timbers were waterlogged. Samples were taken from each timber for species identification and the results are summarised in Table 21. In addition, one sample from timber 2025 (well 322) was processed for radiocarbon dating by Scottish Universities Research and Reactor Centre at East Kilbride. The radiocarbon date obtained (GU-4362, 1290±50BP; cal. AD 650–870) has been calibrated with the 20 year atmospheric calibration curve using the University of Washington Quaternary Isotope Laboratory Radiocarbon Dating Program (1987). The date is expressed at the 95% confidence level with end points rounded outwards to ten years, following the recommended form (Mook 1986).

All the timbers were worn and abraded, making difficult the positive identification of signs of working. Most appear to represent planks of varying sizes and shapes; one piece with a triangular section (Obj. No. 2008) could have functioned either as a stake or a plank. Two planks from well 301 are radially split; the remainder appear to be tangentially split, with sections ranging from triangular to rectangular. Five show possible or definite cut-marks at one end, mostly oblique cuts. One piece seems to represent something more elaborate (Obj. No. 2011): a large, thick timber from well 301 with rectangular section, one end cut obliquely with

Table 21 Summary of worked timbers

Provenance	*Obj. no.*	*Sample no.*	*Dimensions (mm)*	*Species*	*Comments*
Well 301	2005	–	450x100x40	*Quercus* ?h	Tangential plank, rectangular section, both ends worn
	2006	–	34x–x<20	*Quercus*	3 thinnish planks: 2 radially cut/split, 1 wider fragment
	2007	–	470x120x40	*Quercus* h	Tangential plank, rectangular section, obliquely cut one end
	2008	–	580x90x60	*Quercus* h	Stake or thick plank, triangular section, ?obliquely cut one end
	2009	–	–	(1 bark)	Not obviously worked
	2010	–	380x55x<10	*Quercus* h	Short plank or lath
	2011	–	340x140x80	*Quercus* h	Thick tangential plank, rectangular section, obliquely cut one end with ?rebate; hollowed out on one face
Well 322	2025	1084	560x350x70	*Quercus* h	?Tangential plank, wide
	2026	1085	210x100x30	*Quercus* h	?Tangential plank, wide

a possible small rebate, and apparently hollowed out above the oblique cut to give a fairly regular, sub-rectangular depression on one side.

All timbers for which species identification was possible (9 out of the total 11) are of oak (*Quercus*) and all are heartwood. Oak, one of the strongest and most durable of British timbers (Edlin 1949), appears to have been one of the most frequently used timbers for building wells in southern England during the Saxon period. Urban examples have included wells at Hamwic, Southampton (ie Morton 1992, 43-4; Andrews forthcoming) and Ipswich, Suffolk (Wade 1993, 145). Timber-lined Saxon wells in rural contexts are comparatively rare, with two examples from Wicken, Bonhunt, Essex (Wade 1974, 75) perhaps providing parallels with the examples at Wickhams Field.

Discussion of the Artefactual Evidence, by Lorraine Mepham

This section attempts to summarise the artefactual evidence from the site in order to present an overall picture of the material culture represented in each period of site activity, to highlight evidence for artefact production, exchange, and use, and to set this evidence in its local and regional context.

Earlier prehistoric

Material evidence for earlier prehistoric activity on the site is restricted to worked flint diagnostic of both the Early and Late Neolithic, and two joining rim sherds which possibly derive from a Late Neolithic Fengate-style vessel. Other flintwork, such as a small blade component, has been considered as 'earlier prehistoric' and could potentially include Mesolithic material but there is no conclusive evidence to suggest that it is not later. The pottery has been used to date pit 9, the only feature on the site which can definitely be assigned to the early prehistoric period. None of the flintwork came from *in situ* contexts. This rather scanty evidence can be set within the wider picture of the increasing settlement of the area from the later Neolithic onwards; at nearby Field Farm, a Late Neolithic Mortlake Ware bowl was excavated from the area within a later ring-ditch (Butterworth and Lobb 1992, 11), while flintwork associated with Peterborough Ware was recovered from the upper fills of a ring-ditch at Englefield, about 5 km to the west (Healy 1993).

Later prehistoric

Evidence from the later prehistoric period is more common, but still restricted in range, comprising a substantial ceramic assemblage with associated worked flint, much of it *in situ*. The pottery assemblage can be viewed within what is now a well-established ceramic framework for the Late Bronze Age and Early Iron Age in the region, based on Barrett's proposed post-Deverel-Rimbury sequence (1980). Within a 10 km radius of the site, comparable assemblages have been recovered from Field Farm, Anslow's Cottages, Knight's Farm, Aldermaston Wharf, and Reading Business Park (Mep- ham 1992a; 1992b; Bradley *et al* 1980; Hall 1992). A relatively late date range within this sequence seems likely for Wickhams Field, potentially contemporary with the nearby Knight's Farm assemblage. There is little within the assemblage which would indicate anything other than local production, although one distinctive fabric containing glauconite could be taken as an indication of more regional production and exchange. This is echoed within the flint assemblage, which again reflects the exploitation of local resources. One significant piece of evidence for on-site activity is the large quantity of iron-smithing slag from pit 430. The evidence for ironworking at this early period is interesting, although not without parallel in the area. There is evidence for bronzeworking on a small scale at Aldermaston Wharf (Bradley *et al.* 1980, 244), and for ironworking from a Middle Iron Age context at Riseley Farm, Swallowfield (Lobb and Morris 1991–93, 55), but so far the only other evidence for ironworking at this date comes from Cooper's Farm near Thatcham, about 15 km along the Kennet valley to the west, where a small quantity of slag was recovered from a 7th-century BC pit (Fitzpatrick 1995).

Other material evidence of functional significance is restricted to finds of burnt, unworked flint, primarily the large deposit from pit 416. The dating of this feature relies on a single later prehistoric sherd from the upper fill, and the function of this pit is uncertain, but a similarly extensive and ambiguous deposit of burnt flint, albeit not from a pit, was excavated at Anslow's Cottages (Butterworth and Lobb 1992, 90).

Romano-British

This period provides a greater range of artefactual evidence. The primary dating evidence is again the ceramic assemblage, although closely datable finewares are very scarce. The early Romano-British assemblage demonstrates the innate conservatism of ceramic production in the area, with a significant proportion of flint-tempered and grog-tempered vessels of native Iron Age inspiration, probably of local manufacture, alongside the Romanised coarsewares from further afield (eg Alice Holt). Similar ceramic evidence from nearby sites at Pingewood and Ufton Nervet has been taken as an indication of low social status for these sites (Johnston 1985; Manning 1974). However, this is contrasted by the structural evidence from the site, both the *in situ* structure 3007 and the small quantity of ceramic building material, possibly also deriving from this structure, found within the late Roman midden 3009. This structural evidence is significant, since other sites in the Kennet Valley producing ceramic building material have been situated almost exclusively off the valley floor (Lobb and Rose forthcoming), although finds of *tesserae* from a site at Theale Green may represent a similar site (Peake 1931, 99 and 234).

In the later Roman period, there is a slightly heavier emphasis on finewares, with sources in Oxfordshire and the New Forest represented. Coarsewares may have come from these centres, as well as the Poole Harbour area of south-east Dorset and Alice Holt. This evidence of wider contacts in the late Roman period, including evidence of cross-Channel trade in the form of the lava querns, coupled with a higher proportion of finewares could be taken as an indication of a wider sphere of influence for the site at this time and a higher place within the local settlement hierarchy. The coins recovered from the colluvium also belong to this period. Objects of functional significance within the Romano-British artefactual assemblage comprise loomweight fragments, quernstones and a possible chisel; small quantities of iron-smithing slag are not sufficient to postulate ironworking on site at this period. Finally, the use of part of the site for cremation of the dead can be suggested, although no actual burials were recovered, nor is this evidence securely dated.

Saxon

The evidence for Saxon activity on the site is limited to a handful of sherds, concentrated in three pits, and a timber-lined well. The pottery sherds have tentatively been dated to the early/middle Saxon period, although their potential identification as Early Iron Age has been noted. The well, one of a pair that are considered contemporaneous, has been radiocarbon dated to cal. AD 650–870; GU-4362, 1290±50 BP, a date range broadly comparable with the early/middle Saxon span proposed for the pottery. Saxon timber-lined wells are a comparatively rare find from rural excavations, and their presence at Wickhams Field is considered as conclusive evidence for the presence of an associated settlement in the immediate vicinity. The pottery sherds, if their identification as Saxon is to be accepted, act as another pointer to the as yet undiscovered Saxon settlement in the area, to which the cemetery at Field Farm belonged, and with which the evidence for fish trapping on the Kennet in the 7th and 8th centuries AD at Anslow's Cottage may be associated (Butterworth and Lobb 1992).

4. Environmental Evidence

The Landscape Background, by Michael J. Allen

Soils

The excavated area lies partly on the north-eastern edge of a small low-lying spur of Reading Beds and partly on the edge of the Kennet valley on which valley gravels occur. The spur is aligned north–south and parallel to the Clayhill Brook, at a height of *c.* 46 m OD, approximately 4.5 m above the lower valley gravel. The intervening slope is masked with Holocene colluvial deposits (described below).

The soils are mapped as typical stagnogley soils of the Wickham 4 Association on the Reading Beds and include seasonally waterlogged thin argillic brown earths, with coarse typical argillic brown earths of the Hucklesbrook Association on the Valley Gravels (Allen *et al.* 1983; Jarvis *et al.* 1984). Relatively stonefree, fine-grained Holocene colluvium occurred as a broad band nearly 100 m wide at the base of the slope, sealing the Reading Beds and the more recent valley gravel, and locally supported typical colluvial brown earths.

Relict palaeo-channels

At the base of the slope, and adjacent to the possible Early Iron Age group of features, 3015, was an approximately east–west aligned palaeo-channel (feature 3028) (Fig. 63). A similar feature was aligned north–south towards the northern edge of the excavated area (feature 303). Palaeo-channel 3028 was sectioned at three locations and was seen to be at least 0.6 m deep, and up to 11 m wide, with shallow sloping sides and a slightly rounded base. Excavation of feature 303 revealed it to be *c.* 6.5 m wide and only 0.14 m deep.

The main channel infill within palaeo-channel 3028 (context 291) was a sandy loam with common small and medium stones and weak massive blocky structure. Below this, the basal layer (context 243) of silty sandy loam contained a few small flint gravels. Neither structure nor laminations were evident and the layer was heavily mottled with medium to large amorphous, sharply defined, mottles of iron (Fe) and manganese (Mn). Few coarse gleyed macropores were noted, although medium gleyed macropores were common.

Interpretation

The deposits are Lateglacial or Holocene and are not drift deposits of London Clay or Reading Beds. Although the basal horizon showed no positive evidence of laminations or waterlain origin, the dense gleying and evidence of water percolation is indicative of fluvial deposits of standing, if not running water. Although the main infill provided no positive evidence of the mode of deposition, the very fine texture and 'alluvial' nature of the deposit indicate that it is probably fluvially deposited.

The east–west aligned palaeo-channel is probably a channel of the former Kennet river system on the Beenham Grange terrace which lies 1–3m above the floodplain (Cheetham 1980). This is the lowest terrace of the Kennet, but in the Wickhams Field area it is morphologically indistinguishable from the floodplain (Cheetham 1975). Molluscan analysis and radiocarbon determinations from the braided river system on this terrace have shown that it was inactive by early Flandrian (ie Postglacial) times (Cheetham 1975; Holyoak 1980). It seems likely that the north–south palaeo-channel is a part of the same, intermittently surviving relict system described by Cheetham.

The channels have not been dated at Wickhams Field but, as part of the large braided system mapped over the Beenham Grange terrace noted above, are of probable Pre-boreal (ie Early Mesolithic) or earlier date. The dimensions of these channels accord well with recorded data from others of the same system (Cheetham 1980, table 2). It is therefore unlikely that either palaeo-channel is contemporary with the adjacent later prehistoric features and this hypothesis is supported by the absence of archaeological artefacts from the channel fills. This does not, however, negate the possibility that these channels contained standing water on a seasonal basis, but by analogy with Cheet-

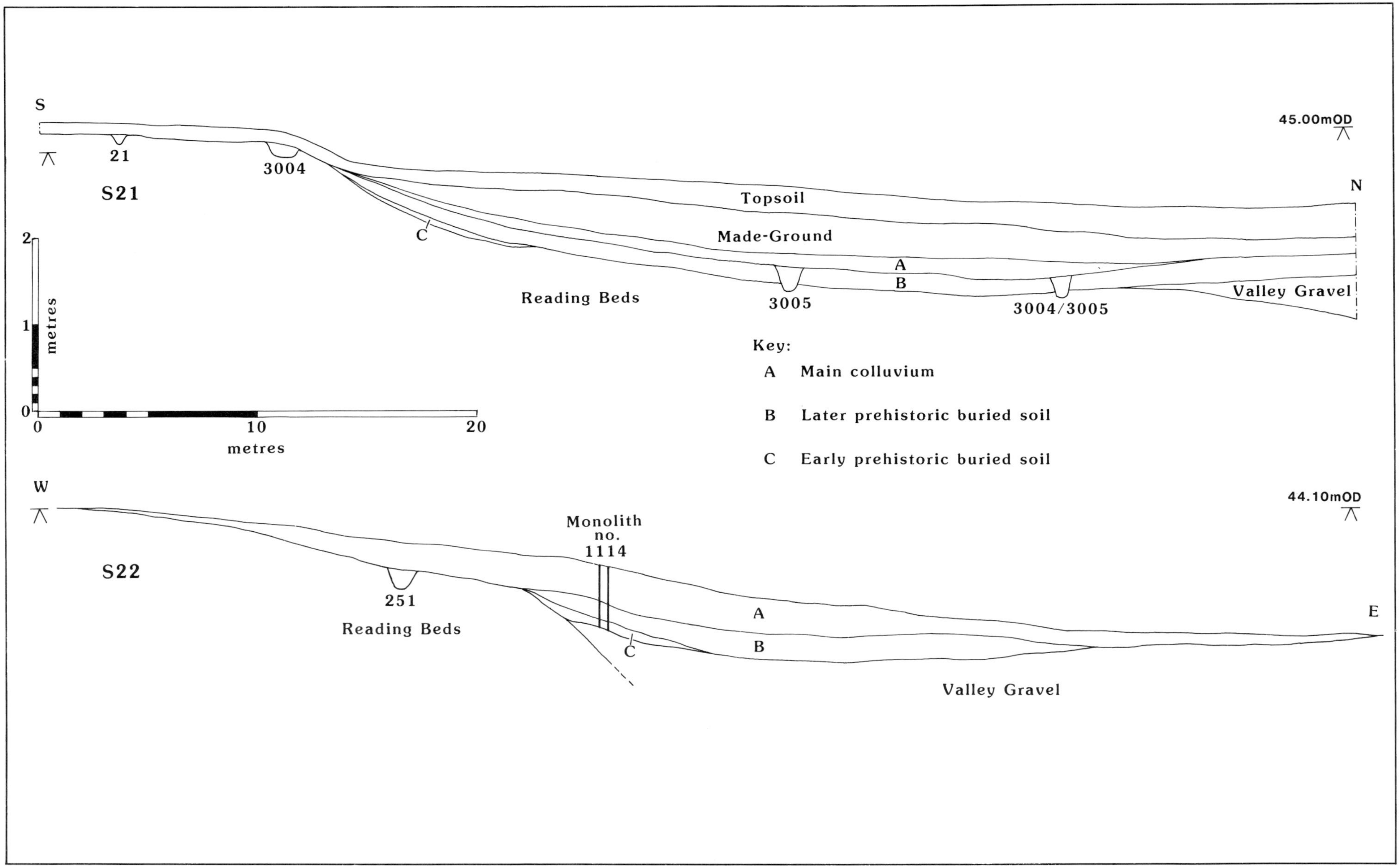

Figure 82 Schematic east-facing (S21) and south-facing (S22) sections through the colluvial deposits (for location of sections refer to Figure 62)

Plate 24 Colluvium section showing four identifiable contexts

ham's work, were not alluvially active (ie no major sedimentation facies can be recognised in the Flandrian epoch).

Colluvial deposits

Footslope colluvium occurred as a band up to 100 m wide and derived from the soils over the Reading Beds (*see* Fig. 62). This footslope deposit was exposed in plan and sample excavated (*c.* 15%) by means of a series of radiating trenches. Although visually uniform, the excavated transects revealed that the colluvium comprised a number of separate units which are described below.

Sequence description

Although the colluvium was broadly uniform in plan a number of discrete episodes of deposition could be detected from detailed examination of the excavated sections (Fig. 82, S21, S22; Pl. 24). The full sequence did not occur in all the excavated sections, suggesting that episodes of colluviation were very limited in their distribution. Towards the southern limit of the excavation area all episodes of colluviation appeared to be represented (Fig. 82, S22) with least disturbance from subsequent archaeological activity. As such, this key sequence is described (top to base) following the terminology outlined in Hodgson (1976) and interpreted below. The description excludes the topsoil horizon since it had already been stripped from the site.

Post-Romano-British massive fine grained main colluvial layer (Fig. 82, horizon A)
0–540 mm, contexts 546 and 547
These two contexts are texturally identical but the lower horizon (547) has a brighter hue. The boundary between the two contexts is diffuse and they are described as a single unit. Silty sandy loam, weak coarse massive blocky structure, 0.5% fine macropores, virtually stonefree, but very rare small flint gravel, no obvious inclusions, gradual smooth boundary.

Later prehistoric buried soil (colluvial brown earth) (Fig. 82, horizon B)
540–690 mm, context 548
Silty sand, strong medium blocky structure, 2% fine macropores, many very fine and fine charcoal pieces and fine to medium burnt soil fragments, stonefree, darker colour possibly indicates higher organic content, gradual wavy boundary.

Earlier prehistoric buried soil (colluvial brown earth) (Fig. 82, horizon C)
690–900 mm, context 549
Silty sand, weak massive blocky structure, becoming very weak, massive structure at about 750–900 mm. Some evidence of sand and silty translocation from inter-ped surfaces (hand lens and x 30 laboratory microscope). No inclusions, 2% fine macropores some localised gleying, abrupt wavy boundary.

Valley gravel
900 mm+
Loose unconsolidated flint gravel.

Interpretation of the sequence

The basal layer sealing the gravel (Fig. 82, S22 — horizon C) appears to be a stonefree brown earth profile developed *in situ* with the addition of soil as a result of colluviation. The sandy content and translocated fine sand/coarse silt component may, in part, indicate the sandy and loamy nature of the former soils over the Reading Beds spur. The colluvial element of this unit probably relates to initial clearance and activity associated with the Late Neolithic period (for which the site has produced slight evidence). This erosion phase has probably partially truncated and reworked the original brown earth soil profile. Elsewhere on the site this primary deposit was only identified with confidence at a few other locations (eg *see* Fig. 82, S21). Its recognition was largely reliant on the occurrence of the later prehistoric buried soil which sealed it and without which it was very difficult to distinguish from the main colluvial layer.

A second brown earth buried soil (Fig. 82, S22 — horizon B) is formed in fine-grained stonefree decalcified colluvium and is tentatively dated to the Late Bronze Age and/or Early Iron Age. Stabilisation and pedogenesis is evident from the strong soil structure, high macropores, and darker (presumably organic) nature, and may represent a grassland soil. It therefore undoubtedly represents a stabilisation horizon and the inclusions of relatively high quantities of very small comminuted charcoal and burnt soil fragments strongly suggest the presence of human activity. On this basis, it is possible to interpret this layer as an 'occupation horizon'.

The overlying deposit of massive fine-grained colluvium (Fig. 82, S22 — horizon A) is dated, on the basis of stratigraphic relationships, as post-Romano-British. However, it is likely that colluviation continued to occur throughout the later prehistoric and Romano-British periods, although it is not possible to recognise any such events within the main colluvial layer. Any such deposits may be caused by tillage upslope, or even constant trampling leading to the local destruction of the protective grass and vegetative cover which might accompany any settlement site.

Pollen assessment from the colluvium

A monolith sample was taken directly from the colluvial sequence and buried soil towards the southern limit of the excavation (Fig. 82, S22 — sample no. 1114). This was examined by R. Scaife for preservation of sub-fossil pollen and spores. Full details of the sampling and methods for the pollen assessment are held in the archive.

Despite rigorous extraction procedures, no preserved pollen or spores were recorded in any of the three horizons (as defined above). Specks of charcoal were noted in the upper colluvial levels. It is likely that a fluctuating ground water table has caused the oxidation of any pollen and spores which may have been contained in the soil. This process appears to have been extreme enough to have removed even spores of ferns and the more robust pollen taxa such as Lactucoideae (Liguliflorae) which frequently remain in generally poor preserving conditions.

Cremated Human Bone, by Jacqueline I. McKinley

Cremated bone from five contexts was examined. Layer 329 (feature 328, probably part of Romano-British ditch 3011) was subject to 50% examination. The remaining contexts (layer 641 — ditch 640; layers 338, 340, 341 — Romano-British pit 337) were excavated in total. Methods of recording and oste- ological analysis are as detailed in Chapter 3.

Results

A summary of the results is presented in Table 22. All weights are given in grammes (g). All measurements are given in millimetres (mm). Unless stated as otherwise, all bone, human and animal, is cremated/burnt.

Disturbance and condition of bone

Layers 329 (feature 328) and 338 (pit 337) were subject to some degree of disturbance. The bone appeared to be in good condition.

Nature of deposits

The contexts comprised fairly homogeneous fills in which the archaeological components of frequent charcoal, cremated bone and, in 338 and 340 (pit 337), burnt clay, were mixed, with no detectable concentrations of cremated bone. Generally, the deposits have the appearance of pyre debris. In the case of layers 329 (feature 328) and 641 (pit 640) this is all that is indicated, layer 329 probably being redeposited material, while layer 641 may constitute a deliberate dump of debris into the upper ditch fill.

The form of Romano-British pit 337 (filled with 338, 340, and 341) suggests it may represent a pyre site (see above for full description). The feature is sub-rectangular with an 'outline' of reddish burnt clay (silty clay soil) and three consecutive charcoal-rich fills, in which the upper-most (layer 338) contained most bone and least charcoal, the charcoal becoming progressively denser and the bone less frequent through the depth of the feature (*see* Fig. 76). This corresponds with what one would expect to find at a pyre site.

Experimental pyre cremations conducted by Alistair Marshall and the writer in 1993 and 1994, over a soil of silty clay composition, showed a very clear reddish outline of the pyre after the site was cleared (McKinley forthcoming b), similar to that noted (albeit disturbed) here. On burning, a pyre collapses down on itself in a fairly ordered manner, the cremated bone remaining in roughly correct anatomical order on top of the other debris (*ibid*). The general aspect is a layered deposition, charcoal and charred wood with a few fragments of cremated bone forming the major lower deposit, with the cremated bone and pyre goods concentrated in the upper levels.

Number of individuals

Although no burials were recovered, the presence of a possible pyre site and dumps of what appear to be pyre debris, demonstrate that at least one adult was cremated, and probably buried, in the area.

Pyre technology and ritual

Most of the bone was the buff–white colour indicative of full oxidation. A few fragments of upper and lower limb bone from 338 (pit 337) did show slight blue or grey coloration but the variation is of little significance.

The majority of bone was recovered in the 5 mm fraction and the maximum fragment size recorded was 29 mm. Although the small quantity of bone recovered from the contexts precludes detailed observations, these figures are relatively low and, whilst probably reflecting the nature of the deposit (McKinley 1994b) they may

Table 22 Summary results for cremated human bone

Provenance	*Type*	*Total wt. (g)*	*Age*	*Sex*	*Animal*
Upper fill 642, ditch 640	pyre debris	57.9	adult	?	–
Fill 329, poss. ditch 328	pyre debris	1.7	older subadult/adult	?	–
Upper fill 338, pit 337	pyre site	135.9	adult	?	?bird
Secondary fill 340, pit 337	pyre site	4.8	adult	?	–
Primary fill 341, pit 337	pyre site	0.2	adult	?	–

illustrate increased fragmentation resulting from trampling of the essentially 'unburied' material.

The inclusion of bone from all skeletal areas in the upper fill of pit 337 (the only sizeable collection of bone) corresponds with a similar composition noted in most cremation burials (as noted in chapter above).

The presence of cremated animal bone in burials of both Bronze Age and Romano-British date is well recorded, the occurrence being more frequent in the latter. The recovery of cremated human bone from the pyre debris supports evidence from burials that it was apparently not considered necessary to include all the cremated remains of the deceased in the burial. The presence of cremated animal bone in the pyre debris similarly indicates that it was not considered necessary to include all the pyre goods/offerings in the burial either.

Coloured staining

Slight blue/green spot staining was noted on a fragment of femur shaft from 338. The nature of this staining is under consideration. The similarity of the coloration to that resulting from copper alloy staining may indicate one-time proximity to the metal (McKinley 1994a), although the staining may be caused by manganese in the apatite (bone mineral) (Herrmann pers. comm.).

Animal Bones, by Sheila Hamilton-Dyer

Animal bone was recovered from 57 contexts, mainly from Romano-British pit and ditch fills and the midden deposit. Preservation varies from good to poor with most fragments under 50 mm in length. Few butchery marks were observed. The methods employed for animal bone analysis is as outlined in the Prospect Park report in this volume. The archive contains full details of anatomy, butchery, measurements, and other details.

A total of 211 bones was recorded. Most contexts produced fewer than 10 fragments. The distribution of the species in each feature is summarised in Table 23, whilst quantifications by context are contained in the archive.

Early Iron Age

Just 10 fragments were recovered from excavated Early Iron Age features; these include two fragments each of cattle, sheep/goat, and pig. In addition, a horn core from the later prehistoric colluvial layer has been positively identified as goat. Although no bones of dog were found, two fragments had been gnawed.

Romano-British

Contexts from the early, late, and unphased Romano-British periods produced the bulk of the animal bone assemblage, in broadly similar proportions for each phase (Table 23). Cattle and cattle-sized fragments dominate, followed by sheep/goat fragments; there are also eight fragments of pig and five of horse. One dog bone was recovered, a jaw in the early enclosure 3004 (segment 40) and many fragments had been gnawed, though none from the later midden 3009. The unphased pit 88 contained the jaw of a roe deer, whilst the unphased pit 98 contained a beaver lower incisor.

Saxon

A cattle bone and a sheep-sized bone were the only remains recovered from Saxon pit group 3025. Well 301 (context 320) contained a complete cattle radius, which gave an estimated withers height of 1.213 m, indicative of comparatively large stock. The bones from well contexts were very dark in colour, consistent with some degree of waterlogging.

Summary

This assemblage is broadly similar in species and proportions to that of the slightly larger collection from the nearby Anslow's Cottages (Coy 1992), although that site suffered from some residuality in the Saxon contexts and has very little Romano-British material. The most notable difference is the presence of red deer in several Bronze Age and middle Saxon contexts at Anslow's Cottages, but the sample size is very small at Wickhams Field and this may not be significant.

Charred and Waterlogged Plant Remains, by Robert G. Scaife

Charred plant remains

A total of 31 bulk samples from early prehistoric, Early Iron Age, Romano-British, and Saxon features was processed for charred and/or carbonised plant remains. Of these, 15 samples (Table 24) yielded seeds attributable to the Early Iron Age, Romano-British, and Saxon periods and are discussed below.

Processing of the bulk samples followed the standard flotation procedures carried out by Wessex Archaeology, with the flots being retained on a 0.5 mm mesh and the residues fractionated into 5.6 mm, 2 mm, and 1 mm categories and sorted under a x10–x30 stereo-binocular microscope. Following rapid assessment of the flots (S. Wyles and M.J. Allen) to broadly quantify the environmental constituents, both the flots and residues were

Table 23 Animal bone, species distribution

Provenance	*Context*	*Horse*	*Cattle*	*Sheep/goat*	*Pig*	*Cow size*	*Sheep size*	*Mammal*	*Dog/roe*	*Beaver*	*Total*
Early Iron Age											
Trackway 3012 (seg. 613, ditch 3003)	612	–	–	–	–	–	1	–	–	–	1
Pit 61	46	–	1	1	–	1	–	–	–	–	3
Pit 62	54	–	–	–	–	1	–	–	–	–	1
Pit 93	67	–	1	1	2	1	–	–	–	–	5
EARLY IRON AGE TOTAL		–	2	2	2	3	1	–	–	–	10
Early Iron Age %		–	20	20	30	30	10	–	–	–	
Early Romano-British											
Enclosure 3004 (seg. 40)	35	–	1	–	–	–	–	–	1 (dog)	–	5
Structure 3007 (post-hole 214)	206	–	1	–	–	–	–	–	–	–	1
Structure 3022 (post-hole 57)	52	–	–	–	–	1	–	–	–	–	1
Group 3006 (pit 674)	672	–	1	–	–	2	1	–	–	–	4
Group 3006 (pit 687)	690/691	–	2	–	–	4	–	–	–	–	6
Group 3006 (pit 751)	749	–	–	–	–	–	1	–	–	–	1
Ditch 3008 (seg. 667)	665	–	4	3	1	25	–	–	–	–	33
Ditch 3008 (seg. 745)	744	1	–	–	–	7	–	7	–	–	15
Ditch 3017 (seg. 518)	508	–	2	2	–	1	–	–	–	–	5
EARLY ROMANO-BRITISH TOTAL		1	11	5	1	40	2	10	1	–	71
Early Romano-British %		1	15	7	1	56	3	14	1	–	
Late Romano-British											
Enclosure 3005 (seg. 47)	45	–	3	–	–	1	–	–	–	–	4
Enclosure 3005 (seg. 399)	398/752	–	1	–	–	1	1	–	–	–	3
Enclosure 3005 (seg. 512)	504	–	–	1	–	–	–	–	–	–	1
Enclosure 3005 (seg. 670)	668	–	2	–	–	–	–	–	–	–	2
Enclosure 3005 (seg. 696)	694	1	4	–	–	2	–	–	–	–	7
Midden 3009	all	–	12	3	1	13	–	2	–	–	31
Ditch 515	510	–	–	–	–	1	–	–	–	–	1
Pit 49	48	–	1	–	4	–	–	–	–	–	5
Pit 85	83/84	1	3	–	–	2	1	–	–	–	7

Table 23 continued

Provenance	*Context*	*Horse*	*Cattle*	*Sheep/goat*	*Pig*	*Cow size*	*Sheep size*	*Mammal*	*Dog/roe*	*Beaver*	*Total*
Late Romano-British contd											
Pit 688	692	–	1	–	–	5	–	–	–	–	6
LATE ROMANO-BRITISH TOTAL		2	27	4	5	25	2	2	–	–	67
Late Romano-British %		3	40	6	7	37	3	3	–	–	
Unphased Romano-British											
Pit 88	87	–	–	–	2	–	–	–	1(roe)	–	3
Pit 98	all	1	10	2	2	10	1	–	1(roe)	1	28
Pit 272	230	–	3	4	–	–	–	–	–	–	7
Pit 342	352	1	–	–	–	1	–	–	–	–	2
UNPHASED ROMANO-BRITISH TOTAL		2	13	6	4	11	1	–	2	1	40
Unphased Romano-British %		3	33	15	10	28	3	–	5	3	
Saxon											
Group 3025 (pit 542)	all	–	1	–	–	–	1	–	–	–	2
Well 301	319/320	–	4	–	–	1	–	–	–	–	5
Well 322	738	–	–	–	–	–	2	–	–	–	2
SAXON TOTAL		–	5	–	–	1	3	–	–	–	9
Saxon %		–	56	–	–	11	33	–	–	–	
Unphased											
Pit 664	663	–	2	–	–	–	–	–	–	–	2
Colluvium	44	–	–	–	–	1	–	–	–	–	1
Colluvium	65	–	–	1	–	2	–	–	–	–	3
Colluvium	505	–	1	–	–	1	1	–	–	–	3
Colluvium	722	1	1	–	–	–	–	–	–	–	2
Topsoil	–	1	1	–	–	–	–	–	–	–	2
UNPHASED TOTAL		2	5	1	–	4	1	–	–	–	13
Unphased %		15	38	8	–	31	8	–	–	–	
OVERALL TOTAL		7	63	18	12	85	10	12	3	1	211
OVERALL %		3.3	29.9	8.5	5.7	40.3	4.7	5.7	1.4	0.5	

Table 24 Charred plant remains: summary of features producing identifiable remains

Phase	*Provenance*	*Sample no.*
Early Iron Age	Group 3015 (pit 416)	1040
Early Iron Age	Group 3015 (pit 430)	1078
Early Iron Age	Pit 61	1034
Romano-British	Group 3006 (pit 397)	1007
Romano-British	Group 3006 (pit 674)	1009
Romano-British	Midden 3009	1096
Romano-British	Ditch 640	1088
Romano-British	Pit 85	1048
Romano-British	Pit 98	1065
Romano-British	Pit 251: upper fill	1012
Romano-British	Pit 251: primary fill	1013
Romano-British	Pit 337	1045
Saxon	Group 3025 (pit 536)	1019
Saxon	Group 3025 (pit 542)	1020
Unphased	Main colluvial layer	1076

sorted (RGS) in detail under a low power microscope. Identification was carried out by comparison with reference collections of charred seeds.

For the purposes of this report, *Hordeum* is classified under *Hordeum vulgare* according to contemporary thinking that allows barley, whether 2 or 6-rowed, to be referable to the single crop species, ie *Hordeum vulgare* L. (Zohary and Hopf 1994, 58). However, it can be noted that the grains were in general 'straight' forms and may thus be attributed to the 2-rowed variety.

Other than Saxon features, samples from contexts of all other phases contained intrusive, non-charred weed seeds, including those of *Veronica hederifolia, Chenopodium (*cf. *album), Polygonum convolvulus,* and *Cerastium* sp. This implies some soil disturbance, or mixing of soil, perhaps through earthworm activity. Given this fact, it is possible that some reworking of the charred seed assemblages may also have occurred. However, as discussed below, it is apparent that the assemblages/types are typical of the phases to which the archaeological contexts have been attributed.

Results of the analysis (Table 25)

Early prehistoric

The single sample examined of probable early prehistoric date (pit 9, sample 1001) produced only modern intrusive seeds of *Veronica hederifolia, Chenopodium* sp. and *Cerastium* sp.

Early Iron Age

Remains obtained from Early Iron Age features are comparatively few, with the exception of pit 61 (sample 1034). This 10 litre sample contained substantial numbers of chaff elements, including spikelet forks (51), glume bases (172), miscellaneous chaff debris (palea and lemma), and a small number of cereal grains (12). This is quite clearly the burnt chaff remains subsequent to processing of the grain; hence the few complete cereal grains in relation to chaff debris. The assemblage is dominated by *Triticum spelta* (spelt wheat) which is readily identifiable from the glume bases and spikelet forks.

Other crop remains include sporadic occurrences of *T. dicoccum* (emmer wheat) and *Hordeum vulgare* (barley), which may be 'weeds' of the spelt crop. This appears to be a typical assemblage of cereal types which might be expected during this period from the region (Helbaek 1952; Murphy 1977; Carruthers 1992; Scaife in press).

Although a variety of different contexts were sampled and examined, it appears that the remainder of samples from this phase only contain background 'noise'; that is waste chaff, grain, and weed seeds which were distributed in features across the site.

Romano-British

As with the majority of Early Iron Age features, the Romano-British samples contained only traces of charred cereal grain, chaff debris, and weed seeds, again appearing to represent the 'background noise' of waste material that occurs across the site.

Saxon

Pit 542 (sample 1020) in group 3025 produced the most interesting assemblage of grain and weed seeds and, in particular *Hordeum* (*H. vulgare* L.) which forms the dominant taxon. However, given the small overall numbers of cereal grains present throughout, this cannot be given any statistical significance. The assemblage almost entirely comprised carbonised grains and grain fragments (55 examples), including *Hordeum* (barley), *T. spelta* (spelt wheat), *T. aestivum* (hexaploid bread wheat) and *Secale* (rye).

No waste chaff was recorded from this sample, with only a few seeds found that are characteristic of those weeds associated with the arable crops noted above. The single fruit seed of *Prunus spinosa* L. (sloe) may be associated with scrub wood used in domestic fires.

Discussion

Little differentiation can be made between the plant assemblages recovered from the Early Iron Age and Romano-British features. This is possibly because of the overall paucity of charred plant remains in most of the samples analysed. However, the consistent background record of *Triticum spelta L.* (spelt wheat) and its dominance in the one 'rich' sample from Early Iron Age pit 61 (sample 1034) is consistent with our existing knowledge of cereal cultivation in this region.

There is little doubt, based on existing data, that spelt formed the principal cultivated wheat during the Iron Age and Romano-British periods in southern and eastern England (Helbaek 1952; Murphy 1977; Jones 1981; Carruthers 1992; Scaife 1994). This may have been accompanied by emmer wheat but its presence at this site is minor. The origin and interpretation of charred seed assemblages in archaeological contexts are

Table 25 Charred plant remains: quantification by phase

Type	*Taxon*	*Early prehistoric*	*Early Iron Age*	*Romano-British*	*Saxon*	*Total*
Grain	*Hordeum* cf. *vulgare*	–	1	1	16	18
	Triticum spelta type	–	3	–	2	5
	Triticum aestivum type	–	–	1	1	2
	Triticum indet.	–	3	1	4	8
	Secale sp.	–	–	–	2	2
	Indet. whole	–	5	5	7	17
	Indet. frags	–	4	28	23	55
Glume bases	*Triticum spelta*	–	146	8	–	154
	Triticum cf. *dioccum*	–	13	2	–	15
	Indet frags	–	13	5	–	18
Spikelet forks	*Triticum spelta*	–	7	–	–	7
	Triticum indet.	–	44	5	–	49
Rachis	*Hordeum* cf. *vulgare*	–	1	2	–	3
	Triticum sp.	–	–	1	–	1
Seeds	*Bromus secalinus*	–	2	–	–	2
	Bromus/Avena type	–	1	–	–	1
	Eleocharis sp.	–	–	–	1	1
	Galium sp.	–	–	–	1	1
	Polygonum sp. indet.	–	1	–	1	2
	Lolium sp.	–	1	–	–	1
	Corylus avellana L.	–	1	1	–	2
	Gramineae (large)	–	–	3	–	3
	Gramineae (small)	–	–	2	–	2
	Rumex sp. indet.	–	1	1	2	4
	Prunus spinosa	–	–	–	1	1
	Vicia/Lathyrus	–	–	–	4	4
	Intrusive weed seeds	*	*	*	–	–

* denotes the presence of non-charred intrusive weed seeds

caused largely by the vicissitudes of human behaviour and chance preservation. Thus the absence of crop types does not necessarily imply that they were not cultivated.

Spelt wheat is frequently encountered for two reasons; firstly, there was an undoubted predilection for spelt during the Iron Age and Roman periods; and secondly, spelt is a glume wheat and requires parching for the release of the grain from the caryopses. Thus, there is a greater likelihood of it being charred and preserved.

In addition, particularly during the Iron Age, it is probable that spelt would have been stored as complete ears in pits. Once the whole grain caryopses had been exhumed and processed for use, the storage pits were probably sterilised by fire prior to reuse. This process would provide a greater chance for the preservation, though charring of residual material left remaining in the storage pits.

The preponderance of chaff remains with few grains in Early Iron Age pit 61 implies that this is true waste from crop processing rather than evidence of stored material. The relative absence of seeds of segetal weeds; that is herbs typically associated with cereal cultivation, may suggest that unprocessed material is being transported to the site, from a separate area of cultivation.

It might be expected that *Triticum aestivum* (bread wheat) would be more frequent in the Romano-British contexts. However, the fact that this wheat type is free-threshing and, therefore, does not require parching, means that there is less likelihood of its preservation by accidental burning.

The only other crop type which is consistently present in contexts from all phases is *Hordeum* (barley). This is likely to be *Hordeum vulgare* L., the two-rowed, hulled variety, although the grains were not wholly diagnostic as preservation was generally poor. The majority of these remains were in Saxon pit 542 (sample 1020) of group 3025. These appeared to be hulled barley which, as with *T. spelta*, would require parching to release the grain, providing greater possibilities for preservation. The absence of waste chaff from this feature may suggest that it served as a storage pit for processed

Table 26 Waterlogged plant remains: quantification by feature

Taxon		*Feature*		
		Well 301 Sample 1016 (1lt)	Well 322 Sample 1086 (5lt)	Pit 664 Sample 1106 (1lt)
RANUNCULACEAE	*Ranunculus a / r / b*	3	3	–
	Ranunculus lingua	1	–	–
	Caltha pulustris	–	1	–
SOLANACEAE	*Utrica dioica*	257	45	–
CORYLACEAE	*Corylus avellana* (nut frag.)	1	–	–
CHENOPODIADEAE	*Chenopodium* sp. *(small)*	30	11	–
	Chenopodium cf *album*	49	12	–
	Atriplex sp.	5	–	–
CARYOPHYLLACEAE	*Cerastium* sp. (cf *glomeratum*)	–	2	–
POLYGONACEAE	*Polygonum persicaria / mite / lapathifolium* type	3	–	–
	Polygonum cf *mite*	–	–	–
	Polygonum aviculare	5	–	–
	Fallopia convolvulus	7	8	–
	Rumex acetosells group	82	30	–
	Rumex acetosa group	6	–	–
	Rumex sp. perianth frag.	–	1	–
HYPERICACEAE	*Hypericum* sp.	–	1	–
MALVACEAE	*Malva* sp.	1	–	–
BRASSICACEAE	Indet.	1	–	–
	cf. *Brassica oleraceus*	1	–	–
PRIMULCACEAE	*Anagallis arvensis*	13	3	–
ROSACEAE	*Rubus fruticosus* agg.	1	–	–
APIACEAE	*Aethusa cynapium*	1	1	–
LABIATAE	*Galeopsis* sp.	3	–	–
	Ajuga reptans	2	–	–
	Prunella vulgaris	–	1	–
PLANTAGINACEAE	*Plantago major*	5	–	–
	Plantago lanceolata	1	–	–
CAPRIFOLIACEAE	*Sambucus nigra*	2	–	–
ASTERACEAE	cr *Senecio*	1	–	–
JUNCACEAE	*Juncus articulatus* type	–	10	2
CYPERACEAE	*Eleocharis* sp.	11	1	–
	Carex flacca	1	–	–
POACEAE	*Poaceae* indet.	4	1	–
MISCELLANEOUS	Fungal sclerotia	–	–	–
	Daphnia eggs	present	present	–

grain, a function which is similarly suggested by its undercutting profile.

Waterlogged Plant Remains

Plant remains, comprising largely 'seeds' (nutlets, fruits, achenes) were extracted from deposits associated with a small a number of deep features on the site. These features comprise two Saxon timber-lined wells (well 301 and 322) and a large unphased pit, 664. In addition, a large oak tree bole was recovered from one of the upper fills of unphased Romano-British pit 342, although this was discarded after identification and recording. All environmental samples contained waterlogged organic deposits and silts and thus, the seed remains extracted were preserved through waterlogging.

Four samples of between 1 litre and 5 litres were washed through sieves of 250 mm, 500 mm and 1.0 mm. The respective fractions were sorted under a low power binocular microscope. Identifications were made using comparative collections of recent material. Absolute numbers of seeds were too low to permit sub-sampling of the 'flot' and thus all material was sorted. The data are presented in Table 26, where total volume of sample and numbers of seeds identified and counted are given.

Environmental samples from pit 664 produced only seeds of *Juncus articulatus* type whilst samples from the wells produced well preserved assemblages of waterlogged seeds. Well 301 produced the greater number of seeds with a total of 499 from 27 taxa, whilst well 322 yielded fewer seeds, a total of 128 from 16 taxa. The results are presented in Table 26.

Although the floristic assemblages of the two wells are broadly similar, well 301 exhibited a greater taxonomic diversity. The taxa largely comprise typical and characteristic plants of waste ground (ruderals). *Urtica dioica* (nettle), *Chenopodium* spp. (goosefoots), and *Rumex acetosella* (docks) type are dominant with lesser numbers of also diagnostic ruderals. These include *Ranunculus acris / bulbosus / repens* (buttercups), *Fallopia convolvulus* (black bindweed), *Polygonum aviculare, P. persicaria / mite / lapathifolium, Anagallis arvensis* (knotweeds), and *Aethusa cynapium* (pimpernel). Shrubs/trees are represented by *Sambucus nigra* (elder), *Corylus avellana* (hazel), and *Rubus fruticosus* agg. (blackberry), although the number of specimens is small. Seeds of marginal aquatic or marsh taxa are also present in small numbers with *Caltha palustris* (marsh marigold), *Ranunculus lingua* (buttercup), *Eleocharis* indet. and possibly *Juncus articulatus* type. Daphina (water flea) eggs were also noted.

The seed assemblages obtained from the wells comprise typical weeds of dry, waste ground, often found growing in proximity to occupation. The large numbers of *Urtica dioica* (nettle) seeds and, to a lesser extent *Chenopodium* spp. (goosefoots), are possibly indicative of nitrogen enriched environments again typical of areas of human habitation and associated with animal rearing (nitrogen enrichment from dung and urine). Preservation of this material is attributed to waterlogging and it is likely that these seeds accumulated 'naturally' and were preserved in these two contexts. It is interesting to note that there are no real indications of weeds specifically related to arable cropping or of cereals and chaff debris from processing and also that few weed seeds were present in the carbonised assemblages.

Conclusion

The oak tree bole recovered from pit 342 cannot only be interpreted as evidence of tree-felling during the Romano-British period, but, on the presumption that such a substantial object would not be transported far before disposal, also the presence of mature oak woodland in the immediate vicinity. The samples from two Saxon wells (well 301 and 322) have yielded assemblages of waterlogged seeds. The floristic assemblages comprise largely weeds typical of dry, waste ground (ruderals) and dominated by *Urtica dioica*, and *Chenopodium* spp. These may also be indicative of nitrogen enriched soils from animal/stock rearing. A very small number of herbs of wet ground are present and reflect the depositional environment. Evidence for woodland, scrub, or even hedgerows is minimal. There is similarly, no evidence for crop cultivation in these assemblages.

Charcoal, by Rowena Gale

Charcoal remains were found in pits, ditches, hearths, middens, and post-holes from early prehistoric, Early Iron Age, Romano-British, and Saxon features. Waterlogged oak planks and posts from two Saxon wells are reported separately above (Mepham and Gale). Ten samples of charcoal, representing all phases, were examined to identify the contemporaneous woodland vegetation and the use of woodland resources.

The charcoal was mainly rather friable and permeated with fine sediments (probably caused by sporadic or seasonal fluctuations of the water table) which overlaid cell walls and often hindered identification. The

Table 27 Charcoal: quantification by feature

Provenance	*Sample*	*Corylus*	*Fraxinus*	*Pomoideae*	*Prunus*	*Quercus*	*Salicaceae*
Early prehistoric							
Pit 9	1001	1	–	–	6	1	–
Early Iron Age							
Group 3015 (pit 430)	1078	–	–	–	–	27h	–
Pit 62	1035	4	–	–	–	37hr	–
Romano-British							
Midden 3009	1096	8	1	1	–	17	8
Ditch 640	1088	17	–	–	–	–	–
Hearth 377	1101	5	–	8	8	7hr	–
Pit 251	1012	6	–	?1	–	21s	6
Pit 337	1051	–	–	–	–	31hs	–
Saxon							
Group 3025 (pit 536)	1019	21	2	–	–	28hs	21
Group 3025 (pit 542)	1020	8	–	–	–	8hr	–

Abbreviations: h = heartwood s = sapwood r = roundwood/stem (diameter = <20 mm)

methods employed for processing and analysis have already been outlined in this volume (Prospect Park).

The results are summarised in Table 27. The taxa identified included: *Corylus* sp. (hazel), *Fraxinus* sp. (ash), Pomoideae — a sub-family of the Rosaceae, which includes *Crateagus* sp. (hawthorn), *Malus* sp. (apple), *Pyrus* sp. (pear), *Sorbus* spp. (rowan, whitebeam, and wild service) — these genera are anatomically similar. *Prunus* spp. (cherry, bird cherry, and blackthorn) — the broad rays suggested *P. spinosa* (blackthorn) rather than *P. avium* or *P. padus*, *Quercus* sp. (oak), and Salicaceae which includes *Salix* sp. (willow) and *Populus* sp. (poplar) (these genera cannot be separated using anatomical methods).

Early prehistoric

Fragments from pit 9 (sample 1001) included blackthorn, hazel, and oak.

Early Iron Age

Features attributable to this phase (pit 430 of group 3015, sample 1078; pit 62, sample 1035) contained predominantly charred oak (heartwood and stem), with a few examples of hazel recorded from pit 62. The charred oak from pit 430 was found in association with a considerable quantity of slag, burnt flint, and daub.

Romano-British

A sample from midden 3009 (sample 1096) produced a range of material, including oak, hazel, willow/poplar, ash, and Pomoideae, whilst hazel charcoal, in association with cremated human bone, was found in the secondary fill of ditch 640 (sample 1088). Charcoal from the basal fill of hearth 377 (sample 1101) within structure 3007 consisted of oak (heartwood and sapwood), blackthorn, Pomoideae and hazel, whilst charcoal from pit 251 (sample 1012), associated with burnt flint and pottery, included oak (sapwood), hazel, willow/poplar and ?Pomoideae. Sample 1051 from the fill of pit 337, interpreted as the truncated remains of a pyre base, produced abundant and large lumps of charred oak (heartwood and sapwood) with no other timber present; many fragments of the charcoal were gnarled and knotty.

Saxon

Charcoal from the fill of pit 536 (sample 1019) included oak (heartwood and sapwood), willow/poplar, hazel, and ash. The fill of pit 542 included burnt flint, burnt daub and charcoal (sample 1020), which consisted of oak (heartwood and narrow stem/twig) and hazel.

Discussion

Charcoal from the possible earlier prehistoric feature was relatively sparse but indicated the presence of oak, blackthorn, and hazel. Oak woodlands probably grew on the damp valley floor with hazel either as understorey or in association with blackthorn in marginal woodland. Hazel and blackthorn may also have grown in woodland glades or more open areas. In the latter environment, blackthorn can form dense thickets.

Similar taxa and also ash, Pomoideae, and willow and/or poplar were identified from the Early Iron Age, Romano-British, and Saxon periods. Ash became more common in Britain after the Neolithic period (Godwin 1956) and, at Wickhams Field, may have infiltrated the oak woodland. The similarity in anatomical structure of the members of the Pomoideae group does not permit identification to genus level; one or more may have grown at or near the site. Willows and poplars thrive on damp or seasonally flooded land such as that offered by the low lying floodplain of the nearby River Kennet or possibly by local pools, streams, and springs. Both may have been present.

The origin of the charcoal, mostly excavated from pits is unknown, but it is probable that some was redeposited from the remains of hearth debris; sample 1101 was more securely associated with a hearth feature. Oak was common to most samples and usually in larger quantities than other taxa which, with the exception of hazel, were only sporadic. The common use of oak heartwood, from either trunk or cord wood, suggested that wood was gathered from semi-mature or mature trees rather than coppiced or pollarded specimens. This suggestion is supported by the recovery of an oak tree bole from the upper fill of Romano-British pit 342 (*see* Scaife this Chapter). Some waste or recycled wood from, for example, building materials may have been used but since heartwood was consistently noted throughout the samples (although material from two samples was too small to assess), the former conclusion seems more plausible. With the exception of willow and poplar, these trees and shrubs would have provided efficient fuel woods, when seasoned (Edlin 1949).

The range of taxa identified at Wickhams Field is similar, if narrower, to those identified from the broadly contemporaneous and nearby sites of Field Farm and Anslow's Cottages (Butterworth and Lobb 1992) and Riseley Farm (Lobb and Morris 1991–3). However, since fewer samples were examined from Wickhams Field, comparative assessments of the local environments or specific selection of the woodland resources may not be realistic. The identification of the charcoal from Wickhams Field contributes data from an area adjacent to sites previously excavated (named above), thereby providing a more comprehensive picture of the ancient landscapes of this region.

Discussion, by Michael J. Allen

It is unfortunate that the deposits encountered at Wickhams Field were not conducive to the preservation of land snails or pollen. As a result, our understanding of the nature of the local landscape during the prehistoric, Romano-British, and Saxon periods is largely based on the field interpretation of the colluvial deposits (*cf* Allen 1992; 1994) and the soils. More detailed information about the farming economy and the local environment of the site is provided by the animal bone, charred and waterlogged seeds, and charcoal.

Soils and colluvium; distribution and interpretation

The occurrence of the probable Neolithic brown earth beneath the later colluvial deposits appears to be highly localised, surviving predominantly in slight depressions. Except where it was sealed by a distinctive

Table 28 Local environment and economy; indications from the environmental evidence

Date	*Deposit*	*Cause*	*Distribution*
Late Neolithic	Typical brown earth and colluvium	Initial clearance and associated activity	Highly localised
Late Bronze Age/Early Iron Age	Colluvium and colluvial brown earth	Occupation activity	Localised
Post Romano-British	Main colluvium, comprised of a number of minor episodes	Occupation/trampling and possibly tillage	Main footslope deposit

Late Bronze Age/Early Iron Age occupation surface, the brown earth horizon was very difficult to differentiate from the overlying massive fine-grained main colluvial layer.

The Late Bronze Age/Early Iron Age occupation surface was also localised, again predominantly surviving within slight depressions, but also perhaps indicating localised deposition of these deposits. The fact that the sequence was not spatially uniform across the site supports this interpretation. At Wickhams Field, we can therefore suggest that the discrete deposits of colluvium across the hillside represent localised areas of human activity, such as tree clearance and ploughing. From the colluvial sequences examined, three main periods of deposition may be postulated, as summarised in Table 28.

Earlier prehistoric

Argillic brown earths survived over the area and probably supported oak woodland, especially in the damp valley floor, with an understorey of hazel and possibly buckthorn. It can be postulated that some local clearance of the woodland took place because of the evidence for limited sporadic activities. These activities, although small in scale, may have resulted in the initial destabilisation of the soil cover and led to localised erosion and the initiation of the colluvial sequence seen around the footslope. There is no evidence for tillage and cereal cultivation at this period, but cultivation of the soil following clearance would certainly enhance the likelihood of the localised erosion events and deposition of colluvium at the foot of the slope.

Later prehistoric

The presence of colluvium along the base of the slope may be taken to indicate further localised clearance, as well as the activities associated with the archaeological activity recorded. The local woodlands were more diverse in species, with the presence of ash (charcoal), sloe (charred seeds), and willow which were probably in the valley adjacent to either the river or pools of water.

The nature of the hillwash deposits recorded is in accordance with the evidence for activities such as farming (especially tillage and cereal cultivation) or local intensive occupation activity. The presence of an *in situ* developed brown earth soil profile in the colluvium, suggests that deposition had ceased locally during the occupation and the small comminuted, unidentified charcoal fragments in the buried soil are indicative of the occupation of the site. From the available evidence, barley was the most common cereal cultivated but was accompanied by spelt and bread wheat.

The sparse evidence for animal husbandry is largely due to preservation (that is, the lack of) rather than a genuine lack of animal husbandry. Nevertheless, there is evidence for cattle, sheep/goat, and pig. Although no dogs were found, some of the bones were gnawed and might indicate that they were present, possibly as sheep dogs. The environmental evidence, limited as it is, does indicate small scale farming typical of prehistoric communities, as recorded at Field Farm, Anslow's Cottages, Knight's Farm, and Aldermaston. The small scale of the activity may be contrasted with the more extensive waterlogged deposits seen on other sites in the Kennet valley.

Romano-British

The woodland remained broadly similar in character, although it is suspected that larger areas had been clear felled at this time, as indicated by the large oak tree bole recovered during the excavation. The woodland seems to have been more open with evidence for hazel, which requires open conditions to flower, being recovered as both charcoal and charred hazel nuts. The range of cereals cultivated is also similar to that recovered from the later prehistoric periods. The predominance of spelt is typical, being the principal cultivated wheat in southern England at this time. However, it is possible that the grain may have been stored as whole ears, and as such it may not necessarily have been cultivated locally. The lack of weed seeds supports this interpretation.

Cattle are the main animals herded, with sheep and goat also present. The recovery of dog remains within the earlier Romano-British settlement may indicate the presence of sheep dogs, although as roe deer was also recovered, the dogs may have been used for hunting. This evidence suggests a community with an established but still small-scale farming economy, which probably reflects the size of the community. In addition, the beaver remains indicate the presence of watercourses in the vicinity, such as the River Kennet.

Saxon

The evidence for Saxon animal husbandry is restricted to a few bone fragments of cattle and sheep/goat, including a complete cattle radius indicative of comparatively large stock. Carbonised plant remains, however, indicate cultivation and storage of barley, with some spelt, bread wheat, and rye. The complete absence of chaff associated with these remains suggests that processing of the crop occurred elsewhere. The wells could have provided drinking water for both humans and animals, and yielded a number of waterlogged seeds. Apart from those seeds merely indicative of the wet nature of these features, those of dry ground surrounding the wells included high numbers of nettles and other species that are typical of areas of both human habitation and nitrogen rich areas (ie dung and urine) typical of farmyards.

Conclusions
There is only tentative evidence for limited activity in the Neolithic, but this probably included some farming, leading to soil disturbance. In the later prehistoric and Romano-British periods, Wickhams Field appears to have supported small communities undertaking small-scale local farming. Some cereals may have been imported and stored on the ear. The episodic settlement at Wickhams Field may have relied largely on its ability to be self-sufficient, with little evidence of either animals or crops being taken, traded, or bought, to or from market. During the Saxon period, the limited evidence available suggests a mix of arable farming, and in particular barley, with some cattle and sheep also present. The waterlogged seed assemblages recovered from the timber-lined wells are typical of a nitrogen-rich farmyard environment. Although the evidence from Wickhams Field only provides a general idea of the farming economy and the nature of the surrounding landscape, it provides a more detailed picture of the nature of the settlement itself.

5. Discussion, by Andrew Crockett

The excavation at Wickhams Field has provided stratigraphic, artefactual, environmental and archaeometric evidence for several periods of activity ranging from the earlier prehistoric to Saxon. As such, these results can be compared and contrasted with the excavations at both Prospect Park and Hurst Park, for which similar date ranges were recorded. All three excavations combine to make a significant contribution to the study of development in land use and settlement pattern within the floodplain of the River Thames and its major tributaries. The evidence from Wickhams Field is summarised below, more detailed commentaries on the artefactual and environmental evidence have already been presented above.

Early Postglacial

There were no diagnostic Mesolithic finds recovered from the site. The palaeo-channels recorded cutting through the lower valley gravel forming the northern and eastern portions of the excavation area probably belong to the Theale Palaeo-channel Series (Cheetham 1980, 212–7). This comprises a network of braided river channels and streams, crossing the Beenham Grange terrace, and situated 1–3 m above the present River Kennet floodplain. Although at Wickhams Field these features are not dated, work elsewhere (Cheetham 1975; Holyoak 1980) has suggested that the channel system was inactive by the Early Mesolithic period. The lack of Mesolithic activity is perhaps surprising in view of known distributions in the Reading area (see for instance Wymer 1977, 5–16) and the concentration of sites higher up the Kennet valley around Newbury.

Neolithic

The only feature that can be confidently ascribed to this phase was a shallow, probably truncated pit that produced Late Neolithic Fengate-style pottery. In addition, several pieces of diagnostic flintwork, including both leaf-shaped and oblique arrowheads, were recovered, although these were either residual finds or unstratified. Similarly, evidence from the immediate area for Neolithic activity predominantly comprises stray finds and isolated features; for example, a pair of shallow pits, similar to the example at Wickhams Field, and a hearth dated to 3900–3000 cal BC (archaeomagnetic date, ref. AJC-63) at Field Farm (Butterworth and Lobb 1992, 68).

A further 118 pits recorded during excavations at Reading Business Park to the east (Jennings 1992, 6–8) have been assigned a Neolithic date, many of which were morphologically similar to the example at Wickhams Field. Although this concentration of features appears to be highly significant, none have been dated from ceramic evidence, even though a number contained Late Bronze Age pottery that has been interpreted as intrusive. As such, the interpretation of these features as Neolithic must be viewed with caution.

The local vegetation at the time has been demonstrated from evidence recovered at the site and at Field Farm to have been predominantly oak woodland, with an understorey of blackthorn and hazel, and occasional damp grassy clearings. However, the earliest colluvial deposits recorded at Wickhams Field appear to indicate the early stages of woodland clearance in the area, which, although as yet undated, probably began during this period. The non-uniform nature of the earliest colluvial layer suggests that it was not a single phase development, with discrete deposits accumulating along the base of the slope as small areas of woodland were cleared.

Pollen has not survived within the colluvial deposits, probably as a result of oxidation brought about by a fluctuating water table. As such it is not possible to chart the developing landscape through the pollen record. It may be suggested, however, that the recovery of Neolithic stone axes, during fieldwalking for the Kennet valley Survey (Lobb and Rose forthcoming) and in the vicinity of Anslow's Cottages (Butterworth and Lobb 1992, fig. 26), is further evidence for tree clearance. The overall picture appears to be of sporadic human activity, probably including hunting, within a predominantly wooded landscape, with episodes of forest clearance probably occurring towards the end of the Neolithic period.

Bronze Age

Although Early Bronze Age remains were not recorded at Wickhams Field, a large ring-ditch has been excavated to the north, at Field Farm (Butterworth and Lobb 1992). This feature contained a central pit dated to HAR-9139, 365±80 BP, cal.BC 2280–1780 from which several sherds of Collared Urn and Beaker pottery were recovered. It has been suggested that the feature was more of a monument than a grave. On the basis of cropmark evidence, similar though smaller ring-ditch features were known to exist in the vicinity, primarily concentrated to the north-east of the excavation area. These were examined in 1969 by R.A. Rutland, producing pottery of probable Late Neolithic and Early Bronze Age date (Lobb 1983–5, 15). In the following year the ring-ditches were destroyed during the construction of the M4, as were possibly associated features in 1973–4 during gravel extraction (Gates 1975, 33).

Environmental evidence indicates that during the Early Bronze Age period at least, the landscape was still predominantly oak woodland, although cereal crops such as barley, emmer, and spelt are represented by small quantities of carbonised material. This suggests that small scale settlement was taking place in the immediate vicinity, perhaps in the area of Knight's Farm, for which a radiocarbon date of BM-1593, 3630±50 BP was obtained from an oven (Bradley *et al.* 1980, 260). A comparable radiocarbon date of HAR-9142, 3569±70 BP was obtained from a sample in a deposit sealing the primary fill of the excavated ring-ditch at Field Farm (Butterworth and Lobb 1992, 69).

By the middle of the Bronze Age, several smaller ring-ditches had been constructed in the area, with additional satellite cremation burials also inserted into the main ring-ditch mound. The recorded increase in burial features at Field Farm suggests an associated expansion in settlement for the area. At Wickhams Field, however, the Middle Bronze Age is only represented by a very small collection of coarse, thick-walled sherds which may derive from urns of Deverel-Rimbury type. Environmental evidence indicates continued woodland clearance taking place, with associated grassland characteristic of abandoned grazing or arable and some evidence for scrub regeneration.

By the Late Bronze Age, the Kennet valley is known to have been relatively intensively settled, with both occupational evidence and burials recorded at many sites in the immediate vicinity, such as Field Farm, Anslow's Cottages, Small Mead Farm (Butterworth and Lobb 1992, fig. 58), and Knight's Farm (Bradley *et al.* 1980). Of these sites, Knight's Farm appears to represent the nucleus of the local settlement distribution, with the remainder producing what can perhaps be interpreted as more 'marginal' activities (Butterworth and Lobb 1992, 70). Occupation at these sites is likely to span the transitional Late Bronze Age/Early Iron Age period.

In a broader context, the majority of later Bronze Age/Early Iron Age sites and finds within the region appear to be concentrated on gravel terraces associated with the principal watercourses, such as the rivers Thames, Kennet, and Loddon (Moore and Jennings 1992, fig. 58). By implication, this preference for free-draining land associated with the underlying gravel produces occupation evidence concentrated away from land prone to seasonal flooding, or considered by modern standards to have been poorly drained soils (Bradley *et al.* 1980, fig. 39).

The later Bronze Age period is not coherently represented at Wickhams Field. Data from the nearby sites noted above suggest that the environment remained relatively unchanged from the earlier Bronze Age period. At Knight's Farm, pollen analysis has demonstrated the presence of several ponds situated in grassland with trees and scrub still forming a significant component of the landscape. Although arable farming may have been taking place, it is likely that the area around the Knight's Farm settlement was predominantly used as pasture (Bradley *et al.* 1980, 279).

Iron Age

The Early Iron Age sees a marked expansion in activity at Wickhams Field. This is manifested by the establishment of a substantial trackway and associated enclosure, together with numerous other features indicating settlement in the area, including refuse pits and features possibly associated with domestic industrial processes. This phase of occupation also appears to be associated with a shift in settlement, the majority of the features being situated on the higher ground formed by the Reading Beds to the south of the Kennet floodplain.

It may therefore be reasonable to assume that the Early Iron Age evidence represents part of a continual period of expansion throughout the Late Bronze Age and Early Iron Age, centred on the river valley floor and extending beyond this margin as pressure on the available resources grew. Such an interpretation is supported by the ceramic evidence which can be described as broadly contemporaneous with the material from Knight's Farm. The increase in settlement activity is also reflected in the development of a 'stabilisation' horizon within the colluvial deposits at the base of the slope below the trackway and enclosure. This stabilisation phase may have been caused, in part at least, by the establishment of the trackway along the brow of the north-east facing slope, as the delimiting ditches (and associated banks if in existence) would have hindered downslope movement of soil whilst they survived as continuing features

Although part of what appeared to be a sub-rectangular enclosure was identified, no structural remains were recorded in association, and many of the pits examined in the immediate vicinity failed to produce datable material. As such, it is probable that the remains recorded at Wickhams Field represent the outer margins of a settlement, the nucleus for which may be assumed to be towards the higher ground to the south, west, and south-west, perhaps concentrated in the vicinity of Dean's Copse (*see* Fig. 61).

Faunal evidence, although not extensive, indicates the presence of a typical range of animals such as cattle, sheep/goat, and pig. Evidence for arable farming was also recorded, with spelt dominating the assemblage, as well as emmer and barley, primarily in the form of waste products generated during crop processing. The comparative absence of weed seeds from the plant remains may suggest that the spelt and other crops were harvested somewhere else, and transported to the site once the weeds had been removed. Other than the various crops noted above, charcoal samples demonstrate the continued presence of oak woodland in the vicinity, together with hazel.

Of particular note is the probable Early Iron Age group of features recorded on the valley gravel towards the south-eastern corner of the excavation, which included a clay-lined pit, containing large quantities of burnt flint, and a smaller pit which produced nearly 1.5 kg of iron smithing slag. Burnt flint-filled features are a common occurrence on prehistoric sites, such as at Hurst Park (this volume) and Dunston Park (Mepham 1995, 77), and whilst the examples from Wickhams Field are not securely dated, the possibility of iron smithing of Early Iron Age date is notable. No evidence was found for an associated hearth, although fragments of vitrified hearth lining and bottom were recovered from the smaller pit and it may be assumed that the associated hearth was located nearby. A limited correlation between the distribution of slag and burnt flint within Iron Age features has already been demonstrated at Riseley Farm (Lobb and Morris 1991–3, 49) and it might be suggested from Wickhams Field that the two materials represent by-products of related industrial processes.

The slag finds its best parallels, perhaps, with the evidence at Cooper's Farm, Dunston Park, Thatcham, also in the Kennet valley, where a small pit of Early Iron Age date, containing a quantity of iron smithing slag, was located *c.* 1 km from a contemporaneous settlement (Fitzpatrick 1995, 89–92). It is unclear whether the features at Wickhams Field were associated with the settlement identified on the higher ground to the west, or perhaps relate to other occupation areas beyond the limit of the excavation. The clay-lined pit has few close parallels in the vicinity, although it can be broadly compared with F37, a morphologically similar, though larger, feature recorded at Aldermaston Wharf (Cowell *et al.* 1978, 7). This clay-filled Late Iron Age rectangular feature, interpreted as a pond or tank, was cut into the natural gravel and measured *c.* 7.2 x 2.4 m and 0.5 m deep.

Romano-British

At Wickhams Field there is no evidence to suggest any continuity in settlement from the Early Iron Age through into the Romano-British period. As such, it must be assumed that an hiatus in the settlement pattern occurred, perhaps lasting *c.* 500–600 years. This is reflected in the immediate area, with very little Middle and Late Iron Age evidence recorded, other than a pair of cremation burials at Pingewood (Johnston 1985). An isolated Late Iron Age cremation was also found to the north-east near Anslow's Cottages (Whimster 1981, 357), although with a date range defined as *c.* AD 25–50, this feature may more properly be described as early Romano-British.

The Romano-British settlement evidence from Wickhams Field indicates occupation in the area throughout this period and can be broadly subdivided into early (ie 1st and 2nd centuries AD) and late (ie 3rd and 4th centuries AD) periods. Of these, the early Romano-British period represents the dominant phase and includes the majority of recorded features. Settlement evidence is concentrated towards the western limit of the excavation area, towards the base of the slope below the higher Reading Beds, though not fully located on the lower valley gravel. The concentration of remains within the margin between the valley gravel and higher ground is a pattern reflected in other neighbouring sites such as Pingewood (Johnston 1985; Lobb and Mills forthcoming), and demonstrated as cropmark evidence from aerial photographs (Gates 1975, 32).

The early Romano-British evidence is broadly similar to the results from excavations and other observations along the Kennet valley (ie Aldermaston, Ufton Nervet, Pingewood etc.). However, unlike some of these sites, the Wickhams Field settlement evidence is not complemented by the presence of a complex field system. This is perhaps reflected in the comparative absence of environmental evidence to indicate arable farming in the area.

The centre of the settlement is clearly identified to the west of the excavation area and, as such, it is not possible to fully determine the nature of the evidence. It is probable, however, that the structural, artefactual, and environmental evidence indicates the presence of a small farmstead, possibly representing a single family farm or 'compound' (cf Hingley 1989, 55–74). Such compounds have been identified as generally comprising between one and five dwellings with associated ancillary buildings, usually situated within a ditched enclosure and/or defined by trackways.

In this context, Wickhams Field has demonstrated at least one early Romano-British ditched enclosure, a timber-framed building, possibly with wattle and daub walls and a tiled roof, and a west–east trackway, with a possible second enclosure formed by a ditch connecting the south side of the trackway to the building. The building is situated towards the eastern periphery of the recorded enclosure(s), and it may therefore be reasonable to assume that it performed a storage or 'workshop' function rather than being used for occupation. It is likely that the prehistoric trackway continued in existence, even if only as a low denuded earthwork, and it is probable that the earliest Romano-British occupation initially exploited this route for access.

Additional remains included numerous pits for refuse and/or storage, and a massive pit situated approximately central to the excavation area and cutting into the valley gravel. Although not fully excavated, this feature may represent a principal water source for the excavated settlement to the west.

In a wider context, the settlement is located within the region delimited to the west by the Roman road from *Calleva* (Silchester) to Dorchester-on-Thames, and to the east by the presumed line of another road from the east gate of *Calleva* towards Reading and ultimately St Albans (Phillips 1993, 20). The line of the route from Silchester towards Reading has never been firmly established, although recent research has suggested that it passes through Mortimer, Goddard's Green, and Burghfield Place towards Knight's Farm and Searles Farm, ie passing within *c.* 6–700 m of Wickhams Field (D. Richards, pers. comm.).

The early Romano-British ceramic evidence indicates locally produced vessels (based on native Iron Age forms) and coarsewares probably brought in from further afield, and is typical of a small rural settlement of low social status. This is reflected in the relative absence of objects that may be considered of 'high status', restricted to a single 1st or 2nd century AD brooch recovered from the late Romano-British midden. Very little evidence was recorded for arable farming, with only low levels of waste chaff and preserved grains to indicate cultivation of spelt, barley, and bread wheat. Very little evidence exists for extensive woodland, although the recovery of an oak tree bole indicates the felling of at least one substantial tree in the vicinity. Furthermore, scrub or hedgerows are poorly represented in the archaeological record.

As suggested by the low-level evidence for arable farming, the faunal remains indicate an economy more closely linked to animal husbandry with cattle dominating the assemblage. Sheep and/or goat are also present, as well as isolated examples of roe deer, beaver, and dog. Further evidence for dogs is provided by a number of animal bones that have been gnawed. It can be tentatively suggested that the dogs were working animals used for herding sheep. The examples of deer and beaver may well represent localised exploitation of the surrounding landscape to supplement the diet, and the dogs could alternatively have served as hunting animals.

Late Romano-British evidence is primarily artefactual, with the bulk of the ceramic assemblage from this phase recovered from a large midden identified to the east of the earlier Romano-British remains. This assemblage includes a greater proportion of finewares and imports, as well as occasional fragments of lava that may represent the remains of lava querns of continental origin. In addition, the majority of coins and diagnostic metalwork recovered are of late 3rd or 4th century date.

The apparent increase in status demonstrated from the artefactual evidence conflicts with the structural evidence which appears to indicate a reduction in settlement activity within the excavation area. The larger early Romano-British enclosure is replaced by a smaller version, with no evidence to suggest that the earlier building continued in use into this phase. Although the west–east trackway may have continued in use into this phase, examinations have indicated that features were excavated through the partially filled remains of the roadside ditches. These features include a shallow truncated pit containing considerable quantities of charcoal, partially fired clay, and cremated human bone. This has been interpreted as a pyre base and, although undated, attributed to this period on the basis of its stratigraphic relationship with the earlier feature. Despite the presence of a pyre base, *in situ* burials were not identified within the excavation area, although small pockets of cremated human bone were recovered within the fills of other features. All the charcoal from this pyre base has been identified as oak, which would have provided an efficient fuel for cremation when seasoned.

In general, the environmental information demonstrates continuity with the earlier period, with perhaps even an increased dependence on a cattle based economy on the evidence of the assemblage recovered from the midden. It is interesting to note the absence of any gnawed bones from this deposit; it might be suggested that this is a reflection of the reduced numbers of sheep present, therefore removing the need for 'sheep dogs'.

As with the preceding phases, it is clear that the later Romano-British activity recorded at the site represents the limits of a settlement that presumably extended further west. What is not clear is whether the apparent reduction in settlement activity from the early to later Romano-British periods represented at Wickhams Field is a true reflection of events. The artefact evidence appears to indicate a higher status for the *later* settlement; this might suggest that the excavated evidence is not a true reflection of contemporaneous settlement on the site, in terms of its intensity and/or extent. In view of these considerations, it is reasonable to propose that the focus of settlement merely shifted to the west in the later Romano-British period, and was associated with a rise in its status. Whether such an increase in status represents a shift from a family farm to something more substantial, possibly even the establishment of a villa settlement, will probably never be known. Considerable ground disturbance occurred to the west during the construction of the M4 in 1970 and, as such, any further remains are unlikely to have survived.

Saxon

Although only three pits and two wells can be placed confidently within the Saxon period, they nevertheless represent some of the few tangible pieces of Saxon settlement evidence in an area otherwise dominated by contemporaneous sepulchral remains and isolated findspots. The most significant local site is the 7th century AD Saxon inhumation cemetery primarily concentrated within the limits of the Early Bronze Age ring-ditch at Field Farm (Butterworth and Lobb 1992, 70–2). Prior to the excavation at Wickhams Field settlement evidence contemporaneous with the cemetery had not been identified, although the settlement was presumed to lie in the Burghfield area. References to *Sewelle* (?Sheffield) and *Borgefelle* (Burghfield) can be found in *Domesday* (AD 1086; *op. cit.* 177), though neither confidently demonstrate the presence of early Saxon occupation. It is now possible to suggest that the settlement associated with the inhumation cemetery at Field Farm lay in the immediate vicinity of the well and pits excavated at Wickhams Field.

The pits are situated on the higher Reading Beds and all demonstrate at least partially undercutting profiles, a characteristic perhaps more usually associated with Iron Age 'beehive' storage pits. A similar storage function is proposed for the Wickhams Field examples, with carbonised remains demonstrating an assemblage consisting almost entirely of barley grains, with some grains of spelt, bread wheat, and rye. No chaff was found in association with these grains, suggesting that crop processing was probably taking place a considerable distance from these features. Very few animal bones were recovered, comprising single examples of cow and sheep/goat, whilst charcoal fragments demonstrate the presence of oak, hazel, and ash woodland, with some willow/poplar evidence indicative of wetter, marshy environments.

A single fragment of lava, similar to the examples recorded from securely dated Romano-British features, may on that basis be residual. However, excavations elsewhere, such as at Hamwic (Morton 1992) and Swaythling in Southampton (Crockett in press) have demonstrated that *Niedermendig* lava querns were a common import from the continent during the Saxon period. Although the Wickhams Field example has not been positively identified as *Neidermendig*, it is nevertheless possible that the fragment recovered in association with carbonised grain is of Saxon date.

The large timber-lined wells, one of which has been radiocarbon dated to GU-4362, 1290±50 BP; cal AD 650–870, were recorded towards the northern limit of the excavation, a considerable distance to the north-east of the contemporaneous pits. All of the identifiable timbers from the wells were oak. Both wells had, shallow, timber-lined shafts at the base of larger pits cutting into the valley gravel, but the construction technique for each differed. One comprised a subcircular shaft lined with upright staves and posts, the other was a rectilinear 'box' formed with edge-on wide planks.

Whilst many parallels for Saxon wells can be found in urban contexts (ie Morton 1992; Wade 1993; Andrews forthcoming), they are a comparatively rare find from rural sites. This rarity may in part be explained by the preference for rural Saxon sites to be adjacent to exploitable watersources such as rivers and streams. Examples of Saxon wells in rural contexts have been recorded at Bonhunt, Essex (Wade 1974) and North Elmham, Norfolk (Wade-Martins 1980). As with the examples at Wickhams Field, each site revealed two wells, comprising both a subcircular shaft formed with uprights and a rectangular shaft formed with edge-on planks.

It is almost certain that the storage pits and wells at Wickhams Field represent features associated with a dispersed settlement which was probably unenclosed. The focus of settlement activity has not as yet been identified but it is likely that the nearby cemetery at Field Farm and fish trapping evidence at Anslow's Cottage (Butterworth and Lobb 1992) represent elements of a broadly contemporaneous settlement landscape. It is possible that the apparently dispersed nature of the evidence may be such that it is difficult to identify the 'centre' of the settlement.

The apparent absence of similarly dated remains elsewhere within the region is interesting and may be related to the comparative difficulty experienced at Wickhams Field in differentiating between Late Bronze Age/Early Iron Age and Saxon pottery. It may be valid to suggest that isolated Saxon features similar to those excavated may inadvertently have been overlooked if situated in areas of intensive and/or extensive late prehistoric activity.

Bibliography

Adkins, L. and Needham, S., 1985, 'New research on a Late Bronze Age enclosure at Queen Mary's Hospital, Carshalton', *Surrey Archaeol.Collect.* 76, 11–50.

Adkins, R. and Jackson, R., 1978, *Neolithic Stone and Flint axes from the River Thames*, British Museum Occ. Paper 1.

Akerman, J.W., 1855, 'Notes on antiquarian researches in the summer and autumn of 1854', *Archaeologia* 36, 175–186.

Allen, M.J., 1992, 'Products of erosion and the prehistoric land-use of the Wessex Chalk', in Bell, M.G. and Boardman, J. (eds), *Past and Present Soil Erosion: Archaeological and Geographical Perspectives,* Oxford, Oxbow Books, 37–52.

——, 1994, *The land-use history of the southern English chalklands with an evaluation of the Beaker period using environmental data: colluvial deposits as environmental and cultural indicators*, unpubl. Ph.D. thesis, Univ. Southampton, 1994.

Allen, R.H., Fordham, S.J., Hazelden, J., Moffat, A.J. and Sturdy, R.G., 1983, *Soils of England and Wales; Sheet 6, South-East England (1:250 000),* Soil Survey of England and Wales.

Astill, G. and Lobb, S., 1989, 'Excavation of prehistoric, Roman and Saxon deposits at Wraysbury, Berkshire', *Archaeol. J.* 146, 95–126.

Barfield, L. and Hodder, M., 1987, 'Burnt mounds as saunas, and the prehistory of bathing', *Antiquity* 61, 370–9.

Barnes, I., Boismier, W.A., Cleal, R.M.J., Fitzpatrick, A.P. and Roberts, M.R., 1995, *Early Settlement in Berkshire: Mesolithic–Roman Occupation Sites in the Thames and Kennet Valleys*, Salisbury, Wessex Archaeology Report 6.

Barnatt, J., 1994, 'Excavation of a Bronze Age unenclosed cemetery, cairns and field boundaries at Eaglestone Flat, Curbar, Derbyshire', *Proc. Prehist. Soc.* 60, 287–370.

Barrett, J.C., 1973, 'Four Bronze Age cremation cemeteries from Middlesex', *Trans. London Middlesex Archaeol. Soc.* 24, 111–134.

——, 1980, 'The pottery of the later Bronze Age in lowland England', *Proc. Prehist. Soc.* 46, 297–320.

—— and Bradley, R., 1980, 'The Late Bronze Age in the Thames valley', in Barrett and Bradley 1980, 247–265.

—— and —— (eds), 1980, *Settlement and Society in the British Later Bronze Age,* Oxford, Brit. Archaeol. Rep. 83.

Bass, W.M., 1987, *Human Osteology,* Missouri Archaeol. Soc.

Bird, D.G., 1987, 'The Romano-British period in Surrey', in Bird and Bird (eds), 1987, 165–196.

Bird, J. and Bird, D.G. (eds), 1987, *The Archaeology of Surrey to 1540*, Guildford, Surrey Archaeol. Soc.

Blackmore, L., 1993, 'La céramique du Vème au Xème siècle a Londres et dans la région Londonienne', in Piton, D. (ed.), *Travaux du Groupe de Recherches et d'Études sur la Céramique dans le Nord-Pas-De-Calais* (Actes du Colloque d'Outreau, 1992), 129–50.

——, forthcoming, 'The post-Roman pottery', in Milne, G. (ed.), *Archaeological Excavations and Associated Research 1952–4 and 1992–5*, English Heritage Archaeol. Reps: Grimes London Archive Vol. 2.

Blair, J., 1994, *Anglo-Saxon Oxfordshire*, Stroud.

Bond, D., 1988, *Excavation at the North Ring, Mucking, Essex,* Gressenhall, E. Anglian Archaeol. 43.

Bowsher, J.M.C., 1991, 'A burnt mound at the Phoenix Wharf, South East London: a preliminary report', in Hodder, M.A. and Barfield, L.H. (eds), *Burnt Mounds and Hot Stone Technology,* 11–19, Sandwell Metropolitan Borough Council.

Bradley, R., 1984, *Social Foundations of Prehistoric Britain*, London, Longman

—— and Richards, J.C., 1979–80, 'The excavation of two ring ditches at Heron's House, Burghfield', *Berkshire Archaeol. J.* 70, 1–7.

——, Lobb, S., Richards, J. and Robinson, M., 1980, 'Two Late Bronze Age settlements on the Kennet gravels: excavations at Aldermaston Wharf and Knight's Farm, Burghfield, Berkshire', *Proc. Prehist. Soc.* 46, 217–296.

——, Entwistle, R. and Raymond, F., 1994, *Prehistoric Land Divisions on Salisbury Plain: the Work of the Wessex Linear Ditches Project,* English Heritage Archaeol. Rep. 2.

Brisbane, M., 1994, 'The cremation pottery fabrics: a note', in Hills, C., Penn, K. and Rickett, R., *The Anglo-Saxon Cemetery at Spong Hill, North Elmham. Part V: Catalogue of Cremations*, Gressenhall, E. Anglian Archaeol. 67.

Brown, L., 1984, 'Objects of stone', in Cunliffe, B., 1984, 407–426.

Brown, N., 1988, 'A Late Bronze Age enclosure at Lofts Farm, Essex', *Proc. Prehist. Soc.* 54, 249–302.

Burgess, C., 1986, '"Urnes of no small variety": Collared Urns reviewed', *Proc. Prehist. Soc. 52,* 339–351.

Butterworth, C.A., 1990, *Berkyn Manor Farm, Horton: archaeological evaluation,* Salisbury, unpubl. Wessex Archaeology report.

—— and Lobb, S.J., 1992, *Excavations in the Burghfield Area, Berkshire: Developments in the Bronze Age and Saxon Landscapes,* Salisbury, Wessex Archaeology Report 1.

Canham, R., 1978, 'Excavations at London (Heathrow) Airport 1969', *Trans London Middlesex Archaeol. Soc.* 29, 1–44.

——, 1979, 'Excavations at Shepperton Green 1967 and 1973', *Trans London Middlesex Archaeol. Soc.* 30, 97–134.

Carruthers, W.J., 1992, 'Plant remains', in Butterworth, C.A. and Lobb, S.J., 1992, 149–158.

Chadwick, P., 1993, *Desk-based assessment, brief and research framework for the archaeological evaluation of the British Airways PLC, Combined Business Centre, Prospect Park, Harmondsworth, West London,* unpubl. client report.

——, 1994, *Project Design in support of mitigation measures, British Airways Combined Business Centre, Prospect Park, Harmondsworth, West London,* unpubl. client report.

Champion, T.C, 1975, 'Britain in the European Iron Age', *Archaeologia Atlantica* 1:2, 127–45

——, 1980, 'Settlement and environment in later Bronze Age Kent', in Barrett and Bradley 1980, 223–246.

Charles, D., 1979, *Aspects of the chronology and distribution of Silchester ware Roman pottery,* unpubl. undergrad. dissertation, Univ. Reading.

Cheetham, G.H., 1975, *Late Quaternary palaeo-hydrology, with reference to the Kennet Valley,* unpubl. Ph.D. thesis, Univ. Reading.

——, 1980, 'Late Quaternary palaeo-hydrology; the Kennet valley case study', in Jones, D.K.C. (ed.), *The Shaping of Southern England,* London: Academic Press, 203–223.

Christie, P.M., 1967, 'A barrow cemetery of the second millennium BC in Wiltshire, England', *Proc. Prehist. Soc.* 33, 336–367.

Cleal, R.M.J., 1993, 'Pottery and fired clay', in Bradley, R., Chowne, P., Cleal, R.M.J., Healey, F. and Kinnes, I., *Excavations on Redgate Hill, Hunstanton, Norfolk, and at Tattershall Thorpe, Lincolnshire,* Gressenhall, E. Anglian. Archaeol. 57, 40–60.

——, in press, 'Beaker pottery', in Cleal, R.M.J., Fitzpatrick, A.P., Harding, P.A. and Rawlings, M.N., 'A deposit of Beakers and the Earls Farm Down Linear at Butterfield Down East, Amesbury, Wiltshire', *Wiltshire Archaeol. Natur. Hist. Mag.*

Cook, A.M. and Dacre, M.W., 1985, *Excavations at Portway, Andover 1973–1975,* Oxford, Univ. Comm. Archaeol. Monog. 4.

Cool, H., 1993, 'The copper alloy and silver gravegoods', in Farwell, D.E. and Molleson, T.L., 1993, *Excavations at Poundbury 1966–80, Volume II: The Cemeteries,* Dorset Natur. Hist. Archaeol. Soc. Monog. 11, 89–96.

Cotswold Archaeological Trust 1994a, *Hurst Park, Surrey: archaeological evaluation report,* Cirencester, unpubl. client report.

——, 1994b, *Hurst Park, Surrey: archaeological evaluation report, phase 2,* Cirencester, unpubl.client report.

Cotton, J., 1991, 'Prehistory in Greater London', *Current Archeaol.* 124, Vol. XI No. 4, 151–154.

——, Mills, J. and Clegg, G., 1986, *Archaeology in West Middlesex: the London Borough of Hillingdon from the Earliest Hunters to the Late Medieval Period,* London.

Cowell, R.W., Fulford, M.G. and Lobb, S., 1978, 'Excavations of prehistoric and Roman settlement at Aldermaston Wharf', *Berkshire Archaeol. J.* 69, 1–35.

Coy, J., 1992, 'Faunal remains', in Butterworth and Lobb 1992, 128-130.

Crockett, A.D., in press, *Excavations at Montefiore New Halls of Residence, Swaythling, Southampton, 1992,* Proc. Hampshire Fld Club Archaeol. Soc.

Crummy, N., 1983, *The Roman Small Finds from Excavations in Colchester 1971–9,* Colchester Archaeol. Rep. 2.

Cunliffe, B., 1984, *Danebury: an Iron Age Hillfort in Hampshire. Vol 2. The Excavations 1969–1978: the Finds,* Counc. Brit. Archaeol. Res. Rep. 52.

Davies, S.M., 1980, 'Excavations at Old Down Farm, Andover, Part 1: Saxon', *Proc. Hampshire Fld Club Archaeol. Soc.* 36, 161–180.

Dewey, H. and Bromehead, C.E.N., 1915, *The Geology of the Country Around Windsor and Chertsey,* London, Mem. Geol. Survey, HMSO.

Dickinson, T.M., 1973, 'Excavations at Standlake Down in 1954: the Anglo-Saxon graves', *Oxoniensia* 38, 239–257.

Down, A., 1989, *Chichester Excavations VI,* Chichester.

Drewett, P.L., 1970, 'The excavation of two round barrows and associated fieldwork on Ashley Down, Isle of Wight', *Proc. Hampshire Fld Club Archaeol. Soc.* 27, 33–50.

——, 1982, 'Later Bronze Age downland economy and excavations at Black Patch, east Sussex'. *Proc. Prehist. Soc.* 48, 321–409.

Edlin, H.L., 1949, *Woodland Crafts in England*

Egan, G. and Pritchard, F., 1991, 'Dress Accessories c. 1150–1450', in *Medieval Finds from Excavations in London 3.*

Ellison, A.B., 1975, *Pottery and settlements of the later Bronze Age in southern England,* unpubl. Ph.D. thesis, Univ. Cambridge.

Evison, V.I., 1987, *Dover: the Buckland Anglo-Saxon Cemetery,* London, HBMCE Archaeol. Rep. 3.

Fairbrother, J.R., 1990, *Faccombe Netherton: Excavations of a Saxon and Medieval Manorial Complex, Volume 2*, London, Brit. Mus. Occ. Paper 74.

Field, D. and Cotton, J., 1987, 'Neolithic Surrey: a survey of the evidence', in Bird and Bird (eds), 1987, 97–137.

Field, D. and Needham, S., 1986, 'Evidence for Bronze Age settlement on Coombe Warren, Kingston Hill', *Surrey Archaeol. Collect.* 77, 127–151.

Fitzpatrick, A.P., 1995, 'An Early Iron Age (7th century BC) pit with ironworking debris from Cooper's Farm, Dunston Park, Thatcham, Berkshire', in Barnes *et al.*, 1995, 89–92.

Ford, S., 1986, 'A newly-discovered causewayed enclosure at Eton Wick, near Windsor, Berkshire', *Proc. Prehist. Soc.* 52, 319-320.

Fowler, E., 1960, 'The origins and development of the Penannular Brooch in Europe', *Proc. Prehist. Soc.* 26, 149–177.

Frere, S., 1984, *Verulamium Excavations 3*, Oxford, Oxford Univ. Comm. Archaeol. Monog. 1.

Fulford, M.G., 1975, *New Forest Roman Pottery,* Brit. Archaeol. Rep. 17, Oxford.

Gardner, E., 1924, 'Bronze Age urns of Surrey', *Surrey Archaeol. Collect.* 35, 1–29.

Gates, T., 1975, *The Middle Thames Valley: an Archaeological Survey of the River Gravels,* Berkshire Archaeol. Committee Publ. 1.

Gejvall, N.G., 1981, 'Determination of burnt bones from prehistoric graves', *Ossa Letters* 2, 1–13.

Gelling, M., 1973, *The Place-Names of Berkshire* 1, Cambridge.

Gingell, C., 1992, *The Marlborough Downs; a Later Bronze Age Landscape and its Origins,* Wiltshire Archaol. and Natur. Hist. Soc. Monog. 1.

Godwin, H., 1956, *The History of the British Flora,* Cambridge.

Goodall, I.H., 1984, 'Iron objects', in Rogerson and Dallas 1984, 77–106.

——,1990, 'Iron objects', in Fairbrother 1990, 403–425.

Gover, J.E.B., Mawer, A. and Stenton, F.M., 1982, *The Place-names of Surrey,* English Place-name Soc. Vol. XI.

Gray, H., 1977, *Anatomy,* New York.

Greene, K., 1978, 'Imported fine wares in Britain to AD 250: a guide to identification', in Arthur, P. and Marsh, G. (eds), *Early Fine Wares in Roman Britain,* Oxford, Brit. Archaeol. Rep. 57, 15–30

Greig, J., 1991a, 'The botanical remains', in Needham 1991, 234–261.

——, 1991b, 'The British Isles', in Van Zeist, W., Wasylikowa, K. and Behre, K. (eds), *Progress in Old World Palaeoethnobotany,* 299–334.

Grimes, W.F., 1960, *Excavations on Defence Sites 1939–45, Part 1: Mainly Neolithic–Bronze Age,* London, Ministry of Works Archaeol. Rep. 3.

—— and Close-Brooks, J., 1993, 'The excavation of Caesar's Camp, Heathrow, Harmondsworth, Middlesex, 1944', *Proc. Prehist. Soc.* 59, 303–360.

Grinsell, L.V., 1932, 'Some Surrey bellbarrows', *Surrey Archaeol. Collect.* 40, 56–64.

——, 1934, 'An analysis and list of Surrey barrows', *Surrey Archaeol. Collect.* 42, 26–60.

——, 1941, 'The Bronze Age round barrows of Wessex', *Proc. Prehist. Soc.* 7, 73–113.

Haddon Reece, D., 1982, *The identification of wood samples from the cattlemarket site, Chichester,* unpubl. Ancient Monuments Laboratory Rep. 3722.

Hall, M., 1992, 'The prehistoric pottery', in Moore, J. and Jennings, D., *Reading Busines Park: a Bronze Age Landscape,* Thames Valley Landscapes: the Kennet Valley, Vol 1, Oxford, Oxford Archaeol. Unit Monog. 63–82.

Hamerow, H.F., 1991, 'Settlement mobility and the "Middle Saxon Shift": rural settlements and settlement patterns in Anglo-Saxon England', *Anglo-Saxon England* 20, 1–19.

——, 1993, *Excavations at Mucking. Volume 2: the Anglo-Saxon Settlement*, English Heritage Rep. 21.

Healy, F., 1993, 'The excavation of a ring-ditch at Englefield by John Wymer and Paul Ashbee, 1963', *Berkshire Archaeol. J.* 74, 1991–3, 9–25.

Helbaek, H., 1952, 'Early crops in southern England', *Proc. Prehist. Soc.* 18, 194–233.

Henig, M., 1993, 'Copper-alloy and non-ferrous metalwork', in Woodward, P.J., Davies, S.M. and Graham, A.H., 1993, *Excavations at The Old Methodist Chapel and Greyhound Yard, Dorchester, 1981–84,* Dorset Natur. Hist. Archaeol. Soc. Monog. 12, 117–132.

Hillam, J., 1978, *Tree-ring analysis of a timber-lined well from Canterbury,* unpubl. Ancient Monumets Laboratory Rep. 2551.

——, 1981, *Lower Brook Street, Ipswich, tree-ring analysis of well timbers*, unpubl. Ancient Monuments Laboratory Rep. 3651.

Hingley, R., 1989, *Rural Settlement in Roman Britain,* London, Seaby.

Hodgson, J.H., 1976, *Soil Survey Field Handbook,* Harpenden: Soil Survey Technical Monog. 5.

Holyoak, D.T., 1980, *Late Pleistocene changes and biostraitgraphy of the Kennet valley, England,* unpubl. Ph.D. thesis, Univ. Reading.

Homer, *Odyssey,* 1972 trans Rieu, E.V., Penguin.

Jarvis, M.G., Allen, R.H., Fordham, S.J., Hazelden, J., Moffat, A.J. and Sturdy, A.G., 1984, *Soils and their Use in South East England,* Harpenden: Soil Survey of England and Wales Bulletin No 15.

Jennings, D., 1992, 'Area 7000', in Moore and Jennings 1992.

Johnson, B., 1975, *Archaeology and the M25, 1971–5,* Guildford, Res. Vol. Surrey Archaeol. Soc. 2.

Johnston, J., 1985, 'Excavations at Pingewood', *Berkshire Archaeol. J.* 72, 17–52.

Jones, M.K., 1981, 'The development of crop husbandry', in Jones, M. and Dimbleby, G.W. (eds), *The Environment of Man: the Iron Age to the Anglo-Saxon Period,* Brit. Archaeol. Rep., Brit. Ser. 87, 95–127.

Lobb, S.J., 1983–85, 'Excavation of two ring ditches at Burghfield by R.A. Rutland, 1969', *Berkshire Archaeol. J.* 72, 9–16.

—— and Mills, J., forthcoming, 'Observations and excavations in the Pingewood area', *Berkshire Archaeol. J.*

—— and Morris, E.L., 1991–3, 'Investigation of Bronze Age and Iron Age features at Riseley Farm, Swallowfield', *Berkshire Archaeol. J.* 74, 37–68.

—— and Rose, P.G., forthcoming, *Archaeological Survey of the Lower Kennet Valley, Berkshire,* Salisbury, Wessex Archaeology Report 9.

Longley, D., 1976, *The Archaeological Implications of Gravel Extraction in North-west Surrey*, Guildford, Res. Vol. Surrey Archaeol. Soc 3.

——, 1980, *Runnymede Bridge 1976: Excavations on the Site of a Late Bronze Age Settlement*, Guildford, Res. Vol. Surrey Archaeol. Soc. 6.

——, 1991, 'The Late Bronze Age pottery', in Needham 1991, 162–212.

—— and Poulton, R., 1982, 'The Saxon cemetery at Upper West Field, Shepperton', *Trans London Middlesex Archaeol. Soc.* 33, 177–185.

Longworth, I.H., 1984, *Collared Urns of the Bronze Age in Great Britain and Ireland,* Cambridge.

Lowther, A.W.G., 1935, 'Excavations at Ewell in 1934. The Saxon cemetery and Stane Street', *Surrey Archaeol. Collect.* 43, 16–35.

Macphail, R.I. and Scaife, R.G., 1987, 'The geographical and environmental background', in Bird and Bird 1987, 31–52.

Manning, W.H., 1974, 'Excavations on Late Iron Age, Roman and Saxon sites at Ufton Nervet, Berkshire, 1961–3', *Berkshire Archaeol. J.* 67, 1–61.

——, 1985, *Catalogue of the Romano-British Iron Tools, Fittings and Weapons in the British Museum,* London.

McKinley, J.I., 1989, 'Cremations: expectations, methodologies and realities', in Roberts, C.A., Lee, F. and Bintliff, J. (eds), *Burial Archaeology: Current Research, Methods and Developments*, Oxford, Brit. Archaeol. Rep. 211, 65–76.

——, 1991, 'Cremated Bone from the Area 15 cemetery, Baldock', unpubl. report for Letchworth Museum.

——, 1992, 'Cremation and inhumation burials from St Stephen's cemetery, St Alban's', unpubl. report for Verulamium Museum.

——, 1993a, 'Bone fragment size and weights of bone from modern British cremations and its implications for the interpretation of archaeological cremations', *International J. Osteoarchaeology* 3, 283–287.

——, 1993b, 'Cremation', unpubl. paper presented to the Prehistoric Society at the Iron Age Research Day, November 1993.

——, 1994a, *The Anglo-Saxon Cemetery at Spong Hill, North Elmham. Part VIII: the Cremations*, Gressenhall, E. Anglian Archaeol. 69.

——, 1994b, 'Bone fragment size in British cremation burials and its implication for pyre technology and ritual', *J. Archaeol. Sci.* 21, 339–342.

——, 1995, *The East London Romano-British cemeteries: cremated bone and cremations*, unpubl. report for Museum of London Archaeological Services.

——, forthcoming a, 'Human bone and funerary deposits', in Walker, K.E., *M3, Bar End to Compton: Archaeological Investigation on Twyford Down*, Winchester, Hampshire Fld Club Monog.

——, forthcoming b, 'Pyre technology and ritual', in Fitzpatrick, A.P. and Powell, A., *Westhampnett, West Sussex, Vol. II: the Iron Age, Romano-British, and Anglo-Saxon Cemeteries, Excavated 1992*, Salisbury, Wessex Archaeology Report.

McMinn, R.M.H. and Hutchings, R.T., 1985, *A Colour Atlas of Human Anatomy*, Wolfe Medical Pub.

Mepham, L.N., 1992a, 'Pottery', in Butterworth and Lobb 1992, 40–48.

——, 1992b, 'Pottery', in Butterworth and Lobb 1992, 108–114.

——, 1995, 'Burnt flint', in Fitzpatrick, A.P., Barnes, I. and Cleal, R.M.J., *An Early Iron Age Settlement at Dunston Park, Thatcham*, Salisbury, Wessex Archaeology Report 6, 77.

——, forthcoming, 'Iron Age and Roman pottery', in Barnes, I., Butterworth, C.A., Hawkes, J.W. and Smith, L., *Excavations at Thames Valley Park, Reading 1986–1988,* Salisbury, Wessex Archaeology Report.

Merriman, N., 1990, *Prehistoric London,* London.

Monk, M., 1991, 'The archaeobotanical work carried out for the M3 Project', in Fasham, P.J. and Whinney, R.J.B., *Archaeology and the M3*, Hampshire Fld Club Archaeol. Soc. Monog. 7, 105–110.

Moore, J. and Jennings, D., 1992, *Reading Business Park: a Bronze Age Landscape,* Oxford, Oxford Univ. Comm. Archaeol., Thames Valley Landscapes: the Kennet Valley 1.

Moore, P.D., Webb, J.A. and Collinson, M.E., 1991, *Pollen Analysis,* Second edition, Oxford, Blackwell Scientific.

Morgan, R.A., 1975, *Tree-ring analysis of timbers from two Roman wells at Scole, Norfolk,* unpubl. Ancient Monuments Laboratory Rep. 1807.

Morris, E.L., 1992, *The analysis of pottery,* Salisbury, unpubl. Wessex Archaeology guideline 4.

—— and Mepham, L.N., 1995, 'The pottery', in Barnes, I. *et al.*, 1995., 77–84.

Morton, A.D. (ed.), 1992, *Excavations at Hamwic: Volume 1,* Counc. Brit. Archaeol. Res. Rep. 84

Murphy, P.L., 1977, *Early agriculture and environment on the Hampshire chalklands: circa. 800 BC–400 AD,* unpubl. M.Phil. thesis, Univ. Southampton.

Myres, J.N.L., 1977, *A Corpus of Anglo-Saxon Pottery of the Pagan Period,* Cambridge.

Needham, S., 1987, 'The Bronze Age', in Bird and Bird, 1987, 97–138.

——, 1991, *Excavation and Salvage at Runnymede Bridge, 1978; the Late Bronze Age Waterfront Site,* London, Brit. Mus. Press/English Heritage.

——, 1992, 'Holocene alluviation and interstratified settlement, evidence in the Thames Valley at Runnymede Bridge', in Needham, S. and Macklin, M. (eds), *Alluvial Archaeology in Britain,* Oxford, Oxbow Monog. 47, 249–260.

—— and Trott, M.R., 1987, 'Structure and sequence in the Neolithic deposits at Runnymede', *Proc. Prehist. Soc.* 53, 479–482.

Nicholls, J., 1987, 'Two Bronze Age urns from Portsdown', *Proc. Hampshire Fld Club Archaeol. Soc.* 43, 15–20.

Oakley, G.E. and Webster, L.E., 1979, 'The copper alloy objects', in Williams, J.H., *St Peter's Street, Northampton. Excavations 1973–1976,* Northampton Archaeol. Monog. 2, 248–64

O'Connell, M., 1990, 'Excavations during 1979–1985 of a multi-period site at Stanwell', *Surrey Archaeol. Collect.* 80, 1–62.

——, 1986, *Petters Sports Field, Egham; Excavation of a Late Bronze Age / Early Iron Age Site,* Guildford, Res. Vol. Surrey Archaeol. Soc. 10.

O'Drisceoil, D., 1988, 'Burnt mounds: cooking or bathing?', *Antiquity* 62, 671–80.

Peacock, D.P.S., 1987, 'Iron Age and Roman quern production at Lodsworth, West Sussex', *Antiq. J.* 67, 61–85.

Peake, H., 1931, *The Archaeology of Berkshire,* London.

Penn, J., Field, D. and Serjeantson, D., 1984, 'Evidence of Neolithic occupation in Kingston: excavations at Eden Walk, 1965', *Surrey Archaeol. Collect.* 75, 207–224.

Petersen, F.F., 1981, *The Excavation of a Bronze Age Cemetery on Knighton Heath, Dorset,* Oxford, Brit. Archaeol. Rep. 98.

Phillips, D., 1993, *Berkshire — a County History,* Newbury.

Plouviez, J., 1985, 'The late Roman pottery', in West 1985, 82–85.

Poulton, R.J., 1987a, 'Saxon Surrey' in Bird and Bird 1987, 197–222.

——, 1987b, 'Saxon County School, Shepperton', *Surrey Archaeol. Soc. Bull.,* 216.

Rackham, J, 1994, 'Economy and environment in Saxon London' in Rackham, J. (ed.), *Environment and Economy in Anglo-Saxon England,* Counc. Brit. Archaeol. Res. Rep. 89, 126–35.

Rashbrook, C., 1983, *A discussion of the pottery found at Hamstead Marshall, near Newbury, Berkshire,* unpubl. undergrad. dissertation, Univ. Reading.

Reece, R., 1991, *Roman Coins from 140 Sites in Britain,* Cirencester, Cotswold Studies 4.

Robertson-Mackay, R., 1987, 'A Neolithic causewayed enclosure at Staines, Surrey: excavations 1961–1963', *Proc. Prehist. Soc.* 53, 23–128.

Robinson, M., 1988, 'The significance of tubers of *Arrhenatherum elatius* (L.) *Beavu.* from Site 4, cremation 15/11', in Lambrick, G., *The Rollright Stones,* English Heritage Archaeol. Report 6, 102.

Rocque, J., 1754, *Map of the County of Middlesex,* BM Maps 175. T1(2).

Rogerson, A. and Dallas, C., 1984, *Excavations in Thetford 1948–59 and 1973–80,* Gressenhall, E. Anglian Archaeol. 22.

Russell, M.J.G., 1989, 'Excavation of a multi-period site in Weston Wood, Albury: the pottery', *Surrey Archaeol. Collect.* 79, 3–51.

Scaife, R.G., 1994, 'The plant remains', in French, C.A.I., *The Haddon Farmstead and a Prehistoric Landscape at Elton. The Archaeology Along the A605 Elton–Haddon Bypass, Cambridgeshire,* Fenland Archaeological Trust/Cambridgshire County Council, 154–167.

——, in press, 'The charred plant remains', in Powell, A.B., Allen, M.J. and Barnes I., *Archaeology in the Avebury Area, Wiltshire: Recent Discoveries Along the Line of the Kennet Valley Foul Sewer Pipeline, 1993,* Salisbury, Wessex Archaeology Report 8.

Serjeantson, D., Field, D., Penn, J. and Shipley, M., 1992, 'Excavations at Eden Walk II, Kingston: environmental reconstruction and prehistoric finds', *Surrey Archaeol. Collect.* 81, 71–90.

Shipman, P., Forster, G. and Schoeninger, M., 1984, 'Burnt bones and teeth, an experimental study of colour, morphology, crystal structure and shrinkage', *J. Archaeol. Sci.* 11, 307–325.

Smith, I.F. and Darvill, T.C., 1990, 'The prehistoric pottery', in Saville, A., *Hazleton North: the Excavation of a Neolithic Long Cairn of the Cotswold-Severn Group*, English Heritage Archaeol. Rep. 13, 141–52.

Sorenson, M-L.S. and Thomas R. (eds), 1989, *The Bronze Age–Iron Age Transition in Europe,* Oxford, Brit. Archaeol. Rep. S484.

Timby, J., 1988, 'The Middle Saxon pottery', in Andrews, P. (ed.), *The Coins and Pottery from Hamwic, Southampton*, Southampton Finds, Vol. 1, 73–124.

Van Beek, G.C., 1983, *Dental Morphology: an Illustrated Guide,* Bristol, Wright PSG.

Van Es, W.A., 1967, *Wijster, a Native Village Beyond the Imperial Frontier, 150–425 AD*, Palaeohistoria XI.

Victoria County History, 1911, *Victoria County History of the Counties of England: Middlesex Vol.2.*

Viner, L., 1986, 'Objects of copper alloy', in McWhirr, A., 1986, *Houses in Roman Cirencester: Cirencester Excavations III,* Cirencester Excavation Committee, 106–111.

Wainwright, G.J. and Longworth, I.H., 1971, *Durrington Walls Excavations 1966–1968*, London, Antiq. Soc. Res. Rep. 29.

Webb, P.A.O. and Suchey, J.M., 1985, 'Epiphyseal union of the anterior ileac crest and medial clavicle in a modern multiracial sample of American males and females', *American J. Phys. Anth.* 68, 457–466.

Wessex Archaeology 1992, *M4 Service Area (Field Farm), Berkshire — archaeological review of application area*, Salisbury, unpubl. Wessex Archaeology report.

——, 1993, *British Airways PLC Combined Business Centre, Prospect Park, Harmondsworth, West London, archaeological evaluation (36661),* Salisbury, unpbl. Wessex Archaeology report.

——, 1994, *Theale Motorway Service Area (M4), Berkshire — archaeological excavation assessment report*, Salisbury, unpubl. Wessex Archaeology report.

West, S., 1985, *West Stow*, Gressenhall, E. Anglian Archaeol. 24.

Whimster, R., 1981, *Burial Practices in Iron Age Britain: a Discussion and Gazetteer of the Evidence c. 700 BC–AD 43*, Brit. Archaeol. Rep., Brit. Ser. 90(ii).

White, H.J.O., 1907, *The Geology of the Country Around Hungerford and Newbury*

Williams, D.F., 1993, 'Note on the petrology', in Grimes and Close-Brooks 1993, 351–352.

Woodward, A., 1992, 'Discussion' in Lobb, S.J., 'Excavation at Shortheath Lane, Abbotts Farm, Sulhamstead', in Butterworth and Lobb 1992, 75–7.

Young, C. J., 1977, *Oxfordshire Roman Pottery,* Brit. Archaeol. Rep. 43, Oxford.

Zohary, D. and Hopf, M., 1994, *Domestication of Plants in the Old World,* Oxford, Oxford Science Publications, Clarendon Press.

Index

by Lesley and Roy Adkins

Entries are largely in alphabetical order. Periods, such as Late Bronze Age and Iron Age, are given in chronological order within subentries wherever practical.